Exploring Id

C000092120

MANAGEMENT, WORK AND ORGANISATIONS

Series editors: **Gibson Burrell**, The Management Centre, University of Leicester
Mick Marchington, Manchester Business School
Paul Thompson, Department of Human Resource Management, University of Strathclyde

This series of new textbooks covers the areas of human resource management, employee relations, organisational behaviour and related business and management fields. Each text has been specially commissioned to be written by leading experts in a clear and accessible way. The books contain serious and challenging material, take an analytical rather than prescriptive approach and are particularly suitable for use by students with no prior specialist knowledge.

The series is relevant for many business and management courses, including MBA and post-experience courses, specialist masters and postgraduate diplomas, professional courses and final-year undergraduate courses. These texts have become essential reading at business and management schools worldwide.

Published

Paul Blyton and Peter Turnbull **The Dynamics of Employee Relations** (3rd edn)
Sharon C. Bolton **Emotion Management in the Workplace**
Sharon Bolton and Maeve Houlihan **Searching for the Human in Human Resource
    Management**
Peter Boxall and John Purcell **Strategy and Human Resource Management**
J. Martin Corbett **Critical Cases in Organisational Behaviour**
Keith Grint **Leadership**
Irena Grugulis **Skills, Training and Human Resource Development**
Damian Hodgson and Svetlana Cicmil **Making Projects Critical**
Marek Korczynski **Human Resource Management in Service Work**
Karen Legge **Human Resource Management**: anniversary edition
Patricia Lewis and Ruth Simpson (eds) **Gendering Emotions in Organizations**
Helen Rainbird (ed.) **Training in the Workplace**
Jill Rubery and Damian Grimshaw **The Organisation of Employment**
Harry Scarbrough (ed.) **The Management of Expertise**
Hugh Scullion and Margaret Linehan **International Human Resource Management**
Adrian Wilkinson, Mick Marchington, Tom Redman and Ed Snape **Managing with Total
    Quality Management**
Colin C. Williams **Rethinking the Future of Work**
Diana Winstanley and Jean Woodall (eds) **Ethical Issues in Contemporary Human
    Resource Management**
Patricia Lewis and Ruth Simpson **Gendering Emotions in Organizations**

For more information on titles in the Series please go to www.palgrave.com/busines/mwo

Invitation to authors

The Series Editors welcome proposals for new books within the Managment, Work and Organisations series. These should be sent to Paul Thompson (p.thompson@strath.ac.uk) at the Dept of HRM, Strathclyde Business School, University of Strathclyde, 50 Richmond St Glasgow G1 1XT

Series Standing Order

If you would like to receive future titles in this series as they are published, you can make use of our standing order facility. To place a standing order please contact your bookseller or, in case of difficulty, write to us at the address below with your name and address and the name of the series. Please state with which title you wish to begin your standing order.

Customer Services Department, Macmillan Distribution Ltd
Houndmills, Basingstoke, Hampshire RG21 6XS, England

Exploring Identity
Concepts and Methods

Edited by

Alison Pullen
School of Management, University of Technology, Sydney, Australia

Nic Beech
The Management School, St Andrews University, Scotland

David Sims
Centre for Leadership, Learning and Change, Cass Business School, London

First published 2007 by
PALGRAVE MACMILLAN
Houndmills, Basingstoke, Hampshire RG21 6XS and
175 Fifth Avenue, New York, N.Y. 10010
Companies and representatives throughout the world

PALGRAVE MACMILLAN is the global academic imprint of the Palgrave
Macmillan division of St. Martin's Press, LLC and of Palgrave Macmillan Ltd.
Macmillan® is a registered trademark in the United States, United Kingdom
and other countries. Palgrave is a registered trademark in the European
Union and other countries.

ISBN-13: 978–1–403–98983–3
ISBN-10: 1–403–98983–4

This book is printed on paper suitable for recycling and made from fully
managed and sustained forest sources. Logging, pulping and manufacturing
processes are expected to conform to the environmental regulations of the
country of origin.

A catalogue record for this book is available from the British Library.

A catalog record for this book is available from the Library of Congress.

10   9   8   7   6   5   4   3   2   1
16   15   14   13   12   11   10   09   08   07

Printed in China

In Memoriam

In memory of Professor Diana Winstanley

Contents

List of figures and table

Acknowledgements

Martin Parker offers a revised version of 'Dividing Organisations and Multiplying Identities' (from K. Hetherington and R. Munro (eds) (1997) *Ideas of Difference*. Oxford: Blackwell, 114–138) in Chapter 3.

Alison Pullen has been granted permission by Blackwell to revise 'Gendering the Research Self: social practice and corporeal multiplicity in the writing of organizational research', which appeared in *Gender, Work and Organization* (2006) 13: 3, 277–298, in Chapter 18.

List of contributors

Nic Beech is Professor of Management at St Andrews University, Scotland. His research is mainly focused on the social dynamics of organizational life – the intertwining of people's identities, relationships and practices. He has a particular interest in cultural industries and the health sector. His books include *The Essence of HRM* (1995), *HRM: A Concise Analysis* (2002) and *Reflective Learning in Practice* (2002). Nic is the founding chair of the British Academy of Management special interest group on identity.

Robin Burrow is a PhD researcher in the IROB group at Warwick Business School, University of Warwick. Robin's research focuses on practices of 'direct marketing' and applies methodological resources from conversation analysis.

Adrian N. Carr is an Associate Professor (Organisation Studies and Applied Social Sciences) and holds the research-only position of Principal Research Fellow in the School of Applied Social and Human Sciences at the University of Western Sydney, Australia. Dr Carr's major area of research interest is psychodynamic theory and its implications for organizational application. Dr Carr's PhD was in the area of psychodynamic theory and he has been the author of over 200 refereed journal publications and a number of books, the most recent of which are *Leadership is a matter of life and death: The psychodynamics of Eros and Thanatos working in organisations* (with Cheryl Lapp), *Cyberspace romance: The psychology of online relationships* (with Monica Whitty) and *Art and aesthetics at work* (co-edited with Philip Hancock). In addition to his five university degrees, Dr Carr holds an advanced accreditation to administer and purchase the Myers–Briggs Type Indicator. Dr Carr is a member of a number of professional associations and editorial boards, the latter including *Policy, Organisation & Society*; the *Journal of Management Development*; *Administrative Theory & Praxis: A*

Journal of Dialogue in Public Administration; Journal of Organizational Change Management; Radical Psychology: A Journal of Psychology (founding co-editor); Politics and Radicalism; TAMARA: Journal of Critical Postmodern Organization Science; Global Business & Economics Review; Journal of Managerial Psychology; Human Relations; Critical Perspectives on International Business.

Gail P. Clarkson earned her PhD at Leeds University Business School, the University of Leeds, UK, where she is currently employed as a Lecturer in Organisational Behaviour. Gail's research is focused on gaining a deeper understanding of how managers can engage employees in employment relationships that will enhance individual and organizational performance and well-being. A second stream of research is related to the development and validation of research methods that will support the generation of a strong evidence base in this regard.

Bill Cooke is Professor of Management and Society at Lancaster University Management School. He researches and publishes on the history of management ideas, the internationalization of managerialism, and the uses of participatory methodologies like action research.

Joep P. Cornelissen is Reader in Corporate Communications at Leeds University Business School. His research interests include corporate communications and the use of metaphor in management and organization theory and practice. He is author of *Corporate Communications: Theory and Practice*. His research articles on metaphor have appeared in *Academy of Management Review, Organization Studies, the British Journal of Management, Psychology and Marketing* and the *Journal of Management Studies*. He is editing a special issue of the *British Journal of Management* (2007) on advances in organizational and corporate identity scholarship with Alex Haslam and John Balmer.

Christine Coupland is Associate Professor in Organizational Behaviour at the University of Nottingham Business School. Her research interests include a broad range of contexts and are based on an interest in identity as a socially constructed phenomenon. This has led to work in the areas of entrepreneurship, corporate Web-based texts, newcomer socialization and careers. She is a co-founder of the British Academy of Management, Special Interest Group on Identity and a member of the editorial board for *Organization Studies*. Her work has been published in a number of journals including *Human Relations, Journal of Management Studies and Organization Studies.*

Stefano Harney, PhD, teaches at the University of London in the Queen Mary School of Business and Management.

Paul Hibbert is Lecturer in Management at the University of Strathclyde. He is also convenor of the British Academy of Management's Special Interest Group on Inter-Organizational Relations. He is interested in how managers can develop strategies for addressing the challenges of organizational and interorganizational life, through reflective and reflexive practice perspectives – and in supporting such perspectives through revealing how management practice is constructed. Paul has received a best-paper award from the Identity Division of the British Academy of Management and (with co-author, Chris Huxham) the Academy of Management's Rupert F. Chisholm award for the best theory-to-practice article.

Rick Iedema is Professor of Communication and Associate Dean (Research) in the Faculty of Humanities and Social Sciences at the University of Technology, Sydney. His work focuses on how (health) professionals communicate about the organization of their work. He publishes his work in *Social Science & Medicine, British Medical Journal, Communication and Medicine, Discourse and Society, Text & Talk* and *Visual Communication,* and he has two edited volumes out with Palgrave: *The Discourse of Hospital Communication* (2007) and (with Carmen Caldas-Coulthard) *Identity Trouble* (forthcoming).

Cheryl A. Lapp has a Master's of Education degree in Adult and Higher Education, a Bachelor of Commerce degree from the University of Alberta, Edmonton, Canada and honors management certification from Grant MacEwan College, Edmonton, Alberta, Canada. She is also a Canadian Certified Human Resource Professional who has been an instructor, researcher and practitioner of organizational leadership, followership, management and change for more than 20 years in universities and the telecommunications industry. As president and principal consultant for Labyrinth Consulting, which conducts research, reports and coaches on leadership, followership and management processes for profit and not-for-profit organizations, Cheryl has co-researched and co-authored numerous manuscripts published in the *Journal of Organizational Change Management, Emergence: Complexity* and *Organization* and has presented research papers around the world. Cheryl's most recent book publication is *Leadership is a matter of life and death: The psychodynamics of Eros and Thanatos working in organisations* (with Adrian Carr).

Stephen Linstead began researching identity issues in the 1980s, albeit sans la lettre. Working on organizational culture, he turned toward identity after the publication of Wally Olins's 'The Corporate Personality' and worked on image and symbol with Bob Grafton-Small, shifting emphasis gradually from the organizational to the interpersonal. He has produced two books with an identity focus – *Sex, Work and Sex Work* (2000, with Joanna Brewis) and *Organization and Identity* (2006 ed. with Alison Pullen). He is currently Professor of Critical Management at the York Management School, University of York, UK.

Nick Llewellyn is Associate Professor in the Industrial Relations and Organisational Behaviour group at Warwick Business School, University of Warwick. His research examines talk and interaction in institutional and public settings. He has published research in journals such as *Sociology, Human Relations, Organization Studies* and *Discourse Studies.* His current projects are examining public meetings and recruitment interviews.

Robert MacIntosh holds a Chair in Strategic Management at the University of Glasgow. He began his academic career as a researcher at Strathclyde and completed his PhD in engineering. He was recently Director of the MBA Programme at the University of Strathclyde and his two main areas of research interest are strategic change and the methods which underpin practice-relevant management research. He has researched change processes with a variety of organizations from the public, private and voluntary sectors and at the moment is working on a longitudinal study of change within the National Health Service in Glasgow. He lives in Glasgow with his wife, Anne, and their children, Euan, Eilidh and Eva. He is happiest when he is at home and in their company. Undermining his credibility as a management researcher, however, is his status as a shareholder in Aberdeen Football Club – not the wisest investment decision, but one filled with hope!

Peter McInnes is a Lecturer in Management in the University of Strathclyde Business School. He is currently the Director of Teaching and Learning for postgraduate courses within the Department of Management. Peter's research interests lie in exploring the impact of identity dynamics upon the way in which people understand themselves, each other and the organizations that they are part of. This has seen Peter undertake action research in a number of organizations within both the public and private sectors. His research has been published in journals such as the *International Journal of Public Administration* and *The International Journal of Public Sector Management.*

Nceku "Q" Nyathi is a doctoral candidate in Management at Leicester University, School of Management. He has a long-standing interest in both postcolonialism and organization studies, with much of his research focusing on ways in which postcolonialism could bring much more generous conceptualizations of organization studies.

Cliff Oswick is Chair in Organization Theory and Discourse at the University of London, Queen Mary School of Business and Management. His research interests focus on the application of aspects of discourse, dramaturgy, tropes, narrative and rhetoric to the study of organizations, organizing processes and organizational change. In addition to co-editing a number of books and contributing to various edited collections, he has published in a range of national and international journals, including recent and forthcoming contributions to *Academy of Management Review*, *Human Relations*, *Journal of Management Studies*, *Organization* and *Organization Studies*.

Martin Parker is Professor of Culture and Organization at Leicester University School of Management. He has written on various things, and recent books are *Against Management* (2002), *For Business Ethics* (2005, with Jones and ten Bos) and *A Dictionary of Alternatives* (2007, with Fournier and Reedy). His identity and his organization are both uncomplicated and transparent, and there is nothing else to add.

Alexandra Pitsis is a writer, completing her PhD at the University of Technology, Sydney, Australia. Her current studies look at poetics in organizational coaching. Her writing mainly revolves around notions of fictocriticism in exploring subjectivity.

Alison Pullen works at the University of Technology, Sydney, and holds an honorary fellowship at the University of Bristol, UK. She is author of *Managing Identity* (Palgrave, 2006), and co-editor of *Organization and Identity* and *Thinking Organization* (both 2005, with Stephen Linstead).

Carl Rhodes is Professor of Organization Studies and works at the School of Management, the University of Technology, Sydney. His research interests relate to the subjective and cultural meaning of work, management and organization. Current projects focus on the ethics of managerial work and the representation of work and organizations in popular culture.

Maxine Robertson is Professor of Management, Queen Mary University, London. Her main research interests include the management of knowledge workers, management of innovation, and professional identity. She has published extensively in all of these areas in journals such as *Organization Studies*, *Journal of Management Studies* and *Management Learning*.

Michael Saren is Professor of Marketing at Leicester University. He has a doctorate from the University of Bath and previously held Chairs in Marketing at the universities of Stirling and Strathclyde. His research covers critical marketing, marketing of technology, consumer culture and marketing theory. He is co-author with David Ford of *Marketing and Managing Technology* (Thomson Business Press, 2001), co-editor with Douglas Brownlie, Robin Wensley and Richard Whittington of *Rethinking Marketing*, (Sage Publications, 1999) and a founding editor of the journal *Marketing Theory*. He was also convener of the marketing stream at the first four Critical Management Studies International Conferences, 1999–2005 and one of the 'Gang of Six' who organized the ESRC Seminar Series on Critical Marketing. He was Chair of the 2003 European Marketing Academy Conference and a member of the organizing committee for the 2005 and 2007 European Association of Consumer Research conferences in Gotenberg and Milan. His recent book is an introductory student text, *Marketing Graffiti: The View From The Street* (Butterworth Heinemann, 2006).

Hermine Scheeres leads the Changing Practices Research Cluster in the Faculty of Education, University of Technology, Sydney, where she is an Associate Professor. Hermine uses ethnographic and discourse analytic approaches to research culture, communication, identity and learning, particularly in post-bureaucratic workplaces and organizations. Her current government-funded research projects focus on communication flows in hospital emergency departments, and the relationships between employee and organizational learning across a range of workplaces. Hermine's publications cross the disciplinary areas and fields of practice of organization studies, applied linguistics and adult learning.

Stephanie Schreven is a PhD student at The Maxwell School of Citizenship and Public Affairs, Syracuse University, Syracuse, New York. Her PhD is on culture jamming and piracy as sites of struggle in response to contemporary capitalism. Her work is informed by an interest in and concern for emancipatory struggles in their political as well as economic larger historical context, and the psychoanalytic dynamics at play therein.

David Sims is Professor of Organisational Behaviour, Associate Dean, and Director of the Centre for Leadership, Learning and Change at Cass Business School, City University, London. He has an academic background in operational research and organizational behaviour. His research and consulting interests are in the relationship between managerial identity, living, leading, thinking, learning and storying. He has applied these interests to topics as diverse as why people get angry in organizations, the motivation of middle managers, how people love their organizations, life, agenda shaping, problem construction, consulting skills and mergers.

Natasha Slutskaya is completing her PhD at the University of Exeter. Her research interests can be divided into three broad areas: art, creativity and innovation; embodiment; philosophy and social theory; in as far as they pertain to empirical and/or theoretical dilemmas in the field of organization studies.

James H. Ward, PhD, is a visiting research fellow at Kingston University and a managing consultant with PA Consulting Group. He has written a number of articles on identity published in *Human Relations, Culture & Organization, Business & Professional Ethics, Sociological Review* and other journals. He continues to follow his research interests in the areas of identity, minority sexuality and diversity, and consults in the people aspects of organizational change. He has a PhD and MBA from Imperial College, London, and a BA in Modern Languages from Leeds University. He can be contacted on james@outoftheearth.demon.co.uk

Diana C. Winstanley (1961–2006) was Professor of Human Resource Management and Director of Postgraduate Programmes at Kingston Business School. She co-authored this chapter before her death in July 2006. It is published posthumously and dedicated to her memory.

Tony Watson is Professor of Organisational Behaviour at Nottingham University Business School. He teaches, researches and writes about industrial sociology, organizations and managerial and entrepreneurial work. Ethnographic research is a special interest. Recent books include *In Search of Management* (revised edition 2001), *Sociology, Work and Industry* (4th edition 2003) and *Managing and Organising Work* (2nd edition 2006). Current research focuses on issues of identity among managers and entrepreneurs and the relationship between how such people shape their 'whole lives' and aspects of the enterprises within which they work.

Julie Wolfram Cox holds the Chair in Management at Deakin University, Australia. Julie received BA (Honours) and MA (Research) degrees in psychology from the University of Melbourne and holds a PhD in organizational behaviour from Case Western Reserve University in Cleveland, USA. Her research interests include critical and aesthetic perspectives on organization theory and research, particularly organizational change. She co-edited a four-volume collection, *Fundamentals of Action Research* (2005) with Bill Cooke, University of Manchester and is currently co-editing two other books and co-authoring *Disorganization Theory: Alternative Organizational Analysis* (2007, with John Hassard and Mihaela Kelemen). Julie is associate editor for *Qualitative Research in Organizations and Management* and is a member of the editorial boards for *Organization Studies, Journal of Applied Behavioral Science, Group and Organization Management* and *Tamara*.

Introduction

You, me, us and identity: introducing *Exploring Identity*

Alison Pullen, Nic Beech and David Sims

Identity is a concept that speaks to all of us – it is about who we are, who we are not and the features that differentiate us as 'individuals'. But identity is a paradox – we can all make claims to having identity, but each of our claims is one of uniqueness. Identity thus makes us the same as others, at the same time as it makes each of us different from everyone else. In contemporary times, work and organizations are a key part of this. We have been told to self-actualize and to realize our own unique potential in the pursuit of our professional and work ambitions. We are also told that our identities rely on identification with the culture of the organizations where we work, and that organizational identity is a key part of this culture management. As 'identity' we are comparable to others – we identify with them as being the same as us. And, as 'identity', we render ourselves as being just us – particular individuals who can be thought of without comparison.

In writing the introduction to this book we too are called upon to account for our identities as academics, thinkers and editors. We speak in this introductory chapter with one voice as if we might inhabit one identity, without separate names. We speak as authorities who are able to gather together the variety, complexity and difference that constitutes theoretical and methodological approaches to researching identity. But we are three people, each with our individual identity, no matter how they might be collectivized in our shared editorial identity. Yet, as three, our organization as editors renders us in terms of a certain 'sameness' that might make you think of us as one. And these concerns, materialized in these few paragraphs of introduction, speak to the heart of theoretical concerns about identity.

1

These are concerns that imply a conflicting desire – a desire to be identity as a 'one of a kind', and a simultaneous desire to be known as one who is part of a social formation.

But it is not just us three that are at stake. In terms of all of the contributors to this book, we can 'identify' with each other – identify enough to hold our names within the boundaries of a book written by people who think they have something to say about 'identity'. Identity both liberates and enslaves. Identity makes us different from all those others who also have their own identities. So too it makes us the same as we also can only possibly know ourselves in relation to the categories that we inherit from culture and experience. And these categories include, most especially, those we inherit from our work – and even those who do not work are 'identified' as the unemployed. Indeed, who might answer the question 'who are you?' without referring to some occupational, professional, educational or other work-related categories? But coming back to the people who contributed chapters to this book, yes, we can collect them all together under some identity category as being people who research identity. But politics are at play, as they always are with identity. This is an identity politics that presumes to render plural difference under a common moniker. But identity also means respect for difference. In this vein our introductory comments are intended to refer to this concept – *identity* – in a way that respects the sameness and difference that it implies and works within the tension between the two. We wish to introduce this volume in terms of the way that it takes the common notion of identity in relation to the variety and contestable ways that it can be theorized, conceived, understood and researched.

The focus of this book is on examining the concepts and methods that have been used to study identity as it relates to work, management and organizations. Indeed, the changing nature of organizations and changing meanings of work have led scholars and students alike to consider the nature of identity and to question how it informs our current thinking and practices in organizations. Many activities in organizations impact on people's identities, just as the identities of people impact organizations. Organizational change, leadership, improving services, developing new products, enhancing corporate social responsibility and sustainability all entail people doing things differently, thinking in new ways and, in a sense, *being* different. The effects of such activities will depend in part on how people react, and their reactions relate to the way they see themselves and others. Understanding such dynamics also means understanding identity, and the ways that it is formed, manipulated, developed and put to work. This puts precedence on exploring identity as one of the fundamental concepts that lies at the heart of organizations, and is central to people's experience of work-life. And it is this concept that is concerned with the way that people might ask themselves questions such as: Who am I? Who was I? How and why are you different from me? And, who can I become?

The purpose of this book is to offer contributions that reflect the wide range of ways that identity has and can be researched, and to appreciate their theoretical, empirical and methodological diversity – the diversity and difference that has come to characterize the way that identity has been researched. In this spirit the chapters are intended, both collectively and in some cases individually, to be both multi- and cross-disciplinary. The book is organized so that the chapters can be read in any order rather than following a single linear argument. This is designed to enable you to reflect on the conceptual and methodological choices that are open in exploring identity. In doing this we have structured the book in two parts: *Concepts* and *Methods*. But, as you will discover, some of the chapters in the 'Concepts' section raise methodological issues, and in the 'Methods' section authors use different concepts and theoretical influences in their execution of their identity research. The book is designed for students and researchers of identity alike. As such, the various chapters seek to address the most up to date and relevant issues for identity research. While these are meant to be of interest to both new and experienced researchers, they are written in a manner that is accessible for those who are not yet immersed in the debates.

Part I of *Exploring Identity* covers the fundamental *Concepts of Identity* as they are applied in current research in organization and management research. Many of the chapters derive from, or are sympathetic to, a broadly critical perspective. From this perspective the focus is on interrogating and questioning how and why identities (for example, personal, managerial, academic, organizational, consumer, sexual) are constructed and reconstructed and what the consequences for these identity projects are. The contributions in this section range from critical marketing, organization theory, critical theory, management, sociology, psychoanalysis and philosophy.

Part I starts with Mike Saren's critique of consumer identity. The chapter explores the subjective nature of consumers' identities and the nature of self in its relationship *with and in* consumption. This chapter draws from across social science authors and disciplines – from Goffman and Maffesoli in sociology, Baudrillard in philosophy, Elliot in marketing, to Bauman and Belk on identity. These sources are used to explore how consumption is related to the identity for consumers. In doing this Saren analyses the processes of performing identity as a consumer in the marketplace, displaying identity in terms of social or cultural status using consumption, and creating identity through consumption: 'we are what we consume'. Chapter 2 discusses the metaphorical construction of organizational identity. Joep Cornelissen shows the theoretical diversity informing the notion of 'organizational identity' in terms of its wide-ranging different theoretical perspectives, influences (ranging from cognitive framing, discursive psychology, organizational communication, social identity, organizational behavior, institutional theory) and conceptual objects such as beliefs and discourses. Cornelissen suggests that considering the nature and capacity of 'organizational identity' as a metaphor appreciates this diversity as a particular discursive construction of organizational reality. Cornelissen argues that the 'metaphorical correlation of concepts in the "organizational identity" metaphor has not only schematized theoretical perspectives in very different ways, but has also provided a conceptual logic (of 'identity') for reasoning about organizations and their manifestations' (p. 45).

In the next chapter Cliff Oswick and Maxine Robertson conduct a textual analysis of popular books on 'branding oneself', arguing that personal branding is a form of identity work which has implications for the construction, negotiation and re-negotiation of management identities. They also consider the way in which personal branding texts have a detrimental impact upon on the ongoing processes of managing, organizing and identity construction insofar as they engender anxiety, encourage dissimulation and promote 'safe' and compliant behavior. Methodologically, Oswick and Robertson also consider the implications of adopting the textual approach of popular books to the analysis of identity work. In Chapter 4 Martin Parker offers a critique of the dualism between identity being thought of as relatively fixed and stable, and identity as fluid and complex. Parker analyses what structuralism can show us about organization and identity, and considers why such structuralist forms of argument seem to be less fashionable than declarations about change, multiplicity and creativity. Parker argues that the shift in attention from identity as fixed to fluid depends on assumptions about human agency. To do so, he also provides an empirical demonstration of identity construction at work to explore the relations between self and other. Through an analysis of spatial and functional divides, generational divides and occupational/professional divides, Parker reveals how dividing is central to identification processes that individuals employ in doing organization.

Chapter 5 sees Carl Rhodes, Rick Iedema and Hermine Scheeres explore the relationship between identity, surveillance and resistance. Rhodes *et al.*, informed by a Foucauldian approach to power and surveillance, explore the way that surveillance is at play in organizations and how it is seen to influence subject formation. Rhodes *et al.* discuss various forms and degrees of resistance against 'the gaze' of surveillance from a relational perspective. In particular, they consider how cynicism has been understood as a mode of internal distancing that, while maintaining the external appearance of compliance, inserts a critical space into being at work. Moreover, they discuss the possibilities of how identity might also be located outside of the compliance-resistance binary. In Chapter 6 Adrian Carr and Cheryl Lapp provide a psychoanalytic approach to explore leadership and the psychodynamic behavioral expressions constituent of the death instinct. According to Carr and Lapp, this needs to be reflexively predicted and interpreted if the 'organization' (i.e. psychic and organizational workplaces) is to regenerate healthy attitudes toward leadership change and, indeed, to understand individual and group identity dynamics during organizational change more generally. Methodologically they achieve this through a re-reading of a case study 'As Leadership Dies' by Hyde.

Tony Watson's Chapter 7 explores the interplay between the 'self' and the 'social' in studying human *identity work*. He does so through an autobiographical account of how his own identity work has influenced and been influenced by the research work he has done on managerial identity work. Chapter 8 explores sexual identity in organizations by drawing on empirical research conducted by James Ward in a major banking corporation, a police department and the fire service – organizations which are all considered to have masculinist workplace cultures. The author explore the processes of sexual minorities – neglected and marginalized identities – coming out at work. This empirical study uses narrative methodology and a focus group method to analyse how dominant discourses of the workplace inform sexual identities and how discourses emerge through the process of 'coming out'. The chapter concludes by suggesting another methodology for gay identity research in organizations focusing on general discourse about sexual minorities rather than lesbians and gay men themselves.

Chapter 9 brings the body back into focus when exploring identity. Natasha Slutskaya and Stephanie Schreven, drawing almost exclusively on Merleau-Ponty's work, explore embodied identity by using the concepts of repetition and loss through the event of modern dance to show that the investigation of those concepts challenges the dichotomization of verbal and nonverbal cultural practices. It does so, they argue, by asserting the unlived possibilities of movement and the theoretical potential of bodily action. In the final chapter of Part I, Nceku 'Q' Nyathi and Stefano Harney ask the question: 'What anti-racist, queer activist, or feminist has not been faced with the charge of being a one-issue scholar, of bringing up the same question again and again, of being caught in "identity politics?" '(p. 185). In a critique of a sample of fundamental studies of identities in work and organization, Nyathi and Harney offer a disidentity politics which 'seek to make us uncomfortable, to insert a silence, to undermine a position, to redouble our efforts' (p. 185). Drawing on postcolonial theorists including Spivak and others, the relationships between the subject and agency are analysed to ascertain that 'disidentity critiques seek the superadequation of the subject that might release agency. The aim is the production of a social individual who would have no need of this category of identity, for whom any question about it, any struggle over it, becomes archaic' (p. 85).

In Part II of *Exploring Identity* some of the *Research Methods* that are currently being employed in research on identity are presented. In studying identity there is an extensive range of research approaches with different ontological, epistemological and methodological implications. The aim of Part II is to discuss a sufficiently broad range of these methods to enable an appreciation of the diversity of possibilities that are available. The chapters explain the processes that researchers use, and where relevant they also give illustrations of the methods in action. In presenting the range of chapters, the reader may develop their own understanding of how they might want to research identity. This may endorse and reinforce existing methodological and paradigmatic preferences or may challenge the reader to explore new methodological options.

Part II starts with Chapter 11 by Gail Clarkson on large-scale identity research using causal cognitive mapping methods. The choices available to researchers are discussed, and by researching a call-center organization, explores issues of personal and organizational identity. Using causal cognitive mapping techniques, individual causal cognitive maps are presented to offer a comparative analysis of generalizability of identity constructs. In Chapter 12 Julie Wolfram Cox and Bill Cooke propose an understanding of action research as an ongoing project of identity formation. In a thorough review of action research role from the 1940s and 1950s Wolfram Cox and Cooke map out some of the changes in representation that have been a part of how this form of research has been practiced. The authors contrast current efforts and the varieties of types of action research (e.g. participatory action research, action learning, and appreciative inquiry) in terms of their relative modesty/ambition, and the implicit and explicit identity claims embedded therein. They argue that the nature of action research and the identities of the action researcher cannot be disentangled, and conclude by arguing for a return to greater modesty in action research.

Chapter 13, by Paul Hibbert, Robert MacIntosh and Peter McInnes, looks at identity trajectories in participative organizational research. Hibbert *et al.* discuss participative modes of research to outline their understanding of the identity dynamics entailed, and analyse these issues of identity in an organization in the cultural sector. In Chapter 14 Stephen Linstead uses performance ethnography and the Radio Ballads (a series of radio programmes from the 1950s and 1960s re-broadcasted on the BBC in 2006) for the study of collective identity. Furthermore, Ewan MacColl (writer, lyricist and singer) and Charles Parker's (editor and producer) writing on their own research methods, together with some transcriptions from the programmes, are used to surface the significance of recording the background culture; listening to language (rather than discourse); intermittent interrogative methods; collective identity and narrative myth; collective self-discovery and catalytic interviewing. Linstead concludes by addressing some potential criticisms of the approach.

Chapter 15 is Christine Coupland's examination of the concept of self-identity as co-construction and its relationship to doing interviews. Starting from the perspective that identity practices are narrative, Coupland draws on Ricoeur to show how 'speakers occupy a position from which we are able to mediate between looking backwards to practical concerns while looking forwards to ethical concerns – that is character, or sedimented acts of the past, are recounted with a concern for what they say about the speaker today and for the future' (p. 274–5). This is considered in terms of its relevance to the narrative nature of the material constructed from interviews. Furthermore, as Coupland shows, the research interview highlights questions surrounding the extent that we are able to construct our selves in interaction. Following suit, Nic Beech and David Sims in Chapter 16 discuss narrative methods for identity research, focusing on the nature of *homo narrans narratur* as the person who understands himself or herself and others by telling stories about themselves, both to themselves and to others. Beech and Sims analyse techniques for analysing stories and narratives to show how they can be used for researching identity – in particular, the gathering of narrative data, the process of analysis and nature of the conclusion that can be drawn from this type of research are discussed.

In Chapter 17 Nick Llewellyn and Robin Burrow present a novel study, drawing on audio/video recordings that capture the work of buying and selling the *Big Issue* magazine in a busy urban street in a British city. In a conversation analysis of the micro-processes of interaction of work identities on the street (a less conventional setting for the study of work), the chapter considers different ways in which magazine sellers and those who engage with them orient to identities including 'Catholic', 'guy', 'customer', 'regular', 'donor' and 'homeless'. Such identities are approached as positions within a fluid web of accountabilities that are locally invoked and negotiated; not as deeply embedded features of personal biographies or psyches. The next chapter by Alison Pullen is offered in the spirit of rewriting the feminine into the research process, arguing that the research self is gendered. To explore the conceptualization of 'self' and 'gender' Pullen presents a discursive/textual approach, a social practice/performance approach, and a 'corporeal multiplicity' approach which reintroduces the body into the research process. To conclude, Pullen offers three strategies to operationalize an embodied identity in reflexive research texts – *re-citing*, *re-siting* and *re-sighting*. These strategies both foreground and problematize the very character of what it might mean to enter the identity of the researcher. The book closes with a piece of creative writing by Alexandra Pitsis written in a 'fictocritical' style. Pitsis explores the relationship between 'cartography' and 'identity' not as metaphor but as an attempt to describe a process of how she experiences subjectivity and identity, particularly when attempting to locate herself in the field of a text. Cartography here is seen as a kind of spatialization of what takes place in the complex process of writing. By drawing on her autobiographical experiences, Pitsis reveals the illusions surrounding knowledge, subjectivity and text.

In having introduced and outlined what it is you can expect to find in this book, what we are sure about is that there is no 'one best way' of exploring identity. There are always choices that need to be made as to what concepts and methods we employ. In *Exploring Identity* this diversity speaks for itself – whether we are doing research on identity or exploring the implications of identity when doing research on other topics, there is a range of options for formulating research questions, conducting literature reviews, justifying research methodologies, collecting and analysing data, developing theory and disseminating research. In having edited this book it is our hope that it will enable readers to understand and appreciate some of this diversity, and be able to use this to further develop their own work.

part **1**

Concepts

1

The obscure subject of consumer identity

Michael Saren

Introduction

Like Bunuel's *Object of Desire*, the subject of consumer identity is obscure in the sense that it is never fully revealed in any description or definition. Attempts to define it or 'pin it down' always seem to fail because either they miss out some important aspects or forms of the subjective consumers' identities or, at the other extreme, they resort to such generalized tautologies that they cease to reflect the variety of types and manifestations of 'the self' in its relationship with and in consumption. I shall return to this essential incompleteness of the consumer identity concept later in the final section of this chapter which explores some problematic issues and a critique of the notion of consumer identity.

The first question is how is consumption related to identity for consumers? There are at least three aspects as follows:

i) **performing identity** as a consumer in the marketplace.
ii) **displaying identity** in terms of social or cultural status using consumption
iii) **creating identity** through consumption: 'we are what we consume'.

Performing the role of the consumer

We are all consumers. Unless we go and live on a desert island we cannot avoid consuming and we all play a role, or roles, in the marketing process as consumers. In this way consumption is an activity which involves a constant and highly repetitive everyday performance into which we all become socialized (Goffman 1959). In a groundbreaking article, Deighton (1992) pointed out that in marketing although the word 'performance' often occurs in accounts of consumption, it is seldom brought into the foreground of the discussion or analysis. Many consumer transactions involve performances, not simply possessions as such. Yet, marketers have in the past tended to study things – products, consumers, adverts, demands, distribution channels – not events (Vargo and Lusch 2004).

Deighton (1992) gives several examples of consumer performance.

1. Consumers attend performances that are staged for them, such as sports events, music concerts, religious services, theatre, college lectures, circuses.
2. Consumers participate in performances that require them to play an active role. In many service markets, consumers have to play their part in the 'performance' of the service operation, such as restaurants, weddings, workshops and sales demonstrations.
3. Consumers perform with products, such as clothes, using them as props in performances which they enact to influence others – and it is the others who actually consume the performance.
4. Products perform for consumers as they use them. Detergents perform by cleaning. A product is the 'frozen potential for performance'. The marketer's purpose in designing and delivering the products is to direct their performance well.

In all these examples, performance is the core element in the consumption experience. Deighton argues that frequently it is performances, not products, that are the objects of consumption:

> In its concern with performance, marketing reveals itself as an inherently dramatistic discipline it scripts, produces and directs performances for and with consumers and manages the motives consumers attribute to the decision to perform. From this perspective, consumers behave as if they were audiences responding to or participating in performances. ..... Consumers may be said to choose products, but they consume performances
>
> (Deighton 1992: 362).

The notion of performance is a useful way of looking at consumption because it encompasses and unites many of the concepts inherent within the consumption experience. All performances take place within a setting or on a stage. One of the phenomena associated with consumer communities or subcultures is that important places are transformed and resignified, for example, the 'rendezvous' of mountain men in the USA (Belk and Costa 1998). Performances also depend on stories, plays, narratives or myth; such as the 'easy rider' myth that feeds US biker culture (Schouten and McAlexander 1995), or the science fiction–based story that has inspired and seen the Star Trek phenomenon develop and grow (Kozinets 2001). Myths allow for fantasy and escape (Belk and Costa 1998) which is central to both performance and observation of performance. This performance allows for the construction and enactment of alternative identities through the adoption of temporary roles. Performances involve spectacle and can be acted out in a carnivalesque atmosphere (Bakhtin 1984) that provides the opportunity to reverse the codes and norms of everyday behavior. Thus, participants can shed their everyday identities and become 'actors' for a temporary period of time.

This view regards consumer identity as the performance of the role of consumer in the marketplace. Through the repeated *performance* of buying, using and evaluating products, we *become* consumers – our performance enacts our consumer identity. Playing the 'role' of consumer gives us certain expectations about our own and others' behavior and confers on us certain rights and responsibilities and an identity.

Displaying social status and cultural identity

Many contemporary commentators have pointed to marketing as one of the key cultural architects of our time. They suggest that marketing since the 1950s has come to play a significant role in the creation, maintenance and/or reproduction of taste, dreams and aspirations (Ewen 1988), needs (Packard 1957), selves and identities (Elliot 1999), desiring consumers (Bauman 1988), morality (Grafton Small and Linstead 1989), hedonism and sign systems (Baudrillard 1981, 1998). The abundance of marketing messages and signs for which the so-called 'culture industries' are responsible in everyday life may even qualify marketing professionals for carrying the label 'ministers of propaganda of the consumer culture'.

Consumer goods are used to signify social status as demonstrated through the choice of a particular selection of goods that classifies the consumer according to various socio-economic hierarchies – such as their wealth, knowledge, social position, taste and refinement. It is not simply the display of the material possessions themselves that is important, nor simply economic capability or the price paid. According to Bourdieu (1984) modern consumption is primarily concerned with the establishment and maintenance of 'distinction' or difference between social classes and status groups. The maintenance of difference thus not only implies a competitive relationship between consumers who perceive themselves to inhabit different groups and identities, but also has the effect of 'bonding' consumers more closely within these subcultures and social communities. By seeking to align themselves with certain group norms, consumers must share with the others in that group such things as their common consumption ambitions and adopt similar behaviors and lifestyles. As Woodward notes, identities are *produced*, *consumed* and *regulated* within culture and they create meanings through symbolic systems of representation (Woodward 1997).

The notion that consumer goods are employed to signify social position and their use by individuals demonstrates the taste and distinction of the users is not a particularly modern phenomenon. Several classic anthropological studies have shown that the primary function of material culture is not the satisfaction of 'needs' but the role in social rituals and the establishment of social hierarchies both within and between groups (Mauss 1966). It was Veblen (1899) who first detailed the modern 'conspicuous consumption' behavior of the *nouveau riches*, and the manner in which they employed certain types of goods and services as registers of their new social position. The success of early department stores as centers for taste and fashion was largely a consequence of the vast appetite for status symbols among the newly emerging affluent middle class in the nineteenth century (Laermans 1993).

Although the power and influence of the marketing profession is undoubtedly very great in creating the cultural language and 'setting the scene' for consumers (Svensson 2004), one criticism of the argument and observations above is that they *understate the role of the consumer* in determining their own culture. For example, Elliot (1999) points out that 'consumers do not passively accept marketing communications but may actively renegotiate the meaning subjectively and construct their own interpretations' (p. 114). This view of the culturally active consumer has supported other studies of 'marketplace' cultures in which consumers are seen as culture producers, in contrast to traditional anthropological views of people as culture bearers (Arnould and Thompson 2005).

Subcultures of consumption

The study of subcultures, their activities, power relations, hierarchies and constitute identities has a long tradition of analysis within the discipline of sociology. In the UK several studies have focused on youth subcultures as a form of resistance to cultural domination (e.g. Hebdige 1979, on the Mods of the 1960s). Other authors have regarded music-based youth subcultures as 'the culture industry's commodification of dissent' (Frank and Weiland 1997). Beyond 'sites of resistance', subcultures are also a form of consumer culture at the micro-level. They are responsible for the creation of micro-markets and the products and services to meet these demands. They have opinion leaders, innovators and imitators of the latest trends in specialized clothing, jewellery and accessories.

Marketing and consumer researchers have more recently begun to focus on the material artefacts and consumption practices that underpin, support and define the very existence of many subcultures and the consumption experiences of those involved. Such studies that look at how consumers forge feelings of social solidarity and create self-selected, sometimes transitory and fragmented, (sub)cultural worlds involving the pursuit of common consumption interests.

Various different terms have been used to describe this phenomenon; such as, subcultures of consumption, consumption micro-cultures, brand communities and consumption tribes. Much of this work is based on Maffesoli's (1996) concept of the 'neo-tribe'. Maffesoli argues that traditional bonds of community between individuals have been eroded and the free market ethos promotes a continual quest for personal autonomy and difference. Consumers, however, find such conditions lonely and alienating; therefore, they form looser grouping of shared interests and engage in joint activities and rituals based on lifestyle choices and leisure pursuits. The neo-tribe provides affectual bonds between people based on leisure activities, cultural pursuits, religion and intellectual interests. The process of feeling emotions together provides an 'emotional glue' that creates a reconnection between people who are otherwise disparate in today's individualistic society. Members are bound together by a process called 'Proxemics' which develops from being close to someone because you share the same space/sentiment – for example, a common interest in surfing or driving the same car. Marketing has recognised these tribes and advertising addresses them directly – and tribes recognize themselves in these messages and images (Cova and Cova 2002).

Social meanings found in material possessions can be viewed as cultural communicators, which has opened the way for their investigation using ethnographic methods. Ethnographic research into the consumer aspects of subcultures include Arnould and Price's (1993) 'River Magic' study of white-river rafters, Hill's (1991) study of homeless women and the meaning of possessions, and Schouten and McAlexander's (1995) longitudinal study of the US 'biker' culture. Other consumer researchers looking at contemporary subcultural groupings have studied heavy metal music fans, gay consumers, skydivers, *Star Trek* followers, mountain men, the rave music scene, Goths, surfers and freerunners. There are a number of themes that emerge from these studies of different consumer subcultures or tribes:

1. Subcultures are based around product constellations, places, events and services. Businesses emerge to serve the wants and needs of participants.
2. Tribal aspects of consumption are pervasive, fostering collective identifications grounded in shared beliefs, meanings, myths, rituals, practices and status hierarchies.
3. Subcultures are made up of diverse groups of people – not gender- or class based. Subcultures provide a platform for the display and construction of alternative consumer activity–based identities.
4. There are different levels of commitment which reflect the individual's identity. People can escape from their 'everyday life' – for example, the subculture enables the bank manager during the week to become a biker at the weekend.

This section has outlined the various ways in which consumption activities within society and subcultures are used by consumers to display their social status or cultural identity. Such 'conspicuous consumption' behavior, of buying, using, showing off products and brands, can be used to 'say something' about the person's social or cultural identity.

Creating identity through consumption

Some argue that consumers are doing more than displaying their status or identity through products – they are creating a part of their identity. One of the most important strands of consumer research in marketing studies and attempts to understand 'the co-constitutive, co-productive ways in which consumers, working with market-generated materials, forge a coherent, if diversified and often fragmented sense of self' (Arnould and Thompson 2005: 13). Within this branch of research in marketing, consumers are viewed as *identity seekers* and makers and it is the *marketplace* that is regarded as the primary source of 'mythic and symbolic resources' through which people construct 'narratives of identity' (Holt 2002).

For Bauman (1988), individual freedom in modern society takes the form of 'consumer freedom', through which the individuals are able to invent and create their own self-identity. People are free to use consumer goods to 'become' any of their 'possible selves'; they are able to *create* their own perceived self by *identifying with* the objects and symbols of their consumption. People may identify themselves with objects of consumption through many forms in their everyday life. If 'lifestyle' TV programmes and magazines are to be believed, for many people these are often consumer objects such as their home, possessions, decoration, furniture, clothes, garden, car and jewellery. Of course, the most immediate and intimate physical manifestation of one's identity is the body.

Consuming the body

The body is the site of *all* consumption. Consumption itself is 'embodied', takes place in and through the body (Falk 1994). Some sensory organ must ingest, take into the body; thus the body is 'contaminated' by the object of consumption. So any performative enactment of the consumer's identity must occur *through the body*, thus identity must be linked in a material form to the body itself. Therefore, another means of creating identity is through 'consuming' the body.

Consider how much consumer and marketing activity is centered on the body and the consumer's 'self-image' – adornment, clothing, perfumery, cosmetics, tattoos, body modification. The use of products and services to make the body look better and 'improve' ones 'self-image' is a means of identity construction using the body as a site of consumption. Identity is often related nowadays to body image and thus to the consumption of particular beauty, health care and cosmetic products. People's identities and 'self-esteem' are so closely associated with their bodies that it can strongly motivate peoples' choice of food consumption, diet, sports, fitness, and medical and surgical products, aimed at affecting or changing their body image. There has been a growth in interest on the part of consumer researchers in the relationship between the body, identity and symbolic consumption (e.g. Thompson and Hirschman 1995) – and in particular the role of the *'embodied self'* (Featherstone 2000, Mauss 1979/1936) which includes body modification such as cosmetic surgery (Schouten 1991) and body art (Velliquette and Bamossy 2001). The field of body modification provides a wealth of possible case studies for understanding the degree of consumer involvement in the production, creation and consumption of a new highly visible 'identity'.

One popular form of body adornment, which has a long and well-documented history, is that of tattooing. With more recent shifts in fashion towards body adornment, including body piercing and tattooing, acquiring a tattoo is now seen as part of contemporary popular culture and is a global multi-billion pound industry (DeMello 2000). Unlike other objects of consumption, the tattoo is unique both in its concept and in its practice, and has very few comparisons, largely due to the permanency of the act. Tattoos are permanent. Research with producers and consumers of tattoos, conducted by Goulding and Follett (2001), has found tattoos are considered by most recipients to be works of art – that are created by 'artists' upon a canvass, the body. They are both public and private statements about the individual's identity, and, significantly, the act of tattooing involves an often-extended period of pain and potential risk of infection.

There are other connections between consumption, the body and identity beyond these various types of body adornment, such as the notion of the 'extended self'.

The extended self

The seminal marketing studies of the relationship between possessions and the sense of self are contained in the publications based on the extensive research on consumer behavior reported by Russell Belk of the University of Utah. Belk (1988) employs the term 'extended self' to encompass the role of possessions in the consumer's identity. He argues that knowingly or unknowingly we regard our possessions as part of ourselves – in other words, 'we are what we have'. In order to demonstrate that possessions play a powerful and complex role and are 'an important component of sense of self', Belk (1988: 139) draws on several forms of evidence, which can be summarized in three parts as follows.

1. The nature of self-perception encompasses possessions. The subjective existence of an extended identity is highlighted by phenomena such as the investment of psychic or physical energy in the products we make or own, the diminished sense of self when certain possessions are lost and the ritual function of objects which anthropological studies have found in all societies. The ritual role of possessions and the person can be observed most clearly when the objects are associated with birth, matrimony and death: points of the transformation of 'self'.
2. The relationships between having, doing and being. Objects in our possession also enable us to do things we otherwise could not, for example an axe to chop wood, a horse to travel. Beyond a functional role of extending one's capacity for '*doing*', possessions are also used symbolically to demonstrate or reinforce *who* we are. This is most obviously the case with a uniform or a badge, but many other apparently functional products are nowadays used symbolically to extend the owner's identity or *being*

in some way, for example clothes, hairstyles, automobiles, houses and furnishing.

3. Processes of self-extension incorporating objects. Building on the relationship between having and being, Belk cites Sartre's (1943) proposition of three primary ways through which we learn to regard an object as part of self. First, by owning, controlling or mastering objects, such as a car, a computer or even by climbing a mountain, one 'masters' them and they 'add' to our sense of self. Purchasing something transfers ownership and control to the buyer and therefore money itself can be regarded as having a *potential* for self-extension through acquisition of objects. Viewed in this manner, gift giving also involves extending the self towards the other, or more negatively, a corresponding loss of control – and thus self – on the part of the recipient (Mauss 1966). The second way of incorporating an object into self is by creating it. Whether it is a physical object or an abstract idea, the creator retains an identity with the object as long as it is associated with that person. The third way in which objects become part of the self, according to Sartre, is by *knowing* them. To 'know' about something or someone contains elements of both desire (Lacan 1977) and power (Foucault 1980) on the part of the knower over the object.

In these ways it is argued that consumers are doing more than displaying their status or identity through products; they are *creating* an 'extended self' by *appropriating and incorporating* the objects and symbols of their consumption; that is 'we are what we consume'.

Critique

This final section presents some problematic issues for the concept of consumer identity.

1. Branding
2. Disadvantaged Consumers
3. Consumer Choice
4. The Incomplete Consumer

Branding has an image problem

In this Chapter I could have explored the relationship between consumer identity and the so-called brand personality (see Holt 2002). The concept of the personality or identity of the brand is not the same thing as the consumer's identity, however, and – for the purpose of this chapter – would take us some distance away from the latter. (For more on identity and branding, see Elliott and Davies 2005; also Schroeder and Salzer-Morling 2005). Another problem is that the term 'branding' has evolved to such an extent that the word itself has become ubiquitous. In the marketing literature you can read about consumer brands, high street brands, virtual brands, brand value, corporate brands, personal brands, celebrity brands, household brands, sub-brands, brand extensions, fashion brands, brand 'fever', brand communities, own-label brands, diffusion brands, brand stretching and lifestyle brands (Saren 2006). In everyday use the term is applied to political parties, movies, TV programmes, footballers, nations, pop stars, military regiments, science, works of art, artists, cartoons, fictional characters and literary icons. As Baudrillard (1981) starkly illustrates, once a concept gains totality and becomes appropriate to everything and anything, it also becomes appropriate to nothing.

There but for fortune: disadvantaged consumers

Not all consumer identities are equal – and some are more unequal than others. According to consumer studies, whatever personal problems some people may face – whether it is loss of community, lack of self-esteem, unhappiness or boredom – can be 'solved' by adopting a particular consumer lifestyle and constructing a 'better' self through the products and services associated with it (Elliott and Wattanasuwan 1998). On the other hand, others argue that the 'freedom' to construct their identity through consumption is in fact quite limited by the 'structuring influence of the marketplace' and that while consumers can pursue personal goals through the market they are in fact 'enacting and personalizing' from a choice of 'cultural scripts' or lifestyles, many of which are set by marketers (Arnould and Thompson 2005). Phenomena such as Marx's commodity fetishism explain how the real social relations which, as it were, lie behind the marketing process are hidden from consumers who are nevertheless constrained and conditioned by them (Marx 1976).

Another aspect when viewed from a global perspective is that the 'issue' of consumer identity is an overwhelmingly ethnocentric one for the rich, advanced economies of the North. The vast majority of consumers in the world desperately want to consume more, not to complete or complement some notional 'identity', but in *order to survive*. For them freedom is not some notion of 'liberation' from the ideological chains of the consumer culture; on the contrary, freedom certainly *is* the realization of material necessity (Marx 1976).

There is a further issue of disadvantage in relation to consumer identity in the advanced economies such as the US and the UK, where many people are unable to fully participate in the consumer society because they have little discretionary spending or choice. Some of this is due to low incomes; however, consumer disadvantage may take several forms including lack of access to markets, information and education, availability of finance and credit, exploitative practices of business and other personal factors such as immobility or illness. The problems faced by poor consumers go beyond the resource scarcity and meagre consumption opportunities.

From his extensive studies of the poor and the wider 'culture of poverty' in which they are said to exist, Hill (2002) concludes that living in an inescapable consumer culture further exacerbates their plight; for example, by the role of the media which all too effectively communicates the standards and opportunities for material accumulation in society through television, movie and music, demonstrating the vivid contrast between their culture of poverty and the consumer abundance that surrounds them. Not only are they materially deprived but also they are thus unable to fully participate in the so-called 'semiotic democracy' that Fiske (1987) suggests is provided by television and other mass communications.

A further cause for concern regarding disadvantaged consumers is the role and emphasis of consumption in the process of identity, self-esteem and connectedness to other consumers who are unable to fully participate in consumer choice and who are also potentially further handicapped by their exclusion from the symbolic and cultural aspects of consumption. In this sense the 'subaltern' consumer of the rich North can have little identity of which to 'speak' (Spivak 1988) through consumption any more than 'wretched of the earth' in the poor South (Fanon 1961).

The court of the Crimson King: consumer Identity and choice

One espoused value underpinning the concept of marketing is the belief in choice: the right of consumers to have the freedom to choose from a selection of options in what they buy, from where and from whom. The phrase often employed to represent the customer as *the* chooser, the one in control, is the term '*the customer is king*'. This royal metaphor goes back a long way and it is deeply rooted in ideas of exchange, customer service and free market choice. As early as Shakespeare's *Merchant of Venice*, Antonio is described as a 'royal merchant'. Adam Smith (1961), who was after all a moral philosopher, described the consumer as 'sovereign' in the marketplace. The royal title was also applied by Horkheimer to describe the 'courting' and 'majesty' of the customer in the pre–nineteenth century era. Far from today's customer being 'king', Horkheimer (1967) observed marketing now has such a powerful control apparatus ('technologies of governance') of the 'free' market that it has resulted in consumers becoming dependent on the knowledge of experts, technologies and systems – that their freedom, 'inner as well as empirical', has been lost.

Hirschman (1993) goes one step further in her discussion of the language employed to discuss the consumer in many marketing texts which, she argues, are littered with metaphors of war, combat and captivity. Market segments are 'targeted' for 'penetration'. Market share must be 'fought for' and 'won'. Customers must be 'locked-in' lest they 'defect' to the opposition. Thus, consumers are worked upon until they are 'captive', although unaware of this captivity (Du Gay 2001). If consumers' freedom – *inner and empirical* – is lost and they exercise 'choice' only as captives, then the customer is not king, not an autonomous subject, but merely a 'royal' subject. And the 'subject' of the consumer's identity is no longer so obscure, not so fragmented, partial and in process. On the contrary, it is all too apparent, more like Hegel's (1977) bondsman subject to the lordship of marketing ideology. To paraphrase Erich Fromm (1978), the choice for the consumer is not 'to have or to be' because now to have *is* to be.

In every dream home a heartache: the incomplete consumer

> The emotion-laden experiences of the consumer: irrational, incoherent and driven by unconscious desire.....able to build a *DIY self* through consumption, yet suffering an expansion of inadequacy through adverting
>
> (Elliot 1999: 121).

It is tempting to conclude that consumer identity is only ever partially constituted, and always in process. First, one might argue, it is partial because the individual's identity as a consumer does not make up the whole person; they are also citizen, parent, professional, sister, neighbour and so on. Secondly, that 'part' of the self which is the consumer is also necessarily *in process* because it changes according to life-stages, expenditure opportunities, outside influences, contexts and so on. The child, for example, has a very different understanding of their self as a 'consumer' compared to their later adult consumer 'self' (e.g. meanings , fantasies, desires and more mundanely regarding financial implications, responsibilities and waste). Thirdly, the consumer self may be compared to a bricolage, being constructed by mixing 'bits and pieces' from commodities and products available in the marketplace (Hebdige 1979). Fourthly, there are various aspects of self related to consumer – social self, self-concept, cognitive self, ideal self, self-image; therefore, many conclude that the consumer has multiple identities (Desmond 2003).

For marketing to provide consumer choice (which as we have seen is one of its core values) it must deliver lots of supplies and products onto the market and therefore the implicit assumption is that more choice is always 'better', that is *more* is valorized *per se*. Thus, consumer marketing values do not just lead to more choice, they also arguably lead to *abundance and excess* and the necessary provision of *more* than consumers need or want. Bataille (1988) argues that all human systems lead to excess and waste. Thus, in this respect, consumption is merely reflecting the human condition, which always creates more than is needed and therefore produces waste. Thus consumers are necessarily 'incomplete' in the sense that they can never consume all, not materially, nor the *surplus of meaning and symbols*.

> If the objects in our lives have no worth or meaning or longevity, if they are perpetually replaced by shiny new ones, what effect does this have on our sense of self?
>
> (Turner 2006).

One way of viewing the partiality and dynamic of consumers' identity is to recognize that the inherent gap, the essential incompleteness, *is* the consumer identity; that is that absence or lack which in modern society's restricted economy the human being *tries to fill* through consumption. Thus, the role of marketing is in stimulating desires, the need for fantasy and fetishism in the commodity form (Marx 1976). And finally – far from the espoused 'satisfaction of needs', what results is the necessary eventual *dissatisfaction* on the part of the consumer, because of the logic of the market which always must create yet more demand, thus never fully satisfying it. This inherent incompleteness, movement, unpinnablilty, can be explained by the inability of any linguistic form to include, or exclude, all of its 'meaning' (Derrida 1976, 1978) or by Althusser's (1966) interpellation – a calling from the ideology, discourse or episteme to *be*, to act, to perform, as a consumer. Thus, consumer identity may be decentered in form, manifested in the unconscious (but not entirely unaware) behavior of consumers as subjects of marketing ideology (Zizek 1989). As Kozinets (2002) ponders: 'Can Consumers Escape the Market?'

References

Althusser, L. (1966) *For Marx*. London: Verso.
Arnould, E. J. and Price, L. L. (1993) 'River magic: extraordinary experience and the extended service encounter'. *Journal of Consumer Research* 20 (June): 24–45.

Arnould, E. and Thompson, C. J. (2005) 'Consumer culture theory: twenty years of research'. *Journal of Consumer Research* 31 (March): 868–883.

Bakhtin, M. (1984/1965) *Rabelais and his World*, Trans. Iswolsky, H., Bloomingdale: Indiana University Press.

Bataille, G. (1988) *The Accursed Share*, Trans. Hurley, R., New York: Zone Books.

Baudrillard, J. (1981) *For a Critique of the Political Economy of the Sign*. St Lois: Telos Press.

Baudrillard, J. (1998) *The Consumer Society: Myths and Structures*. London: Sage.

Bauman, Z. (1988) *Freedom*. Milton Keynes: Open University Press.

Bourdieu, P. (1984) *Distinction: A Social Critique of the Judgement of Taste*. London: Routledge.

Belk, R. W. (1988) 'Possessions and the extended sense of self'. *Journal of Consumer Research* 15: 139–168.

Belk, R. W. and Costa, J. A. (1998) 'The mountain man myth: a contemporary consuming fantasy'. *Journal of Consumer Research* 25 (December): 218–252.

Cova, B. and Cova, V. (2002) 'Tribal marketing: the tribalization of society and its impact on the conduct of marketing'. *European Journal of Marketing* 36(5/6): 595–620.

Deighton, J. (1992) 'The consumption of performance'. *Journal of Consumer Research* 19 (December): 362–372.

DeMello, M. (2000) *Bodies of Inscription: A Cultural History of the Modern Tattoo Community*. Durham and London: Duke University Press.

Derrida, J. (1976) *Of Grammatology*, Trans. Spivak, G. C., Baltimore, MD: Johns Hopkins University Press.

Derrida, J. (1978) *Writing and Difference*. Chicago: University of Chicago Press.

Desmond, J. (2003) *Consuming Behaviour*. Basingstoke: Palgrave.

Du Gay, P. (2001) 'Servicing as cultural economy'. In Sturdy, A. *et al.* (eds) *Customer Service: Empowerment and Entrapment*. Basingstoke: Palgrave, pp. 200–204.

Elliot, R. (1999) 'Symbolic meaning'. In Brownlie, D. *et al.* (eds) *Rethinking Marketing*. London: Sage, pp. 112–125.

Elliott, R. and Davies, A. (2005) 'Symbolic brands and authenticity of identity performance'. In Schroeder, J. and Salzer-Morling, M. (eds) *Brand Culture*. London: Routledge.

Elliott, R. and Wattanasuwan, K. (1998) 'Brands as resources for the symbolic construction of identity'. *International Journal of Advertising* 17(2): 131–144.

Ewen, S. (1988) *All Consuming Images: The Politics of Style in Contemporary Culture*. New York: Basic Books.

Falk, P. (1994) *The Consuming Body*. London: Sage.

Fanon, F. (1961) *Les Damnes De La Terre* , Trans. Farrington, C., The Wretched of the Earth, Paris.

Featherstone, M. (ed.) (2000) *Body Modification*. London: Sage.

Fiske, J. (1987) *Television Culture*. London: Routledge.

Foucault, M. (1980) *Power/Knowledge: Selected Interviews and Other Writings*, Gordon, C. (ed.), New York: Pantheon Books.

Frank, T. and Weiland, M. (eds) (1997) *Commodify Your Dissent The Business of Culture in the New Guilded Inn*. New York: Norton.

Fromm, E. (1978) *To Have or To Be*? London: Abacus.

Grafton-Small, R. and Linstead, S. (1989) 'Advertisements as artefacts: everyday understanding and the creative consumer'. *International Journal of Advertising* 8(3): 205–218.

Goffman, E. (1959) *The Presentation of Self in Everyday Life*. New York: Doubleday.

Goulding, C. and Follett, J. (2001) 'Subcultures, women and tattoos: an exploratory study'. *Gender Marketing and Consumption*, Association for Consumer Research, 6: 37–54.

Hebdige, D. (1979) 'Subcultures: the meaning of style'. In Gelder, K. and Thornton, S. (eds) *The Subcultures Reader*. London: Routledge.

Hegel, G. W. F. (1977) *Phenomenology of Spirit*, Trans. Miller, A. V., Oxford: Clarendon Press.

Hill, R. P. (1991) 'Homeless women, special possessions, and the meaning of home: an ethnographic case study'. *Journal of Consumer Research* 18 (December): 298–310.

Hill, R. P. (2002) 'Consumer culture and the culture of poverty: implications for marketing theory and practice'. *Marketing Theory* 2(3): 273–293.

Hirschman, E. C. (1993) 'Ideology in consumer research, 1980 and 1990: a Marxist and Feminist critique'. *Journal of Consumer Research* 19 (March): 537–555.

Horkheimer, M. (1967) *Zur kritik der instrumentellen Vernunft*. Frankfurt am Meine.

Holt, D. B. (2002) 'Why do brands cause trouble? A dialectical theory of consumer culture and branding'. *Journal of Consumer Research* 29 (June): 70–90.

Kozinets, R. V. (2001) 'Articulating the meanings of Star Trek's culture of consumption'. *Journal of Consumer Research* 28(1): 67–88.

Kozinets, R. V. (2002) 'Can consumers escape the market? Emancipatory illuminations from burning man'. *Journal of Consumer Research* 29(1): 20–38.

Lacan, J. (1977) *Ecrits: A Selection*. New York: Norton.

Laermans, R. (1993) 'Learning to consume: early department stores and the shaping of modern consumer culture (1860–1914)'. *Theory, Culture and Society* 10: 79–112.

Maffesoli, M. (1996) *The Time of the Tribes: The Decline of Individualism in Mass Society*. London: Sage.

Marx, K. (1976) *Capital: A Critique of Political Economy*. Vol 1, Trans. Fowkes, B., London: Penguin.

Mauss, M. (1966) *The Gift: Forms and Functions of Exchange in Archaic Societies*. London: Routeldge and Kegan Paul.

Mauss, M. (1979/1936) *Body Techniques, in Sociology and Psychology*, Trans. Brewster, B., London: Routledge and Kegan Paul.

Packard, V. (1957) *The Hidden Persuaders*. New York: Pocket Books.

Saren, M. (2006) *Marketing Graffiti*. Oxford: Butterworth Heinemann.

Sartre, J. -P. (1943) *Being and Nothingness: A Phenomenological Ontology*. New York: Philosophical Library.

Schouten, J. (1991) 'Selves in transition: symbolic consumption in personal rites of passage and identity reconstruction'. *Journal of Consumer Research* 17 (March): 412–425.

Schouten, J. and McAlexander, J. (1995) 'Subcultures of consumption: an ethnography of the new bikers'. *Journal of Consumer Research* 22(1): 43–61.

Schroeder, J. and Salzer-Morlin, M. (eds) (2005) *Brand Culture*. London: Routledge.

Smith, A. (1961) *The Wealth of Nations*, Edwin Cannan (ed.), London: Methuen.

Spivak, G. C. (1988) 'Can the Subaltern Speak?'. In Nelson, C. and Grossberg, L. (eds) *Marxism and the Interpretation of Culture*. Chicago: Univ of Illinois Press, pp. 271–313.

Svensson, P. (2004) *Setting the Marketing Scene: Reality Production in Everyday Marketing Work*. Lund: Lund Business Press.

Thompson, C. and Hirschman, B. (1995) 'Understanding the Socialised Body: A Poststructuralist Analysis of Consumer's Self Conceptions, Body Images and Self Care Practices', *Journal of Consumer Research*, 32, September, pp. 139–153.

Turner, J. (2006) 'It's all splurge and sod the future', *The Times*, 29th July, p. 24.

Vargo, S. L. and Lusch, R. F. (2004) 'Evolving to a new dominant logic for marketing'. *Journal of Marketing* 68 (January): 1–17.

Veblen, T. (1899/1995) *The Theory of The Leisure Class: An Economic Study of Institutions*. Penguin: London.

Velliquette, A. and Bamossy, G. (2001) 'The role of body adornment and the self reflexive body in life-style cultures and identity'. *European Advances in Consumer Research* 5: 21.

Woodward, K. (ed.) (1997) *Identity and Difference*. London: Sage Publications.

Zizek, S. (1989) *The Sublime Object of Ideology*. London: Verso.

2

Personal branding and identity: a textual analysis

Cliff Oswick and Maxine Robertson

Within the realms of marketing the concept of branding has gained considerable prominence. The emergence of corporate branding has spawned both prescriptive 'positivist texts' (e.g. Aaker 1996, Haig 2003, Murphy 1987, 1990) and 'critical counter-texts' (e.g. Bakan 2004, Boyle 2003, Klein 2000, Schlosser 2001) on the subject. Moreover, the growth of interest in branding has led to the formation of 'personal branding' (Andrusia and Haskings 2000). The central premise explored in this chapter is that 'personal branding' as a form of identity work has significant implications for the construction, negotiation and re-negotiation of management identities. In particular, we consider the way in which personal branding texts have a decidedly detrimental impact upon the ongoing processes of managing, organizing and identity construction insofar as they engender anxiety, encourage dissimulation, and promote 'safe' and compliant behavior. We will also consider the methodological implications of a textual approach to the analysis of identity work.

There are four main parts to this chapter. First, the recent proliferation of books on 'how to brand oneself' (Sampson 2002) is discussed and some contextual consideration is given to their emergence and appeal to a management audience. Second, the collection of branding books which form the basis for analysis is described and the discourse-based methodology used to interrogate the sample of texts is explained. Third, the central themes, recipes and prescriptions offered within personal branding texts are articulated and critiqued. Finally, the politically imbued imperatives associated with this approach for the 'identity branding' of managers are explored and, in terms of methodology, we consider the benefits and limitations of employing a text-based approach to study this phenomenon.

The emergence of personal branding

The notion of a personal brand is a relatively new phenomenon. It first came to mainstream prominence in Tom Peters' book, *The Brand You 50*, published in 1999. Since then, a number of books that explicitly address the topic have appeared (e.g. Gross 2001, McNally and Speak 2002, Montoya and Vanderhey 2003). The common feature of all these contributions is that they can be characterized as 'popular management' texts insofar as their target audience is practicing managers and they offer prescriptive advice to the reader. In this regard, they represent a specific strand of the more general plethora of 'how to' texts for managers (Garsten and Grey 1997). However, rather than prescribing and promoting the development of specific management techniques that will solve particular organizational problems, these 'how to' texts target the managers themselves, prescribing and promoting the idea of the necessity to develop a personal brand. In order to consider their growing appeal, some consideration needs to be given to the organizational context in which managers have been operating since the early 1990s.

At the beginning of the 1990s numerous management gurus (including Tom Peters 1992) began to promote recipes for organizational success and the personal effectiveness of managers. This occurred against a backdrop of downsizing which focused attention on individual employability and personal career management. In particular, the 'organizational restructuring imperative', characterized by the removal of hierarchical layers in order to achieve efficiency gains through improved horizontal communication and co-ordination, gained momentum.

The evidence, however, regarding the effects of restructuring, has been mixed. Insights from the US have suggested that managerial downsizing was a myth and US corporations were in fact growing 'fat and mean' during the 1990s (Gordon 1996). However, in the UK and Australia there does seem to be evidence for significant restructuring and delayering (Worrall and Cooper 2001). For example, longitudinal research conducted in Australia across the 1990s (Littler and Innes 2004) highlights that 88% of firms experienced restructuring between 1994 and 1998, which typically included delayering such that the total number of managerial positions in the Australian labor market did actually decline significantly in that period. Whether real or mythical, the overriding conclusion that can be derived about corporate restructuring during the 1990s is that whilst 'at the aggregate level, apparent labour market continuity exists, ... many managers experienced dramatic changes involving career disruption, loss of job security, and even loss of managerial status' (Littler and Innes 2004: 1180). This research does then give a flavour of the general context within which the fertile ground for popular management texts was created. In particular, it helps to explain the growing popularity of the personal branding phenomenon, emphasizing as it does the increasing uncertainty and precariousness of managerial positions during the 1990s which is likely to have focused managers' attention on how they might enhance their employability and stand out from the crowd. In short, personal branding has emerged as a response to the uncertainty created through structural change and as a potential source of individualized competitive advantage.

Analysing personal branding texts: the sample and the approach

An extensive systematic review of the literature revealed a total of 12 books on personal branding. These texts constitute the sample that is analysed in this paper. The particular texts subjected to critical scrutiny being:

The Brand You 50: Reinventing Work

by Tom Peters (1999).

Brand Yourself: How to Create an Identity for a Brilliant Career
by David and Rick Hastings (2000).

Build Your Own Life Brand

by Stedman Graham (2001).

Microbranding: Build a Powerful Personal Brand and Beat Your Competition
by T. Scott Gross (2001).

Build Your Personal Brand

by Eleri Sampson (2002).

Managing Brand Me
by Thomas Gad and Annette Rosencreutz (2002).

Be Your Own Brand: A Breakthrough Formula for Standing Out from the Crowd
by David McNally and Karl Speak (2002).

The Personal Branding Phenomenon
by Peter Montoya (2002).

Branding Yourself: How to Look, Sound and Behave Your Way to Success
by Mary Spillane (2002).

The Brand Called You: The Ultimate Brand-Building and Business Development Handbook to Transform Anyone into an Indispensable Personal Brand
by Peter Montoya and Tim Vanderhey (2003).

The Leader's Edge: Using Personal Branding to Drive Performance and Profit
by Susan Hodgkinson (2005).

Personal Branding for Extraordinary Results
by Anthony Warren (2005).

The examination of the sample of personal branding books was undertaken via textual analysis. More specifically, the books were analysed using a general approach based upon critical discourse analysis (Fairclough 1992, 1995). This perspective is pertinent because any written material, including books, can be 'seen as being simultaneously a piece of text, an instance of discursive practice, and an instance of social practice' (Fairclough 1992: 4). Hence, critical discourse analysis positions written and spoken language as being three dimensional: the *text dimension* – which attends to the analysis of language; the *discursive practice dimension* – which addresses the processes of text production and text consumption; and, the *social practice dimension* – which considers the wider institutional and organizational circumstances and context of the text. In effect, using a critical discourse analysis framework as a basis for undertaking a systematic examination of personal branding texts encourages us to focus on several key questions, namely: What is actually said (the text dimension)? Who is saying it, to whom are they saying it and in what ways are they saying it (the discursive practice dimension)? And, what is the broader management context and social backdrop against which, and within which, this is occurring (the social practice dimension)?

Although critical discourse analysis offers a general mode of inquiry, the specific technique used to classify and explore the texts is 'thematic analysis' (Aronson 1994, Boje 2001, Boyatzis 1998). According to Braun and Clarke (2006), thematic analysis is 'a method for identifying, analyzing and reporting patterns (themes) within data' (p. 79). It typically involves trawling for themes via a copious reading and re-reading, the noting down of interpretations and the listing of tentative themes (Kaufman 1992).

In terms of the structure of the research, there were three practical phases to the analysis. First, the books were read in their entirety in order to get an overall sense of the body of work. Then, a more detailed second reading was undertaken of all of the books and the underlying central themes and patterns were provisionally highlighted. The final phase involved a selective reading of parts of the books where specific passages were identified, coded and unpacked in relation to the dominant themes. In actuality, the processes of highlighting themes and identifying and coding data were iterative and difficult to disentangle as discrete temporal stages. That said, the basic process was consistent with Braun and Clarke's (2006) description of the key stages of thematic analysis as being: (1) familiarizing yourself with the data; (2) generating initial codes; (3) searching for themes; (4) reviewing themes; (5) defining and naming themes; and (6) producing the report.

Several interesting themes emerged from the thematic analysis of the personal branding texts. They can be summarized as centring on issues related to anxiety, dissimulation, authenticity and conformity. These focal areas are discussed in the subsequent sections.

Anxiety, opportunity and change: don't miss the boat!

A common feature of all the personal branding texts is the way in which they subliminally operate as anxiety-inducing devices. Given the organizational changes that occurred during the 1990s, discussed earlier, it is perhaps not surprising that a fairly overt approach is adopted in the personal branding literature. The implication is that if the reader does not develop a personal brand he or she will be disadvantaged by those who do. This is exemplified in the book by Andrusia and Haskins:

> So, why do I need to brand myself? Why can't I get ahead simply on the basis of my job performance? . . . because if you don't create your own brand, someone else will create their own, and steal the show
>
> (2000: 23).

Within the texts, the need for personal branding is predicated on the notion of an impending threat rather than simply focusing on the intrinsic benefits of branding oneself. In assimilating the justification for action, the texts amplify the negative aspects of the working environment, and more broadly the economy, and in doing so portray personal branding techniques as a necessity. For example, an excerpt from the opening introduction in *Brand Yourself* asserts:

> Despite what politicians tell us about job growth, competition for positions in all fields is fiercer than ever before. We'll spare you the macroeconomic analysis; the key reasons for this hypercompetitiveness are:
>
> - a greater number than ever before of college-educated men and women
> - corporate downsizing, begun in the 1980s and continuing today
> - consolidation and takeover of companies is reducing the workforce considerably, a trend that will continue well into the millennium
> - automation and computerization that has reduced the number of human bodies required in many industries and fields
>
> (Andrusia and Haskins 2000: 1).

Interestingly, offering to 'spare us the macroeconomic analysis' could be read as a 'rhetorical strategy' (Cheney *et al.* 2004) for avoiding rigor and also avoiding serious and sustained interrogation of the postulations made. More importantly, Andrusia and Haskins (2000) seem to seek to induce reader anxiety by playing on conditions that undermine the confidence the audience has in the working environment. The inclusion of words such as 'competition' and 'downsizing' serves to remind the reader that jobs are not secure, and that the economic environment and job markets are unstable. Given the earlier discussion, it is likely that most managers are conversant with corporate buzzwords such as downsizing. Even if we take the US as an example, where Gordon (1996) argues for the myth of downsizing in practice, by highlighting the 'fat cat' syndrome of many US corporations, there is also the suggestion that downsizing and delayering need to be put onto the corporate agenda. What promotes anxiety, however, in this instance is not the words themselves, but the supposition that without participating in personal branding the manager is susceptible to becoming a victim of these hazards.

Similar sentiments are expressed by Tom Peters in *The Brand You 50*. In a characteristically provocative manner, he suggests:

> Your job probably won't evaporate between now and the time you finish reading this book. (At least if you're a fast reader.) But it is going to . . . evaporate . . . or at the very least be redefined beyond recognition . . . in the next ten years
>
> (1999: 22).

Having generated a degree of anxiety by positing 'the problem', Peters goes on to provide a 'personal branding solution':

> Thus: Those of us – starting with me! – who want to survive The Flood will grasp the gauntlet of personal reinvention . . . before we become obsolete
>
> (1999: 22).

Somewhat unsurprisingly, Peters is not alone in offering up personal branding as a remedy for anxiety and/or an opportunity to overcome uncertainty:

> What will happen [if you create a personal brand] is that you might even avoid some of the traumatic experiences
>
> (Gad and Rosencreutz 2002: 4).

> It's about taking as much risk and chance out of the complex dynamic of human interaction and perception
>
> (Montoya 2002: 216).

Nobody can control what happens *to* them, but we can control how we respond. Building a Life Brand helps you to understand your own strengths and your own weaknesses. It encourages you to keep building upon your strengths throughout your lifetime so that you are prepared to take advantage of the opportunities

(Graham 2001: 15).

The propensity for self-improvement texts to feed off anxiety has been noted by Garsten and Grey (1997). They observe:

those exposed to recurrent claims about the changing nature of work face particular worries. These worries are compounded by an intellectual and cultural terrain of post-modernism, which simultaneously suggests a collapse of certainty whilst promoting the role of expertise. Taken together, this provides a fertile soil for an individualistic form of self help . . .

(1997: 212).

An interesting aspect of the discursive construction of anxiety in the personal branding literature is the way in which it frames itself as an essential prescription to combat organizational and social ills. In effect, it produces what has been referred to elsewhere as a 'grammar of imperatives' (Collins 2000: 380). The message to the reader, which is embedded within the texts, is simple: you have to take action and the action has to be personal branding. When viewed in this way the books might be more aptly thought of as 'have to' texts for managers rather than simply as 'how to' texts.

The imperative is apparent in many of the earlier quotes and it also underlies Montoya's observation in *The Personal Branding Phenomenon*: 'In this world there is little or no job security, so people have started changing the rules' (2002: 13). Sampson (2002) similarly states: 'Whatever the job, being successful requires more than just doing it well' (p. 40). It is worth noting that within this discourse 'the problem' always remains ephemeral – never to be tied down – and hence, only the sorts of magical solutions sold by what might be referred to as 'snake-oil salesmen' can work because 'the problem' is not amenable to other types of rational solution.

A fundamental facet of the anxiety-inducing potential of the sample of texts, which underpins the formation of a grammar of imperatives, is the use of a particular rhetorical strategy highlighted by Cheney *et al.* (2004). The rhetorical approach in question is 'identification' which involves linking one issue with another. Cheney *et al.* illustrate how this rhetorical strategy works through the example of 'how often "sex and violence on television" is expressed as an indivisible unit'(2004: 96). If we take the following extract from *Brand Yourself,* by Andrusia and Haskins, there appears to be a similar process of identification in play:

You can hope and pray that you'll rise to the top by sheer dint of your merits and good work alone. Perhaps, in the best of all possible worlds, that is how things would work. But in the hypercompetitive atmosphere of today's retrenched times, you need to do far more than that to make the most out of your career

(2000: 2).

Just as 'sex' and 'violence' are different phenomena that become inextricably linked in talk and text about television, it would seem that personal branding is rhetorically identified with the 'turbulent' and 'hypercompetitive' world of work by the authors of texts on the subject. The need for personal branding is depicted as indivisible from work and wider socio-economic change. Yet, none of the 12 books that comprise the sample explain the nature of the causal connection between the two. There is a distinct absence of any articulation as to how having a robust personal brand would make an employee more 'promotable' or less vulnerable to the machinations of the market or the whims of global capitalism. Indeed, even at a local level it is far more likely that, for example, decisions regarding redundancy are going to be made on the basis of factors such as length of service, skills and the profitability of particular departments, rather than simply on one's individualized image or brand. In short, the link between the changing context of work (e.g. corporate competitiveness, downsizing and social change) and personal branding is at best a tenuous one. However, the psychological link of a 'magical' solution to an ephemeral, but deeply felt, threat is clearly apparent here.

Dissimulation and authenticity: being yourself by being someone else!

One might expect the potential disjuncture between dissimulation and authenticity in the carrying off of a personal brand to be ignored in the extant literature. However, the question of authenticity is a recurring theme within the sample of personal branding books. These texts present authenticity as being important, if not essential, to the technique of creating a personal brand. The books seek to actively distance themselves from inauthentic behavior and dissemblance. Moreover, authenticity is placed center stage as an integral part of the process. Not only is authenticity claimed to be important for the creation of a personal brand, it is also heralded by the authors as the cornerstone upon which the success of the brand rests. This is evident in the various quotes, such as:

Creating a lasting, great Personal Brand requires absolute authenticity.

(Montoya 2002: 7).

A successful brand is an accurate, genuine representation of the substance at the core of the originator

(McNally and Speak 2002: 460).

You don't have to be someone else to be successful – the power in personal branding is that you are most successful when you are really being you and being visible to your target market. No manipulation required

(Warren 2005: 15).

Real authenticity?

Much of the literature suggests that the notion of authenticity is integral to creating a brand that will work and bring success, but beyond this it is framed as being essential to the psychological well-being of the brander. As Montoya asserts:

Brands built on lies inevitably crash and burn. A Personal Brand built on the person's true character, values, strengths and flaws is a brand that person can live with

(2002: 16).

In claiming this, Montoya implies being genuine in the creation of a brand is the only way for the reader to brand effectively. He reiterates this later in the book: 'Whether you are lying to yourself or others, the effect is the same: a Personal Brand you cannot live with' (2002: 122).

In addition to the problems that a lack of authenticity can cause for the individual brander, it is suggested that brands based on falsity run the risk of being exposed by others. As Montoya comments:

principles become null and void if built on falsehood. It is possible to create Gestalts based on deceptive brand attributes . . . But it's dangerous. Give people the slightest hint they've been misled about a brand and their Gestalts can swing to the other extreme

(2002: 50).

This notion of falsity being hard to sustain is also identified by Gad and Rosencreutz in *Managing Brand Me*. They explain: 'Even if you have been good up to now in matching a special personality to a special group of stakeholders, one of these days you are bound to screw up' (2002: 18). Again, this statement frames a lack of authenticity as a potential pitfall. The danger of 'being found out' also simultaneously acts as an anxiety-inducing mechanism which ensures a degree of conformity.

Presentation and image

Taking a slightly different line of argument, Sampson (2002) anticipates the difficulty that some readers might find the idea of developing a brand as engaging in dissimulation. She states:

> Some people might find the idea of treating themselves as a product rather distasteful and consider the activity dishonest.... Do not allow such things as a natural reluctance to blow your own trumpet...., ignorance of the process.... stop you building your brand
>
> (Sampson 2002: 2).

This extract links concerns about honesty with modesty (i.e. 'reluctance to blow your own trumpet') and a lack of knowledge (i.e. 'ignorance of the process'). In short, apprehensions about legitimacy of personal branding are dismissed as unwarranted. Other authors seek to allay fears about branding oneself by presenting branding as a 'natural', ongoing and pervasive activity, for example:

> Each of us has a personal brand . . . We didn't know we were creating it, but it has been building for years
>
> (Montoya 2002: 14).

> It's [personal branding] simply managing a process that's happening anyway and turning it to your advantage
>
> (Montoya 2002: 16).

This rendition of personal branding raises a fundamental question: If personal branding is so natural, inevitable and commonplace why do we need books that tell us how to do it? Arguably, although not meaningfully addressed within the personal branding books, there is an inherent, unspoken tension between advice which says 'be yourself' and that which advocates that you embrace the general recipes for improved personal effectiveness offered by the authors of these books.

The potential incongruence of prescription and authenticity is apparent in Sampson's *Build Your Personal Brand*. Consider, for example, this excerpt on why navy is an ideal color for business:

> Because it [navy] is a combination of blue and black. Blue has the ability to create calm and symbolises dignity and truth (it is no accident that so many financial institutions, banks and insurance companies incorporate medium-blue tones into their corporate logo). Black adds weight and power, both symbolically and visually
>
> (Sampson 2002: 70–71).

What if you prefer earth colors? This highly prescriptive advice is an extreme example, but it succinctly illustrates how following advice to present an image (i.e. dissimulation) can be at odds with personal preferences (i.e. being yourself).

We find similar presentational advice being given by Hodgkinson (2005) who devotes a complete chapter to the importance of 'packaging' to a personal brand:

> It may help us understand the importance of your wrapping (your clothing and appearance) if we liken them to consumer goods packaging, which is created to enhance the product and reinforce the image of the brand. Similarly, your clothing and your appearance speak volumes about your personal brand
>
> (2005: 66).

Acting or being?

Authenticity and dissimulation can be viewed as elements of a dramaturgical perspective on social and organizational life (Burke 1945, Goffman 1959, Mangham and Overington 1987). Moreover, the way in which an individual chooses to engage with others can be construed as constituting either 'a form of "acting" or a state of "being" (Oswick *et al.* 2001: 218). The dramaturgical overtones of personal branding become explicit in Sampson's book:

> Goffman refers to this as 'dramaturgical control'. Like an actor, we costume and script our performance for the outside world in a considered way. . . . He calls this theme 'impression management', and this is the recurring theme for building your personal brand. We learn to manage the impression we create because we know it will influence how we are treated by other people
>
> (2002: 22–23).

Sampson's text endorses impression management and it undeniably promotes a form of 'acting' rather than 'being'. The theatrical intent is embedded within the language used (i.e. 'costume', 'script' and 'performance'). The obvious inference to be drawn from this is that different situations require the branded individual (or actor) to play different roles. The enactment of a repertoire of performances is arguably contrary to the notion of authenticity espoused elsewhere in the texts.

Gad and Rosencreutz (2002) seem to be against the use of varying performances in personal branding. They assert that it is 'confusing' and difficult to sustain:

> We adapt to different situations, pleasing different people in a way that makes life confusing, not only for our many different 'audiences', but also for ourselves
>
> (2002: xxi).

They go on to suggest that acting out different roles for different situations is no longer tenable:

> To live the life of a chameleon, to have sub-personalities, will become impossible. In the old days we could be one person at work, one person at home and a third person among our friends at the club: no longer!
>
> (2002: 17).

As Gad and Rosencreutz follow this with notions of authenticity, they really set apart that 'being', rather than 'acting', is what is at the core of creating a personal brand. However, whilst they assert a need for 'being', there are passages in their book that contradict this stance. For example, in discussing how you can be of benefit to others, they state: 'And of course, this means how you can be perceived to be beneficial, not necessarily what good you do' (Gad and Rosencreutz 2002: 39). By highlighting a difference between perceived and actual benefit, a distinction is perhaps made between 'being' authentic and 'acting'. The orientation towards acting becomes even more pronounced and overt in a subsequent extract:

> Packaging a personality is all about dramatization; it's acting out the character described in the script. To sell yourself successfully you have to truly act out what is you, or rather, what you have just decided that you want to be
>
> (Gad and Rosencreutz 2002: 86).

In being able to decide what you want to be, rather than what you truly are, this also suggests that there is considerable latitude when it comes to authenticity claims in the personal branding literature. If we accept that acting is an inescapable and unavoidable facet of social interaction, it is rather surprising that its role in creating a personal brand is downplayed while the need for authenticity is inappropriately fore-grounded. Given that the rationale for creating a brand is to make a product (or person) appealing to a group of consumers, it is inevitable that this is contingent, at least to a certain extent, upon their preferences rather than one's core characteristics. The requirement of being malleable to the needs of consumers accentuates the need to perform. This pragmatic need for dissimulation is, however, only directly acknowledged by one of the personal branding texts:

> In a perfect world, every Personal Brand would be based on natural behaviours. But sometimes appealing to an audience means adopting a new characteristic
>
> (2002: 120).

Conformity and homophily: being different by being the same!

The demands of top managers are relatively predictable and consistent, which means that the efforts of the various personal branders have to be aligned with, and tapered to, the needs of this particular audience. Hence, the individuals who develop personal brands will have to employ more or less similar branding recipes and strategies. This, in turn, leads to a high level of conformity and homogeneity of branding behavior. The irony in play here is that the pursuit of being different and authentic, as advocated in the texts, is subsumed in a sea of personal branders exhibiting 'dissimulated sameness' in an effort to impress their bosses. Whilst ironic it is not particularly surprising, resonating well with the notion of homophily and its importance in the organizational context. It has long been acknowledged, for example, that in order to survive and get on in organizations – particularly at a managerial level – there is a need to be similar to others (Kanter 1977). Kanter, referring to the gendered nature of work in large US corporations in the 1970s, focused attention on the 'homosexual reproduction' of managers. She highlighted that management was an occupation characterized by uncertainty, uncertainty in terms of the nature of the role and uncertainty regarding evaluation of the role. One important characteristic of managerial work was communication, and here Kanter suggests that 'one way to ensure acceptance and ease of communication was to limit jobs to those who were socially homogeneous. Social certainty, at least, could compensate from some of the other sources of uncertainty in the task of management' (p. 58). With regard to uncertainty of evaluation, Kanter also suggests the pressures to conform and be like others are enormous. Peer acceptance in the managerial ranks is paramount and this is only achieved by being similar. The problems of establishing the criteria by which managers are evaluated are then resolved as 'by keeping management positions in the hands of people of one's kind provides reinforcement for the belief that people like oneself actually deserve to have such authority' (p. 63). In this way, then, the homosexual reproduction of managers is sustained.

Whilst inroads have been made with regard to the inclusion of women in management positions, forms of homophily still persist in organizations. Homophily is a broad concept meaning, in simple terms, that similarity promotes connection and contact between similar people occurs at a higher rate than among dissimilar people (McPherson et al. 2001). Homophily is considered to be a basic organizing principle, operating at the institutional, organizational and individual level and there has been considerable research conducted around the phenomenon since the early twentieth century (Almack 1922, Bott 1928, Lazarsfeld and Merton 1954, Richardson 1940). In an organizational context, networks and networking relationships are fundamental to organizational life, the advancement of careers (Ibarra 1995, 1997) and the accomplishment of organizational tasks, and arguably more so as organizational boundaries become blurred and organizations become increasingly distributed around the world (Castells 1996). Thus, it follows that to be successful at networking and involved in the right organizational networks that might secure or enhance one's position in the organization, then, conforming in terms of identity is paramount. This implies conformity not only in dress and appearance but also values, attitudes and behavior.

Identity, self and personal branding

In many ways, aspects of identification, selfhood and personal branding are inextricably linked. Indeed, personal branding is, arguably, all about the construction of identity. However, this particular form of identity work is rather intricate and requires further unpacking.

As Bendle (2002) has pointed out, there remains 'an inherent contradiction between a valuing of identity as something so fundamental that it is crucial to personal well-being and collective action, and a theorization of "identity" that sees it as something constructed, fluid, multiple, impermanent and fragmentary' (p. 1). The concept of personal branding exemplifies the tension between an essentialist and a constructivist view of identity (Cerulo 1997, Giddens 1991). On the one hand, the essentialist position which presents identity as a relatively stable and enduring phenomenon (Oswick *et al.* 2006) resonates with the portrayal of personal branding by the producers of texts as being about the presentation of self as a matter of authenticity. On the other hand, the implicit emphases on re-presenting oneself through processes of dissimulation and changing one's image are consistent with a view of identity as something which is more fluid and malleable (Ainsworth and Hardy 2004).

It is interesting that the focus in the personal branding literature is on creating one's own identity (i.e. the formation of a personal brand, and de facto identity change, is a self-initiated and self-regulated process). By implication, this suggests that we decide who we are or who we want to be. However, given that the advice offered by the authors of branding texts is largely prescriptive and promotes conformity, it is difficult to see how this domain of identity work can be regarded as an internal manifestation which is 'personal' or 'self-determined'. Arguably, the personal branding literature serves to remind us that 'our identities are importantly fashioned by the texts of media representation' (Gergen 1999: 43) and highlights the often subtle and indirect pressure placed upon employees in terms of identity management (Sveningsson and Alvesson 2003).

Conclusions and implications

The development of a personal brand, and de facto one's identity as a manager, is implicitly presented within the texts as an unproblematic journey of self-improvement. In this regard, it is almost as if identity construction is univocal, coherent and takes place within a social vacuum insofar as identity is not seen as being shaped by processes of interaction with others. In short, personal branding is positioned as a self-determined, and self-determining, process. Moreover, it is portrayed as a necessary journey. The anxiety engendered through the projection of a rapidly changing world and a hypercompetitive work environment acts as a catalyst for individuals to brand themselves in order to survive (i.e. to keep a job) or flourish (i.e. to be promoted). The drive to make oneself employable or more promotable means that the audience to whom one's brand is inevitably targeted is top management.

The lure of competitive advantage through personal branding means that the gaze of the brander is firmly fixed in an upward direction within the organizational hierarchy, yet the role of peers is nevertheless a significant one. In the personal branding texts, peers are presented as one's rivals for rewards and promotion. An unfortunate consequence of this perception of peers (i.e. work colleagues) is that competition is privileged over collaboration. Paradoxically, if managers display 'dissimulated sameness' it actually becomes harder to differentiate between them and hence promotion and retention decisions become more arbitrary.

The focus of personal branding texts on anxiety, and indirectly dissimulation, propagates a sense of individualism (i.e. strong peer competition) and a high level of compliance (i.e. meeting the needs of senior management as brand consumers). The net result is a subtle subordination and colonization of the needs of the individual to the demands of corporate capitalism.

In conclusion, it should also be noted that the methodology employed in this chapter has certain strengths and limitations. Like any textual method applied to the study of identity, the approach adopted deals primarily with the 'espoused' and 'transcribed' elements of identity work rather than the 'actual' or the 'enacted'. Hence, a limitation of the textual-analytic approach is that it addresses what is said rather than what is actually done and, therefore, does not incorporate insights into how managers put into action the prescriptions offered in personal branding texts. In effect, the research focus on secondary data insofar as the everyday, situated practice of personal branding, as a form of identity work, is not explored and detailed inferences about the direct impact upon managers are not possible.

Ironically, the main advantage of the sort of textual analysis undertaken is directly related to the source of weakness. The fact texts, as secondary sources, are given prominence means that the externally stimulated processes at play in the social production of identity can be privileged. By focusing on media representations (i.e. personal branding texts) of how managers should act and behave (i.e. the subtle imposition of prescribed identity), alternative perspectives on the phenomenon (i.e. beyond those revealed through the direct study of managers) are rendered analytically possible. In addition to offering a different point of analysis, a further compelling reason for enlisting text-based analysis is that this mode of inquiry remains an under-utilized and under-represented means of studying aspects of identity.

References

Aaker, D. A. (1996) *Building Strong Brands*. New York: Free Press.

Ainsworth, S. and Hardy, C. (2004) 'Discourse and identities'. In Grant, D., Hardy, C., Oswick, C. and Putnam, L. (eds) *The Sage Handbook of Organizational Discourse*. London: Sage.

Almack, J. (1922) 'The influence of intelligence on the selection of associates'. *Sociology* 16: 529–30.

Andrusia, D. and Haskins, R. (2000) *Brand Yourself: How to Create an Identity for a Brilliant Career*. New York: Ballantine Publishing.

Aronson, J. (1994) 'A pragmatic view of thematic analysis'. *Qualitative Report* 2(1).

Bakan, J. (2004) *The Corporation: The Pathological Pursuit of Profit and Power*. New York: Free Press.

Bendle, M. F. (2002) 'The crisis of "identity" in high modernity'. *British Journal of Sociology* 53(1): 1–18.

Boje, D. (2001) *Narrative Methods for Organizational and Communication Research*. London: Sage.

Bott, H. (1928) 'Observation of play activities in a nursery school'. *Genetic Psychology Monographs* 4: 44–88.

Boyatzis, R. E. (1998) *Transforming Qualitative Information: Thematic Analysis and Code Development*. London: Sage.

Boyle, D. (2003) *Authenticity: Brands, Fakes, Spin and the Lust for Real Life*. London: Harper Perennial.

Braun, V. and Clarke, V. (2006) 'Using thematic analysis in psychology'. *Qualitative Research in Psychology* 3: 77–101.

Burke, K. (1945) *A Grammar of Motives*. New York: Prentice-Hall.

Castells, M. (1996) *Rise of the Network Society*. Cambridge, MA: Blackwell.

Cerulo, K. (1997) 'Identity construction: new issues, new directions'. *Annual Review of Sociology* 23: 385–409.

Cheney, G., Christensen, L., Conrad, C., and Lair, D. (2004) 'Corporate rhetoric as organizational discourse'. In Grant, D., Hardy, C., Oswick, C., and Putnam, L. (eds) *The Handbook of Organizational Discourse*. London: Sage.

Collins, D. (2000) *Management Fads and Buzzwords*. London: Routledge.

Fairclough, N. (1992) *Discourse and Social Change*. Cambridge: Polity.

Fairclough, N. (1995) *Critical Discourse Analysis*. London: Longman.

Gad, T. and Rosencreutz, A. (2002) *Managing Brand Me*. Harlow: Pearson Education.

Garsten, C. and Grey, C. (1997). 'How to become oneself: discourses of subjectivity in post-bureaucratic organizations'. *Organization* 4(2): 211–28.

Gergen, K. J. (1999) *An Invitation to Social Construction*. London: Sage.

Giddens, A. (1991) *Modernity and Self-identity*. Cambridge: Polity.

Goffman, E. (1959) *The Presentation of Self in Everyday Life*. New York: Anchor Books.

Gordon, D. (1996) *Fat and Mean: The Corporate Squeeze of Working Americans and the Myth of Managerial Downsizing*. New York: Free Press.

Graham, S. (2001) *Build Your Own Life Brand*. New York: Free Press.

Gross, T. S. (2001) *Microbranding: Build a Powerful Personal Brand and Beat Your Competition*. Washington, DC: Leading Authorities Press.

Haig, M. (2003) *Brand Failures: The Truth about the 100 Biggest Branding Mistakes of All Time*. London: Kogan Page.

Hodgkinson, S. (2005) *The Leader's Edge: Using Personal Branding to Drive Performance and Profit*. New York: iUniverse Inc.

Klein, N. (2000) *No LOGO: taking aim at the brand bullies*. New York: Picador.

Ibarra, H. (1995) 'Race, opportunity and diversity of social circles in managerial networks'. *Academy of Management Journal* 38(3): 673–704.

Ibarra, H. (1997) Paving an alternative route: gender difference in managerial networks. *Sociology, Psychology Quarterly*, 60: 90–102.

Kanter, R. M. (1977) *Men and Women of the Corporation*. New York: Basic Books.

Kaufman, B. A. (1992) 'In pursuit of aesthetic research provocations'. *Qualitative Report* 1(4).

Lazarsfeld, P. and Merton, R. (1954) 'Friendship as a social process: a substantive and methodological analysis'. In Berger, M. (ed.) *Freedom and Control in Modern Society*. New York: Van Nostrand.

Littler, C. and Innes, P. (2004) 'The paradox of managerial downsizing'. *Organization Studies* 25(7): 1159–84.

Mangham, I. L. and Overington, M. A. (1987) *Organizations as Theatre: A Social Psychology of Dramatic Appearances*. Chichester: Wiley.

McNally, D. and Speak, K. (2002) *Be Your Own Brand: A Breakthrough Formula for Standing Out from the Crowd*. San Francisco, CA: Berrett-Koehler.

McPherson, M., Smith-Lovin, L., and Cook, J. (2001) 'Birds of a feather: homophily in social networks'. *Annual Review of Sociology* 27: 415–44.

Montoya, P. (2002) *The Personal Branding Phenomenon*. Corona del Mar, CA: Personal Branding Press.

Montoya, P. and Vanderhey, T. (2003) *The Brand Called You: The Ultimate Brand-building and Business Development Handbook to Transform Anyone into An Indispensable Personal Brand*. Corona del Mar, CA: Personal Branding Press.

Murphy, J. (1987) *Branding: A Key Marketing Tool*. New York: McGraw-Hill.

Murphy, J. (1990) *Brand Strategy*. Englewood Cliffs, NJ: Prentice-Hall.

Oswick, C., Gale, J., and Beech, N. (2006) 'Relationships, discourse and identity work: from multiple interpretation to mutual implication'. In Kornberger, M. and Gudergan, S. (eds) *Only Connect: Neat Words, Networks and Identities*. Copenhagen Business School Press: Universitetforlaget.

Oswick, C., Keenoy, T., and Grant, D. (2001) 'Dramatizing and organizing: acting and being'. *Journal of Organizational Change Management* 14(3): 218–24.

Peters, T. (1992) *Liberation Management: Necessary Disorganization for the Nanosecond Nineties*. London: Macmillan.

Peters, T. (1999) *The Brand You 50: Reinventing Work*. New York: Alfred Knopf.

Richardson, H. (1940) 'Community of values as a factor in friendships of college and adult women'. *Journal of Social Psychology* 11: 303–312.

Sampson, E. (2002) *Build Your Personal Brand*. London: Kogan Page.

Schlosser, E. (2001) *Fast Food Nation*. London: Penguin.

Spillane, M. (2002) *Branding Yourself: How to Look, Sound and Behave Your Way to Success*. London: Pan Books.

Sveningsson, S. and Alvesson, M. (2003) 'Managing managerial identities'. *Human Relations* 56(10): 1163–93.

Warren, A. (2005) *Personal Branding for Extraordinary Results*. Eastbourne: Byzantion Books.

Worrall, L. and Cooper, C. (2001) 'The impact of organizational change on UK managers' perceptions of their working lives'. In Burke, R. and Cooper, C. (eds) *The Organization in Crisis*. Oxford: Blackwell.

3

The metaphorical construction of organizational identity

Joep P. Cornelissen

Introduction

The metaphor of 'organizational identity', paraphrased as 'organization' as '(personal) identity', has moved center stage in organization theory in recent years. Since the watershed article of Albert and Whetten (1985: 293) raised the issue of whether we can metaphorically project an 'identity' upon organizations to describe and explain their dynamics, organization theory has seen a rash and marked increase of conceptual and empirical work using and referring to the 'organizational identity' metaphor (e.g. Albert and Whetten 1985, Dutton and Dukerich 1991, Gioia, Schultz and Corley 2000, Whetten and Godfrey 1998). The concept of 'organizational identity' is considered metaphorical in that it involves a linguistic utterance in which the combination of words is conjunctive, semantically anomalous at first (organizations do not literally have an identity) and also literally deviant in the sense that the source or vehicle term of 'identity' has originally or conventionally been employed in relation to different concepts and domains (i.e. individuals and groups within social psychology) before it was applied and connected to the target term of 'organization' (cf. Gibbs 1996).

The increase in theoretical and research attention on 'organizational identity' has been attributed to the depth and profundity of the covering 'identity' concept that integrates different levels of analysis – individual (i.e. people's individual identity within an organizational context), collective (i.e. the social identity of groups within an organizational context) and organizational (i.e. the identity of the whole organization) (Brown 2001) – and the generative and versatile nature of the 'organizational

44

identity' metaphor itself that is credited as having opened up various avenues for theoretical development and revelation (Albert, Ashforth and Dutton 2000: 13). Indeed, theoretical development on 'organizational identity' is characterized by an 'amazing theoretical diversity' (Pratt and Foreman 2000b: 141) where the same term ('organizational identity') is conceptualized from very different theoretical perspectives and refers to different conceptual objects (e.g. beliefs held by individuals, the discourse of individuals, bundles of capabilities of an organization, etc.).

Both the increased attention and the ensuing theoretical diversity can be understood, I suggest, by appreciating, to a greater extent than before, the very nature and capacity of 'organizational identity' as a metaphor (Cornelissen 2002a, b, 2004, 2005, 2006). The surge of attention, first of all, can be attributed to the 'organizational identity' metaphor's linguistic characteristics including its novelty, creativity (in the play of words), figurative nature and, importantly, its polysemy. From the linguistic perspective, this polysemy, or 'interpretive viability', refers to the plurality and openness of interpretation that a metaphor exhibits which effectively allows for a metaphor's rapid and wide distribution whenever it links up with other meanings in existing academic discourses and research traditions (e.g. the communities of organizational behavior, organizational psychology) and whenever it provides a sounding board that resonates (cf. Maasen and Weingart 1995, 2000). The theoretical diversity encountered by the 'organizational identity' metaphor is, on the other hand, the result of the very different ways in which various authors comprehend and apply the metaphor, where they are working from very different images and assumptions concerning 'identity' and 'organization'. I will demonstrate below that the metaphorical correlation of concepts in the 'organizational identity' metaphor has not only schematized theoretical perspectives in very different ways, but has also provided a conceptual logic (of 'identity') for reasoning about organizations and their manifestations.

Research traditions on organizational identity

The purpose of this chapter, then, is to identify and draw out the different ways in which authors have theorized and researched 'organizational identity' in a far more comprehensive manner than previous commentaries (Cornelissen 2002a, Gioia 1998, Gioia, Schultz and Corley 2000, 2002). To give this shape, I started with a search of four databases (Social Sciences

Citation Index, Science Citation Index, Psyc-INFO and ABI-Inform) using the keywords 'organizational' and 'identity' either in a string or separately to identify articles where mention was made of 'organizational identity' in the title, abstract or keywords of the article. In this way, 132 articles were initially identified (October 2003). These 132 articles were further screened, and articles that made only a passing reference to 'organizational identity' (rather than using it as a metaphor or construct in the article's theoretical claims and analysis) were deleted from the list, as were articles that turned out to focus instead on the topics of organizational identification and organizational commitment of individuals or groups within the organization. Eighty-one articles remained after this screening. All of these articles were read by my research assistant and me working on the project with the purpose of both identifying the basic images and assumptions lying at the root of the 'organizational identity' metaphor's use in each of these articles and of understanding the different interpretations made. Each of us subsequently wrote down the identified base definitions – or image-schemata[1] as we call them – of 'organization' and 'identity' for each article together with the meaning ascribed to the 'organizational identity' metaphor, and then ordered and named the written material into categories. After a discussion between us about the identified categories, the six categories displayed in Table 3.1 below emerged (for a full overview of the analytical procedures that were used for coding and categorizing the data, see Cornelissen [2006]). The objective of this exercise was to identify the different ways in which the metaphor of 'organizational identity' is used and understood. A close reading of published articles allowed us to identify the uses of the 'organizational identity' metaphor in different texts and to infer the meanings or image-schemata underlying the correlation of 'organization' and 'identity'. The latter put us in a position to say whether interpretations of 'organizational identity' are restricted to one or two meanings or indeed are more variable across writings.

The six significant categories in Table 3.1 represent the general ways in which the metaphor of 'organizational identity' is used and understood, as emerging from the content analysis (i.e. our reading of the 81 articles). Here, we identified and named several 'research traditions' as separate analytical categories that are sufficiently distinct from one another. Each of these 'research traditions' was abstracted from the data of our content

---

1 An image-schema is an abstract imaginative structure that is triggered by the target ('organization') and source ('identity') concepts that are correlated in a metaphor (see also Johnson 1987).

Table 3.1 An image-schematic view of the 'organizational identity' metaphor

Research tradition	Image-Schema of 'organization'	Image-Schema of 'identity'	Emergent meaning	Selected references
Organizational communication	Organization is constituted in and through language	The identity of an entity exists in and through language	Organizational identity is the imposition of an actor ('corporate rhetor') in and through corporate language	Cheney (1991), Levitt and Nass (1994), Taylor (1999), Taylor and Cooren (1997)
Organizational behavior	Organization as a physical system consisting of specific features and characteristics (competencies, products, skills, etc.)	Identity is housed in the unique and distinctive character traits of an individual	Organizational identity refers to those unique characteristics and features of a company that give it specificity, stability and coherence	Larçon and Reitter (1979), Albert and Whetten (1985), Kogut and Zander (1996), Balmer and Greyser (2002)
Cognitive framing	Organization as a cognitive lens for scanning, shifting, filtering and relaying information (sense-making)	Sense-making or framing process of 'who one is'	Organizational identity is a self-referential cognitive frame or perceptual lens for sense-making	Dutton and Dukerich (1991), Elsbach and Kramer (1996), Gioia and Thomas (1996), Dukerich, Golden and Shortell (2002)

Table 3.1 (Continued)

Research tradition	Image-Schema of 'organization'	Image-Schema of 'identity'	Emergent meaning	Selected references
Discursive psychology	Organization is discursively constructed through the language and sense-making of its members	Identity is discursively (re)constructed in talk and discourse between actors in a social context	Organizational identity is the social and discursive construction of collective meaning	Maguire, Phillips and Hardy (2001), Philips and Hardy (1997), Humphreys and Brown (2002a, b)
Institutional theory	Organization as an actor in institutional fields	An identity is symbolically enacted, and thus constituted, within a social context	Organizational identity is the symbolic projection and enactment of the organization as a unitary actor in its environment	Czarniawska and Wolff (1998), Lounsbury and Glynn (2001), Hatch and Schultz (2002), Glynn and Abzug (2002), Fiol (2001), Glynn (2000)
Social identity	Organization is the collective product of group cognitions, sense-making and behavior	Identity is established through categorization of individuals in groups (in- and out-groups) and a social comparison between them	Organizational identity resides in shared group cognition ('oneness with the organization') and connected behaviors	Ashforth and Mael (1989), Hogg and Terry (2000a, b), Haslam, Postmes and Ellemers (2003)

analysis as significant and coherent categories (and labeled subsequently), although of course the research that is classified within them may be more diverse and heterogeneous in terms of specific theoretical perspectives and methodologies. Each of these categories can furthermore be considered as representative of the theorizing and research of a group of academic researchers – in a sense indicating a 'research tradition' as I will argue below – although, it needs to be noted, individual researchers may not always neatly fall into one of the categories. That is, individual researchers may over time be more diffuse and variable in their interpretation and use of the 'organizational identity' metaphor. The communications scholar Taylor, for instance, initially based his work in a language-based account of the metaphor of 'organizational identity' (in his work with Cooren 1997, see below), but has now shifted toward a position where the concept of 'organization', and as a corollary the concept of 'organizational identity', is not only seen to reside in language but also in physical systems and contexts (Taylor personal communication). Bearing this caveat in mind, the data from the content analysis and the general categories that we constructed provides a representative overview of the variety of ways in which the metaphor of 'organizational identity' is constructed and understood.

Our reading of published articles on organizational identity revealed a wide variety in the embedded image-schemata of 'identity' and 'organization', as such pointing to considerable differences in the way in which the metaphor of 'organizational identity' itself is understood. Table 3.1 shows the different image-schemata in use that we identified, and that we labeled with names to depict the very different 'research traditions' in play. These are the 'organizational communication' (5 articles), 'organizational behavior' (21 articles), 'cognitive framing' (28 articles), 'discursive psychology' (10 articles), 'institutional theory' (11 articles) and the 'social identity' (6 articles) research traditions. These identified 'research traditions' incorporate the 'institutional', 'cognitive framing' (or 'sensemaking') and 'social identity' perspectives on 'organizational identity' that have frequently been mentioned as dominant streams in literature on the subject (Gioia 1998, Gioia, Schultz and Corley 2000, 2002, Haslam, Postmes and Ellemers 2003, Whetten and Godfrey 1998, Whetten and Mackey 2002).

Table 3.1 illustrates that the concept of 'organization' itself evokes very different image-schemata (cf. Morgan 1980, 1983, 1996). Furthermore, Table 3.1 shows that each of the image-schemata evoked for 'identity' singularly match up with each of the different image-schemata evoked for 'organization', a process that I define as image-schematic matching, and subsequently has led to further blending, elaboration and completion of the construed metaphorical image into an emergent meaning (see Table 3.1).

Due to this 'image-schematic matching', which allows for the combination of different image-schemata into congruent metaphorical images, the academic literature on 'organizational identity' is, as mentioned, diverse, as theorists work from different image-schemata of 'organization' and 'identity' (and, as a corollary, use and refer to different constructs and conjectures), and is also far from coherent. This diversity can perhaps best be understood when we consider the different embedded image-schemata of the target concept of 'organization' (that the 'organizational identity' metaphor is projected upon) in terms of where 'organization' is located and wherein it is constituted: in language, cognitions and/or behavior. Figure 3.1 visualizes and displays the positioning of the different research traditions identified in Table 3.1 along these three dimensions (language, cognition and behavior) on the basis of their root image-schema of 'organization'.

Organizational communication tradition

At the language end of the three-dimensional space in Figure 3.1, the assumption driven by 'organizational communication' researchers is that 'communication' or language use is constitutive of 'organization' and that both concepts should be seen as a duality (i.e. communicating is organizing and organizing is communicating) (Cheney 1991, Levitt and Nass 1994, Taylor 1999, Taylor and Cooren 1997). In this sense, communication and the use of language (i.e. speech, discourse and rhetoric) becomes the basis

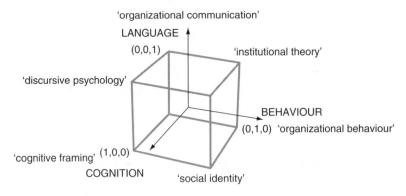

Figure 3.1   Different research traditions on the 'organizational identity' metaphor
Note: The figure visualizes the general categories of 'research traditions' that were identified. Here, each of these traditions is considered as an analytically separate category, although these research traditions may at least to some degree overlap and interpenetrate in the actual practice of theorizing and research on 'organizational identity'.

of 'organization' and, therefore, it is only possible to conceive and talk of an 'organizational identity' as grounded in language and as having 'no existence other than in discourse, where [its] reality is created, and sustained, to believe otherwise is to fall victim to reification' (Taylor and Cooren 1997: 429). This particular metaphorical interpretation (see Table 3.1) of 'organizational identity' emerges from the blending of the 'organization' and 'identity' image-schemata identified in Table 3.1, and further completion and elaboration. Through further completion and elaboration, an image or meaning effectively emerges of a 'corporate rhetoric' being (re)presented in all language, including advertisements and corporate texts, of the organization.

Organizational behavior tradition

The views expressed by the 'organizational behavior' research tradition, positioned at the far end of the behavioral dimension, are obviously at odds with an extreme language position, or indeed a cognitive grounding of 'organization' for that matter. In a behavioral tradition, it is possible to speak of 'organizational identity' in material and aspectual terms (outside of the cognitions and language use of members of an organization), denoting certain characteristic tangible and intangible features of an organization, as 'organization' itself is conceived in those terms. Theorists in this behavioral tradition refer to specific identity characteristics or 'traits' of an organization in all of its strategies, artifacts, values and practices that give the company its specificity, stability and coherence (Albert and Whetten 1985, Alvesson and Willmott 2002, Balmer and Greyser 2002, Carroll and Swaminathan 2000, Cornelissen, 2002a, Kogut and Zander 1996: 506, Larçon and Reitter 1979: 43, Moingeon and Ramanantsoa 1997, Peteraf and Shanley 1997: 167, Rohlinger 2002: 481). This interpretation of the 'organizational identity' metaphor is based upon the blending of the image-schemata identified in Table 3.1, and is further completed and elaborated on to form an interpretation of organizations as unique, coherent and stable sets of activities, values and people.

Cognitive framing tradition

At the cognition end of the three-dimensional space, the 'cognitive framing' tradition sees 'organization' as constituted in the cognitions of individual organizational members which together (when aggregated) constitute a collective cognitive lens for processing information and organizational sense-making (see Putnam, Phillips and Chapman 1996). 'Organizational identity', on the back of this image-schema of 'organization', is itself seen as a cognitive frame (Dutton and Dukerich 1991, Dutton, Dukerich and Harquail 1994, Elsbach and Kramer 1996, Golden-Biddle and Rao 1997, Scott and Lane 2000) or perceptual lens (Dukerich, Golden and Shortell 2002, Fiol 2002, Fox-Wolfgramm, Boal and Hunt 1998, Gioia and Thomas 1996, Gioia, Schultz and Corley 2000, Labianca et al. 2001) for organizational and individual sense-making activities. That is, through the blending of the image-schemata of 'organization' and 'identity' (Table 3.1), and further completion and elaboration, 'organizational identity' is interpreted as a collective self-definition or cognitive self-representation of organizational members ('who are we?') that is 'generally embedded in deeply ingrained and hidden assumptions' (Fiol and Huff 1992: 278) and refers to those features that are perceived 'as ostensibly central, enduring, and distinctive in character [and] that contribute to how they define the organization and their identification with it' (Gioia and Thomas 1996: 372).

The 'organizational behavior', 'organizational communication' and 'cognitive framing' traditions all occupy extreme positions in Figure 3.1, emphasizing either behavior, language or cognition as constitutive of 'organization'. The other three identified research traditions ('discursive psychology', 'institutional theory' and 'social identity') occupy more intermediate positions.

Discursive psychology tradition

The 'discursive psychological' strand considers 'organizations are socially constructed from networks of conversations or dialogues; the intertextuality, continuities and consistencies of which serve to maintain and objectify reality for participants' (Humphreys and Brown 2002a: 422). In other words, 'organization' in this sense is constituted not only through discursive acts (i.e. language), but also through the sense-making of the members of the organization as interactants (i.e. cognition) (cf. Edwards and Potter 1992). Working from this image-schema of 'organization', the metaphorical interpretation that subsequently emerges after blending with the image-schema of 'identity', and further completion and elaboration (see Table 3.1), is that 'organizational identity' refers to collective meaning that is discursively (re)constructed in a social context. And with this metaphorical interpretation, theorists in this tradition have also taken issue with 'behaviorist' objective and material conceptions of 'organizational identity' as 'essential' and 'fixed', as in a discursive sense identity is continuously (re)structured and therefore processual, situational, fractured, contested, dynamic, precarious and fluid

(Czarniawska 1997, Czarniawska-Joerges 1994, Holmer-Nadesan 1996, Humphreys and Brown 2002a, b, Kärreman and Alvesson 2001: 63, Martin 2002, Maguire, Phillips and Hardy 2001: 304, Phillips and Hardy 1997).

Institutional theory tradition

The research strand informed by 'institutional theory' sees organizations as unitary actors in and through connected language and behavior rather than as systems, shared cognitions or bundles of practices and routines negotiated and contested through the daily interaction of their members (Powell and DiMaggio 1991). Based on this image-schema of 'organization' as a unitary actor, and coupled with the notion that an 'identity' is symbolically enacted (Table 3.1), the metaphorical interpretation that emerges after blending, and further completion and elaboration, is that an organization is seen to symbolically construct an identity through behavior and language use within organizational fields (Czarniawska and Wolff 1998). Within this interpretation, the symbolic construction of 'organizational identity' happens through language (e.g. corporate names, rhetorics, narratives, stories) (Glynn and Abzug 2002) and culturally patterned practices (e.g. organizational dress, ideological script, rites and rituals, artifacts) (Glynn 2000, Pratt and Rafaeli 1997) with the overall objective of differentiating and legitimizing the organization with stakeholders in its environment (Fiol 2001, Hatch and Schultz 2002, Lounsbury and Glynn 2001, Randel 2002). A number of institutional theorists have argued in this respect that an account of 'organizational identity' effectively 'needs to be situated within institutional dynamics' (Glynn and Abzug 2002: 277) over and beyond alternative theoretical perspectives and research traditions, as such an institutional perspective alone can capture organizations' unique status as 'social actors' (Hatch and Schultz 2002: 1004, Whetten and Mackey 2002: 395).

Social identity tradition

The 'social identity' approach, lastly, interprets, in line with its embedded image-schema of 'organization' (see Table 3.1), an 'organizational identity' as a property of a collective of individual organizational members, which resides not only in both cognitions and perceptions of what is shared, but also in behavioral roles, symbols, artifacts and other material products within the organization (Haslam, Postmes and Ellemers 2003, Pratt and

Foreman 2000a: 20). This interpretation is based on the blending of the image-schemata of 'organization' as encompassing both collective cognition and behavior cognition, and 'identity' as a (self-)categorization process, and further completion and elaboration of the image thus construed. In this sense, the 'social identity' interpretation of 'organizational identity' extends and progresses on traditional cognitive social identity approaches that strictly focus on the ways in which individuals can be seen as part of a collective entity in the mind of themselves and others by analyzing processes of (self-)categorization and psychological commitment (Ashforth and Mael 1989, Tajfel 1972), to consider how such social identity categorizations give rise to patterns of organizational behavior (Bartel 2001, Haslam and Ellemers 2005, Haslam, Postmes and Ellemers 2003, Hogg and Terry 2000a, b, Pratt 1998). Working from this theoretical extension of 'social identity' theory, 'organizational identity' is, as Haslam, Postmes and Ellemers (2003) have recently suggested, both a 'psychological and social reality' and a 'mental and material fact', as it embodies both cognitive categorization processes that take place in the minds of individuals, and collective products of those processes and the activities they encourage. The guiding premise in this regard is that once a particular organizational identity has become salient for a particular group of members of the organization and once particular norms and values have come to define it, 'organizational identity' not only has an impact on the psychological make-up of individuals but should also help translate that psychology into collective products such as plans and visions, goods and services, practices, institutions and organizations (Haslam 2001).

> as a form of social identity, shared organizational identity is a basis not only for people to perceive and interpret their world in similar ways, but also for processes of mutual social influence which allow them to coordinate (and expect to coordinate) their behavior in ways that lead to concerted social action and collective products
>
> (Haslam, Postmes and Ellemers 2003: 364).

Discussion

In all, the above discussion of the different research traditions in 'organizational identity' points out that this particular metaphor has spiraled out into different research communities and has been translated and comprehended in very different ways. Furthermore, with each of these research traditions working from very different image-schemata of 'organization' and 'identity', and consequently using very different theoretical frameworks and constructs, knowledge development and theoretical progress is often confined to the particular research tradition and community of theorists and researchers working within it. There has been fairly little interaction or conceptual borrowing between research traditions – the only exception being that Albert and Whetten's (1985) conception of identity, as referring to features that are fundamental (central), uniquely descriptive (distinctive), and persistent over time (enduring), has found its way into different research traditions where it has been accommodated and integrated with existing schemata of those importing traditions. Glynn (2000: 285), for instance, reworked this concept, initially stemming from a behaviorist tradition, into a discursive and language-based account where it refers to that which is 'claimed' as central, distinctive and enduring in and through narratives issued by the organization. And Gioia and Thomas (1996: 372), from a cognitive framing perspective, have reworked and accommodated it into their research tradition by referring to cognitive representations of individuals of what they perceive as ostensibly central, enduring, and distinctive in character about the organization. Due to these divergent image-schemata, going back to root, fundamental assumptions of 'organization' and 'identity', I also found that at the time of the content analysis (2003) there were little if any signs of a greater convergence between research traditions and the theoretical frameworks that these traditions espouse. Recently, however, there have been conscious attempts at bridging the various research traditions. Brickson (2005, 2006), for example, with her work on organizational identity orientation, which presumes that firms construct an identity of themselves that determines whether and how they relate to stakeholder groups in the environment, blends a 'cognitive' (2005: 580) definition with an institutional orientation on organizational form, behaviors and stakeholder relationships. Similarly, Corley et al. (2006) and Hatch and Yanow (2006) have stressed the need to bridge the different ontological and epistemological foundations underlying organizational identity research, and have argued that these foundations now need to be made explicit. I argue that these different ontological and epistemological foundations are in effect structured by different metaphorical interpretations of 'organizational identity' and the constituent terms of 'organization' and 'identity'.

Indeed, the content analysis of the use of the 'organizational identity' metaphor in published articles has shown the specific, yet related, ways in which individual academic discourses and communities ('research traditions') have experimented with this metaphor. More specifically, the content analysis has accounted, at a linguistic level, for the linkage function of metaphor by pointing to the discourse-specific, yet (at times) related, processing of metaphor within different academic realms. That is, as diverse as each of these academic discourses as 'organizational communication' and 'organizational behavior' are, what they have in common is that they all resonate with the 'organizational identity' metaphor (because of the linguistic appeal and interpretive viability of the metaphor), albeit each with certain aspects of it because of the varied background of their research traditions. At a semantic level, the content analysis demonstrates the creative and transformative effect of the 'organizational identity' metaphor where through its schematizing of mental representations it has provided for various novel perspectives across these research traditions, as well as for prospects for extended theorizing and research.

A final point that is worth stressing about the organizational identity metaphor and its appropriation in different research traditions is that it questions whether knowledge development is a simple, linear process (Pfeffer 1993) and rather suggests that it is a cultural project – that is, knowledge is produced at a multiplicity of discursive sites, interspersed with different background assumptions, capacities, practices and resident knowledge of the community involved (see also Hassard and Kelemen 2002, Maasen and Weingart 2000). From this perspective, knowledge development consists of a structured, yet unpredictable, process based on the import and export of metaphors across research traditions and the locally specific processing of metaphors within them. This process is likely to be a non-linear one: each research tradition will give its own slant on a certain metaphor, which altogether makes for a diffuse and heterogeneous picture, and will also interact with each other in unforeseeable ways. The locally specific processing and interpretation of a metaphor furthermore suggests that although different research traditions may resonate with a single metaphor like 'organizational identity', the different meanings that they attach to it may make their respective accounts inconsistent, and perhaps even contradictory with one another. As such, theorizing and research that is based on metaphors may be fraught with inconsistencies and contradictions across research traditions, and may be difficult to synthesize and integrate at a higher level – at the level of the entire body of organization theory. In one sense, this may not be seen as problematic from the perspective of the local research tradition, where a metaphor becomes apt and useful when it is interpreted and integrated with the background assumptions, practices and resident knowledge of the research tradition involved. The currency of a metaphor will then be assessed in terms of the new insights and research pathways that it has contributed to theorizing and research within the local research tradition. At a more global level, however, the contradictions across research traditions, and the fundamentally different ways in which a single metaphorical concept is understood, may, as mentioned, be seen as problematic where such differences hinder the global accumulation and progress of knowledge. For organizational identity researchers, then, the quest for the coming years is to engage in debate on these different meanings, and to reflect whether these can be synthesized and integrated, or rather whether a plurality of meanings is fruitful or, indeed, inevitable.

Acknowledgments

This chapter is part of a larger research program (Metaphor, Theory and the Evolution of Knowledge on Organizations) supported by a grant from the Economic and Social Research Council (ESRC) in the UK (RES-000-22-0791). I am grateful to James Taylor and the participants in the 'organizational identity' colloquium at EGOS 2004 for their valuable comments upon a previous version of this manuscript. I also wish to acknowledge the contribution of Susanne Broekhuizen in the data collection.

References

Albert, S., Ashforth, B. E., and Dutton, J. E. (2000) 'Organizational identity and identification: charting new waters and building new bridges'. *Academy of Management Review* 25: 13–17.

Albert, S. and Whetten, D. A. (1985) 'Organizational identity'. In Cummings, L. L. and Staw, B. M. (eds) *Research in Organizational Behavior* (pp. 263–295). Greenwich, CT: JAI Press.

Alvesson, M. and Willmott, H. (2002) 'Identity regulation as organizational control: producing the appropriate individual'. *Journal of Management Studies* 39: 619–644.

Ashforth, B. and Mael, F. (1989) 'Social identity theory and the organization'. *Academy of Management Review* 14: 20–39.

Balmer, J. M. T. and Greyser, S. (2002) 'Managing the multiple identities of the organization'. *California Management Review* 44: 72–86.

Bartel, C. A. (2001) 'Social comparisons in boundary-spanning work: effects of community outreach on member's organizational identity and identification'. *Administrative Science Quarterly* 46: 379–413.

Brickson, S. L. (2005) 'Organizational identity orientation: forging a link between organizational identity and organizational relations with stakeholders'. *Administrative Science Quarterly* 50: 576–609.

Brickson, S. L. (2006) 'Organizational identity orientation: the genesis of the role of the firm and distinct forms of social value'. *Academy of Management Review* 31.

Brown, A. D. (2001) 'Organization studies and identity: towards a research agenda'. *Human Relations* 54: 113–121.

Carroll, G. R. and Swaminathan, A. (2000) 'Why the microbrewery movement? Organizational dynamics of resource partitioning in the US brewery industry'. *American Journal of Sociology* 106: 715–762.

Cheney, G. (1991) *Rhetoric in An Organizational Society: Managing Multiple Identities.* Columbia, SC: University of South Carolina Press.

Corley, K. G., Harquail, C. V., Pratt, M. G., Glynn, M. A., Fiol, C. M., and Hatch, M. J. (2006) 'Guiding organizational identity through aged adolescence'. *Journal of Management Inquiry.* 15(2): 85–99.

Cornelissen, J. P. (2002a) 'On the organizational identity metaphor'. *British Journal of Management* 13: 259–268.

Cornelissen, J. P. (2002b) 'The merit and mischief of metaphor: a reply to Gioia, Schultz and Corley'. *British Journal of Management* 13(3): 277–279.

Cornelissen, J. P. (2004) 'What are we playing at? Theatre, organization and the use of metaphor'. *Organization Studies* 25: 705–726.

Cornelissen, J. P. (2005) 'Beyond compare: metaphor in organization theory'. *Academy of Management Review* 30(4): 751–764.

Cornelissen, J. P. (2006) 'Metaphor and the dynamics of knowledge in organization theory: a case study of the organizational identity Metaphor'. *Journal of Management Studies,* 43 (4): 683–709.

Czarniawska, B. (1997) *Narrating the Organization: Dramas of Institutional Identity.* Chicago: University of Chicago Press.

Czarniawska, B. and Wolff, R. (1998) 'Constructing new identities in established organization fields'. *International Studies of Management and Organization* 28: 32–56.

Czarniawska-Joerges, B. (1994) 'Narratives of individual and organizational identities'. In Deetz, S. A. (ed.) *Communication Yearbook* (pp. 193–221). Thousand Oaks: Sage.

Dukerich, J. M., Golden, B. R., and Shortell, S. M. (2002) 'Beauty is in the eye of the beholder: the impact of organizational identification, identity, and image on the cooperative behaviors of physicians'. *Administrative Science Quarterly* 47: 507–533.

Dutton, J. E. and Dukerich, J. M. (1991) 'Keeping an eye on the mirror: image and identity in organizational adaptation'. *Academy of Management Journal* 34: 517–554.

Dutton, J.E., Dukerich, J.M., and Harquail, C.V. (1994) 'Organizational images and member identification'. *Administrative Science Quarterly* 39: 239–263.

Edwards, D. and Potter, J. (1992) *Discursive Psychology.* London: Sage.

Elsbach, K. D. and Kramer, R. M. (1996) 'Member's responses to organizational identity threats: encountering and countering the Business Week rankings'. *Administrative Science Quarterly* 41: 442–476.

Fiol, C. M. (2001) 'Revisiting an identity-based view of sustainable competitive advantage'. *Journal of Management* 27: 691–699.

Fiol, C. M. (2002) 'Capitalizing on paradox: the role of language in transforming organizational identities'. *Organizational Science* 13: 653–666.

Fiol, M. and Huff, A. S. (1992) 'Maps for managers: Where are we? Where do we go from here?'. *Journal of Management Studies* 29: 269–285.

Fox-Wolfgramm, S. J., Boal, K. B., and Hunt, J. G. (1998) 'Organizational adaptation to institutional change: a comparative study of first-order change in prospector and defender banks'. *Administrative Science Quarterly* 43: 87–126.

Gibbs, R. W. Jr. (1996) 'Why many concepts are metaphorical'. *Cognition* 61, 309–319.

Gioia, D. A. (1998) 'From individual to organizational identity'. In Whetten, D. and Godfrey, P. (eds) *Identity in Organizations: Building Theory Through Conversations* (pp. 17–31). Thousand Oaks: Sage.

Gioia, D. A., Schultz, M., and Corley, K. G. (2000) 'Organizational identity, image and adaptive instability'. *Academy of Management Review* 25: 63–81.

Gioia, D. A., Schultz, M., and Corley, K. G. (2002) 'On celebrating the organizational identity metaphor: A rejoinder to Cornelissen', *British Journal of Management,* 13, 269–275.

Gioia, D. A. and Thomas, J. B. (1996) 'Identity, image and issue interpretation: sensemaking during strategic change in academia'. *Administrative Science Quarterly* 41: 370–403.

Glynn, M. A. and Abzug, R. (2002) 'Institutionalizing identity: symbolic isomorphism and organizational names'. *Academy of Management Journal* 45: 267–280.

Glynn, M. A. (2000) 'When cymbals become symbols: conflict over organizational identity within a symphony orchestra'. *Organization Science* 11: 285–298.

Golden-Biddle, K. and Rao, H. (1997) 'Breaches in the boardroom: organizational identity and conflicts of commitment in a nonprofit organization'. *Organization Science* 8: 593–611.

Haslam, A. S. (2001) *Psychology in Organizations: The Social Identity Approach*. London: Sage.

Haslam, A. S. and Ellemers, N. (2005) 'Social identity in industrial and organizational psychology: concepts, controversies and contributions'. In Hodgkinson, G. P. and Ford, J. K. (eds) *International Review of Industrial and Organizational Psychology*. New York: John Wiley and Sons. (pp. 39–118).

Haslam, A. S., Postmes, T., and Ellemers, N. (2003) 'More than a metaphor: organizational identity makes organizational life possible'. *British Journal of Management* 14: 357–369.

Hassard, J. S. and Kelemen, M. L. (2002) 'Production and consumption in organizational knowledge: the case of the "paradigms debate"'. *Organization* 9: 331–355.

Hatch, M. J. and Schultz, M. (2002) 'The dynamics of organizational identity'. *Human Relations* 55: 989–1018.

Hatch, M. J. and Yanow, D. (2006) 'Methodology and metaphor, or can painting help us study organizational identity?' Paper presented at *EGOS 2006*, Bergen.

Hogg, M. A. and Terry, D. J. (2000a) 'Social identity and self-categorization processes in organizational contexts'. *Academy of Management Review* 25: 121–140.

Hogg, M. A. and Terry, D. J. (2000b) 'The dynamic, diverse, and variable faces of organizational identity'. *Academy of Management Review* 25: 150–152.

Holmer-Nadesan, M. (1996) 'Organizational identity and space of action'. *Organization Studies* 17: 49–81.

Humphreys, M. and Brown, A. D. (2002a) 'Narratives of organizational identity and identification: a case study of hegemony and resistance'. *Organization Studies* 23: 421–447.

Humphreys, M. and Brown, A. D. (2002b) 'Dress and identity: a Turkish case study'. *Journal of Management Studies* 39: 927–952.

Johnson, M. (1987) *The Body in the Mind: The Bodily Basis of Meaning, Imagination, and Reason*. Chicago: University of Chicago Press.

Kärreman, D. and Alvesson, M. (2001) 'Making newsmakers: conversational identity at work'. *Organization Studies* 22: 59–89.

Kogut, B. and Zander, U. (1996) 'What firms do? Coordination, identity and learning'. *Organization Science* 7: 502–518.

Labianca, G., Fairbank, J. F., Thomas, J. B., Gioia, D. A., and Umphress, E. E. (2001) 'Emulation in academia: balancing structure and identity'. *Organization Science* 12: 312–330.

Larçon, J. P. and Reitter, R. (1979) *Structures de pouvoir et identité de l'enterprise*. Paris: Nathan.

Levitt, B. and Nass, C. (1994) 'Organizational narratives and the person/identity distinction'. In Deetz, S. A. (ed.) *Communication Yearbook* (pp. 236–246). Thousand Oaks: Sage.

Lounsbury, M. and Glynn, M. A. (2001) 'Cultural entrepreneurship: stories, legitimacy, and the acquisition of resources'. *Strategic Management Journal* 22: 545–564.

Maasen, S. and Weingart, P. (1995) 'Metaphors – messengers of meaning. A contribution to an evolutionary sociology of science'. *Science Communication* 17: 9–31.

Maasen, S. and Weingart, P. (2000) *Metaphors and the Dynamics of Knowledge*. London: Routledge.

Maguire, S., Phillips, N., and Hardy, C. (2001). 'When "silence = death", keep talking: trust, control and the discursive construction of identity in the Canadian HIV/AIDS treatment domain'. *Organization Studies* 22: 287–312.

Martin, D. D. (2002) 'From appearance tales to oppression tales – Frame alignment and organizational identity'. *Journal of Contemporary Ethnography* 31: 158–206.

Moingeon, B. and Ramanantsoa, B. (1997) 'Understanding corporate identity: the French school of thought'. *European Journal of Marketing* 32: 383–395.

Morgan, G. (1980) 'Paradigms, metaphors and puzzle solving in organization theory'. *Administrative Science Quarterly* 25: 605–622.

Morgan, G. (1983) 'More on metaphor: why we cannot control tropes in administrative science'. *Administrative Science Quarterly* 28: 601–607.

Morgan, G. (1996) 'Is there anything more to be said about metaphor?'. In Grant, D. and Oswick, C. (eds) *Metaphor and Organizations* (pp. 227–240). London: Sage.

Peteraf, M. and Shanley, M. (1997) 'Getting to know you: a theory of strategic group identity'. *Strategic Management Journal* 18: 165–186.

Pfeffer, J. (1993) 'Barriers to the advance of organizational science: paradigm development as a dependent variable'. *Academy of Management Review* 18: 599–620.

Phillips, N. and Hardy, C. (1997) 'Managing multiple identities: discourse, legitimacy and resources in the UK refugee system'. *Organization* 4: 159–185.

Powell, W. W. and DiMaggio, P. J. (1991) *The New Institutionalism in Organization Theory*. Chicago: University of Chicago Press.

Pratt, M. G. (1998) 'To be or not to be: central questions in organizational identification'. In Whetten, D. A. and Godfrey, P. C. (eds) *Identity in Organizations: Building Theory Through Conversations* (pp. 171–207). Thousand Oaks: Sage.

Pratt, M. G. and Foreman, P. O. (2000a) 'Classifying managerial responses to multiple organizational identities'. *Academy of Management Review* 25: 18–42.

Pratt, M. G. and Foreman, P. O. (2000b) 'The beauty of and barriers to organizational theories of identity'. *Academy of Management Review* 25: 141–152.

Pratt, M. G. and Rafaeli, A. (1997) 'Organizational dress as a symbol of multilayered social identities'. *Academy of Management Journal* 40: 862–898.

Putnam, L. Phillips, N. and Chapman, P. (1996) *Metaphors of Communication and Organization*. London: Sage.

Randel, A. E. (2002) 'The maintenance of an organization's socially responsible practice'. *Business and Society* 41: 61–83.

Rohlinger, D. A. (2002) 'Framing the abortion debate: organizational resources, media strategies and movement-countermovement dynamics'. *Sociological Quarterly* 43: 479–507.

Scott, S. G. and Lane, V. R. (2000) 'A stakeholder approach to organizational identity'. *Academy of Management Review* 25: 43–62.

Tajfel, H. (1972) 'La catégorization sociale'. In Moscovici, S. (ed.) *Introduction à la psychologie sociale* (vol 1, pp. 272–302). Paris: Larousse.

Taylor, J. R. (1999) 'What is "organizational communication"? Communication as a dialogic of text and conversation'. *Communication Review* 3: 21–63.

Taylor, J. R. and Cooren, F. (1997) 'What makes communication "organizational"?' *Journal of Pragmatics* 27: 409–438.

Whetten, D. A. and Godfrey, P. C. (eds) (1998) *Identity in Organizations: Building Theory Through Conversations*. Thousand Oaks: Sage.

Whetten, D. A. and Mackey, A. (2002) 'A social actor conception of organizational identity and its implications for the study of organizational reputation'. *Business and Society* 41: 393–414.

4

Identification: organizations and structuralisms

Martin Parker

Positioning

There is an odd thing going on in many of the debates about identity.[1] It can be summarized by suggesting that the identity of identity is changing. That is to say, the concept 'identity' is sometimes claimed to have referred to something relatively fixed and stable, and now it is becoming more fluid and complex. Crucially, the new identity of identity is identified in terms of its difference from the previous identity of identity. We can only know the difference through comparison. If there had not been a previous identity of identity we would not have been able to know the new identity of identity. The word 'identity' adds a particular flavour to such claims, because it (like all concepts) not only produces a certain 'thing-ness' by being applied but also (like fewer concepts) recursively refers to that very 'thing-ness'. Any-thing can be identified, whether molecule, star or person, and in such identification identity is created. It does not always matter what the molecule, star or person thinks about this, because the identifying can happen at a distance. A human does not suddenly think of itself as a meal because it has been spotted by a tiger. However, it always happens as a division, a separation of foreground from background, of this from that and us from them.

This, it seems to me, is the central insight of structuralism. In this chapter I want to do two broad things with this (now elderly) idea. The first is

---

1 This chapter is a revised version of 'Dividing organizations and multiplying identities' from Hetherington, K. and Munro, R. (eds) (1997) *Ideas of Difference*. Oxford: Blackwell, 114–138. Thanks to David Sims for his very helpful comments.

to show what a form of structuralism can show us about organization and identity. The second is to consider why such structuralist forms of argument seem to be less fashionable than declarations about change, multiplicity and creativity. These declarations are sometime labelled poststructuralism, but I think this is rather misleading. Instead, I suggest such a position actually relies on certain assumptions about human agency, and particularly on the idea that there is more agency around nowadays than there used to be. This in turn can be related to the broader idea that organizations used to be structural iron cages, whilst they are now flexible and entrepreneurial. In other words, there is more identity around now than there used to be because the structures are receding, and structuralism is not flexible enough to deal with these 'liquid' times (Bauman 2000).

The detail of the argument suggests that the division of labor, which is a precondition of organization, results in a 'labor of division' (Hetherington and Munro 1997) which continually dis-orders. More specifically, I argue that the specialization of function which is found in all organizations produces multiple and contested identities for organizational members. Using empirical material from a study of a hospital, a factory and a building society (Parker 2000a), I suggest that identity in organizations should be understood as a moving pattern of shared differences. In other words, I want to suggest that a theory of identity at work needs to recognize that there are many partial identifications which can be mobilized in cross-cutting and contradictory ways. However, this is not a particularly new phenomenon because human beings have always found many things good to think with, whether formal organizations, food or kinship structures. Furthermore, we can provide a satisfactory account of complex identities by thinking about some simple structural oppositions that appear to play a generative role. We do not need to assume that we are past structuralism, or poststructuralists, in order to think about contemporary organizational identities.

How organizations think

As others have noted, the word 'organization' has two different referents – one a noun, the other a verb (see for example Cooper and Law 1995, Law 1994). In the most general terms, structural theory concentrates on the noun, seen as the more or less stable precondition and outcome of human action. The nouns are those structures 'inside' or 'outside' our heads that constrain human agency. Capitalism, patriarchy, bureaucracy, the state, imperialism, discourse, ideology, '*langue*' and so on can, according to this way of thinking, be conceptualized as social facts with a certain obduracy to them. Not material things certainly, but things with effects that are analogous to material constraint or grammatical rules. Agency theory, on the other hand, tends to concentrate on the verb, on processes of organizing. Organizing here refers to making more or less stable patterns – the use and continual revision of recipes, interpretive frameworks, accounts and so on that allow human beings to act as if the 'buzzing, blooming confusion' is ordered. In the most general sense, but again depending on the fluidity of the theory of agency concerned, 'outcomes' are dissolved into a flow of interpretive practices. There is nothing stable here, simply a stream of revisable methods for sense making, for doing '*parole*', for organizing.

This diagnosis of the two poles of social theory is overdrawn but certainly widely influential. It has also, of course, led to many attempts to repair or dissolve the supposed breach – within sociological theory, the work of Elias, Bourdieu, Giddens and so on. What is common to the work of these authors is an attempt to develop a theory of nouns as verbs and verbs as nouns, of 'being' and 'becoming' depending on each other in some way (Cooper and Law 1995). Whilst I certainly do not intend to try anything as ambitious as a general theory in this chapter, I do want to illustrate some simple ways in which structures can be seen in identity claims. It seems to me that ideas concerning who a person is and what an organization is can be seen as moments within organized processes. But, crucially, the moments of these processes are structured, and it is in these moments that identity is performed as divisions between 'us' and 'them'.

In a very obvious sense, formal organizations are necessarily sites of division. As Adam Smith's classic example of pin making illustrated, specialization of task is the central principle of modern capitalism. Durkheim's embedding of this concept in a theory of social change further suggested that specialization, the differentiation of persons, was the central principle (and problem) of modernity itself (1991). It is only through task specialization that complex social structures can exist at all, yet the resulting fragmentation of affiliations threatens to dissolve the normative glue that supposedly holds the social contract together. In the contemporary organizational context, the development of division has extended tasks to include a wide variety of activities arranged laterally and hierarchically. The extension of functions – marketing, production, design, purchasing, strategy, accountancy, human resources – together with the vertical extension of status and reward now provides an elastic web in which the organization's persons can be suspended. These divisions of labor (combined with certain material technologies) allow organizations to be globally co-ordinated, institutions exercising remote-control effects over time and space that would otherwise not be possible. However, the extension itself presents problems for management. The more complex the organization the easier it is for individuals to engage in practices that are subversive, costly or peripheral to the interests of those who are supposed to be 'in control'.

So, for the manager who wishes to avoid an organizational version of anomie, we have seen repeated attempts to argue for the importance of (re)strengthening normative coercions. A common theme in the century-long literatures on culture, motivation, leadership, selection, quality and so on has been the attempt to sponsor a version of organizational identification (Beder 2000). In order to be successful, it is said, managers must ensure that their employees believe in the shared mission of the organization. Division is the problem and new articulations of identity are the answer. Division, according to this reading, equals 'segmentalism' – beliefs and consequent behaviors that are oriented to one part of the organization rather than to the whole (see Watson 1994 for a useful discussion). The problem here can be illustrated as that of the organizational member who fights for their territory, department, occupation or whatever without regard for 'the bigger picture'. The organization then ceases to be a body of people oriented towards a common goal and becomes a battleground for sectional interests. Many strategies that attempt to transcend the battle fail because they are interpreted in diverse ways and result in collective frustration. The suggested treatment is the construction of a form of identity that would transcend segmentalist interests – an organizational identity, common culture, sense of community, *esprit de corps*, mission statement and so on. Organizational division is defined as pathological and the employee is made whole through unity with others.

If we leave the 'treatment' aside for a moment, what we have here is a very suggestive theory of the divisions of identification that result from organization. Organizing results in dividing in order to produce organizations. Hence, organizing produces identities in the sense of locations or stations that enable particular classifications of similarity and difference. Identification in this sense is something like 'perspective' – a particular site from which certain things are identified as this and not that. However, the divisions between organizational identities then disrupt the idea of the unified organization. To put it another way, the unintended consequence of organizing is the continual undermining of the very organizations it seeks to produce – the verb continually disrupts the stability of the noun. Now in general terms I suppose this is a fairly poststructuralist claim. Fixed meanings are continually dissolved by the unceasing and unstoppable spillage of signifiers. Organization and disorganization depend on each other, which means in practice that attempts to prevent 'segmentalism' in order to organize more 'efficiently' continually undo themselves.

This may be a broadly poststructuralist picture, but it certainly does not imply that people can do what they want. This is because (symmetrically) the verb is only possible because of the noun. The subject positions established by the organization allow for claims about identity to become possible. Decisions concerning what counts as similarity and what counts as difference can only be made from somewhere, from a moment of organization, a division that allows for vision (Cooper 1997). To claim to be 'us' rather than 'them' is to stake a claim of identification and separation simultaneously.[2] It is drawing a boundary that makes thought possible. In principle, there are a huge number of materials that might be used to decide what difference makes a difference – gender, skin color, dialect, sexuality, clothing, age, yellow armbands and so on. In Levi-Strauss's terms, what is 'good to think with' is a locally contingent issue. Further, the symbolics of these differences will be context dependent because sameness and otherness will be deployed in different ways in different contexts. So both structuralists and poststructuralists should be perfectly happy to claim that a person does not 'have' an identity but engages in endless acts of identification, or as Munro puts it, a 'consumption' of meanings and materials (1996).

In order to do identity, people make claims about membership categories.[3] The categories will be instantiated as suggested unities and differences between others who are inside and outside the boundaries of the formal organization. In addition, these claims are multiple – one person does not have one identity and one identity will not be located in only one person (otherwise the claim would be unintelligible). Cohen has connected this to the idea of the segmentary kinship system that allows for people to be simultaneously members of many different groupings. For him, 'segmentalism', multiple identification, is a fact of organizational and social life – 'a person identifies with different entities, and with different levels of society for different purposes' (1994: 93). Following Van Maanan and Barley (1985), I attempt to crudely illustrate this in the Venn diagrams in Figure 4.1

---

2 For an understanding of such a claim that shows the complementarity of the (so-called) structuralist Aethusser and the (so-called) poststructuralist Foucault, see Hall 1992.
3 Other, older, languages seem to provide similar insights. As Gouldner (1957) and Becker and Geer (1960) argued, individuals have a variety of *role* commitments, some of which will be manifest and others latent at different times. See also Munro (1997).

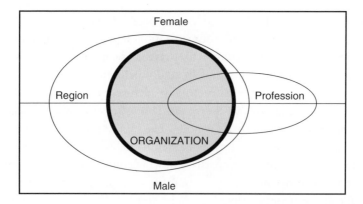

Figure 4.1   An organization with some 'externally' derived identity divisions

below – though remember that the material constraints of ink, paper and two dimensions tend to make these structures much less fluid than I would like them to be.

Think about this as an organization divided and unified by three hypothetical identification categories derived from 'outside' its formal boundaries. First, certain members of the organization share beliefs and values with members of the same profession or occupation working in other organizations which distinguishes them from other professions and occupations within the organization. Secondly, the organization is located in a particular geographic region that distinguishes it from organizations operating in other regions. Finally, the organization, region and profession are cross-cut by assumptions about gender that pervade the wider society.

This is the same organization divided and unified 'internally' by three more hypothetical categories as can be seen from Figure 4.2 It operates from two buildings and one of the buildings contains two departments that can function as markers of difference. Finally, the managers in both buildings and departments are unified by a common hierarchical position and are hence potentially distinguishable from other members. Superimposing the diagrams, it is possible to imagine a female professional manager working in department A of building Two for this organization based in a particular region. Any of these divisions, and lots of others too, may be relevant to her at particular times because they all potentially suggest identifications based on some kind of sharing – and hence some kind of difference. The common beliefs, values or languages of the organization 'as a whole' *may* be the relevant ones sometimes, but are unlikely to be much of the time. That being said, it seems that certain commonalities seem to be more enduring

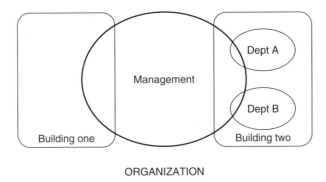

ORGANIZATION

Figure 4.2 An organization with some 'internally' derived identity divisions

than others – femaleness is likely to be a more durable classification than membership of department A. It is also really important to remember that many of these affiliations may be contradictory in their allegiances and imperatives – whether to act as a manager or an inhabitant of building Two may provoke a real dilemma. Finally, what is used to think with will be continually changing. If the chief executive or staff canteen moved from one building to another, then it is likely that the meanings attached to that building would also change (see for example Young 1989).

But it is not enough for me to simply claim that identity is about dividing 'us' from 'them' as if this were a matter of a rational actor calculating the x and y co-ordinates of their position. In the next section I will try to show how some of these ideas might help us think about some complex empirical examples, but without losing sight of the structural relations that underlie them.

Identity construction at work

I looked at three organizations – a hospital, a building society and a factory (for more detail see Parker 2000a). All three existed within a state and society which can be described as capitalist and patriarchal, and in which there are prevalent generalized assumptions about the meaning of age, professionalism, management, technology and so on. In that sense, all the organizations were similar. At the same time, it was clear that people in each of the three organizations responded to these generalized assumptions in different ways. Each organization ordered unique symbols, concerns and practices that made particular sense locally. Transposing talk and action from one organization to another would result in confusion precisely because of

Spatial/Functional	Geographic and/or departmental dividing – 'them over there, us over here'.
Generational	Age and/or historical dividing – 'them from that time, us from this time'.
Occupational/Professional	Vocational and/or professional dividing – 'them who do that, us who do this'.

Figure 4.3   Three divisions of dividing

the importance of this particularity. Understanding the identification and dividing of one organization, hence, involves detailing both specificity and generality – appreciating what made the organization both different and the same. Listening to people talk, I felt that there were three categories through which members appeared to translate the general into the specific as seen in Figure 4.3

It seemed that these classifications of space, time and person were common ways to emplace the identity of self and other, and hence articulate a particular assertion about the distinctiveness of a particular individual or group. But the three forms were not distinct. More than one could be used simultaneously, and occasionally the use of one was dependent on assumptions about another. How they were deployed depended upon local histories and understandings but their use seemed generalizable, and suggested something about the relationship between identity and structure.

Spatial and functional divides

In all three organizations there were assertions about divisions based on space. In the health service it was suggested that those working at the regional level were different from people in the district. Within the hospital district it was suggested that the hospital centre had concerns that were not the same as those working in the smaller units – elderly, mental health, community and so on. Within the hospital centre, members proposed that the Royal Hospital's culture was subtly different to the City Hospital's culture. In the factory a major divide was also expressed in spatial terms – the top site and the bottom site – and in the building society similar assertions of difference were made about head office and branches. Yet these spatial differences were not usually of importance in themselves but were deployed as a marker of some other identity. Of course, in most organizations spatial divisions are also functional divisions, and the use of spatial terms usually involves assertions about the different character of different functions.[4] Hence, within the health service district, region was regarded as centralizing, absorbing too much of the available resource and marginalizing the problems of the periphery. Within the non-acute units of the district, the hospital centre was seen to have the same failings as region. Within the hospital centre, Royal respondents saw the City as having a lower medical status and a more managerialist orientation whilst the City respondents saw the Royal as having poorer accommodation and a less efficient management. Within the factory the bottom-site managers saw the top site as too accountancy and design focused, the reverse was that the bottom site was regarded as too insular and production focused. In the building society the head office regarded the branches as needing more control, whilst the branch managers saw the head office as imposing too much control and not understanding the problems of the 'real world'.

Not all of these divides had immediate implications, for example, the distinction between the City and the Royal was one that was rarely mentioned by doctors and seemed to be more a matter of vague historical allegiance anyway. Other spatial/functional divides appeared to be much more pressing. In the building society, for example, it would have been almost impossible to conduct an interview with a branch manager without them criticizing the staff in head office because it was a matter of continual concern to them. What this seems to indicate is the importance of some kind of us and them polarity with space being used as a metonym for other issues – 'them over there are like that, we over here are like this'. As well as this being a device that could be used on a wide level to encompass large divisions within the organization, it could also be used to indicate more localized senses of difference. Consider this story from a bottom-site manager at the factory.

> The number of times they come down here with such stupid, pathetic ideas, they don't come any more. (. . .) I'll give you example. [*Someone*] bought a panel down here and there was no holes in it. Now that may not be significant to you, but to me as an enameller the point is if there's no holes I've got nowhere to hang it. Which means that the man who bought it down has got to run through the furnace with it in his hands. And he insisted that there could be no holes in this panel. So I give him a mouthful and basically told him to go away and come to his senses.

The speaker based 'here' has an expertise that 'they' (who are not often here) do not have. This leads them to do and say things that are 'stupid'.

---

4 See Ford and Harding (2004) for an elegant discussion of space and organization.

If they really understood the problems of 'here' they would not do and say these things. What is important is that the 'here' can be both used and understood on different levels. The assertion can be classified as one of the general difficulties of communication between top and bottom sites, but it is also referring specifically to the enamel shop itself. The enamel shop manager constructed an 'us and them' as 'the enamel shop' against 'everyone else'. His department had particular problems and skills that no one else understood and appreciated. In a similar way the marketing manager in the factory asserted a difference between his department, which understood the vagaries of a competitive market, and everyone else, who looked inwards and thought products sold themselves. Whether used as large- or small-scale assertions about 'here', the spatial referents are used to indicate something about the relative understandings of the two groups, to assert that rationality can be found here and irrationality there.

Generational divides

> Old age and treachery will overcome youth and skill. (poster in senior hospital managers office)

Another common divide was the use of generational identities – new managers and old administrators in the hospital; new engineers and old engineers in the factory; new managers and old managers in the building society. I will begin by looking at how an older generational identity can be used as a way of criticizing 'now' and then move to look at how a new generational identity can be used to sponsor change.

The dominant theme within an older generational identity was the idea that the organization was currently in danger of throwing away its past – its real mission or heritage. New-style management, technology, professional practice or whatever were inadequate because they did not recognize what customers really wanted, what the organization should be doing or what had worked well in the past. The older group had often been with the organization for some time and were less likely to have formal qualifications. In two cases, the factory and the building society, they also related their particular skills to the idea that the people of the local areas had given the organizations a particularly valuable heritage. They also often held positions of power and were keen to stress that their years of experience were an asset that could not be gained through college or shorter tenure within the organization.

> The one thing you've got with a graduate – you know he's intelligent. But if you accept that he's more than that I think this is where mistakes are very often made. They think somebody that's just graduated from an university, you bring

him out there and stick him into something and he's going to be a whiz kid and that's just not on. (. . .) If you take it that he's going to come in and he's going to change 163 years of experience – he's not going to do that. (factory manager)

Implicit in such a view was that these new people were in danger of sweeping tried and tested values and practices away and this may not be a good thing.

We've gone away from the old bureaucratic organization's rule of precedent. Now in some ways that was an unnecessary constraint but in other instances the precedent was used because it was sensible. It indicated what had worked in the past and, by that definition, what might not work. We just have to be careful that we don't go too far out on a limb with some of what we're about and chop the limb off while we're on it. (hospital manager)

An essential component of this generational divide was nostalgia for a time when things were more certain, when the organization produced quality products or services for grateful customers and really cared about quality. This was exemplified by the hospital manager who asserted that 'this isn't the service I came into', or the older building society manager's nostalgia for the time when –

Things were very straightforward, repetitive, you learnt something and you were confident that it was hardly likely to change much at all. Whereas now things are very different.

Sometimes, this rosy glow could even spread to things, and even things that a particular manager could not have remembered, such as the factory manager who compared their old products with the new ones.

We've got an old cooker in our little museum somewhere up the top. Its a cast iron Hercules and it cost about three pounds in 1899 or something like that. Now if I got that Hercules down here and our latest [*product*] with all the technology we've put in it and you give me a leg of pork (. . .) I could do that ham on the Hercules, it might take a little bit longer. (. . .) I could make you a cup of tea and make a piece of toast on that hotplate and the grill just as good as the [*new product*].

As I suggested above, in two of the cases this nostalgia was also connected with ideas about the particularity of the organization's geographical location. For the factory it was the close-knit community of Tidsbury – 'It used to be a little foundry in a little village' – or the traditional values of the building society were supposed to be based on 'the traditional thinking of thrifty country-folk of the day'. In both cases it was as if social change was affecting these places for the worse and if the organization forgot its roots it would be losing a central part of its reason for existing.[5] In all three of these organizations it was as if the older members felt that they were happier in the old days – things may have been hard but there was pride in a job well done and a sense of community.

Often opposed to this nostalgia was a younger generational identity that was positively oriented to change. This group was likely to have been with the organization for a shorter period of time, was not native to the area, and had formal qualifications for their sector, profession or occupation. They also did not usually hold senior management positions and were less concerned with the organization's history or uniqueness.

> To me the health service is a business, it's just in a business of people's care rather than the business of manufacturing nuts or bricks or bolts or whatever. (hospital administrator)

In the factory, a group of graduate project engineers fitted this characterization fairly closely. They regarded the older engineers as conservative, under qualified and currently doing a bad job.

> At the moment no-one knows what's going on. Tickets all over the place. [*Products*] falling off the end of the line because there is no-one there to take them. (. . .) You've only got to sit in the office to see what problems they've got. People are running around all over the place.

The younger engineers saw the organization differently because they believed that they were not burdened with assumptions about how things should be.

> Since I don't have much industrial experience, or I haven't been in industry, I don't have a narrow mind (. . .) That's the only advantage I have over the people with twenty–thirty years experience.

By implication, the older generation were narrow-minded and change meant persuading them that things could not carry on as they had in the past.

Similar assertions can be found in the building society. In this case the younger generation meant anybody who was appointed since the last general manager retired. Those who were appointed by him were again

---

5 The importance of nostalgia has been mentioned by others writing on organizations. Gouldner briefly referred to what he called the 'Rebecca Myth', the idealisation of past events or leaders (1952: 346). Gabriel has written about the importance of 'organizational nostalgia' (1993) – a longing for home, for past events, certainties and triumphs. Anthony (1994) and Lilley (1995) have noted that organizational change inevitably involves the rewriting of history – the changing of assumptions about the appropriateness of what was done in the past.

conservative – 'dinosaurs' as one manager put it – and doing a bad job of running the organization.

> There are a number of areas in head office where people have become so cloistered and institutionalised in their own departments that they haven't got an awful lot of common sense, and I say that with some feeling.

The younger head-office managers and the branch managers felt that they better understood the problems of the organization and the strategies that were needed to make it prosper.

> We've got to move with the times because the whole financial world has been shaken up over the last few years out of all recognition. And if you don't gear up to change you're going to get left behind really.

Hence in both the factory and the building society a generational identification was also being deployed to sponsor change. This could be characterized as a faith in the future rather than a faith in the past.

A generational identity is a resource that organizational members can deploy to orient themselves for or against a particular issue. Bate characterizes the two sides neatly –

> the elders, those who claim timeless validity for their way of life and struggle to maintain this by pursuing defensive, stability oriented strategies. (…) the champions of change, the young turks, disrespectful of authority and indifferent about history, hell-bent on the pursuit of offensive strategies that will bring down the old regime . . . (1994: 149).

Like the spatial/functional identity, it involves an identification and dividing of 'them and us'. They don't understand because they are the wrong age, because they don't share our understanding of what will work for this organization. They are conservative but we are radical, or, they are naive but we are experienced. I should stress that I am not trying to ironize either of these claims. Whether the past was 'really' better or worse than the present is not a matter that can be adjudicated upon. It is enough to note that members' understandings of the divisions of their organization's history are vital in shaping their understanding of the present.

Occupational/professional divides

In addition to spatial and generational divisions there seemed to be another way in which difference could be articulated, that of an occupational or professional identity. I am treating the two terms as essentially similar here, though I would argue that the former is the inclusive term with the latter being a particularly intense and powerful form of job-related identity (Bloor and Dawson 1994). Unsurprisingly perhaps, this was clearest in the hospital with the clinicians using their professional identity to resist the incursions of managers.

> Now if [*a manager*] comes to me and says 'your hernia waiting list has gone shooting up, and that's bad', my first reaction is to hit him on the nose and say 'well what the hell do you know about it? Do you know how many colo-rectal carcenomas we've had? Do you know how long they stay in a bed? Do you know how long it takes to operate on them? Do you know the average age of them and the medical problems associated with those patients? Those are absorbing all my energies and time. Of course I've got a bloody great hernia waiting list. Have you looked at the number of surgeons we have here? What have you done about trying to increase the number of surgeons?

This doctor is claiming to have an expertise that others do not. This expertise is based on a training and experience that can not be replaced or controlled by management or technology. There is also an implicit claim that only the professional really understands the central purpose of the organization – making patients better. Even in the building society, the organization with least obvious 'professionalization', the three trained accountants – one of whom was the general manager, used the idea of an 'audit environment' to resist change and point to the suggested central task of the organization. As the internal auditor said –

> People here have criticised us for being too conservative, for not getting on to new ideas, but I think there's a lot to be said for being careful. Profitability is important but you've also got to bear in mind the risks.

A professional identity, with its identification beyond the narrow confines of the organization – doctor, engineer, accountant – could hence be used as a resource to resist change, as well as a claim to an unique understanding of what the organization should do.

Of course generational and occupational identities could be related – the older factory engineers were both experts because they knew about production but also because they had 'shop floor education' and 'engineering genes if you come from Tidsbury'. This is hardly surprising because implicit in these defensive occupational claims is the assumption that they were listened to in the past but that the new order marginalizes them and elevates the knowledges of others. The history of different professions is clearly also relevant here as an indicator of their legitimated power. As is well established, doctors have a long history of professionalization whilst engineers and accountants have begun to make such claims more recently (Armstrong

1986, 1987, Dent 1993). The extent to which a particular group in an organization can call upon a professional identification is hence related to wider assumptions about the credibility of such a claim. On the other hand, the extent to which spatial/functional or generational identifications can be called upon is not as contingent on such external validation, being instead a more localized claim that would not necessarily have legitimacy outside the organization.

The examples given so far suggest that an occupational identification is a unified one that can be used to resist change, but there were also examples in which a divide was being talked about within an occupation, between emergent professional engineers and craft-oriented engineering managers. In the factory, all the bottom-site engineers were often opposed to the accountants and designers on the top site, but they were also clearly divided into the older 'shop floor education' engineers and the younger academic engineers. Both these positions were related to claims about occupational expertise, but the younger engineers defined this expertise as insufficiently professional. They suggested that the older engineers – who 'think if you're not in work with jigs and fixtures and machine tools you're not really an engineer as such' – and the top-site accountants – who wanted 'to identify every screw, nut, washer' – both had incorrect assumptions about how the organization should work. For the younger engineers, the organization could best be understood as a series of abstract systems in which information, people and things moved around. Such a system could be efficient or inefficient and such a judgement could only be made rationally if the procedures of systems engineering were followed. Identifying as a 'professional production engineer' hence meant promoting, not resisting, change.

A similar but more generalizable example of occupational identity claims can be seen in the case of management. The professionalization of management is a process that has now gained considerable momentum and again involves claiming access to a unique body of knowledge (Parker 2002). In the hospital, and to a lesser extent in the building society, there was mention of the move from 'administrator' to 'manager'. This particular linguistic and conceptual shift is not limited to these cases, it has been noted by other commentators on public-sector management also (Clarke and Newman 1993, du Gay 1994). If administrators were conservative dinosaurs who followed established rules and procedures, then managers are dynamic leaders.

> They're going to react much more quickly to the demands of people than they would be if it was bureaucratic. (hospital manager)

The development of management as a professional identification, hence, again involves asserting claims to a particular expertise that other groups do not have. In the hospital this meant asserting that doctors may be good at clinical things but they should not have formal management power. It is a manager's job –

> (. . .) to identify the problems and ask the people with the expertise to tell me whether the systems can actually answer those problems. (hospital manager)

Strong echoes of this development of a distinctive management identification can be found in the general manager of the building society attempting to reduce the power of his board because he did not want to be a 'paper fetcher and carrier', whilst his younger head-office managers were sponsoring 'management development' and his branch managers were criticizing the rule-bound 'administrators' at head office. In all three cases new-style managers were being articulated as those who caused change to happen. As noted above, to adopt a management identification means being for 'excellence', 'quality' and 'dynamism'. It meant being against conservatism and insularity, against the established assumptions of groups who felt change could not, or should not, happen.

> It was a company that was all these little islands and people did their own thing and the director was king and even another director almost wouldn't want to go into another director's bit of the empire. And that's been swept away. So [the factory] now is a team of people with a common goal.

Most importantly perhaps, it meant being able to understand the 'real' needs and environment of the organization. As noted above, being a manager meant understanding the turbulence of the organization's market, being able to look outwards and into the future and see things that those who only looked inwards could not see.

As might be expected, the assertion of a distinctive management identification did not go unchallenged – though the challenges themselves sometimes worked to talk management into existence. In all three organizations there were examples of employees denying that a particular occupational group were really 'managers' at all. This was clearest in the hospital with doctors asserting that those who called themselves managers were really administrators because they worked within a bureaucratic welfare structure and could never make profits to reinvest. Similarly, in the factory, the new engineers asserted –

> They use the term manager to mean foreman. (. . .) 90% of the managers here would be termed supervisors elsewhere.

The implication was that these 'managers' were not performing management tasks and hence did not deserve the title. Finally, in the building society, branch managers criticized the 'glorified typists' who 'shouldn't be in charge' and again used the term 'administrator' with derogatory connotations. In each of the cases the claim to a management identity was being denied and it was instead being suggested that these people were 'time-servers' or 'bureaucrats'. As I suggested, implicit in such claims is the recognition of precisely the management identification that was being claimed. It was not being denied that there could be entrepreneurial leaders, simply that these examples did not fit the bill and should therefore not be granted that status. Hence, denying an occupational identification to a particular group did not mean denying the existence of that occupation as a whole and neither did it necessarily imply a particular orientation to change. For example, the doctors wished to deny managers' claims in order to resist change, but the new engineers and branch managers were doing the same thing in order to explain why their changes were not being adopted more rapidly.

Like spatial/functional or generational claims, occupational claims provide a shorthand for saying 'we understand and they do not'. They can be used both to sponsor 'change' (new engineers, managers) and to hinder it (doctors). This fits well with the idea that professionalism is a collective strategy for social mobility by establishing a monopoly over a particular service (Johnson 1972). Using a professional identification meant protecting or sponsoring the centrality of a particular group. It, hence, also meant asserting that this group best understood the real needs of the organization and that other groups did not. In other words, to use a professional identification is to comment on the inabilities of others just as it elevates the expertise of self.

Staking the posts

In this chapter I have argued that dividing is central to the identifications that members deploy in doing organization.[6] In other words, organizations are always sites of laboring over divisions, and hence over identities. Various resources can be called on to articulate these senses of dividing and I have suggested that they can be broadly classified as spatial/functional,

---

6 I would argue that these ideas have application beyond the work organization. For an application to an urban identity, see Parker 2000b.

generational and professional. In each of these cases a marker of difference is used to articulate a distinct view of what the organization should be doing and to suggest that some other group does not understand this 'truth'. In addition to this I have suggested that three kinds of claim can be deployed in a combination of ways – using a spatial claim does not preclude the use of a professional claim simultaneously or on another occasion. Hence, the older factory managers could identify themselves not only spatially as 'bottom site managers' but also as generationally different to the younger engineers in being 'older engineers'. The younger engineers could not only make the same spatial/functional claim for a production focus but also differentiate themselves professionally as 'new engineers'. An organization member was able to use a combination of these divisions in different ways to articulate senses of who they were and who others were. Orientations to change, to the past, to the 'mission' of the organization could all be expressed with different combinations of claims. So who was 'us' and who was 'them' for a single member could differ according to the context in which they were talking – who they were talking to, what was being discussed, what had happened that morning and so on. This certainly results in a complex picture of the organizing of identification, but it is surely naive to suggest that some people or groups within an organization are for change and others are not, or that this department thought X and that department thought Y. Organization is a contested process, a continually shifting set of claims and counter claims, and there is no place or time from which it can be finally captured and presented as fact.

Of course, if we accept a broadly poststructuralist view of language then any claims to explanation are situated, but not all are situated equally. Some claims do seem to have more persuasive power than others, especially when they are put forward by high-status or well-resourced members or groups within the organization and/or because they echo claims being made by high-status or well-resourced individuals or groups 'outside' the organization. (Politicians, state functionaries and management gurus are in the business of making 'us' and 'them' claims too.) Organizations are populated and influenced by actors who occupy different power positions, depending on their access to wider assumptions that help to legitimize certain actions and beliefs but not others. Organizational identifications are hence not a democratic, stable outcome of multiple claims, but a continuing process of articulating contested versions of what the organization should be doing, who it should be responsible to and who does what for what sort of reward. The sense members make of their organization (and that I make of it) is therefore bounded by the context of these more pervasive, yet still contingent, divisions – between men and women, the old and the young, managers and workers, professionals and administrators and so on.

A development of this argument would be that any pattern of identifications and divisions is unique, yet all these patterns are likely to be constructed through similar dividing strategies. Using a structuralist conception of language foregrounds precisely this kind of assertion. Grammar is a set of rules that allow linguistic practice to take place. It is functionally necessary that we have a broad agreement on rule use because without them communication would be a very hit and miss affair. Yet, the use of these rules does not commit us to agreement on the definition of particular terms or the substance of any given conversation. Analogously, organization (the process of organizing) is a set of rules that allows organizations (more or less stable institutions) to be produced. Yet, simply because of this it does not mean that there is stable and enduring agreement concerning the identity of people and things. In theoretical terms, this metaphor suggests that the structuralist question 'how is social order possible?' is pretty much the same as asking 'what are the rules of disorder?' (Marsh, Rosser and Harré 1978). How is an organization recognized by its members and others as a (more or less) agreed upon entity, but yet also a 'plurality of heterogeneous mentalities' (Bate 1994: 136) or 'temporary and fraught coalition of coalitions' (Watson 1994: 111)? Organization is an endless process of identifications and divisions – not *either* one *or* the other.

These identifications and divisions, like languages themselves, spill across state and geographic boundaries, are cut through with regional dialects as well as vocabularies of occupation, gender, class, ethnicity, age and so on. Defining 'a language' is never a simple matter of suggesting a physical boundary. Similarly with identification. 'British identity' is not confined to the boundaries of the British state and is internally divided along a multiplicity of lines. The same argument might be made for any other form of identity which is seen as contained within a space, category of people, period in history and so on. Identity is hence a term that must necessarily always be located as a moving identification which employs whatever local categories are 'good to think with'. But identifications are also divisions – a cut that divides 'us' from 'them'. Beyond certain requirements of durability and distinctiveness, a huge variety of identification claims are supportable. Specifying exactly what the 'bottom limits' of such claims might be is therefore very difficult. The plausibility of such claims depends entirely on whether they are deemed credible, given durability, by the definer, the defined and the audience. As noted earlier, Cohen suggests that segmentary lineage structures are resources for deciding who is 'us' and 'them' in matters of 'grazing herds, feuding, contracting marriages, making war, and so on' (1994: 93). So is organizational segmentation used for different identification work at different times.

But, and this is of considerable importance I think, none of what I have argued suggests that identity is now liquid when it used to be solid. It certainly suggests that, as organizing becomes more complex, so do the resources for identity construction become more complex. But complexity does not imply a lack of structure. This might be a fine distinction, but I think it is an important one. Consider someone who asserts that people and organizations are different nowadays, that people are used to having autonomy and require new forms of management, and that changing notions of career, globalization and new technology mean that identity matters more than it used to. All this begins to sound like the idea that we have more agency now, and that the dull rule of hierarchical bureaucrats has ended and been replaced by organizational democracy and individualization. No wonder then that structuralism is seen as old fashioned, and that poststructuralism is sometimes understood as the theoretical recognition of creative agency. No wonder that management and social theorists can so easily slide into suggesting that expressions of identity within organizations are further examples of the humanization of management, and of progressive advances in management theory.

The logical mistake that reads complexity as freedom can so easily be propelled by a political desire to write modern organizations as sites for authenticity and self-actualization. But, as any game player knows,[7] complexity does not mean that there are no rules, it means there are more rules. It does not mean that we are somehow 'after' structure, but that we need to understand structure as a process of structuring. What I have attempted to do in this chapter is to attend to three local organizations of identities. This involves understanding the huge variety, and contested nature, of 'us' and 'them' claims that are the necessary and continual outcome of organizing processes. In some cases the organization will be 'us', but in many others ideas about similarity and difference will call upon dividings or identifications from other sources. Identification is the product of division and division the product of identification.[8] For organizations, like any human organizing process, there is no vision without division.

---

7 As many writers on complexity and chaos theory in management appear to forget.
8 See Munro 1997 for further discussion of what it might mean to 'see' difference, and how making claims about difference must be seen as an aspect of claims about membership and belonging. So this chapter is a labour of division too, an attempt to indicate where the author belongs.

References

Anthony, P. (1994) *Managing Culture*. Buckingham: Open University Press.

Armstrong, P. (1986) 'Management control strategies and inter-professional competition'. In Knights, D. and Willmott, H. (eds) *Managing the Labour Process*. Aldershot: Gower.

Armstrong, P. (1987) 'Engineers, managers and trust'. *Work, Employment and Society* 1: 421–440.

Bate, P. (1994) *Strategies for Cultural Change*. Oxford: Butterworth-Heinemann.

Bauman, Z. (2000) *Liquid Modernity*. Oxford: Polity.

Becker, H. and Geer, B. (1960) 'Latent culture'. *Administrative Science Quarterly* 5: 304–313.

Beder, S. (2000) *Selling the Work Ethic: From Puritan Pulpit to Corporate PR*. London: Zed Books.

Bloor, G. and Dawson, P. (1994) 'Understanding professional culture in organizational context'. *Organization Studies* 15(2): 275–295.

Clarke, J. and Newman, J. (1993) 'The right to manage: a second managerial revolution'. *Cultural Studies* 7(3): 427–441.

Cohen, A. (1994) *Self Consciousness*. London: Routledge.

Cooper, B. (1997) 'The visibility of social systems'. In Hetherington, K. and Munro, R. (eds) *Ideas of Difference*. Oxford: Blackwell, 32–41.

Cooper, R. and Law, J. (1995) 'Organization: distal and proximal views'. *Research in the Sociology of Organizations* 13: 237–274.

Dent, M. (1993) 'Professionalism, educated labour and the state: hospital medicine and the new managerialism'. *Sociological Review* 41: 244–273.

du Gay, P. (1994) 'Colossal immodesties and hopeful monsters'. *Organization* 1(1): 125–148.

Durkheim, E. (1991) *The Division of Labour in Society*. Basingstoke: Macmillan.

Ford, J. and Harding, N. (2004) 'We went looking for an organization and could only find the metaphysics of its presence'. *Sociology* 38: 815–830.

Gabriel, Y. (1993) 'Organizational nostalgia'. In Fineman, S. (ed.) *Emotion in Organizations*. London: Sage.

Gouldner, A. (1952) 'The problem of succession in bureaucracy'. In Merton, R. *et al.* (eds) *Reader in Bureaucracy*. New York: Free Press.

Gouldner, A. (1957) 'Cosmopolitans and locals'. *Administrative Science Quarterly* 2: 281–306.

Hall, S. (1992) 'The question of cultural identity'. In Hall, S., Held, D., and McGrew, T. (eds) *Modernity and its Futures*. Oxford: Polity.

Hetherington, K. and Munro, R. (eds) (1997) *Ideas of Difference*. Oxford: Blackwell.

Johnson, T. (1972) *Professions and Power*. London: Macmillan.

Law, J. (1994) *Organizing Modernity*. Oxford: Blackwell.

Lilley, S. (1995) 'Disintegrating chronology'. *Studies in Cultures, Organizations and Societies* 2: 1–33.

P. Marsh, Rosser, E., and Harré, R. (1978) *The Rules of Disorder*. London: Routledge & Kegan Paul.

Munro, R. (1996) 'A consumption view of self: extension, exchange and identity'. In Edgell, S., Warde, A., and Hetherington, K. (eds) *Consumption Matters*. Oxford: Blackwell.

Munro, R. (1997) 'Ideas of difference: stability, social spaces and labour of division'. In Hetherington, K. and Munro, R. (eds) *Ideas of Difference*. Oxford: Blackwell, pp. 3–24.

Parker, M. (2000a) *Organizational Culture and Identity: Unity and Division at Work*. London: Sage.

Parker, M. (2000b) 'Identifying Stoke: contesting North Staffordshire'. In Edensor, T. (ed.) *Reclaiming Stoke-on-Trent: Leisure, Space and Identity in the Potteries*. Stoke-on-Trent: Staffordshire University Press, pp. 255–270.

Parker, M. (2002) *Against Management*. Oxford: Polity.

Van Maanan, J. and Barley, S. (1985) 'Cultural organization'. In Frost, P., Moore, L., Louis, M., Lundberg, C., and Martin, J. (eds) *Organizational Culture*. Beverly Hills: Sage, pp. 31–53.

Watson, T. (1994) *In Search of Management*. London: Routledge.

Young, E. (1989) 'On the naming of the rose'. *Organization Studies* 10(2): 187–206.

5

Identity, surveillance and resistance

Carl Rhodes, Rick Iedema and Hermine Scheeres

The front cover of the 1979 Penguin paperback edition of Michel Foucault's renowned book *Discipline and Punish*[1] displays Vincent Van Gogh's painting 'La Ronde de Prisonniers'. On the cover can be seen 15 men – prisoners – walking in a circular route in what appears to be a prison yard. Surrounded by a brick wall that extends to the top of the picture, the arms of these inmates hang aimlessly by their sides, or rest in their pockets. Their mouths are turned down, their shoulders slumped, and their eyes hollow. In the stillness of the picture one can see a circular motion as they walk around this prison yard, just as they did yesterday and will do tomorrow. This is the 'ronde' – the regular course – that they follow with no thoughts to propel them. No one is strolling, but everyone is moving. Not visible on the Penguin cover, but very clear in the original work; is that there is actually a circle of prisoners, apparently going around, and around and around the brick wall–cloistered yard. There are too, just to the right of them, three rather indistinguishable looking men, all wearing brimmed hats, sternly looking on.

The image of men walking was also the subject of the Bruce Springsteen song *Factory* released in 1977. This was the same year as the release of the English translation of Foucault's book; but even some 83 years after Van Gogh's painting, the imagery is remarkably similar. Recalling a vision of his father finishing a hard day's work in a factory, the song's narrator bemoans: 'End of the day, factory whistle cries, Men walk through these gates with death in their eyes. This is a death which is so vividly illustrated by Van

---

1 The book was originally released in France in 1975 as *Surveiller et punir: Naissance de la prison*. The English translation was released in 1977 and then re-released by Penguin in 1979.

Gogh – the motion of the bodies of men routinized into the absurd pointless-ness of the repetition marked on their faces – marks that erase vitality. In Springsteen, this is a walk through factory gates that guide workers 'through the mansions of fear, through the mansions of pain'. Foucault's (1977) well-known account of the similitude between prisons and factories as 'instruments of penalty' (p. 228) is rendered forth in stark artistic and cultural imagery.

But there is an important difference between Van Gogh's prison and Springsteen's factory. In the painting the direct surveillance of the prison guards is both obvious and palpable. The presence of the guards, standing motionless immediately adjacent to the walking prisoners, sets the scene for the whole painting. These prisoners may be exercising to the rhythm of daily repetition, but they do so under a watchful eye. Someone is always ready to intervene should the order be disrupted. But in Springsteen's factory there is no mention of any human overseer. In the factory, work begins when 'early in the morning factory whistle blows', and stops when 'end of the day, factory whistle cries'. This whistle is a disembodied discipline that requires the eye of no one in particular – it rings with the sadness of routine and restriction. Springsteen's workers know fear and pain, and they walk into it each day of their own free will. Their identity is formed through the routines and restrictions that anchor factory life.

The idea that workplaces are quasi-prisons is not limited to popular culture – it is something that is well developed in organization and management theory as a means to characterize work relations, usually in large organizations of western capitalism. This is particularly the case for those theorists influenced by the work of Michel Foucault. Within such theory, the prison is taken as a metaphor for the organization. Most bluntly, the Foucauldian position is that 'since all of us belong to organizations and all organizations are alike and take the prison as their model, we are all imprisoned [...] even as we sit alone' (Burrell 1988: 221). Perhaps the most salient aspect of the prison-organization that has been given attention relates, as with our opening examples, to modes of surveillance that go on at work. In this chapter we offer a critical introduction of those organization studies that have concerned themselves with such forms to surveillance, as it relates to identity and subject-formation of people at work.

The chapter starts with an introduction to Foucault's consideration of surveillance and subjectivity, and then reviews how this has been taken up in relation to studies of organizations. The key thesis that united such studies is that in being watched or being thought of as being watched, people at work become self-disciplining. To capture the different ways this has been theorized, we discuss the broad connection between surveillance and how it is seen to shape identity. First, we rehearse the argument that the absence of direct and open coercion into particular forms of conduct leads workers to not just voluntarily internalize the gaze of surveillance but also, in so doing, to entirely surrender their identities to their organization. We note, however, that other versions leave workers with more room for manoeuvre, allowing for more dynamic kinds of subject formation that are less totalizing, and more opportunistic, calibrated and exploratory. Thus, second, we explore how people, rather than being passively capitulated into complying with 'the gaze' of surveillance, might also partake in various forms and degrees of resistance against it. Indeed, following Foucault, the relational character of power means that power and resistance are not oppositional but rather each requires the other for its existence. Third, we examine some of the more recent work in organization studies that has provided new and more nuanced ways of examining how people might respond to, mobilize and capitalize on organizational surveillance. We consider cynicism as a mode of internal distancing that, while maintaining the external appearance of compliance, inserts a critical space into being at work. Fourth, we turn to work that has situated the surveillance problem at the heart of intensifying demands for communicative-emotional labor on the part of contemporary workers. Here we review the argument that the rising levels of difference and mobility that workers now confront, and have to enact themselves, render irrelevant stable oppositional stances (to management, power, mechanisms of control). This research regards workplace identity as an embodied performance of increasingly mobile, reflexive, learning-oriented and therefore emergent ways of being. We close with a summary of how the notions of surveillance and resistance can be mobilized for studying identity in organizations.

Foucault and surveillance

In his book *Discipline and Punish* (1977) Michel Foucault makes a distinction between modes of surveillance and control that prevailed across the plague-stricken towns and cities of Middle-Ages Europe, and the modes that emerged with the onset of the Renaissance. To illustrate this shift, Foucault honed in on a particular kind of prison that was modelled on an architectural design termed the panopticon, originally conceived of in the nineteenth century by the English philosopher and social reformer Jeremy Bentham. Foucault begins his exposition by describing a city beleaguered by the plague, where control over individuals was achieved through an unceasing functioning of inspection. Here, guards, officers and members of the militia are virtually omnipresent to physically enact the authority of the magistrates. Should a townsperson be sick, have died or be subject to any form of irregularity, then the details are noted and transmitted back to a central authority. Through a precise chain of command every individual in the town is observed and accounted for on a daily basis. Foucault refers to this as a system of surveillance based on 'permanent registration' (p. 196). This registration makes possible that those deemed irregular or abnormal can be identified, portioned off and dealt with accordingly.

Foucault contrasts this exhaustive and direct mode of surveillance with that of the panopticon prison design. The design of the panopticon consists of a central tower that opens onto a ring of cells on its periphery. The windows in the cells are arranged such that once in the tower a supervisor is able to see the shadows and images of all of the inmates. The prisoner is rendered constantly visible, but at the same time the architecture is such that the person observing is never in sight. As Foucault explains, the aim of this arrangement is 'to induce in the inmate a state of conscious and permanent visibility that assures the automatic functioning of power' (p. 201). With the inmate never able to know whether or not observation is taking place, Foucault argues, surveillance is set up such that it is 'permanent in its effects, even if it is discontinuous in its action' (p. 201). Moreover, the power that is in place is both automatic and not borne by a particular inspector – it is a power that becomes internalized in or 'moulds' the observed. For Foucault this panopticon, 'a cruel, ingenious cage', was not only to be regarded as just an architectural form, but rather more generally 'a way of defining power relations in terms of the everyday life of men [sic]' (p. 205). In comparing the mode of power and surveillance in the plague-stricken town to that of the panoptic establishment, it is the latter, Foucault argues, that is 'lighter, more rapid, more effective, a design of subtle coercion for a society to come' (p. 209).

The notion of the panopticon and the disciplinary power that attends it are now common themes in the study of organization. So, following Foucault, there has been considerable discussion of 'subjectivity as the product of a plurality of disciplinary mechanisms, techniques of surveillance and power-knowledge strategies' (Knights and McCabe 1999: 203). Adopting the prison modelled on Bentham's panopticon as metaphor, scholars have regarded organizations as enacting control by positioning employees under the gaze of potential surveillance. As it did in the case of Foucault's prisoners, this physical subjection to the gaze of the (potentially absent) supervisor is argued to transmute into the formation of employees' subjectivity. Put in different terms, their sense of identity is shaped by the constant shadow of surveillance as they come to regard their own conduct as being constantly observed by others. In this way, the suspicion of surveillance by others accrues to self-surveillance, and this, in turn, acts on others working alongside us. Seen from this vantage point, surveillance is a sophisticated and economical mechanism of power. It is realized precisely by those who are the object of control: 'illustrating how power and discipline actively construct conformist selves, [Foucauldian] studies show how forms of power exert control over people, not least by shaping their identities and relationships' (Collinson 2003: 536). In this panoptic scenario, the likelihood that individual employees internalize the disciplinary gaze of supervisory surveillance and psychologize its essence is enhanced by a whole array of surveillance mechanisms: peer-observation, electronic surveillance, team-based organization, performance management, and a whole raft of related rituals and devices that entwine employees in self-generated imaginations of supervisory power and control. Here, the principal source of suspicion is not just a sovereign and embodied supervisory gaze but a diffused power that has begun to predispose employees to 'appropriate' behaviors and dispositions. These considerations have been developed in a body of knowledge that is referred to as 'surveillance theory' (Brocklehurst 2001) – a form of theory dominated by a motif of 'power as domination' (Dixon 2007: 286).

Surveillance and identity in organizations

Most centrally, surveillance theory is concerned with the blurring of sources of control across actors, sites and boundaries. Its focus is on addressing the complexities and ambivalences that come into play for employees embodying and enacting emerging horizontal, and, not just self-directed, but also other-oriented modes of control. This understanding of worker subjectivity in terms of the disciplinary mechanism and techniques of self-directed surveillance has become central to the critical study of contemporary management practices (Knights and Willmott 1989). Much of this work initially emerged out of an attempt to understand the effects of the increased use of direct surveillance in contemporary organizations, and its link to developments in information technology, and peer- and self-management techniques in place of top-down supervision (Sewell and Wilkinson 1992). These new forms of self-management are said to be strategies of 'normative control' (Kunda 1992) or 'concertive control' (Barker 1993) tantamount to nothing less than an 'age of corporate colonization' (Deetz 1992). The spread of self-surveillance in organizations has been seen to derive from practices as varied as corporate culture programmes (Fleming and Spicer 2003, Willmott 1993), human resource management (Barratt 2002, Townley 1998), employment assistance programmes (Weiss 2005), team work and self-management teams (Barker 1993, Ezzamel and Willmott 1998), homeworking (Brocklehurst 2001) and total quality management (Sewell and Wilkinson 1992, Knights and McCabe 1999). These studies portray workers' identification in a way that suggests that, even if organizational values are rarely internalized exhaustively, comprehensively and without modification, worker identity is still defined in their terms. Workers are described as internalizing or resisting values imposed on them by and through organizations, without sustained attention to their ability to interpret, adapt or creatively exploit these values and the media through which they are communicated. In sum, the oppositionality that is inherent in theorizations and descriptions of surveillance, power and resistance 'still remains the accepted orthodoxy in organization studies' (Fleming and Spicer 2003: 165).

Within this orthodoxy the argument is that besides supervisors, employees' peers come to embody the disciplinary gaze and assume the role of agents of control. This view leaves limited room for doubt, multiple meanings, shades of reasonableness or partial adoption of the resources and meanings through which organizational power is realized. In an emblematic study that pursues this line of thought, and taking a particularly dim view of organizations capitalizing on 'concertive' control, Ezzamel and Willmott report the team workers' complaint that 'each machinist was under pressure "to be the supervisor"' (1998: 382). This pressure resulted in '[c]lashes between the high performers and the low performers within groups [...] as teamwork meant that the affirmation of self-identity became increasingly conditional upon the conduct of fellow team members' (1998: 384). As a result, '[m]any of the machinists were unresponsive and even deeply antagonistic to the self-managing aspect of the teamwork ethos' (1998: 385). Their conclusion was that the ethos of team-based work camouflages peer control, thereby disenfranchising individual workers. Ezzamel and Willmott's critique of concertive control extends out from it being embodied by peers to it becoming embedded and rendered non-negotiable in technologized processes. In another study that promotes the same theme, Sewell reports on how horizontal surveillance works in tandem with 'language and symbols derived from new forms of classification that are "electronically wrapped"' (Sewell 1998: 403). For Sewell, technology strengthens organizations' capacity to pressure employees into controlling colleagues and subduing their extra- or anti-organizational tendencies. This becomes possible thanks to 'the 'wrapping' provided by electronic surveillance [that] can support new relations of power and domination in addition to reinforcing existing ones' (Sewell 1998: 404).

In pursuing the concern to reveal the intimidations outlined above, there is a danger of backgrounding the extent to which workers might also seek to capitalize on these circumstances and refract to their advantage the flows of power that they get caught up in. Common here are critiques of panoptic organizational architectures (Hopper and Macintosh 1998), information technology as a new generation of panopticism (Newell *et al.* 2000) and the increasing reach of the digital information that managers and these technologies garner and produce (McKinlay 2000). But in mapping the spread of horizontalized control, these studies risk abrogating emerging sources of surveillance with an effectiveness that rules out the possibility for employees to rethink, reshape or resist these new pressures and the responsibilities and visibilities they harbor. For consideration of this possibility, we turn to a body of literature that turns from the theme of surveillance and worker subjection to one that is concerned with more complex kinds of agency, identity, identity performance and resistance (Starkey and McKinlay 1998).

Resisting disciplinary surveillance

Understanding employees as wholly and inevitably subject to surveillance and control, however much these technologies continue to spread, 'improve' and diversify, has been argued to construct a simplistic view of employees' relationship to power (see Fleming and Sewell 2002). The main point here is that representations of efficacious power and of hoodwinked employees are not unlike traditional Marxist analyses that position work as essentially alienating, and that regard workers as always and inevitably co-opted and exploited through the generation of false consciousness, while locating true consciousness in a utopian world strangely divorced from existing or particular organizational, bureaucratic and industrial structures it nevertheless requires for its realization. Hence, to give credence to the possibility of a dominant organizing principle producing a common purpose amongst employees is to essentialize facets of socio-organizational life that remain dynamic and unpredictable. Indeed a generalizing theory, no matter how comforting, can never capture the particular, personal and embodied character of lived experience. In questioning the deterministic tendencies of surveillance theory, researchers have moved away from such straightforward determinations and turned their attention to resistance – not just in terms of overt recalcitrance, but also in ways that are 'more inconspicuous, subjective, subtle and unorganized' (Fleming and Sewell 2002: 859). This regards surveillance theory as limited because it tends to 'pay little attention to subordinates' strategic agency, knowledgeability and coping strategies' as they are manifested in 'defensive practices' (Collinson 1999: 581) and 'modes of resistance/subversion' (Hodgson 2003: 2). Moreover, when surveillance theory becomes obsessed by 'the subjects' active complicity in producing and reproducing domination' (Deetz 1992: 47) the relational character of power becomes obscured, notions of power and domination become conflated, and resistance can only be conceived of in terms of oppositionality.

What the above discussion points to is how, in conjunction with the growing research on the effects of surveillance, there has been a consideration of the extent to which such practices coexist with multiple resistance practices. These practices can come in the form of 'failure to act when required, acting ritualistically, leaking information to the press, rumour-mongering, or whistle-blowing' (Gabriel 2005: 211). They can also include 'foot dragging, false compliance, feigned ignorance, dissimulation […] that are conducted below the veneer of legitimacy; covert and seditious acts carried out in the silent spaces of everyday life' (Fleming and Sewell 2002: 859). By focussing on the multiplicity of possible modalities of resistance and subversion (e.g. Collinson 1999) this research centres on invoking understandings of agency and power that shift attention to the 'the complex responses of the 'governed' to forms of resistance and the contesting of forms of domination at work' (Barratt 2002: 193). In general this means that this research questions the efficacy and domination of surveillance and has led to an emphasis on worker resistance in the face of neo-liberal or self-disciplinary practices (see Jermier et al. 1994). This also reinvests importance in Foucault's point that resistance is itself 'always already' internal to power (Burrell 1988: 228) such that surveillance cannot be a guarantor for the wholesale reconstitution of organizational members' identity or behavior (Knights and McCabe 1999).

In general, much research has focussed on resistance in its many subtle, indirect and mundane forms – including humor, irony, cynicism, scepticism, parody, hidden transcripts, bitching and fiddles (Hardy and Clegg 2006). While the 'multiplicity of power relations exercised in a number of diverse directions' (Knights and McCabe 2003: 63) is accounted for, what is less researched, however, is the productivity of self and other that exceeds compliance and resistance in directionality and effect. This re-emphasizes that resistance is not a one-dimensional and purely oppositional response to the exercise of managerial power. It also emphasizes that notions of resistance do not exhaust the possibilities of people's conduct even when that conduct is located in power relations. This brings us to a vantage point from where we can begin to discern and outline the contours of emergent practices that disrupt the dichotomies of compliance/resistance and surveillance/worker-invisibility. Moreover, focussing on such emergent practices suggests a research agenda that moves away from generalized theories of surveillance and towards a consideration of embodied and lived experience – the discussion of which cannot be wholly theoretically prefigured.

When (self)surveillance fails: cynicism

In opposition to the view that surveillance practices are necessarily effective in moulding identity on the part of employees, it has also been suggested that a significant response to surveillance-related management practices is 'a reinforcement of instrumentality amongst employees who comply with their demands without internalizing their values' (Willmott 1993: 536). This suggests that 'rather than moving away from a powerful discourse, cynical resistance might actually become contiguous with it' (Fleming 2005: 53) through processes of 'calculative compliance' (Willmott 1993: 537) that are not realized directly through identity alignment. This argument points to dis-identification through cynicism (Kunda 1992, Watson 1994) as a means for workers to counteract having their identities determined by the norms and values espoused by the organization, whilst still enacting the behaviors favored by them. Drawing on studies in the sociology of work by Piccone (1976, 1978), Willis (1977) and Burawoy (1979), Fleming and Spicer (2003) argue that cynicism masks a lack of opportunity to assert one's agency in the face of organizational power: 'rather than reading the deep-seated cynicism of employees as a successful strategy of resistance [...] it may diminish the efficacy of more transformational workplace politics' such that 'some forms of transgression can be a preserving force' (p. 162). The logic here is that cynicism works as a safety valve and a coping mechanism that reconfirms one's agency in circumstances that do not favor self-determination. As Fleming and Spicer describe it: 'in being cynical, we are enlightened about the ways of the world, yet can still enact even the most boorish discourses because we fail to understand that the fantasy is ingrained in our modes of conduct' (p. 164).

A key contribution here is the idea that identification may not be as exclusively central to the achievement of power through subjectification as it is sometimes assumed – power can also work through dis-identification and have disjunctive effects. Here power is not about the colonization of the interiority of employees but works quite nicely on that which is external – objects and actions, rather than thoughts and beliefs. This view regards cynicism as able to disrupt managerial power on an emotional level, but as less likely to be effective on a behavioral level. This provides a compelling counterpoint to much of the accepted wisdom of surveillance theory, according to which power acts by being internalized by workers as a result of being objectified by the managerial gaze, leaving little or no cognitive remainder.

That said, cynicism deserves to be unpacked further both as what it represents and in how it has been theorized. Gabriel remarks that cynicism may be 'based on the individual's acknowledgement of an instrumental dependence on the organization and simultaneous denial of psychological attachment to it' (Gabriel 2005: 210). Here, it is not resistance to managerial power that motivates cynical responses and attitudes, but a resentment of one's dependence, potentially complicated further by an unacknowledged wish to be the object of authority. Gabriel's analysis has penetrating implications for those who mobilize cynicism as organizational response and for those seeking to theorize cynicism as anti-organizational impulse: by being cynical, employees remain ' "unpolluted", [or] untouched by the organization's inequities, even as they profit from its bounty' (Gabriel 2005: 210).

Emergent and embodied identities

For the authors reviewed above, concertive modes of control can invite cynicism, subversion, and potentially other resistant and evasive tactics that can disperse as well as enhance the efficacy of power realized through surveillance and self-surveillance. In an important sense, these latter accounts capture the ambiguities inherent in workplace conduct following the rise in personal and organizational visibility of workers across organizational domains. What they also begin to do is to offer more specific accounts of surveillance that account for the multiplicity of its empirical realities. However, accounts that focus on the multi-variate nature of resistant stances may only partially capture the full implications of emerging and emergent kinds of workplace conduct. Without denying the importance of putting these stances and tactics on the organization theoretical map, a more recent critique foregrounds the dynamic nature of employees' workplace positioning practices. This work places particular emphasis on facets that have thus far received limited attention in the organizational theoretical literature: the complexity of *in situ* conduct, the consequences of this for worker positioning, and the potential of surveillance to produce more than mechanized subjection and relational resistance (Iedema, Rhodes, and Scheeres 2006). This alternative work moves beyond endorsing the notion that we can speak about a progressive horizontalization of the managerial gaze, propagating itself with some perturbations, refractions and inflections, but maintaining the original principle of dichotomous workplace relationships and positionings.

Examining identity in terms of the multiplicity of sources of influence that workers are commonly and ongoingly faced with, raises questions about whether the sophistication attributed to 'soft control' (Courpasson 2000) justifies the leap in organizational and management studies from interactive moments (specific performances of recalcitrance, cynicism, subversion, contradiction, as well as the genesis of interpersonal relationships) to definitive or lasting identity commitments. More generally, what this points to is a central issue for the analysis of identity in organizations: workers' roles in contemporary organizations can be complex, dynamic and intertwined with multiple values, whose analysis only rarely boils down to theoretical singularities such as surveillance and resistance.

Central here is the notion that people at work are 'multiple members of, and participants in, other social and cultural institutions and forms, many of which might be expected to exert a more powerful influence on values and beliefs, if not on behavior and performance, than the organizational credo' (Linstead and Grafton Small 1992: 225). Empirically, this points to a need to attend to the specifics of employee conduct as it may embody diffuse, contradictory and ambivalent performances, experiences and positionings. Such a perspective is bolstered by the view that the 'organizational regulation of identity . . . is a precarious and often contested process involving active identity work [such that] organizational members are not reducible to passive consumers of managerially designed and designated identities' (Alvesson and Willmott 2003: 621), and that identity performance is 'a continually contested process of making claims of difference within and between groups of people who are formally constituted as members of a defined group' (Parker 2000: 233). Following such views, it becomes apparent that *in situ* conduct harbors an inherent and far-reaching undecidability and indeterminability (Deleuze 1995) that cannot be captured once and for all. This line of argument has important implications for how we conceive subject formation and employee identity.

The notion that identity responses to power-laden interactions and organizational structures are in the first instance local and contingent phenomena can be understood in the Heideggerian notion *presencing* (Heidegger 1969; see Iedema, Rhodes, and Scheeres 2005). Such presencing is brought on by being 'confronted with the immediacy of another person's existence' (Thompson 2000) and entails the idea that we do not act from within an originating ego that is already fully formed, but rather that we as identities emerge as our actions unfold through time (Schatzki 2003). Here the 'self's defining quality is what it is about to become rather than what it is' (O'Connor and Hallam 2000: 238). Identity is thus not 'present' but is ongoing 'presenced' in the here-and-now. In a context of the intensification of communicative and interactive work, rising ethnic, educational, religious and other kinds of difference, and mobility, presencing becomes increasingly inevitable as the repetition of stable structures falls away. In effect, employees' involvement in complex forms of interaction at work foregrounds the immediacy of the other, rendering presencing a visible and tangible aspect of identity in organizations. Presencing manifests at values workshops, culture change meetings, conflict resolution sessions, complaints, and also during the unfolding of ordinary kinds of work. The sheer intensity of social-personal difference and the interactive volatilities this engenders inevitably perturb enactments of rituals, power and (self/other) surveillance. It is in this regard that presencing represents a stimulus for incipient and unstable socialities, ontologies and, therefore, identities (Iedema, Rhodes and Scheeres 2005).

Another implication of the argument that work harbors rising levels of undecidability is that it leads to *observance* (Iedema, Rhodes and Scheeres 2006). Emerging from the interactive volatility of work and the presencing this calls forth, observance references a complex, ambivalent and constantly shifting mix of self-steering social conduct – one where identity is re-negotiated on an ongoing basis rather than predictably rolling forth from pre-structured relations and position-takings. This conduct ranges dynamically and opportunistically across conformity to the imperatives of productivity, desire and self-aesthetics, and confrontations with the other through excess difference. This ontological multiplicity, it is hypothesized, may produce attention to the performance of self in the midst of difference, in short: it may produce observance. Observance encapsulates the view that it makes little sense to regard the worker as defending (through resistance) or failing to defend (through compliance) his or her authenticity. Rather than mechanically adopting or rejecting a gaze that is equated with others' disciplinary interests and concerns, observance capitalizes on the impulse and potential that self-surveillance harbors as reflexive strategy. Observance further highlights the contemporary possibility that people 'succeed' in reflexively reconfiguring their identity, practice, norms and future as their participation vacillates between being central and peripheral, centrifugal and centripetal, visible and invisible. Their openness to, and *observance of*, the dynamics of what is 'in' and what is 'out' enables employees to assume and enact a productive subjectivity that is not determinable by a singular or even a consistent stance. The rising rapidity of the turn-over of any one interactive stance, this argues, means observance becomes the medium *par excellence* through which experimental and temporal identity enactments become not just possible and practical, but desirable, necessary and increasingly common.

The direction that the issues outlined above point to is a need for (yet lack of) a more emergent and embodied consideration of identity in relation to organizational power. Dale (2005) makes a telling critique of the forms of theory reviewed in this chapter when she writes: 'changing ideas about control tend to be analysed through the lens of conceptual tools that themselves focus on a predominantly ideational level: discourse, culture and identity' (p. 651). The direction this portends is towards a consideration of the 'embodied subjectivity of organizational members' (p. 658) and focusses on 'the subjective, embodied experience of the workers' (p. 659). Indeed, if we look back on the studies reviewed in this chapter much of the focus is at the ideational level where identity, it would seem, floats above and beyond the embodied person. A problem here of course is that the conventions of theory and analysis that inform organization studies and social science lean easily towards such discourse-centric abstractions. Nevertheless there remains a need to locate the materially and empirically 'real' person into theorizing about power, surveillance and identity lest the particularity of subjective difference gets lost in the desire to theorize people *per se* and without specificity. This points to the way in which much existing theory is both 'de-materialized and disembodied' – it also calls for 'looking at how particular organizational spaces are produced, and control and resistance are 'lived' through the embodied subject' (Dale 2005: 674) as it emerges in practice.

Conclusion

In this chapter we have critically reviewed and explored research on identity in terms of the relations between surveillance and resistance in organizations. In an era where managerial practices have moved from control-and-command to include more cooperative, collegial and team-based discourse, the forms of disciplinary power first discussed by Foucault are increasingly relevant and potent in organizational settings. At the same time, however, theorizing disciplinary control struggles to account for 'the ultrarapid forms of apparently free-floating control that are taking over from the old disciplines at work' (Deleuze 1995: 178). Besides pointing to the modern-day contiguity of intra- and extra-organizational forms of participation and identity performance, Deleuze's comment can also be read to unhinge workers' identity from being contingent on the structure of organizational power relations, freeing them from the dual options of confirming or rejecting the status quo. The ultra-rapid forms of control at issue here are not as self-evidently the preserve of those in power as they used to be, locating power not in stability and certainty, but in mobility and adaptability. In one sense, this development heralds a diffusion and a horizontalization of power. On the other hand, it naturalizes power with the potential effect that traditional divisions between owners and workers, capital and power, disintegrate as free-floating discourses come to reign supreme across previously impenetrable demarcations. In this new world, there appears to be 'no inconsistency in simultaneously promoting teamwork, delayering, commitment, flexibility, loyalty, individualism, greed, empowerment and surveillance' (Keenoy, Oswick and Grant 1997: 147). Control may now be less a function of identifiable structures of power, than of shifting flows of influence and legitimacy that work through the bodies of persons.

If organizational control can be characterized by a thrust towards self-discipline and the internalization of managerialist discourse amongst employees, it is equally clear that such control is never total. There are many complex kinds of compliant, resistant and emergent responses to organizational power – responses that are not limited to the prefiguring imaginations of researchers and theorists. Responses might include oppositional resistance that simply tries to push back with equal or more force. In confronting more diffuse forms of power and free-floating kinds of control, however, stable forms of resistance lack in efficacy, breadth and creativity, and emergent forms transcend traditional oppositions. What this suggests is that while surveillance-based power and resistant practices characterize a good deal of contemporary work, it appears that there are also spaces where surveillance itself is exploited as reflexive resource to enable workers to inhabit the increasingly unstable, difference-enriched and mobility-prone workplaces and work-relationships of the present. The embodied, changeable and unpredictable character of such spaces remains an important part of identity and identity formation in organizations.

References

Alvesson, M. and Willmott, H. (2003) 'Producing the appropriate individual: identity regulation and organizational control'. *Journal of Management Studies* 39(5): 619–644.

Barker, J. (1993) 'Tightening the iron cage: concertive control in self-managing teams'. *Administrative Science Quarterly* 38(3): 408–437.

Barratt, E. (2002) 'Foucault, Foucaldianism and human resource management'. *Personnel Review* 31(2): 189–204.

Brocklehurst, M. (2001) 'Power, identity and new technology homework: Implications for "new forms" of organizing'. *Organization Studies* 22(3): 445–466.

Burawoy, M. (1979) *Manufacturing Consent: Changes in the Labor Process Under Monopoly Capitalism.* Chicago: University of Chicago Press.

Burrell, G. (1988) 'Modernism, post modernism and organizational analysis 2: the contribution of Michel Foucault'. *Organization Studies* 9: 221–235.

Collinson, D. (1999) ' "Surviving the rigs": safety and surveillance on North Sea oil installations'. *Organization Studies* 20(4): 579–600.

Collinson, D. (2003) 'Identities and insecurities: selves at work'. *Organization* 10: 527–547.

Courpasson, D. (2000) 'Managerial strategies of domination: power in soft bureaucracies'. *Organization Studies* 21(1): 141–161.

Dale, K. (2005) 'Building a social materiality: spatial and embodied politics in organizational control'. *Organization* 12(5): 649–678.

Deetz, S. A. (1992) *Democracy in the Age of Corporate Colonization.* New York: SUNY Press.

Deleuze, G. (1995) *Negotiations.* New York: Columbia University Press.

Dixon, M. A. (2007) 'Transforming power: expanding the inheritance of Michel Foucault in organization studies'. *Management Communication Quarterly* 20(3): 283–296.

Ezzamel, M. and Willmott, H. (1998) 'Accounting for teamwork: a critical study of group-based systems of organizational control'. *Administrative Science Quarterly* 43(2): 358–396.

Fleming, P. (2005) 'Metaphors of resistance'. *Management Communication Quarterly* 19(1): 45–66.

Fleming, P. and Sewell, G. (2002) 'Looking for the good soldier, Svejk: alternative modalities of resistance in the contemporary workplace'. *Sociology* 36(4): 857–873.

Fleming, P. and Spicer, A. (2003) 'Working at a cynical distance: implications for power, subjectivity and resistance'. *Organization* 10(1): 157–179.

Foucault, M. (1977) *Discipline and Punish: The Birth of the Prison*, Trans. Alan Sheridan. London: Allen Lane.

Gabriel, Y. (2005) 'Beyond happy families: a critical re-evaluation of the control-resistance-identity triangle'. In Pullen, A. and Linstead, S. (eds) *Organization and Identity* (pp. 199–222). London: Routledge.

Hardy, C. and Clegg, S. R. (2006) 'Some dare call in power'. In Clegg, S. R., Hardy, C., Lawrence, T., and Nord, W. R. (eds) *The Sage Handbook of Organization Studies* (pp. 754–775). London: Sage.

Heidegger, M. (1969) *Identity and Difference.* New York: Harper and Row.

Hodgson, D. (2003). ' "Taking it like a man": masculinity, subjection and resistance in the selling of life insurance'. *Gender, Work and Organization* 10(1): 1–21.

Hopper, T. and Macintosh, N. (1998) 'Managing accounting numbers: freedom or prison – Geneen versus Foucault'. In McKinlay, A. and Starkey, K. (eds) *Foucault, Management and Organization Theory* (pp. 126–150). London: Sage.

Iedema, R., Rhodes, C., and Scheeres, H. (2005) 'Presencing identity: organizational change and immaterial labour'. *Journal of Organizational Change Management* 18(4): 327–337.

Iedema, R., Rhodes, C., and Scheeres, H. (2006) 'Surveillance, resistance, observance: exploring the teleo-affective intensity of identity (at) work'. *Organization Studies* 27(8): 1111–1130.

Jermier, J., Knights, D., and Nord, W. (1994) *Resistance and Power in Organizations.* London: Routledge.

Keenoy, T., Oswick, C., and Grant, D. (1997) 'Organizational discourses: text and context'. *Organization* 4(2): 147–157.

Knights, D. and McCabe, D. (1999) '"Are there no limits to authority": TQM and organizational power'. *Organization Studies* 20: 197–224.

Knights, D. and McCabe, D. (2003) *Organization and Innovation: Guru schemes and American dreams*, UK: Open University Press.

Knights, D. and Willmott, H. (1989) 'Power and subjectivity at work: from degradation to subjugation in social relations'. *Sociology* 23(4): 535–558.

Kunda, G. (1992) *Engineering Culture: Control and Commitment in a High-Tech Corporation.* Philadelphia: Temple University Press.

Linstead, S. and Grafton Small, R. (1992) 'On reading organizational culture'. *Organization Studies* 13(3): 331–355.

McKinlay, A. (2000) 'The bearable lightness of control: organizational reflexivity and the politics of knowledge management'. In Prichard, C., Hull, R., Chumer, M., and Willmott, H. (eds) *Managing Knowledge: Critical Investigations of Work and Learning* (pp. 107–121). London: Macmillan.

Newell, S., Scarbrough, H., Swan, J., and Hislop, D. (2000) 'Intranets and knowledge management: de-centred technologies and the limits of technological discourse'. In Prichard, C., Hull, R., Chumer, M., and Willmott, H. (eds) *Managing Knowledge: Critical Investigations of Work and Learning* (pp. 88–106). London: Macmillan.

O'Connor, K. and Hallam, R. (2000) 'Sorcery of the self: the magic of you'. *Theory and Psychology* 10(2): 238–264.

Parker, M. (2000) *Organizational Culture and Identity.* London: Sage.

Piccone, P. (1976) 'Beyond identity theory'. In O'Neil, J. (ed.) *On Critical Theory* (pp. 129–144). New York: Seabury.

Piccone, P. (1978) 'The crisis of one-dimensionality'. *Telos* 35: 43–54.

Schatzki, T. (2003) 'Living out of the past: Dilthey and Heidegger on life and history'. *Inquiry* 46: 301–323.

Sewell, G. (1998) 'The discipline of teams: the control of team based industrial work through electronic and peer surveillance'. *Administrative Science Quarterly* 43: 397–428.

Sewell, G. and Wilkinson, B. (1992) 'Someone to watch over me': surveillance, discipline and the just-in-time labour process'. *Sociology* 26(2): 271–289.

Starkey, K. and McKinlay, A. (1998) 'Afterword: deconstructing organization – discipline and desire'. In McKinlay, A. and Starkey, K. (eds) *Foucault, Management and Organization Theory* (pp. 230–241). London: Sage.

Thompson, I. (2000) 'Ontotheology? Understanding Heidegger's destruktion of metaphysics'. *International Journal of Philosophical Studies* 8(3): 297–327.

Townley, B. (1998) 'Beyond good and evil: depth and division in the management of human resources'. In McKinlay, A. and Starkey, K. (eds) *Foucault, Management and Organization Theory* (pp. 191–210). London: Sage.

Watson, T. J. (1994) *In Search of Management: Culture, Chaos and Control in Management Work.* London: Routledge.

Weiss, R. M. (2005) 'Overcoming resistance to surveillance: a genealogy of EAP discourse'. *Organization Studies* 26(6): 973–997.

Willis, P. (1977) *Learning to Labour: How Working Class Kids Get Working Class Jobs.* Westmead: Saxon House.

Willmott, H. (1993) 'Strength is ignorance; slavery is freedom: managing culture in modern organizations'. *Journal of Management Studies* 30(4): 515–552.

6

As leadership dies: cases of individual and group identity destruction and construction

Adrian N. Carr and Cheryl A. Lapp

Introduction

In 2003, the journal *Human Relations* published an article authored by Paula Hyde and Alan B. Thomas entitled, 'When a leader dies'. This article used case study data from work that comprised Hyde's doctoral thesis (1999). In a broadly psychoanalytic manner, the article by Hyde and Thomas investigated and described 'the reactions of followers after losing a leader' (Hyde and Thomas 2003: 1005). A study of leadership loss has much to commend itself, in as much as a change in leadership can demonstrably have profound ramifications for an organization, but in particular, for the cohesiveness and identity of the group who are the 'followers'. In reaction to a change in leadership, it is not uncommon to find a group exhibiting a range of defensive and apprehensive behaviors. Such apprehension and defensive behaviors occur because, by and large, people do not fear change in itself but in large measure, they fear being changed in ways that put their self-esteem and sense of security at risk. When self-esteem is affected, so also is self-efficacy and other aspects of self-concept that constitute identity. The erosion of self-esteem is directly connected to feelings of identity dissolution, which we, along with a number of scholars, argue is akin to feeling like one is dying (Alford 1994, Becker 1973/1997, Berzonsky and Adams 1999, Bick 1968, Nitsun 1996, Ogden 1989, Solomon, Greenberg and Pyszczynski 1998, 2003).

This erosion of self-esteem and identity dissolution, we attribute to the effects of what some of the psychodynamic literature refers to as two antagonistic classes of instinct – *Eros* and *Thanatos*. *Eros* is that class of instincts represented by extemporization for life (sex) and self-preservation.

Eros' adversary, *Thanatos* (Jones 1957: 295), is an assemblage of destructive expressions embodied by feelings and behaviors related to dying or mortality and death (Carr 2003b, c, Carr and Lapp 2005, 2006a, Freud 1920/1984, 1923/1984). The significance of these two antagonistic classes of instincts to both destructive and constructive aspects of individual and group identity will become clear, but it is an understanding of the dynamics of these two classes of instincts that provide the fundamental lens to our re-reading of the original case study by Hyde (1999) and some of its subsequent appearance in the *Human Relations* article by Hyde and Thomas (2003). Our re-analysis of the case study is also informed by the work of C. Fred Alford (1991, 1994) as well as earlier psychodynamic work of Sigmund Freud (1920/1984a, 1923/1984b), Melanie Klein (1975 a–d) and the much lesser known work of Sabina Spielrein (1912/1994).

The overall purpose of our chapter is to uncover psychoanalytic and, predominantly, psychodynamic behavioral expressions constituent of the death instinct, which need to be reflexively predicted and interpreted if the 'organization' (i.e. psychic and organizational workplaces) is to regenerate healthy attitudes towards leadership change and, indeed, to understand individual and group identity dynamics during organizational change more generally. Before we examine the case study, it is instructive to first outline the conceptual framework we intend to employ.

Predilections

One wonders if you can overstate the impact of the collective works of Sigmund Freud. Certainly, there is little doubt that Freud's work has had a significant influence upon social and cultural ideas. The topographical and dynamic model of the mind in which he posited the realms of the id, ego and super-ego are now all too familiar and have passed into everyday language. So too the notion of defence mechanisms like projection, regression, denial, sublimation, identification, displacement and also the notions of free association, slip-of-the-tongue (Freudian-slip), Oedipus and Electra complex, cathexis, psychosexual stages, and so on, are all parts of our vernacular as well as becoming part of the general vocabulary of psychology and other fields. His ideas bear the hallmarks of the scientific method with revisions being made when further observations indicated a need to modify his working 'hypotheses'. Notwithstanding, his core ideas have proved remarkably resilient in the face of those who have set out to 'scientifically' discredit them only to discover more substantiation for much of those psychodynamic processes originally described by Freud.

As we have previously noted (see Carr 2002), unlike many of his contemporaries, Freud did not view the unconscious as simply a passive or less active state of being and some kind of brain activity with no connection to mental activity. Freud also did not agree that this was a domain beyond comprehension. His notion of the unconscious was quite different. For Freud, like the proverbial iceberg, the unconscious was the domain of mental activity that lay below the 'surface' and, together with conscious mental processes that were often entwined, was responsible for human behavior. The unconscious was the subterranean strata of the psyche that consisted of previous experiences, memories, feelings and urges, of which the individual was not actively aware due to defensive mechanisms – the most common of which was repression – or other active psychodynamic processes.

The concept of the unconscious was central to the field of psychology founded by Freud called *psychoanalysis* or psychodynamics. Psychodynamics is a preferred term, by many, as the less 'treatment'-oriented synonym that implies the normality and dynamic nature of these processes. Of course, the nature of the psychodynamic theories posited by Freud have extended well beyond the 'consulting room' (see Carr 1998) and we find his work reflected in the development of theories of group behavior, leadership, religion, art, culture and so on. Also, as was noted earlier, we find the hallmarks of his theories even in our language and our everyday comprehension of the world. For all this notoriety and profound insight, the uptake of psychodynamic theory in organization studies and the discourse of management has proceeded at a snail's pace.

In this chapter we demonstrate how the application of psychodynamic insights provides us with a rich comprehension of the dynamics of group identity and the interface with leadership change and behavior. In particular, we define and demonstrate how the psychodynamics of defending against death are both constructive and destructive activities to identity.

While the topic of 'death' is one normally avoided, or wrapped in metaphor or euphemism, in our discussion we note connections between physical and psychic mortality and as such, use terminology fitting such a theme. Where psychical 'dying', 'death' and 'killing' are indicated, we have purposefully chosen these words precisely to make the reader aware of the effects and affects of mortality salience: to accentuate the personality, emotional and self-concept reconstructions that occur as people in the workplace defend themselves against identity dissolution and death.

Research methodology

For the re-reading of the case study, 'As leadership dies', it needs to be understood that in the collecting and analysing of data in a naturalistic manner, we employ what we have dubbed 'pracademics' (Carr and Lapp 2006a). Pracademic is a term used to refer to any approach that seeks to meld a specific application to a specific theory. In this regard we borrow from Burkard Sievers (1999) the term *Thanatospraxis* as a specific instance of pracademics in as much as, in part, we use a specific case to interrogate a theory of *Thanatos*. The paper frames its discussion of the case study using Alford's five dramas of 'acting out the missing leader'. Like a drama, the paper locates a case study as a series of acts and scenes with a specific psychodynamic script that is being played out. In the sequence of events, we will be using a style or approach that is reiterative and recursive.

Much of what we remember needs to be unrepressed from the unconscious and it is for this reason that we set the case study before the literature. In this way, the reader can begin to ask the data questions pertaining to the psychodynamics and thus, enhance reflexivity for subsequent sections. The case study will now be outlined to give the reader a sense of the dramas that will be subsequently read and analysed through the lens of psychodynamic theory. In this first review, it is instructive to first look at the case in terms of the psychodynamics involved. At this point, one question to ask the data is: 'What workplace situations are occurring to make employees feel like their identities are changing?' Following the case study, we will review the literature on the instincts and then examine excerpts from the case and its related organizational theory through the aforementioned lens of the psychodynamics. The chapter concludes with some suggestions for future research in this area.

The case study: *As leadership dies*

As we discussed earlier, our case study of 'As leadership dies' is drawn from the work of Hyde (1999) and Hyde and Thomas (2003), and what now follows is our summary of that case study.

Northern Community Mental Health Team (NCHMT) Overview

Marjorie, the service director of service managers Paul and Anne, suggested that Hyde and Thomas use Anne's group for their study. Northern CMHT[1]

---

1 All names have been replaced with pseudonyms.

(NCMHT) was established five years before the study took place, mainly from ward staff and a small number of existing community staff. It was created in response to complaints from general practitioners about long waiting times for services from community psychiatric nurses (CPNs) and social workers. Anne Evans was well known by her superior and service director, Marjorie, who before being promoted from service manager had worked alongside Anne. Marjorie was located in an administrative office in the center of the city and about five miles away from NCHMT. Marjorie appointed Anne to deal with the perceived service problems at that hospital because the staff there was generally seen as difficult to handle, as well as being unkind or neglectful of the patients.

Anne was allowed to radically restructure part of the larger health care organization to form the newer, smaller NCMHT because of complaints regarding the very 'union', militant CPNs' and social workers' (SWs) inefficiencies surrounding patient care. Theoretically, the new group was to ensure that each patient would be serviced by a one-stop-shop or a one worker: one patient ratio. Instead, patients were passed from one worker to another or they were referred elsewhere. Five months before Anne was diagnosed to be terminally ill, a further restructuring was to take place that would effectually reverse Anne's efforts – psychiatric nurses and social workers were to be repatriated, thus reconstituting the larger CMHT. Anne's response was to spend as much time as she had left at NCMHT, in physical proximity to her core team, where she was cared for primarily by Stella. During Anne's illness, some core-team members tended to her home garden. Less than three months after being diagnosed, Anne passed away. Some male team members were pallbearers at Anne's funeral.

After Anne died, the last known restructuring took place. Management, in general, was looking for change because they disliked results of Anne's leadership, which negatively impacted other parts of the larger organization. 'Anne sat in her wheelchair in the office waiting to die and making sure that her legend lives on' [Marjorie, service director]. Marjorie promoted Susan from social worker to fill the service manager role, with the job description to lead Anne's core group along with others who had recently joined the larger CMHT.

During Anne's leadership

The primary task of NCHMT was to maintain people in the community who were already identified as having a severe mental illness. The NCMHT administered medication, offered social activities and alerted doctors in the event of any decline in the patient's condition. Their task was to contain threats of violence from the patients[2] to themselves or to others. Their patients had long-term illnesses, which meant success was judged by an absence of violence or by the avoidance of readmission to hospital. Such 'failures' in mental health care may, in extreme cases, lead to widespread media exposure and public inquiry.[3]

Although the team was based in the hospital, the majority of their work was in patients' own homes. The patients had conditions that required regular monitoring and they were expected to be involved with the community team for long periods. One worker was expected to provide most of the care for one patient, giving the opportunity for personalized care and the development of long-term working relationships. In reality, patients were regularly passed from one worker to another or referred out to other services.

Part of Anne's re-engineering implementation was to deport CPNs and SWs to other units within the larger organization, including Susan, one of the SWs. The separation caused great resentment among the CPNs. Anne allowed the entry of three experienced outside hospital staff to join the team, but in doing so all three were demoted.

Anne was considered to be an authoritarian, who was revered, feared and competitively inclined. The staff had little discretion and were checked upon and disciplined regularly for minor infractions. Dress codes that included the wearing of shirts and ties for the male staff were imposed. In three years, Anne pushed 29 staff members to strive for and win two service quality awards, which were prominently displayed. More restructuring resulted in two additional units specifically created in the image of Anne's successful NCMHT. Outsiders resented these achievements. They cynically referred to Anne's team as 'Evans' angels'.

The team's immediate manager was Andrea, who was based in the team office and had her own case-load of patients as well as immediate managerial responsibilities. She had been appointed by Anne. Andrea's desk was behind a filing cabinet out of sight of the office door. She had been promoted over other members of the team (some of those members had been demoted).

Although the older and more experienced members seemed to like Andrea, she carried little authority in the team. With Andrea, team members behaved like children, testing the boundaries and drawing her into telling them off

---

2 The term patient is used here for consistency, although staff also used the term client.
3 In a two-week period in 1992, Jonathan Zito was killed by Christopher Clunis, and Ben Silcock was filmed being mauled by lions at London Zoo. More recently, Michael Abram broke into George Harrison's home and stabbed him. In all of these cases mental health workers were severely criticized for failures in care.

for wearing jeans, arriving a few minutes late, or making challenges to her in meetings by moving away from the point, joking or making light of her efforts to improve behavior on the team. Their behavior did not escalate or annoy Andrea. She did not respond in the way Anne was reported to have done (i.e. by taking formal disciplinary action). Rather, Andrea made somewhat ineffectual attempts to get the team working. In effect, her attention was often diverted to those team members who were grieving the most or those who had been most attached to Anne. During data collection after Anne's death, Andrea was applying for other jobs. As an observer, the researcher felt that Andrea had a very difficult job to contain emotions in the team and as the new leader operated at some distance, this role fell to Andrea.

After Anne's leadership

'It was a huge disgusting place with more disgusting staff. It was the norm to sit with a fag in their hand, drinking coffee and doing nothing all day. Everything was a chore, especially if patients asked for anything . . . I'm lucky Anne just left me to get on with it. She'd ask you to do a job and expect you to do it'. 'What's the point now? I want to be here, it suits me for childcare' [Stella, personal assistant].

A series of extramarital affairs sprung up between members of staff who had formed the loyal core of original team members. Paperwork substituted for emotional work, it was used increasingly to facilitate withdrawal from wider society.

Three additional team members had been employed since Anne's death. Two were support staff employed from within the hospital and the third was Penny, an occupational therapist (OT) from outside the local area. Members of the team encouraged me (Hyde) to spend time with Penny, although they emphasized she was unpopular and isolated. Although Anne had been mentioned before, the following conversation was the first indication of how influential to the team she had been: 'Anne set up these teams and died last year. She was held in great esteem. She seemed to rule with a rod of iron and there was a blame culture. If you didn't write your name and date and who you were [in the patient notes] you'd get a letter to discipline you. It was all about getting the quality award. More time doing paperwork – ridiculous!' [Penny, newly hired OT].

Anne's core group was resentful of anyone from the 'enemy camp' or those who were outsiders, such as CPNs and SWs, and appeared to be torn between feelings of disloyalty if they accepted any benefits of the new regime, and wanting to preserve the positive acknowledgements of their work.

There were two other small groupings of staff. The first were made up of the staff appointed after Anne's death who found the strong attachments of the core group of staff, to the past and the service quality awards, perplexing. The second group consisted of people who had not necessarily gained from Anne, such as staff who were disciplined or demoted by her. Both these groups felt less threatened and more optimistic about the future.

Anne's replacement was considered by the team to be indifferent, distant, fallible and an impostor from the enemy camp. Susan, a social worker from one of the staff groups that had been alienated in the past, became the team's new leader, in Anne's place. In contrast to Anne, Susan was less authoritarian and spent little time with the NCMHT as the management role covered many other mental health services. Marjorie, who suggested the team for study and who appointed Susan to replace Anne, later said of the new management arrangements: 'Susan's got a really tough job there, even she's wondering why I put her there' [Marjorie, service director].

Another manager who had worked alongside Anne and took a parallel appointment in the trust said: 'That team though, because her office was physically next door to them, were her special team and they all turned out for her funeral they were all absolutely destroyed by her going and that was why I would never have wanted Susan's job . . . Anne had a particular style and I think it's taking a while for people to come out from living under her shadow' [Paul, service manager].

Susan was attempting to work on this conflict, but was finding the process difficult: 'I'm trying to talk to people to pick out what is good about the service and needs to be continued. I mean Stella [personal assistant], is fine now, but she has tremendous loyalty to Anne and to the original service and has been very upset at the thought of changing it. [She is] enormously proud of the service quality award and all the work that was put into it. I'm not terribly impressed by any of these awards. I have always felt if they think we have to put a carrot like that to make us do the right job, they must think we are idiots' [Susan, service manager].

'From my point of view, we have a new manager who maybe doesn't understand the nature of the service that was created. She maybe wants to mould it into something completely different and doesn't care that you know this work was done and this was achieved' [Jackie, Past NCMHT Nurse].

The theoretical setting: conceptions of the death instinct in primal human relations

The co-construction and co-destruction of both individual and group identities by *Eros and Thanatos* bring forward behaviors that are influenced by the id, the unconscious, in which both classes of instincts reside, psychically:

> The unconscious is to be understood as the subterranean strata of the mind consisting of previous experiences, memories, feelings and urges of which the individual is largely unaware. The hidden meaning of actions, desires and emotions are brought to light through a study of human behaviour that views conscious phenomena as expressions of unconscious ones
>
> (Carr and Lapp 2006a: 5)

The work of Sigmund Freud is seminal to the discussion of the psycho-dynamic building blocks of the mind that in combination serve to shape our identities and it is to the work of Freud that we now direct our attention.

Psychodynamic building blocks of identity: the id, the ego and the super-ego

In psychodynamic terms, identity is constructed and destructed by virtue of humans' inherent reversion to and projections of unconscious manifestations of the class of life and death instincts – instincts that reside in the psyche's id. Sigmund Freud's original notion that human beings are primarily instinctual beings later became modified to recognize that the expression of these instincts was subject to repressive psychodynamics that are themselves culturally shaped. At one point Freud (1933/1988) remarked:

> Instincts are mythical entities, magnificent in their indefiniteness. In our work we cannot for a moment disregard that, yet we are never sure that we are seeing them clearly
>
> (p. 127).

Freud was always unsure of the *degree* to which instincts were themselves amenable to cultural 'modification' – in his view, instincts were certainly open to socio-historical influence – but, that they are definitely the subject of control of agencies of the mind are part of the now familiar realms of the mind he called the *id*, the *ego* and *super-ego*. This topography of the mind is illustrated in Figure 6.1, below. It was because instincts make 'a constant claim on the mind and urges the individual to take certain actions' (A. Freud 1952/1992: 58) that Freud's discourse is not a biological discourse but 'what we are talking now is biological psychology, we are studying the psychical accompaniments of biological processes' (Freud 1933/1988: 128).

In this familiar topography of the mind, it is the ego's responsibility to mediate the demands of the id as they are triggered by aspects of the outside

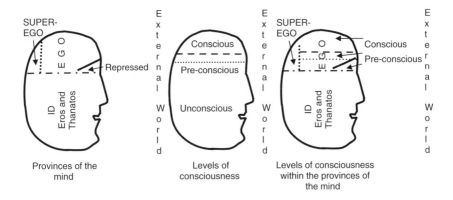

Figure 6.1 Freud's topography of the mind

Adapted from: Carr and Lapp 2006: 28 (see also Carr 1989, Freud 1923/1988, Freud 1933/1988, Jones 1964)

world that push the individual to have pleasure increased and unpleasure decreased (Freud 1900/1986, 1920/1984). Freud (1923/1984) described the relationship of the ego with the id in the following manner:

> The functional importance of the ego is manifested in the fact that normal control over the approaches to motility devolves upon it. Thus in relation to the id it is like a man on horseback, who has to hold in check the superior strength of the horse; with this difference, that the rider tries to do so with his own strength while the ego uses borrowed forces. Often a rider, if he is not to be parted from his horse, is obliged to guide it where it wants to go; so in the same way the ego is in the habit of transforming the id's will into action as it were its own
>
> (p. 364; see also Freud 1933/1988: 109–110).

In dealing with the id's demands for expression of specific instincts, the ego itself also has to have regard for social acceptability and other constraints. It is the realm of the mind, or agency, called the super-ego that seeks to remind the ego of these constraints. The super-ego gains its script from the rules of conduct, morals and other strictures constituent of authority figures – including, but not limited to, parents and their values and worldviews. In attempting to manage the id, the ego absorbs or introjects super-ego schema to suppress, postpone or satisfy the demands of the id. Through the process of identification, the super-ego not only gains a script of what is prohibited or are rules for conduct, but at the same time gains a script of positive 'models' of behavior to be ascribed to or to which one might aspire. This latter positive script is what Freud called the 'ego-ideal'. Thus, the super-ego functions in both a positive and negative manner: in as much as it performs the role of censor to the options and wishes of the ego, it also acts to direct the ego to an idealized self to which the individual aspires. Any failure of the ego to meet the strictures of the super-ego results in 'punishment' in the form of anxiety, guilt and shame. Indeed, if the ego fails to properly manage its own 'house', Freud (1933/1988) noted that a variety of forms of anxiety could result:

> Thus the ego, driven by the id, confined by the super-ego, repulsed by reality, struggles to master its economic task . . . If the ego is obliged to admit its weakness, it breaks out in anxiety – realistic anxiety regarding the external world, moral anxiety regarding the super-ego and neurotic anxiety regarding the strength of the passions of the id
>
> (Freud 1933/1988: 110–111).

It is when the ego fails to successfully repress the id that *Erostic* and *Thanatic* behaviors are most clearly revealed. Positive behaviors are embodied through *Eros* as self-love, self-protection and other-love (i.e. including but not limited to sex) and other-protection, which are *Erostic* such that they are not harmful to self and other. Alternatively, *Thanatos* is the class of death instincts that when acted out are purely destructive (Carr 2003b, c, Carr and Lapp 2006a, Freud 1920/1984, 1923/1984, see also Jones 1957: 295).

When overly influenced by *Thanatos*, the same 'normal' psychodynamic *Erostic* processes combine in ways that are first masochistic and harmful to self, which through 'needed' expulsion from the mind or projection are then transcended into sadistic or outwardly aggressive behaviors enacted upon others. *Eros and Thanatos* are 'fused, blended, and alloyed with one another' (Freud 1923/1984:381); so where one emigrates the other immigrates to cancel each other's energies (Carr and Lapp 2005). Should either accede uncontrollably, the modulated repression would be broken and gratification of pleasure and dispensation of unpleasure would lead primitive sexual and aggressive impulses to take over, thus breaking societal rules (Mitchell and Black 1995). Since it is both *Eros'* and *Thanatos'* jobs to cancel each other's energies before the ego and super-ego would allow such violations to occur, the death instinct is also embodied by repetitive compulsion or the need to reach a state of non-excitation and equilibrium in which neither the acquisition of more pleasure or the elimination of more displeasure is sought.

Competing values and goals or incongruity among various aspects of the super-ego create ambiguity and ambivalence resulting in the ego's inability to meet all demands simultaneously. Synchronistic failure causes the sacrifice of one to obtain another, generating moral anxiety as we noted in the earlier citation from Freud (1933/1988: 110–111). This sacrifice can also be in the form of guilt, which is inwardly turned aggression, or masochism. In extreme cases, guilt is revealed in the neurotic and the melancholic, individuals prone to excessive emotional upset from uncontrollable anxiety and whose super-egos appear 'as it were, a pure culture of the death instinct' (Freud 1923/1984: 394). Guilt erodes self-efficacy, self-esteem and therefore self-concept, a process that parallels the pull towards identity dissolution and fragmentation: examples of the death instinct's frustration of the life instinct in all its semblances.

The lack of self-concept allows the ego to further mismanage the id. Sadism is a phenomenon in which primary masochism is outwardly directed in behaviors ranging from subliminal demonstrations of avoidance and separation to overt, aggressive physical acts. These are examples of ways and means to feed the illusion that one has the will to power or that one can control externality. In other words, to defend against dissolution and to eliminate death fear, the ego turns on the super-ego. If the ego continually separates and re-attaches to similar but different aspects of the super-ego, the death instinct assumes the form of repetitive compulsion expressed as reiterations of masochism transposed into outwardly turned sadistic acts.

To satisfy instinctual satisfaction, action and desire are directed towards the objects believed to be able to fulfill them (Freud 1905/1977, 1933/1988). The corollary is that it is also from this object that an inability to continue identification and transference causes the deepest feelings of persecution and effects the most destructive behaviors through unbridled emergence of the death instinct. This latter issue and the significance of *objects* was subsequently one that Melanie Klein found somewhat intriguing. Although her work was 'strictly based on Freudian psychoanalytic concepts' (Segal 1981/1990:3), she was of the view that *Eros* and *Thanatos* first reveal themselves in the mother–infant interrelationship. It is to the work of Melanie Klein that we now direct our attention.

The first group identity: Melanie Klein and the mother–infant interrelationship

Klein accepted much of Sigmund Freud's orthodoxy including the vision that under the super-ego's rules and strictures, the ego is responsible for mediating the demands of the id, in which instincts are housed (Freud 1923/1984). In Klein's rendering of primal human relations, the mother or *object* represents the super-ego, the newborn's or ego's first attachment. Klein argued that the release of instincts from the id always presupposed the object interacting with the ego such that objects and memories or fantasies they trigger are sources of reassurance and/or persecution.

Klein's aggregate view of human experience (see Klein 1975a–d) was based upon two primitive dispositions of relating to the world: one is adoring, caring and loving or reassuring, and the other is comprised of destructiveness, hatred, envy, spite or persecution. The former parallels *Eros*, the class of instincts comprised of life (sex) and self-preservation; and the latter, the class of instincts embodied by destructive behaviors, or *Thanatos*, the death instinct. It is in the child's all-important first year of development that Klein viewed the death instinct as purely a destructive force summoned forth by fears of dissolution and imminent annihilation, when the infant, in its Manichaean world, cannot adequately resolve ambiguity and conflict posed by the mother's breast.

On the one hand, the infant projects love onto the breast as this 'good' object is idealized: it generates feelings of contentment that are absorbed or introjected by the infant because they represent the mother's reassurance, as through the transfer of milk (Suttie 1935). The infant also becomes confused, perplexed and anxious because it is also the 'good' object that inspires a degree of envy from the emphasis of the infant's need and dependence upon it – the infant experiences the 'good' object as being outside its control, when the infant cannot have it. On the other hand, the breast is simultaneously reminiscent of the 'bad' object that is hated when reassurance is disrupted. These disruptions are terrifying and frustrating so the infant also views the 'bad' object to be a powerful persecutor that can destroy both the infant and the 'good' object, causing separation anxiety during these periods of isolation. This anxiety becomes acute; it threatens to transform isolation into total dissolution, which becomes synonymous with the fear of death. *Thanatos* emerges through destructive defence mechanisms of splitting and projective identification.

To increase clarity, the infant uses splitting to exaggerate differences between 'good' and 'bad' objects, so part of the defence is somewhat schizoid. This early stage of development, characterized by fear and suspicion of the breast, Klein termed the *paranoid-schizoid position*, highlighting 'the persecutory character of the anxiety and . . . the schizoid nature of the mechanisms at work' (Laplanche and Pontalis 1988: 298). In the paranoid-schizoid position, destructive urges emanating from hatred and envy are projected in the same manner originally described by Freud (Laplanche and Pontalis 1967/1988: 427–429, Rycroft 1995: 139–140). They are split off from the ego to remove its 'bad' and contained in the other's 'bad' object (i.e. container or case) as a way to also develop the remaining 'good' object, which is supposed to emerge from the split as a place of refuge and core for ego development. Because the death and life instincts are melded, the death instinct does not yield to a pure split and in the form of envy, becomes a damaging force. It seeks to eliminate the good objects around which the ego attempts to develop and in so doing, destroys hope. Klein declared that of the seven 'deadly sins', envy is 'unconsciously felt to be the greatest sin of all, because it spoils and harms the good object which is the source of life' (Klein 1975c: 189).

Beyond mere projection of 'bad' breast feelings is the simultaneous process called projective identification. With the push of *Thanatos* over *Eros*, projective identification goes further to transcend shame of wanting more into the anxiety of not getting it, thus completing the transcendence, sadistically, as blame. The purpose of projective identification is to induce in the mother the feelings towards the 'bad' object for which she must take responsibility. In this way, without considering its own accountability, the infant attempts to make the mother feel guilty:

> a relationship to the original bad object has been created from the destructive force of the death instinct for the purpose of containing the threats posed by that instinct. There is a malevolent breast trying to destroy me, and I am trying to escape from and also destroy that bad breast
>
> (Mitchell and Black 1995: 93).

As early as the third month of life, the infant may come to the realization that it both loves and hates the same breast, which Klein referred to as the *depressive position*. The infant may, as another defence mechanism for this less developed ego, seek to deny (or as Freud (1940/1986) termed '*disavowal*') the reality of the persecutory object. It is the 'good breast' that becomes the core around which the ego seeks to develop as if it were the grain of sand that yields the pearl (see Klein 1975c: 178-180). Thus

> The frustrating whole object who has been destroyed is also the loved object toward whom the child feels deep gratitude and concern. Out of that love and concern, reparative fantasies are generated, in a desperate effort to heal the damage, to make the mother whole once again
>
> (Mitchell and Black 1995: 95).

Because 'good' can be perceived to be better than 'bad', 'good' can still be 'bad'. And, because 'bad' might be better than worse, it can be considered to be 'good'. The result of introjected projective identification is the construction of false selves or identities (see Laing 1961/1969).

Klein's rendering of development is one that argues that without progression to the depressive position, aggressive impulses will push the individual towards eventual and complete dissolution. Klein's version of the death instinct can be characterized as an anxiety theory generated by the ego's determination to split off and project aggressive impulses, thereby recreating the experience of the persecutory 'bad breast' in and around the individual. While in normal development we pass through this phase, the paranoid-schizoid position is a constant threat because in the sense of always being available to us, it is never truly transcended – even and especially in adulthood when the unconscious becomes unrepressed.[4] As adults, not experiencing others as 'whole' integrated objects may result in a regression to infantile behavior (see Suttie 1935: 32). C. Fred Alford provided an explanation of adults' regression to the paranoid-schizoid position resulting in manifestations of the death instinct during transitions from single- to many-object relations. It is to the work of Alford that we now turn our attention.

Alford's script: conceptions of the death instinct in adult human relations – *acting out the missing leader*

C. Fred Alford has explored the nature of the death instinct in the therapeutic group context. He shed some light on situations where adults are confronted with the anxiety of immigrating to and participating in (i.e. joining) what are perceived to be unstable human interrelationships: unstable, specifically as a result of intrapersonal leadership identity change following interpersonal leadership identity change – including that of the death of the leader. To further define the unstable group, one can turn to Nitsun (1996), who spoke to the characteristics of those who were, upon joining the group, anxious [i.e. perceiving something(s) 'bad' might happen], fearful [i.e. predicting what would go wrong], and/or frightened [i.e. actually being negatively affected by those predictions of group characteristics] of the group and especially its leader (see also Freud 1920/1984: 282). Group instability characteristics included but are not limited to feeling, predicting, and or knowing that: (a) the group and especially its leader (i.e. parent substitute) were untrustworthy; (b) the group does not have adequate direction or purpose; (c) group

---

4 Together, both Freud and Klein would propose that projection and projective identification, since they arise from destructive forces, are ways to reflect 'bad' that has been split away by child or adult into another child or adult. Both Freud and Klein point to self and other being mutually constituted, similar to that of the familiar Hegelian dialectic of the slave subject wishing to be free of the master object (See Hegel 1807/1977). This latter point is important but undeveloped in this chapter due to space considerations. Those interested in this issue are referred to Carr 2003a, Carr and Lapp 2006a, also Modell 1996: 97–120.

members do not have capacities to lead the group; (d) others will not care about the individual; and, because of these (e) there is always inherent, unhelpful and unwanted interpersonal conflict in the group (p. 43; see also Carr and Lapp 2006a: 135).

Leader–follower identity stability develops if individuals and the group are able to simultaneously curb anxiety, fear and fright and reach the depressive position by using projective identification to stimulate 'good breast' memories. Alternatively, projective identification of only 'bad breast' reminders, along with the schizoid compromise, results in dedevelopment from acute fear of either dissolution or engulfment when it is fantasized that the leader refuses to lead. The death instinct is then played out in the *five dramas* of 'acting out the missing leader' (Alford 1994) – dramas that we will discuss presently.

Background to group identity

Eros drives individuals' needs to participate in combined efforts to accomplish something that could not otherwise be achieved through individual performance. The primal group is infant and mother or representation of mother, in which ostensibly mother is leader and infant follower – in as much as the infant continually changes with and because of its environment, transformation is required to maintain self-esteem or love 'between the child and the mother and later to its substitute relationships with its whole social environment' (Suttie 1935: 29; see also Gabriel 1999).

Alford's contention was that the basic adult group is comprised of one subject and one object, in physical or perceptual contiguity, that use interaction to achieve some purpose. In the context of the leader–follower relationship, *Eros* is comprised of both pleasure-seeking and object-seeking states and with mutual causality: 'The mother gives the breast, certainly, but the infant *gives the mouth*, which is equally necessary to the transaction of suckling. The fact that there is a transfer . . . is immaterial to the child's mind, *if the milk comes willingly*' (Suttie 1935: 27). An unstable group is indicative of one in which this transfer in some way has been disrupted.

Joining an unstable group conjures ambiguity. There is a constant need to be a part of a group, continually tempered with the individual's fear of identity loss, 'which means to accept that within each individual is the desire to be an autonomous individual, the desire to submerge oneself in the group, and a perpetual conflict between these two desires' (Alford 1994: 5). Many human behaviors, including expressions of psychological illness, are ambivalent in nature as they often have, simultaneously, two antagonistic tendencies. The whole notion of individual becomes 'dividual' (Carr 2003b, c, Spielrein 1912/1994: 160).

In translation, joining an unstable group can be a destructive-reconstruction or a 'nothing ventured, nothing gained' event: 'Death is horrible; yet death in the service of the sexual instinct, which includes a destructive component, is a salutary blessing since it leads to a coming into being' (Spielrein 1912/1994: 183). In unstable groups, the willingness to risk identity loss or partial dissolution in the wake of creating something new may be based on the ambivalent relationship between *Eros* and *Thanatos*. However, if the personal sacrifice is perceived to come at too great a cost, *Thanatos* expresses itself as an 'instinct of destruction' (Freud 1923/1984: 381).

In diametric opposition to the individual, 'the group seeks first of all its own security. The creation of a less threatening environment is the group's paramount task. Everything else, including the recognition of its individual members, is subordinated to it' (Alford 1994: 27). Fantasies associated with impending identity annihilation recur during change in groups and set the stage for heightened anxiety from the group's 'unlimited power and an insurmountable peril' (Freud 1933/1985). Joining an unstable group can be likened to a life and death situation.

Relational combinations and permutations are positively correlated with the number of group participants: the more people in the group, the more confusion and anxiety generated, as each ego seeks to protect its own egoism and to defend against the needs of many, rather than only one other. The subject's need to protect the self against group threats to amass identities and diminish or even annihilate any differentiation invokes extreme anxiety of identity death, thereby necessitating the requirement of the formal leader. As Alford (1994) noted from his studies of groups:

> *Group development requires leadership, a fact that political theory has worked hard to ignore, evidently because the need for leadership is experienced as humiliating and dangerous.* Humiliating, because the need for leadership questions the autonomy and freedom of individuals, and dangerous, because leadership so often seems to connote the *Führerprinzip*
>
> (p. 5).

'Armed' with the foregoing insight from psychodynamics, we will now revisit the case, *As leadership dies*. Our intention is to initially present key facts regarding organizational structure and primary players' activities, characteristics and perceptions relating to leader–follower relationships when Anne Evans, the core group's leader, dies. We will then analyse these salient factors against the theoretical conceptualizations of the death instinct we have presented. The last segment of our presentation includes important implications for organizational studies and practice more generally.

As leadership dies: death instinct manifestations and leadership change

Thanatos outweighs *Eros* in mortality salient situations that threaten identity. Alford argued that the simultaneous resolve of the individual and the group to eliminate death fear anxiety results in the use of a mutated form of the paranoid schizoid position, the schizoid compromise, which in partnership with projective identification invokes individual egoism that underscores the play of *Acting out the Missing Leader*. The following synthesis of theory and analysis indicates that the first drama played out is *leadership and identity* (Alford 1994: 37–38, 63) in the three scenes of: the case of the missing leader; cases of missing leaders; and the missing formal leader.

Act one, scene one: leadership, identity and the case of the missing leader

Before restructuring was contemplated, Anne, an experienced middle manager, was likely in the feeling state of wisdom (Erikson 1980). Contiguousness of the individual–group relationship precipitated proleptic fantasies of joining an unstable collective long before reaching physical proximity to any others: especially if negative experiences were carried forward from past, non-esteemed interrelationships (Napier and Gershenfeld 2004). It is likely Anne experienced high levels of separation anxiety, while intuiting or understanding that she would also be creating unstable groups in which she would have to survive.

Anne placed herself in the autistic-contiguous position (Ogden 1989) where Alford's first lamina of the schizoid compromise occurs. The non-reflexive individual perceives that the continued refusal to lead is an act of persecution so 'good breast' reminders are more deeply hidden, thereby eliminating progression to the depressive position.

> This represents a superordinate defense in which psychological pain is warded off, not simply through defensive rearrangements of meaning (such as projection and displacement) and interpersonal evacuation of endangered and endangering internal objects (projective identification); in addition, there is an attachment on the psychological processes by which meaning itself is created. The outcome is a state of 'non-experience' in which the individual lives partly in a state of

psychological deadness – that is there are sectors of his personality in which even unconscious meanings and affects cease to be elaborated

(Ogden 1989: 199).

In simpler terms, the autistic-contiguous position is an embodiment of the death instinct and one in which the individual *super-protects* what is believed to be 'good' and *super-projects* what is perceived to be 'bad'. That which is protected is kept outside of the group, thus bringing into the group, mostly or only that which is perceived to be needed to defend against others' perceived persecutory attacks on self-esteem. We consider this to be *primordial* splitting, which is of particular significance because it helps determine why gaps in wisdom – that were not in prior existence – suddenly appear at the mere thought of joining an unstable group. Primordial '. . . splitting off the true self is an alternative to suicide . . . ' (Alford 1994: 55): it is instrumental in protecting the individual from diffusion and dedifferentiation or identity annihilation, suggesting existence of some degree of masochism. Further, in the group setting, primordial splitting is the foundation for the schizoid compromise where:

1. After hiding one's 'best' aspects, part of the self is isolated and withdrawn and barricaded against others' 'good'.
2. Another part of the self sees itself as instrument of the other's malevolent or careless will. The other may be group or leader; but generally the primary fear is of the group, displaced onto the leader.
3. Another part of the self imagines itself to be in an ideal relationship with the other [so as not to be excluded from and unrecognized by the group], so that the other's power, beauty, and so forth becomes an extension of one's own (Alford 1994: 52).

Anne was schizoid compromised and, therefore, enacting primordial splitting, because she was chosen to restructure: a masochistic task seen to feed a narcissistic need to do a good job for the parent company, while simultaneously building perceptions of terror and mortification by creating the NCMHT. Her self-esteem was deflated more than inflated, which induced her to put into 'cold storage' (Alford 1994: 55) some of the best parts of herself, thus giving life to the zombie, a psychologically downsized, fragmented self whose

current identity structure is being disequilibrated. The person may feel confused and scattered, behave impulsively, look for support in inappropriate places, become 'irresponsible,' 'unreliable,' and 'unpredictable'

(Marcia 2002: 15).

Subsequent fears resulted in Anne's regression or dedevelopment all the way back to memories of early childhood and infancy constituted by mistrust, hopelessness (Erikson 1980) and envy of the 'bad breast' (Klein 1975c: 189), hanging the backdrop for Anne's subsequent sadistic actions. While love and hate are viewed as a reflection of the antagonism of life and death instinct, sadism is an instance in which the two classes of instincts have become fused and in which primary masochism is outward-directed (Carr 2003b, c, Freud 1920/1984, 1923/1984):

> Part of Anne's re-engineering implementation was to deport CPNs and SWs to other units within the larger organization, including Susan, one of the social workers. Anne allowed the entry of three, experienced outside hospital staff to join the team but in doing so all three were demoted in the process.

In mortality salient situations, diminutions of self-esteem enhance death fear anxiety, which lead to punitive, outward acts of aggression that are severe (Solomon *et al.* 1998). Anne was becoming dissociated (Kets de Vries 2001b): she became more attached to process and task than to relationship. Anne defended against death fear by separating perceptions of good aspects of both distal and proximal group experiences from the bad, thereby activating the remaining two layers of the schizoid compromise. This is the phase of *primal splitting*, our renaming of Klein's original word. Anne split and projected 'bad breast' representations, so CPNs and SWs were exiled because they were perceived as untrustworthy incompetents. The CPNs' militancy was threatening and powerful, giving rise to competitive authority. Fear and envy were particularly evident in Anne's decisions to demote new members, although their service experience could have helped NCMHT development. Outwardly expressed sadistic acts, among other harmful death instinct manifestations, had ensued to protect the 'ordinary masochist' (Lind 1991). Defence mechanisms, especially early in the group development lifecycle, seem to be unavoidable because adults ' . . . would rather be 'bad somebodies' than 'weak non-entities' – to be human and weak is felt as if it were on the way to loss of identity' (Holbrook 1971: 199).

We interpret act one, scene one of *As leadership dies* to be indicative of the individual's loss of self-leadership, or what is akin to the leader's self-mutilation of identity. This is based on introjective identification of real and imagined *Thanatic* projective identification and these 'bad' identifications need to be projected into others. Alford's therapeutic group setting presupposes that the formal leader has a healthy psychological organization and is thus capable of mentoring the newborn group to become a working group. This may not always be the case when self-leaders allow themselves to be schizoid compromised, a new manifestation of the death instinct. Scene two discusses other such cases of missing leaders.

Act one, scene two: cases of missing leaders

In as much as the schizoid compromise creates holes in the ego to allow instinctual impulses to spill out, the gaps also allow various aspects to seep in. In contrast to Klein's rendition, Alford (1994: 48) assimilated Spillius' (1983) version of projective identification to say that it has the power to virtually project ego parts into others in both highly overt and subliminal ways: to infiltrate others' containers or cases and control them in what is unconsciously and consciously felt to be a coercive process.

> Anne was considered to be an authoritarian who was revered, feared and competitively inclined. In three years, Anne pushed 29 staff members to strive for and win two service quality awards, which were prominently displayed. More restructuring resulted in two additional units specifically created in the image of Anne's successful NCMHT. Outsiders resented these achievements. They cynically referred to Anne's team as 'Evans' angels'.

The death instinct becomes outwardly directed and transposed in the form of seeking control over externality or the will to power (Carr 2003b, c, Freud 1920/1984, 1923/1984), reinforcing masochistic and sadistic expressions, which can be amplified by narcissism and transference (Noer 1993, Kets de Vries 2001a, b, Schwartz 1990). In Arndt, Greenberg, Pyszczynski and Solomon (1997) and Solomon *et al.* (1998), it was shown that defence mechanisms manifested themselves after some period of time had elapsed between the inducement of mortality salience and the manifestations of its effects. As long as Anne was recognized and rewarded for her efforts, and especially in a temporally punctuated manner, a repetitive compulsion that focused on competitive award achievement was reinforced.

Individuals support the values of the person who elevates their self-esteem; individuals feeling highly esteemed are less likely to experience death fear anxiety (Solomon *et al.* 1998). It is in the context of ameliorating death fear that we recognize forms of transference, mirroring and repetition compulsion (Lapp and Carr 2006a). This explains why, even under such oppressive conditions, the core group remained so attached to Anne and her processes while, even at the same time, knowing that the group was being alienated by other organizational members. The core group was also seen to be supported in working against the primary service process, for which restructuring, ostensibly, was implemented. Anne's narcissistic state and the group's need for propping (Holbrook 1971) may have shielded them from the realization that resizing objectives were being ignored.

The more diffused group members' cases, the easier and faster the penetrations of Anne's perceptions of 'bad breast' reminders because primordial splitting helped each individual bury 'good breast' commemorations. Anne's core-group members allowed persecutory dumping of guilt and would have felt shame for not following Anne's authoritative and dictatorial rules. They allowed themselves to be ruled through an inferiority complex: 'Mother *is* good and kind; if she does not love me, that is because *I* am bad' (Suttie 1935: 32). Anne had an easier time of projecting what she fantasized to be 'good breast' images of restructuring, such as conferring self-esteem to her core group by forming and strengthening libidinal ties with awards, which was supported by the group members' willingness to use transference to reinforce Anne's narcissistic tendencies – to ensure the milk would keep flowing (Suttie 1935).

In order to survive Anne's organizational structure, group members needed to reach the depressive position or seek a core around which development could occur. They did so by convincing themselves that Anne's decisions were akin to the 'good breast', thereby disavowing Anne's negatives to preserve the 'lovability of the first loved object' (Suttie 1935: 31). Negatives were projected to other cases in and outside of the core group, which were reflected by the core's unwillingness to perform the service correctly and by outside groups' open disdain or 'bad breast' perceptions of the NCMHT's achievements. Thus, the NCMHT is the *premature group* that is paranoid schizoid and in the 'autistic-contiguous position' (Ogden 1989 cited in Alford 1994: 29). Without transcendence to the depressive position, or without the development of collective reflexivity, the group ego was punctured and its identity fragmented to the extent that

> the group itself, through pervasive projections, embodies a process akin to the death instinct. Here, the group as a whole becomes a poisonous container, acting as a siphon for the self-destructive process
>
> (Nitsun 1996: 151).

Alford would describe Anne's group as a collection of digressed, regressed part individuals, meaning neither group members nor the group itself were whole objects. Alford's (1994: 16, 58) theory is a fragmented-group theory that speaks to the premature group, a group that does not have the reflexive power to self-determine whether it will live to become a more mature group. Consequently, act one, scene two has resulted in many non-reflexive *cases of missing leaders* filled with fantasies of misleading 'good breast' images, a hatred of outsiders and perhaps even envy because non-cores were not shackled to approved and lauded dictatorial processes. The next scene outlines the group's expressed representations of the death instinct.

Act one, scene three: the missing formal leader

The true missing leader is Marjorie. Nowhere in the case does anyone refer to Marjorie as anything but a benign, legitimate leader who, by other group members, was not perceived to be downsize affected, even though it was she who effected the restructuring. By ignoring Marjorie's role in their own identity annihilation, a subliminated and repressed form of the death instinct was expressed in competitive strategy to achieve awards (Carr 2003b, c, Carr and Lapp 2006b, Freud 1920/1984, 1923/1984) and to attract the missing formal leader's attention, especially during the feeling state of envy. The formal leader is both revered and hated for what the group does not have (Alford 1994: 39, 59–60), which is the power to keep from identity dissolution. Reflexive circumvention generated by the schizoid compromise helps receivers fantasize they are being coercively controlled by the formal leader or what must be an 'aggressive imaginer' (Alford 1994: 29, 61–62). To protect her individual egoism, we see Marjorie defending her attachment to her mother, the organization, by using projective identification to not disallow Anne from further continuance of destruction. True to Alford's theory, Anne perceived Marjorie to be too 'brutal and sadistic' (Alford 1994: 73) because by selecting Anne to complete the restructuring, she was alienating Anne from the larger group without giving Anne the time or support to mourn this loss (Carr 2003b, c, Gabriel 1999, Hyde and Thomas 2003, Kets de Vries 2001b).

Marjorie becomes the creative sadist who is necessary to confer the masochist's desires: 'But these desires entail a large measure of frustration: the conductor is there to understand dependency, transference and other longings towards him, not to gratify them' (Nitsun 1996: 135–136). Marjorie was the entire group's missing leader, but for the wrong reasons. In what may have been an unconscious or conscious Machiavellian political parry, Marjorie may have killed off Anne.

The schizoid position, along with projective identification, ensures that rage, hatred and humiliation trigger group members to rip the formal leader into manageable, controllable pieces (Alford 1994: 28). Even though Anne has died, she and that which she embodied, Marjorie, is hated and loved at the same time. Reminders of the formal leader as 'good breast' are introjected and 'bad breast' projected according to each group members' individualized needs: to patch a self-esteem hole in each ego's punctured boundary and to spear other cases with persecutorial images to better control the experience of deindividuation. Although considered to be abnormal or infantile responses for a developed or mature individual, projective identification as embodied by envy, coerciveness and manipulation becomes the norm of individuals in the undeveloped premature group that without collective reflexivity and with *Thanatic* introjective identification has turned into the primal horde (Alford 1994: 59). It is likely that Anne would have been sacrificed by the core group at some point. However, to protect individual and group vestigial identity, we would suggest Anne and her group sacrificed Marjorie well before Anne's somatic death, and in retaliation for Marjorie's willingness to do away with them all. Ambivalence generated by the contemporaneousness of love, hate and envy (Suttie 1935) necessitates the removal of the formal leader (Alford 1994).

Act two: the sacrificial drama

Ambivalence is intolerable and the 'love relationship must be preserved as a matter of life or death . . . so an alternative is to abandon the mother, *as she now appears in reality* . . . ' (Suttie 1935: 31). Group members act out what they do not have and that is the formal leader: 'In this drama, the group is enacting the conflict between its fantasy of the consultant leader as aggressive, intrusive sadist to whom all must submit and its fantasy of the consultant leader as one whom the group must destroy to save itself' (Alford 1994: 62), creating three missing leader roles to be filled: the aggressive, the sadist and the scapegoat. These roles can also be filled by as many as three or one group member, the latter being a more efficient yet a just as effective a choice.

> One of Anne's appointments was her second in command, Andrea, a first line manager who upheld Anne's views and actions ensuring that:
>
> The staff had little discretion and were checked upon and disciplined regularly for minor infractions.

Alford argued that aggressive imaginers are also those who are most able to use projective identification to influence others because others who are dependent upon the leader are more likely to accept these subliminal and overt signals so as not to be rejected by the leader. In regard to the core group, at least one member, Andrea, was also masochistic. At the risk of being alienated by the core group and outsiders, she mirrored Anne's values in the form of promoting and supporting Anne's management style, using transference to identify with Anne.

Strong interpersonal relationships are more likely to diminish death fear anxiety in mortality salient situations (Mikulincer, Florian and Hirschberger 2003). The emergence of a co-dependent relationship between Anne and Andrea is evident, which also brings to mind the master–slave connection (Lapp and Carr 2006b). The conspicuous absence of reasons for Andrea's appointment might also be explained in terms of this likeness.

The group may have been deluded in perceiving Anne to be even more omnipresent because the illusion of there being *two of her* could easily have been invigilated. Solomon *et al.*'s (1998) conclusions argued that in high mortality salient situations, it is more likely that heroism will be rewarded with greater rewards than in low mortality salient situations. This might be why Andrea's character seems not only to be so tolerable of Anne but, in attempting to continue to serve Anne's wishes, is also an amplification, stemming from her courage to try to enforce Anne's rules of sadistic behavior. To even attempt such a feat – to be a mother like Anne – could be perceived by the group members to be an aggressive act.

In an interesting twist, Andrea is swept up in the generality of the discussion about the group dynamics by the group: the group ignores her presence. In other words, Andrea becomes another of group's sacrifices or scapegoats. Alford's contention that the powerfulness of his theory lies in covert influences and psychological communication used in projective identifications is strengthened. This parallels Freud's suggestion that the death instinct may be sublimated, as in the case of one's competitiveness in working relationships (Carr 2003b, c, Carr and Lapp 2006a, b, Freud 1920/1984, 1923/1984). Subliminal reminders of mortality salience are indeed more powerful than overt manipulations: 'Although many people are unaware of, or seem to deny, their concern with death, the evidence from these and other recent studies suggests that it is precisely when people are unaware of this fear that it has the strongest impact on their behaviour' (Arndt *et al.* 1997: 379). Andrea's failure to 'mother' the group like Anne created a group perception that Andrea was yet another missing leader or someone sadistically withholding reassurance, who was deserving of projected retaliation by the group:

> Sacrifices had a double purpose: on the one hand man participated in the creative process, at the same time paying back to the gods contracted by his species; on the other hand he nourished cosmic life and also social life, which was nurtured by the former. Perhaps the most characteristic aspect of this conception is the impersonal nature of the sacrifice. Since their lives did not belong to them, their deaths lacked any personal meaning

> (Paz 1961: 54–55).

In acts three and four, the core group shows the first signs of having potential to come back to life or to re-attaching themselves to something meaningful so 'values, disassociated from the body of the object can then be carried forward' (Hyde and Thomas 2003: 1006).

Act three: despair, deadness and hopelessness

To control shame and guilt at the sacrifice of one their number, despair, deadness and hopelessness all need to be incorporated by up to three group cases – respectively, the mourner, the murderer and the dead formal leader. Smaller groups have a tendency to mourn, which is the first sign of reparation or the core group's awareness that something less destructive might be done to act out the missing leader. During Anne's illness, some core-team members tended to her home garden. Less than three months after being diagnosed, Anne passed away. Some male team members were pallbearers at Anne's funeral.

The mourning process requires consideration of competence and temporality: it is reparative if all group members are able and, given time, use it to reach the depressive position. Larger groups have more cases to project and introject only 'bad breast' reminders. They are also more likely to become enraged murderers, 'which involves aggression, coercion, anger and love protests on the part of the child' (Suttie 1935: 31) that leads to hopelessness when the leader cannot be resurrected:

> It was a huge disgusting place with more disgusting staff. It was the norm to sit with a fag in their hand, drinking coffee and doing nothing all day. Everything was a chore, especially if patients asked for anything... I'm lucky Anne just left me to get on with it. She'd ask you to do a job and expect you to do it [Stella, personal assistant].

> What's the point now? I want to be here, it suits me for childcare [Stella, personal assistant].

To use Alford's (1994) words on our behalf: 'In general, however, the tone of this drama is dominated by the experience of deadness, the group's identification with the dead leader' (p.62):

> Anne sat in her wheelchair in the office waiting to die and making sure that her legend lives on [Marjorie, service director].

With Anne and Andrea no longer in the scene, only remnants of Marjorie remain. This is the dissociated aggressive imaginer who is in no position to lead the entire core group through the mourning process, so the group continues to seek yet another method for reviving the leader, in the next drama.

Act four: sex and death

In this drama the group resorts to having real or metaphorical sex split into life-giving and life-taking potential of, respectively, positive revivification or further destruction. We see this as an attempt to transform the group or re-eroticize the environment (Marcuse 1955, 1970):

> A series of extramarital affairs sprung up between members of staff who had formed the loyal core of original team members.

> The core group created their own processes that stressed assessment completion and interventions to their award winning service such as communicating with patients' relatives or their doctors rather than the patients themselves. Instead of maintaining the one-stop-shop service concept:

> Paperwork substituted for emotional work, it was used increasingly to facilitate withdrawal from wider society.

Real and metaphorical sex was the means to seek a ' "good" substitute for the "bad" ' (Suttie 1935: 31) and to re-manufacture identity. Sex and death can regenerate some reflexivity in potential space: the place between fantasy and reality where creativity or the need to 'play' (Ogden 1989: 199–200) resides and, which initiates movement towards the depressive position. In this sense, striving for something new substantiates that 'Close to our desire to maintain our present condition, there lies a desire for transformation' (Spielrein 1912/1994: 163). Positive transformation manufactures cases of the chaste and beloved (Alford 1994: 63) to supply the group with resources to project 'good breast' memories.

Potential space cannot be created if case boundaries have been fortified to the extent that no one can ever escape their autistic-contiguous paranoid schizoid fantasy. The consequence is generally the male abusive lover's dominance that atomizes self-esteem: 'the sexual predator, who uses sex as a tool to dominate or control others . . . ' (Alford 1994: 63), which further dedifferentiates the group. Death in sex can lead to both positive and negative transformation (Spielrein 1912/1994). In the case of the latter, reversion to the previous drama of despair, deadness and hopelessness is likely to ensue when revivification fails. The death instinct may assume the form of repetition compulsion with an intended conservative effect on what might otherwise be the case if the life instinct were to exert its forms of expression (Freud 1920/1984, 1923/1984). Although sex and death have not transitioned the group to the depressive position, in the interest of parsimony, we move to the fifth act.

Act five: tribal warfare and superficial ideologies

Group members now seek to blame others for this resuscitative impotence and through further projective identification act out the fifth drama, 'tribal warfare and superficial ideologies' (Alford 1994: 63). This drama is characterized by the group splitting into new, smaller untested collectives or good and bad tribes as similarly posed by Freud in *Totem and Taboo*: 'Recall that the real enemy is one's own group and the demands on the member's individuality it makes' (Alford 1994: 64). Tribal warfare can be seen as the primordial regressive state of leadership identity and sacrifice acts that the group itself has developed – '. . . warring tribes are not just fighting each other; they are fighting each other to sacrifice themselves' (Alford 1994: 64):

> The core group was resentful of anyone from the 'enemy camp' or those who were outsiders, such as CPNs and SWs and 'appeared to be torn between feelings of disloyalty if they accepted any benefits of the new regime, and wanting to preserve the positive acknowledgements of their work'.

Group splitting by the group pushes itself, and the individuals within it, further towards engulfment and isolation that eventually results in group suicide or a form of slow death (Quinn 1996). This helps define the process of mortality and identity entropy in the group. In tribal groups, death instinct manifestations push individuals farther towards the pole of submergence or engulfment (Carr 1994). Splitting gives the options of turning into one or the other; projective identification helps the group member choose. Alford's argument in the NCMHT holds true: 'If all can't be leader, then none shall be an individual' (Alford 1994: 63) so group members remain in fragmented states. The best the group can do is split itself into an 'us against them' mentality.

To defend against introjection of the warring tribes' projections of only 'bad breast' reminders, the *group* ego now fortifies its boundaries as a stopgap measure to protect the 'unstable entity within, albeit at the cost of learning from without: from experience and from the consultant' (Alford 1994: 29; see also Ogden 1989: 47–82). Without group development, there can be no individual development, so the 'depressing thing about these dramas is that they just go on and on' (Alford 1994: 64):

> After Anne died, the last known restructuring took place. Management in general, was looking for change because they disliked Anne's results, which negatively impacted other parts of the larger organization. Marjorie promoted Susan from social worker to service manager; with the job description to lead Anne's core

group along with others who had recently joined the larger CMHT. Marjorie, who suggested the team for study and who appointed Susan to replace Anne, later said of the new management arrangements: 'Susan's got a really tough job there, even she's wondering why I put her there' [Marjorie, service director].

From my point of view, we have a new manager who maybe doesn't understand the nature of the service that was created. She maybe wants to mould it into something completely different and doesn't care that you know this work was done and this was achieved [Jackie, CMHT nurse].

The purpose for our discussion is to develop awareness of death's potential: 'The paradox is that the more people become defended against death, and inevitability of their own death, the more it becomes possible for death to be manufactured and split off from life' (Lawrence 1979/2002: 242) and the more likely its group members will be unconscious of their own and others' death-deflecting behaviors. The following section provides a brief summary of our primary theoretical framework on the death instinct that we used to review the case study.

Summary of the death instinct in theory

Alford's conceptualization of group dynamics included Freudian and Kleinian perspectives on the death instinct's manifestations on the individual group member's psyche. However, his renditions of these perspectives are primarily based on influences of schizoid compromise interrelationships with projective identification, or a synthesis of splitting, projection, introjection, projective identification and transference. Alford's undeveloped group is de-differentiated, premature, and based on part-object relations theory or fragmentation of individual and group. This view is in contrast to Klein's whole object relations theory [and Bion's (1961) whole group theory]. Whereas Freud and Klein's renditions of the death instinct are grounded in destruction, Alford's depiction of the 'sex and death' drama indicates a Spielreinian influence as group members engage in real or metaphorical sex leading to something new, but with potential results of positive or negative transformations. Spielrein and Alford's theories are both destructive and expansive in nature. While Alford's theory recognizes the danger of group politics it does not go as far to cover fragmented human interrelationships in multiple groups, nor does it speak to fantasies of many formal leaders or 'skip level' formal leaders, which makes for a much more complex and intriguing read of death instinct manifestations. The synthesis of this group of theories outlines a progression from individual to collective expressions of the death instinct.

Discussion of the death instinct in organizational studies and practice

In as much as organizations are currently occupied and controlled by humans, theories about development and degeneration of personality and human behavior are relevant to the field of organization studies (Christensen and Raynor 2003, Crowell 1998). Issues related to mortality and deaths acted out in interrelationships are important because they frame life itself. Our unconscious motivation can be so strong that we may act in a manner unthinkable to the conscious, yet we remain unaware of the underlying psychodynamics. The following discussion considers some important implications for further understanding of human relations in organization studies and practice, which is framed from the synthesis of many theorists' works on the death instinct.

Acting out the missing leader: the death instinct and organizational leader and follower identities

Because of the interplay between *Eros* and *Thanatos*, instead of the psychodynamics of identification being associated with the parent, they become centred upon authority figures that hold the promise of a loving, protective 'parent' that enhance narcissistic satisfaction. 'The revolt against the primal father eliminated an individual person who could be (and was) replaced by other persons...' (Marcuse 1955: 91). In our work organizations, it is these 'parents' that become leaders to those who must continually be held with love and protection from others. These are followers who do not wish to reconstruct their identities to acknowledge and to act upon other different super-ego, ego-ideal or organizational-ideal aspects to reshape the ego and therefore, self's identity[5] *as well as* the group's identity. Whether *Erostic* or *Thanatic* in nature, the embodiments of life and death

---

5 In keeping with mainstream psychodynamic theory, we are making a distinction between the self and ego, ascribing to the view that:
  The self differs from the ego in that it refers to the subject as he (sic) experiences himself, while the ego refers to his personality as a structure about which impersonal generalizations can be made. (Rycroft 1995: 165)

instincts conclude in establishing self and other in mutually constituted interrelationships, as long as *self or other* perceive he or she is in the group *and* as long as the 'group' perceives he or she is in the group (Alford 1994, Carr and Lapp 2006a). The interplay of the instincts in the id, with the ego and the super-ego and ego-ideal, are socially constructed and therefore, individual identity and group identity are mutually constituted whether we are aware of these interrelationships or not.

Manifestations of the death instinct during battles of 'leadership and identity' (Alford 1994: 37–38, 63) inform us as to why followers, to their detriment, continue to follow. Sievers (1990, 1994) noted that leadership deification is followed by the re-manufacture of workers as production means or things contributing to identity annihilation, which, in the case study, is consistent with Marjorie's ability to isolate Anne and the core group for the sake of protecting organizational productivity (Solomon *et al.* 1998). Fear of identity loss is synonymous with mortality salience brought forward when the leader–follower relationship, and therefore group identity (Alford 1994), has not reached the depressive position (Klein 1975a–d) or is not equilibrated for any meaningful period of time.

Referent power matched with other power bases, such as legitimate or formal and expert power, inflates the perception of the leader's total power base (Hinken and Schriesheim 1989 cited in Schermerhorn, Hunt and Osborn 2003). At the same time, to build referent power (Dumas and Sankowsky 1998), one should appear to be 'warm, friendly, and dynamic' (Robbins and Hunsaker 2003: 29). Because of the schizoid compromise and projective identification, reaction transference (Glenn and Bernstein 1994) becomes most persuasive in the premature group or in one that is about to experience disruptions of transfers of the mother's milk (Suttie 1935), such as those resulting from continuous restructuring and threats of downsizing (Noer 1993, Allen *et al.* 2001). This indicates that trait theory needs to be revisited for its temporal influence as well as for its constituents and its projected purpose: leaders using restructuring as the means to knowingly scramble identity are invoking the death instinct and the pathological organization (Bakan 2004).

Leadership and identity wars from restructuring lead to the practice of sacrifice (Alford 1994) in organizations. However, these sacrifices are now more commonly hidden in the putative need for the reconstitution and then deflation of the labor force in guises of contract workers and other temporary employees. If leader–follower relationships are stratified as the means to protect each other from death fear anxiety (Mikulincer, Florian and Hirschberger 2003), it follows that recruitment and selection practices will be based on hiring in one's own image. Sacrificed group members are those who are fantacised to most resemble their leader. Consequently, a value-matching exercise (Jaffe and Scott 1998) feeds the fantasy and so may be hazardous to one's working health.

Alternatively, a stable of contract workers creates safety in numbers. In the premature group context, the informal leader is the least vulnerable group member relative to others and is therefore perceived as master, and who in a regressive state taps into the death instinct in an aggressively outward manner 'as a wish for self-annihilation in the face of unendurable frustration and suffering' (Segal 1993 cited in Nitsun 1996: 151) to end the longing for the mother's holding or her protection from persecutory anxiety. In this sense, the informal leader is the group's fantasy of the most infantile member who, in competitive terms, is the best schizoid compromised projective identifier or the dialectically twisted, sickest, strongest weakest member who, by the schizoid compromised, has been promoted to a level of incompetence (Peter and Hull 1969). In its many guises, the death instinct's role in the reiterative interchange and development of a group's informal leader adds new dimensions to leadership, group relations and political discourse (Alford 1991, Marcuse 1955, 1964, 1970).

Clearly, an understanding of the synthesis of theories framing the death instinct, by all in the organization, reconstitutes the evidence and the emphasis on the 'me' in team so individual reflexivity, group and organizational identity and effectiveness are not sacrificed for the sake of efficiency. Reflexivity and human praxis (Chessick 1989) can lead to *Thanatospraxis* in the workplace as the means to predict, interpret and curb detrimental death defence behaviors. Most importantly, recognition of the death instinct is necessary to understand how we frame organizational life.

References

Alford, C. F. (1991) *The Self in Social Theory: A Psychoanalytic Account of its Construction in Plato, Hobbes, Lock, Rawls, and Rousseau.* New Haven, CT: Yale University.

Alford, C. F. (1994) *Group Psychology and Political Theory.* New Haven: Yale University.

Allen, T. D., Freeman, D. M., Russell, J. E. A., Reizenstein, R. C., and Rentz, J. O. (2001). 'Survivor reactions to organizational downsizing: Does time ease the pain?' *Journal of Occupational and Organizational Psychology* 74: 145–164.

Arndt, J., Greenberg, J., Pyszczynski, T., and Solomon, S. (1997) 'Subliminal exposure to death-related stimuli increases defense of the cultural worldview.' *American Psychological Society* 8(5): 379–385.

Bakan, J. (2004) *The Corporation: The Pathological Pursuit of Profit and Power.* Toronto, Ont: Viking.

Becker, E. (1997) *The Denial of Death*. New York: Free Press Association. (Original work published 1973).

Berzonsky, M. D. and Adams, G. R. (1999) Reevaluating the identity status paradigm: Still useful after 35 years. *Developmental Review* 19: 557–590.

Bick, E. (1968) 'The experience of the skin in early object-relations.' *International Journal of Psycho-Analysis* 49: 484–486.

Bion, W. (1961) *Experiences in Groups*. New York: Basic Books.

Carr, A. (1994) 'For self or others? The quest for narcissism and the ego-ideal in work organisations.' *Administrative Theory and Praxis* 16: 208–222.

Carr, A. N. (1998) 'Identity, compliance and dissent in organisations: a psychoanalytic perspective.' *Organization* 5: 81–89.

Carr, A. N. (2002) 'Managing in a psychoanalytically informed manner: an overview.' *Journal of Managerial Psychology* 17: 343–347.

Carr, A. N. (2003a) 'The "separation thesis" of self and other: metatheorizing a dialectic alternative.' *Theory and Psychology* 13: 117–138.

Carr, A. N. (2003b) 'Thanatos: the psychodynamic conception of the "death instinct" and its relevance to organizations.' In Biberman, J. and Alkhafaji, A. (eds) *Business Research Yearbook: Global Business Perspectives* (pp. 803–807). Michigan: McNaughton and Gunn.

Carr, A. N. (2003c) 'The psychodynamic conception of the "death instinct" and its relevance to organisations.' *Journal of Psycho-Social Studies* 2: 1–15. Retrieved March 27, 2003, from http://www.btinternet.com/~psycho_social/

Carr, A. N. and Lapp, C. A. (2005) 'Wanted for breaking and entering organizational systems in complexity.' *Eros* and *Thanatos*.' *E:CO* 7(3–4): 43–52.

Carr, A. N. and Lapp, C. A. (2006a) *Leadership is a Matter of Life and Death: The Psychodynamics of Eros and Thanatos Working in Organisations*. Hampshire, England: Palgrave.

Carr, A. N. and Lapp, C. A. (2006b, July) *'Modern Madness' (Examining the Dark-side of Competition Through the Optics of Psychodynamics)*. Paper presented to the 23rd International Society for the Psychoanalytic Study of Organizations (ISPSO) Annual Meeting, Amsterdam/Haarlem, The Netherlands.

Chessick, R. (1989) 'The death instinct and the future of humans.' *American Journal of Psychotherapy XLIII*: 546–561.

Christensen, C. M. and Raynor, M. E. (2003) 'Why hard-nosed executives should care about management theory.' *Harvard Business Review* September: 67–72.

Crowell, D. (1998) 'Organizations are relationships.' *Nursing Management* 29 (5): 29–39.

Dumas, C. and Sankowsky, D. (1998) 'Understanding the charismatic leader–follower relationship: promises and perils.' *Journal of Leadership Studies* 5(4): 1–13.

Erikson, E. (1980) 'Reflections on Dr. Borg's lifecycle.' In Van Tassel, D. (ed.) *Aging, Death and the Completion of Being* (pp. 28–69). USA: University of Pennsylvania Press.

Freud, A. (1992) *The Harvard Lectures*, Sandler, J. (ed.). London: Karnac. (Original work published 1952).

Freud, S. (1977) 'Three essays on the theory of sexuality.' In *On sexuality*. Volume 7 (pp. 33–169). Great Britain: Pelican Freud Library. (Original work published 1905).

Freud, S. (1984a) 'Beyond the pleasure principle.' In Strachey, J. (ed. and Trans.), *On metapsychology: The Theory of Psychoanalysis* (Vol. 11, pp. 269–338). Pelican Freud Library, Harmondsworth, England: Pelican. (Original work published 1920).

Freud, S. (1984b) 'The ego and the id.' In Strachey, J. (ed. and Trans.) *On Metapsychology: The Theory of Psychoanalysis* (Vol. 11, pp. 339–408). Pelican Freud Library, Harmondsworth, England: Pelican. (Original work published 1923).

Freud, S. (1985) 'Why war?' In Strachey, J. (ed. and Trans.) *Civilization, Society and Religion* (Vol. 12, pp. 341–362). Pelican Freud Library, Harmondsworth, England: Pelican. (Original work published 1933).

Freud, S. (1986) *The Interpretation of Dreams* (Strachey, J. ed. and Trans.) (Vol. 4). Pelican Freud Library, Harmondsworth, England: Pelican. (Original work published 1900).

Freud, S. (1986) 'An outline of psychoanalysis.' In Strachey, J. (ed. and Trans.) *Historical and Expository Works on Psychoanalysis* (Vol. 15, pp. 371–443). Pelican Freud Library, Harmondsworth, England: Pelican. (Original work published 1940).

Freud, S. (1988) 'Anxiety and instinctual life.' In Freud, S. *New Introductory Lectures on Psychoanalysis* (Strachey, J. ed. and Trans.) (Vol. 2, pp. 113–144). Pelican Freud Library, Harmondsworth, England: Pelican. (Original work published 1933).

Gabriel, Y. (1999) *Organizations in Depth: The Psychoanalysis of Organizations*. London: Sage.

Glenn, J. and Berstein, I. (1994) 'Sadomasochism.' In Moore, B. and Fine, B. (eds.) *Psychoanalytic Terms and Concepts* (pp. 252–265). New Haven, CT: The American Psychoanalytic Association and Yale University Press.

Hegel, G. (1977) *The Phenomenology of Spirit* (Miller, A. Trans.). Oxford: Oxford University. (Original work published 1807).

Holbrook, D. (1971) *Human Hope and the Death Instinct: An Exploration of Psychoanalytical Theories of Human Nature and their Implications for Culture and Education*. Oxford, UK: Pergamon Press.

Hyde, P. (1999) *Organisational Dynamics of Mental Health Teams*. Unpublished doctoral dissertation, University of Manchester, England.

Hyde, P. and Thomas, A. (2003) 'When a leader dies.' *Human Relations* 56: 1005–1024.

Jaffe, D. T. and Scott, C. D. (1998) 'How to link personal values with team values.' *Training and Development* 52(3): 24–30.

Jones, E. (1957) *Sigmund Freud: Life and Work* (Vol. 3). London, UK: Hogarth Press, 1957.

Kets de Vries, M. (2001a) *The Leadership Mystique: An Owner's Manual*. London, UK: Financial Times, Prentice Hall.

Kets de Vries, M. (2001b) *Struggling with the Demon: Perspectives on Individual and Organizational Irrationality*. Madison, CT: Psychosocial Press.

Klein, M. (1975a) *The Writings of Melanie Klein I: 'Love, Guilt and Reparation' and Other Works 1921–1945*. London: Hogarth.

Klein, M. (1975b) *The Writings of Melanie Klein II: The Psychoanalysis of Children*. London: Hogarth.

Klein, M. (1975c) *The Writings of Melanie Klein III: 'Envy and gratitude' and Other Works 1946–1963*. London: Hogarth.

Klein, M. (1975d) *The Writings of Melanie Klein IV: Narrative of a Child Analysis*. London: Hogarth.

Laing, R. D. (1969) *Self and Others*. London: Penguin. (Original work published 1961)

Laplanche, J. and Pontalis, J. B. (1988) *The Language of Psycho-analysis* (Nicholson-Smith, D. Trans.). London: Karnac.

Lapp, C. A. and Carr, A. N. (2006a) 'Mirror, mirror on the Wall: Reflections on the good, the bad and the ugly of them all.' In ten Bos, R. and Kaulingfreks, R. (eds) *The Good, The Bad and The Ugly: Organizations and Demons* (pp. 375–398) Nijmegen, Holland: Radbound University Press.

Lapp, C. A. and Carr, A. N. (2006b) To have to halve to have: 'Being' in the middle in changing time's space. *Journal of Organizational Change Management*. 19(5): 655–687.

Lawrence, G. W. (2002) 'The management of oneself in role.' In G. W. Lawrence (ed.) *Exploring Individual and Organizational Boundaries: A Tavistock Open Systems Approach* (pp. 235–249). London, UK: Karnac (Books) Ltd. (Original work published 1979).

Lind, L. (1991) 'Thanatos: The drive without a name.' *Scandinavian Psychoanalysis Review* 14: 60–80.

Marcia, J. (2002) 'Identity and psychosocial development in adulthood.' *Identity: An International Journal of Theory and Research* 2(1): 7–28.

Marcuse, H. (1955) *Eros and Civilization*. Boston, MA: Beacon.

Marcuse, H. (1964) *One Dimensional Man: Studies in the Ideology of Advanced Industrial Society*. London: Routledge and Kegan Paul.

Marcuse, H. (1970) *Five Lectures: Psychoanalysis, Politics and Utopia* (Shapiro, J. and Weber, S., Trans.). London: Penguin.

Mikulincer, M., Florian, V., and Hirschberger, G. (2003) 'The existential function of close relationships: introducing death into the science of love.' *Personality and Social Psychology Review* 7(1): 20–40.

Mitchell, S. and Black, M. (1995) *Freud and Beyond: A History of Modern Psychoanalytic Thought*. New York: Basic Books.

Modell, A. (1996) *The Private Self*. Cambridge, MA: Harvard University.

Napier, R. and Gershenfeld, M. (2004) *Groups: Theory and Experience*. Boston, MA: Houghton Mifflin Company.

Nitsun, M. (1996) *The Anti-group: Destructive Forces in the Group and Their Creative Potential*. London, UK: Routledge.

Noer, D. (1993) *Healing the Wounds: Overcoming the Trauma of Layoffs and Revitalizing Downsized Organizations*. San Francisco, CA: Jossey-Bass Inc. Publishers.

Ogden, T. (1989) *The Primitive Edge of Experience*. Northvale NJ: Jason Aronson Inc.

Paz, O. (1961) *The Labyrinth of Solitude: Life and Thought in Mexico* (Kemp, L., Trans.). New York, NY: Greengrove Press, Inc.

Peter, L. and Hull, R. (1969) *The Peter Principle: Why Things Always Go Wrong*. New York, NY: William Morrow and Company, Inc.

Quinn, R. E. (1996) *Deep Change: Discovering the Leader Within*. San Francisco, CA: Jossey Bass.

Robbins, S. P. and Hunsaker, P. L. (2003) *Training in Interpersonal Skills: TIPS for Managing People at Work*. Upper Saddle River, NY: Prentice Hall.

Rycroft, C. (1995) *A Critical Dictionary of Psychoanalysis* (2nd ed.). London: Penguin.

Schermerhorn, J., Hunt, J., and Osborn, R. (2003) *Organizational Behaviour* (8th ed.). Hoboken, NJ: John Wiley and Sons, Inc.

Segal, H. (1990) *The Work of Hanna Segal: A Kleinian Approach to Clinical Practice*. Northvale, NJ: Jason Aronson Inc. (Original work published 1981).

Schwartz, H. (1990) *Narcissistic Process and Organizational Decay: The Theory of the Organizational Ideal*. New York: New York University.

Segal, H. (1993) 'On the clinical usefulness of the concept of the death instinct.' *International Journal of Psycho-Analysis* 74: 55–62.

Sievers, B. (1990) 'Thoughts on the relatedness of work, death and life itself.' *European Journal of Management* 8(3): 321–324.

Sievers, B. (1994) *Work, Death, and Life Itself: Essays on Management and Organization*. Berlin; New York: de Gruyter.

Sievers, B. (1999) 'Psychotic organization as a metaphoric frame for the socioanalysis of organizational and interorganizational dynamics.' *Administration and Society* 31(5): 588–615.

Solomon, S., Greenberg, J., and Pyszczynski, T. (1998) 'Tales from the crypt: on the role of death in life.' *Zygon* 33(1): 9–43.

Solomon, S., Greenberg, J., and Pyszczynski, T. (2003) 'Fear of death and human destructiveness.' *Psychoanalytic Review* 90(4): 457–474.

Spielrein, S. (1994) 'Destruction as the cause of coming into being.' *Journal of Analytical Psychology* 39(2): 155–186. (Original work published 1912).

Spillius, E. (1983) 'Some developments from the work of Melanie Klein.' *International Journal of Psycho-Analysis* 64: 331–332.

Suttie, I. D. (1935) *The Origins of Love and Hate*. New York: The Julian Press, Inc.

7

Identity work, managing and researching

Tony Watson

Introduction

In this chapter I shall illustrate the value of paying attention to the interplay between the 'self' and the 'social category' aspects in studying human *identity work* by reflecting on the way my own identity work over the years has influenced and been influenced by the research work I have done on the identity work of managers. I shall use conceptual tools which I have devised in my most recent work to do this. One can only look back to earlier work from where one is currently conceptually located.

Increasing attention is being paid by organization and management scholars to 'identities'. As well as looking at 'organizational identities' (Hatch and Schultz 2004, for example), researchers are investigating so-called 'professional identities' (Dent and Whitehead 2001, for example), 'entrepreneurial identities' (Cohen and Musson 2000, for example) and 'managerial identities' (Sveningsson and Alvesson 2003, for example). My own research has taken me into each of these latter three areas. But note that I have distanced myself from these expressions with inverted commas and the tag 'so-called'. Why is this? It is because I feel that these terms encourage us to beg the question of whether, say, a 'managerial identity' is part of some people's notions of self or is a social category which exists 'in society'. To what extent is a 'managerial identity' part of what we become as a person if we occupy a managerial role in a work organization and to what extent is it a characterization of a type of individual to be found in novels, newspapers or workplace conversations?

All the issues that arise with regard to human identities, I suggest, have a 'self' dimension and a 'social category' dimension to them. To understand what happens in work organizations and the lives of managerial and other workers, we need to look at both the social categories that relate to those people and the varying ways in which individuals embrace or refuse to embrace those categories. What needs to be investigated is the nature of the relationship between social categories and 'selves'. It is therefore important for research and theorizing to start with concepts that do not prejudge or close off the variety of empirical possibilities that arise. To keep open the relationship between issues of self and issues of social categorization, it would be much more helpful to talk of 'entrepreneurial', 'professional', 'managerial' *aspects of human identities*, rather than of 'managerial identities' and the rest, as such.

Thus, I shall now set out the key concepts to be used and then go back to what I believe are the biographical roots of my research career, moving from childhood through to undergraduate learning and on to participant observation research in managerial settings and to later reflections on what I now choose to conceptualize as 'identity work' as it relates to the working aspects of people's lives.

Identity work, self and social identities

What I mean by *identity work* is the mutually constitutive set of processes whereby people strive to shape a relatively coherent and distinctive notion of personal self-identity. To do this they struggle to come to terms with and – within limits – influence the various social identities which pertain to them in the various milieux in which they conduct their lives. This characterization distinguishes between self-identity and social identities, it will be noticed. These are seen as two aspects of the broad concept of *human identity*. And 'human identity' is simply the notion of who or what a particular person is, in relation to others. It defines the ways in which any given person is like other people and the ways in which they differ from others. *Self-identity* refers to the internal aspects of human identity. It is the individual's own notion of who and what they are and it is something that has to be 'worked at'. To be sane and effective social actors, we all have to achieve a degree of coherence and consistency in our conception of who we are. But we can only achieve this through relating to the social world. And to understand this it is necessary to consider how we are influenced by or choose to relate to *social identities*: cultural, discursive or institutional notions of who or what any individual might be. And these social identities take three different forms. First, there are *category identities* of class, gender, nationality and ethnicity; second there are *formal role identities* of occupation, rank, citizenship and so on; third, there are *local-personal identities* whereby individuals are characterized in terms of what various others make of an individual, in the context of specific situations or events ('the departmental clown', 'a bullying manager'…).

These analytical categories represent a personal attempt to develop a conceptual apparatus to be applied to the people and organizational settings that I am studying. But they can also be understood as revealing my own understanding of the personal and social world in which I exist, all the time privately coming to terms with my own life circumstances and publicly producing analyses of the social world that I hope will be of value to the people who read my work or participate in my classes and my discussions with organizational practitioners – these two aspects of my life, like anyone else's, being tightly interrelated. Making the latter statement is in itself clearly a piece of 'identity work', as that activity was defined earlier. I am presenting a notion of the type of person I am, or aspire to being, both to myself and to you, the reader. I am using social categories like those of 'teacher' and 'writer' and relating these to personal aspects of self: presenting my-self as someone who cares about the people he tries to serve, wants to say things that are relevant to organizational actors and so on. At this point we can move into autobiographical mode to make some sense of this.

Who am I, where do I come from?

The personal identity work that we all do has to answer questions of who we are and where we come from, even if we leave such questions in the background of our personal taken-for-grantedness most of the time. And such questions necessarily take us back into our childhoods. I shall do this shortly but, to help connect this autobiographical reflection to social scientific issues, I shall frame my account in terms of some thinking that I did in my late teen/early adult years as sociology student.

Before settling for a sociology course, I had been tempted some of the time to study English literature, sometimes to study psychology and sometimes to study history, or perhaps politics. But sociology turned out to be precisely the subject to deal with the concerns around which my interests were crystallizing. At the core of this was the issue of the relationship between individual human beings and the bigger patterns of history, society and politics. When I read English literature I was fascinated not only by the texts in their own terms, but also by the writers of those texts and their lives and times. When I thought about history I was fascinated not only by patterns of change, but also by the role that key individuals played in those patterns. This, I was to discover on reading Wright Mills, could be understood in terms of *the sociological imagination* – that style of thinking in which one shifts up from a concern with the 'personal troubles' of individuals to the level of 'public issues' (Mills 1970).

It was reading Bendix's (1966) 'intellectual portrait' of Max Weber and its emphasis on Weber's concern to link individual thinkers, group material interests and massive social change which confirmed for me that sociological ideas were vital for relating who we all are, as unique individuals, to the social world. But how did I link this to my own biography and my desire to make sense of my own life? As I remember, it happened not so much as a result of reading the analytical content of the work of people like Weber, Durkheim, Veblen or Mills, as a result of my reflecting on what it was about the lives of these figures that pushed them towards a sociological style of thinking about the world. To put this question in more contemporary terms: I was wondering about a possible personal *identity work* dimension to their writing. Without now remembering the details of my rough analysis of the lives of these 'founding fathers of sociology' (as the texts of the time tended to characterize them), I remember so clearly coming to the conclusion that they were all in some way socially or psychologically *marginal* in the circumstances of their origins and/or their subsequent lives. They had a capacity or a need to 'stand back' and look with a critical eye at a social world of which they did not feel they were unproblematically a part.

This idea that a sociological (or perhaps an 'anthropological') imagination could relate to some degree of marginality in a writer/researcher's life experience might not stand up to serious intellectual examination. But it was invaluable to me as an 'identity work' resource. It resonated loudly with how I remembered my own childhood. There were practically no other children around in the English East Midlands near-slum back-street in which I spent the first two and a half years of my life. And then, to my delight, I found myself with a whole lot of friends to play with when we eventually moved into a new (and very fine) house on a public housing estate. But I soon became aware of the fact that the other people on the street spoke differently from me. Although my mother is English, she and my father had moved to England from the north of Scotland and lots of the expressions that the people on the street used, and the ways in which they pronounced words, were quite different from what I was used to (both my mother's Wiltshire and my father's Highland speech – and hence, presumably my own, contained rhoticity – the pronouncing of the letter 'r' in words like mother and father – something missing in the English Midlands). I clearly remember seeing puzzled faces when I referred to one friend's baby sister as 'a girning bairn'. And I was equally puzzled myself when I heard another friend being accused of being a 'mardy bum'. I was experiencing here what I later learned to call cultural variation and relativity!

Nothing in these circumstances was powerful enough to be described as 'culture shock'. Nevertheless, continuous recognition of social differences between people, in addition to the more obvious individual differences, led to a life-long tendency to ask 'why is this like this?', 'what is going on here?' A striking memory is that of visiting a friend's home for tea and seeing on the table a plate of bread that had already been cut and buttered. As soon as I got home I asked my parents about what seemed to me to be peculiar behavior. It wasn't just that we cut slices from the loaf as we needed it in our house, and then buttered it. It also seemed to me to be wasteful to butter bread that might not be consumed. When later, as a student, I read Weber's reference to 'the ghosts of dead religious beliefs' haunting our lives, I reflected back on this incident, going beyond my parents' explanations of the bread-buttering phenomenon in terms of English/ Scottish and social class differences to new thoughts about the possible influence in our (non-churchgoing) family of deep-down currents of Scottish Calvinism.

Much later in life I have reflected on this 'bread and butter' experience, and others like it, when people have asked me why doing ethnographic research has been so important to me in my academic career. The truth, I tend to think, is that I find it hard to conceive of 'real research' which does not involve one in thinking/theorizing/explaining events in the process of closely observing and, if possible, experiencing them. I lived in what was effectively a Scottish home in an English town. And, yes, like for so many fellow diaspora semi-Scots there were the Jimmy Shand records and a wee kilt to wear at family weddings. Also, I lived in a council house with a father, who, in spite of his *social category identity* as a factory worker, was well educated and well read. All of this, it could be said, made me marginal in ethnic and class terms. And, generally speaking, I was not uncomfortable with this. I rather liked it, in fact. It was a good training for a participant observation researcher, one could say with hindsight.

Into the field

Within weeks of graduating from the sociology course (in which there was an excellent industrial sociology option), I was working as an industrial relations officer in the foundry of the aero-engine division of Rolls-Royce.

I also registered to do a research degree at a nearby university. Both of these moves were deliberately planned as a preparation for an intended move into an academic post in three years' time (which happened exactly as planned). The research study focused on a major organizational change in the foundry and, as my managerial job was involved with the 'human facilitating' of that change, I quickly found myself doing participant observation research. And what does such research inevitably both push and pull one into? Yes, marginality. Participant observation involves switching back and forth between being a 'native' and being a 'stranger', as we are all told on our research methods courses. It is when one tiptoes along the margin between, in this case, being a fully active junior manager and being a reflective sociological researcher that one produces one's best insights. Well, that is what I persuaded myself as I switched about between the two very divergent *formal role identities* of suited and 'street-wise' (very) young manager and thoughtful, theory-hungry research student. When managers wanted to oppose what I was doing (and the job meant this would inevitably happen) they could attack me by drawing on and pejoratively shaping discursive resources from *category identities* ('typical over-educated graduate'), *formal role identities* ('another Personnel parasite') or a *local-personal identity* ('another straight-out-of-college careerist who will be gone from here as soon as he can get a promotion'). My outward-facing identity work meant countering this with a presentation of self, in *category identity* terms, as 'a boy from a factory-working background who is loyal to his roots'. (This, incidentally, would have been an 'identity of choice' for many sociology students at the time.) And there was a presentation of self in *formal role identity* terms, as 'someone in Personnel who actually wants to support line managers' and, in *local-personal identity* terms as, well, 'a friendly and interested colleague' – or something like that.

I don't remember the identity-management issues in the business context worrying me too much. But I do remember being more challenged, in self-identity terms, when one or two university colleagues tried to make me feel uncomfortable for working for 'a capitalist company' or being 'a servant of power'. To handle this, my external-facing identity work involved my pointing out the necessity of gaining sociological understandings of managerial processes from inside management and by arguing that this could be done without compromising, in any way, one's personal and political values (I argue this further in Watson 2000). And my father helped me significantly in this self-identity maintenance in two respects. First, he said that he had slogged through the heavy factory work and the hours of overtime in part to give his sons the chance to do work above and beyond the working class. And, second, he argued that those people who worked on the shop floor would often be much better placed if the managers in charge of the factory had a better understanding of 'good management'. 'With your education', he said, 'you might be able to do something about that – and have a much more comfortable life than I have had.'

What about the research itself then? This examined the process of the move of more than a thousand employees from Rolls-Royce's 'dirty old foundry' to what they referred to as the 'ultra modern precision casting facility' – the 'PCF'. At the center of the analysis was a consideration of the changing work orientations and implicit contracts of the various groups in the foundry (Watson 1982). The differing social class and work experience aspects of what we might now call these people's 'identities' were central to the analysis. As an illustration of the thinking here, I would pick on one detail of how the senior managers' orientations related to their commitment or otherwise to the new venture. All but two of the senior managers in the foundry were enthusiastic about the new PCF. This made sense, given that they saw involvement in this major business investment as highly career-enhancing. I talked at length, over a period of time, with these two men. After a period of mutual trust-building, they admitted to me that they were unhappy with what was happening. And it became clear that a higher level managerial career was not pertinent to their self-identities. Each of them, we could say, preferred to relate to different *formal role* identities from those embraced by their peers. One of them told me that he valued much more his international reputation as an expert on certain aspects of quality control. And the other man told me how he felt uncomfortable with the managerial level that he was currently at. He saw himself much more as craft plant-management person than as a career line manager. He told me that he was tired of having to present himself to people inside and outside the company as 'a manager'. He would welcome a chance to work at a senior technical level. He had told no one else about this, in part, he explained, because he had 'taken his eye off the ball a couple of times' with costly results. As I understood it, these failures were managerial rather than technical ones.

This piece of detail from my first research study can be interpreted in terms of personal identity issues having implications for managerial behavior and, indeed, managerial effectiveness. And coming back to my own identity work and the importance of this of my claims for the virtues of ethnographic research, I would claim that what I learned here about these two men's identity work would not have been discovered by a researcher simply calling at the plant to interview managers in a more traditional way. This latter type of data collection, however, was what most of the other research students

I knew were doing. They might 'name-call' me 'management boy'. But I could counter this with a claim to be 'the researcher who gets the better data'. Yah boo. Most identity work has an element of this kind of label-sticking and label-resisting to it!

Marginality, management and personnel work

Self-labelling is something in which personnel managers have shown a particular interest over recent decades. They have re-presented themselves to the world as human resource (HR) professionals. And their occupational spokespersons have shown considerable *discursive ingenuity* in building on this – going as far as to redefine the very idea of a 'profession' (Watson 2002). Why have such efforts been so important? It is because members of this occupation have always had to handle the problem of, guess what? Yes, marginality. The analysis which I first set out in my 1970s study of the personnel management occupation (Watson 1977) stands to the present day, I believe. Whether or not particular 'employment management' specialists present themselves to the world as personnel or HR managers, they have continually to struggle to win credibility – above all in the eyes of other managers. These are men and women whom HR managers are required, at the same time, both to advise/assist and to constrain/control. I learned about the implications of this from the very first day of being located in a personnel department at Rolls-Royce. Within days of starting work I realized that being a member of the 'Personnel and Administration' department made one suspect with other managers and required the type of outward-facing identity work to which I referred earlier. Whether one liked it or not, one had to deal with what I called 'conflict, marginality and ambivalence' (Watson 1977: 58) every working day.

The personnel worker is employed as an 'agent' of the employer. Yet it does not always seem as straightforward as that, in practice. It is normal for HR managers to have to come to terms with a situation which, when I joined the Rolls-Royce 'Personnel and Administration' department, immediately reminded me of the classic industrial sociology studies of foremen whom Wray (1949) called the 'marginal men of industry' and Roethlisberger (1945) referred to as 'master[s] and victim[s] of double talk'. Part of the rationale for my undertaking a study of the personnel management occupation was one of making sense *in sociological terms* of what I had experienced as a young manager doing personnel and industrial relations work. (The other part of the rationale, it has to be recognized, was the career-making one of writing a significant book about an occupation that had previously been practically untouched sociologically.) In personnel work one would, in day-to-day terms at least, 'side' with a managerial group at one moment and with trade union representatives at another. One would 'side' on certain occasions with a corporate management initiative and, at another time, with local management resistance (or vice versa). All of these moves, of course, occurred within a logic of strategically servicing long-term corporate interests. This was firmly argued in *The Personnel Managers*. The daily identity work (both inward- and outward-facing) of the personnel managers whom I studied was related to what was conceptualized in that study as the logic of handling aspects of the conflicts and contradictions of an industrial, capitalist, political economy. In the spirit of the sociological imagination (Mills 1970), we can thus see that the 'personal troubles' and individual identity work that I and the hundred personnel managers studied for the book engaged in were only understandable in terms of 'public issues' and societal structures. Although the expression 'identity work' was not used in the study, much of the analysis of the values, orientations and stratagems of the personnel managers can be understood in such terms.

The study of the personnel management occupation was carried out primarily by visiting a range of organizations, from large to small enterprises and from public sector to private sector undertakings, to interview employment management specialists. One of the research aims was to find out the extent to which there were occupational characteristics in common across different organizational settings. In terms of personal identity, I felt a need to gain knowledge of organizations other than a large engineering one. This was important to my authority as an industrial sociologist or organization theorist, I believed, as well as to my credibility as a business school teacher. How could one speak about organizations and management generally to students and others when one only had experience of a large aerospace business?

A question I asked myself about the personnel manager study was whether I might be seen as turning away from the ethnographer/participant observer element of both my self-identity and my social identity within the academic community. The way my internal identity work handled this question was to persuade myself that the interview-based study was deeply rooted in the ethnographic experience of working as a participant in a personnel function. And I remain persuaded of this. In so far as there were hypotheses being examined in the study, they were ones formed during my full-time industrial experience. And what about outward-facing identity work? Here my claimed background as a 'former personnel specialist' or as someone 'who worked for some time in industrial relations' (the precise formula depending on who I was addressing) was invaluable. It was helpful in gaining access to organizations and senior management offices and it was utterly invaluable in establishing a level of rapport with individuals which would not have been possible for a complete 'civilian'. And this rapport enabled me, I believe, rapidly to establish the level of trust which is so vital to the obtaining of high quality information from research respondents. Such a level was going to be even more important in another large research undertaking.

Back to the field: searching for management

After 20 or so years of teaching and researching in a full-time business school post following the publication of the personnel manager study, I remember a sense of unease once again developing around 1990 about the gap between the occupational dimension of my identity as a business school 'expert' on the managing of organizations and the fact that my organizational and managerial experience was now almost completely confined to the organizing and managing of academic activity. At the same time I felt the need to undertake a significant empirical study. What do I mean by 'felt the need'? Perhaps I should recast this in terms of identity work. Yes, I should. I had written two textbooks in a row (three, if one includes a second edition of one of these) and I did not want to take on a work-related identity as 'mainly a textbook writer'. Earlier in this chapter, I conceptualized human identity as the notion of who or what a particular person is, in relation to others. And I emphasized how it defines not only how any particular person is similar to others but also how they differ from them. Establishing who *one is not* is as important in identity work as establishing who *one is*. I did not want to be seen as someone who, after producing one successful research monograph in the 1970s, was in the 1990s producing books which did not present new research material and theorizing.

In the middle of this self-reflection, two opportunities presented themselves to me. The first of these was the opportunity to be released from normal academic duties for a year to concentrate on personal research. 'What about taking a fellowship abroad or getting an attachment to a leading business school somewhere where you can have plenty free time to write another book?', I was asked by the head of the business school. To put it in very simple terms, I felt that neither of these things was 'me'. 'Essentialist' as this statement might seem, it most effectively describes the feeling that I remember (feelings surely being significant parts of all identity-maintenance work). And foolishly puritanical as it may sound, I felt that either of these possibilities would be somewhat parasitic. Could one really take a salary for this? Perhaps I should take a 'real' job for a year. And that really would give me something to write about.

The moral aspect of human identity is perhaps coming into play here: the need to believe that one is a 'good' person. And a good person would not live parasitically off others. But is 'need' the right word? Perhaps not. It might simply have been the old ghost of dead Protestant beliefs coming back to haunt me. It would be unworthy to take time away from one's normal duties without producing something that engaged with the 'this-worldly'. This would not happen if one confined oneself to the 'other-worldly' pseudo-monastic world of the university library or set off on the equivalent of the old leisure-class gentleman's 'grand tour'. There would be little monastic, gentlemanly or 'other-worldly', however, about working in a factory for a year. But perhaps these reflections amount to little more than my putting a moral gloss on a simple desire to satisfy my curiosity about what was going on 'out there' in the big corporate world by going out into the field 'in search of management' – as I came to characterize my research adventure when I later wrote about it (Watson 2001a, originally 1994). But I suspect that all of these factors were important, together with others I do not remember. And this is where the second opportunity came in. I found myself in conversation with the manager in charge of an ambitious 'change programme' in the Nottingham-based businesses of GPT (GEC Plessey Telecommunications or 'ZTC' in earlier publications). To help them with their change programme, the management was proposing to employ consultants to undertake a number of specific tasks. One of these, for example, was to 'identify the management competences that the business needs'. Given the sabbatical opportunity that I had been offered and, I must admit, given that the company was in easy walking range of my own house, I offered to help. I argued that it was a bad idea to think of employing consultants to do such sensitive work. If they were willing to give me a senior post for a year, I would undertake these tasks *from within management*. And after some interesting negotiations, in which I clearly had to establish that I had some really 'practical' ideas about management as well the necessary managerial experience, the deal was done. I once again found myself with an office in the HR function of a large company. And I had a list of research questions on one side of my desk and a list of management tasks to fulfil on the other.

I could write at length about the extremely challenging outward-facing identity work which had to be done for me to establish the necessary credibility and rapport with the managers with whom I was working in GPT. However, I can cut this short by referring to my earlier account of the identity work that had to be done when I was a new sociology graduate and junior manager in Rolls-Royce. The 'distancing' from personnel was again very important. So was the need to establish that someone can be academically accomplished and still capable of 'making a difference' in the rough and tumble of managerial politics and problem solving. At least this time I was a 'senior' man working among people of my own age group. But the main difference from the earlier fieldwork experience lay in the vital need to establish with everyone, at every level, that I was not a consultant. Earlier I referred to how 'internal' identity work has to deal with *who one is not* as much as *who one is*. Here we see the importance of establishing in 'external' identity work what one is not. Someone even offered to make me a badge saying in large bright letters 'I am not a consultant'. This was a label, if not a literal one, that I needed. The managers had to be absolutely sure that I was not a consultant if I was going to be accepted as a working colleague. And without that I would neither be able to carry out effective managerial work nor produce worthwhile research.

As at Rolls-Royce, I worked hard to make it clear that I was being paid to act managerially, as a manager, in management's interest. I was not acting in any way whatsoever as an independent professional 'expert'. I was anxious to remove any ambiguity about this for both ethical reasons and in order to make my research observations fully 'participant'. The difference this time was that I had to overcome the suspicion that I was, as it was put to me, 'yet another consultant who takes up our managerial time and then writes a report saying what crap we managers are'. I heard some grim war stories about consultants they had endured. I thus had to repeat time and again that I was part of the management team and that I would bring to bear on events whatever expertise and outside experience I had during my everyday work with them. In this external identity work I was careful not to throw away the academic part of my social identity. This formed a necessary part of my claim to expertise. But it also enabled me to make sense for them of what I wanted from the project materially. I made a promise, which was well received, that I was never going to write any kind of report to top management. I was, however, going to write a research-based book. This, I said, would be published for academic and public consumption (with the confidences of my informants respected throughout and, as I jokingly put it a couple of times, 'the identities of guilty colleagues protected').

The research carried out at GPT, which combined 12 months of participant observation ethnography with the formal interviewing of managers, focused on the activities and accommodations of managers managing their lives and identities within the structural circumstances which prevailed over the year of the study. A key question was that of how managers were handling the 'double control problem' of having, at the same time, to handle all the personal and existential challenges of their personal lives and all the interpersonal, political and economic challenges of managing the activities and meanings of others in the workplace. The study used the notion of 'identity work' albeit in a rather informal way (Watson 2001a: 58). The term was not used as a formal part of the study's conceptual framework. And the managers themselves did not use an explicit notion of 'identity'. A number of them, however, made significant use of a notion of 'the sort of person I am'. This can be seen as an interesting 'lay' concept which is close to what, in the social sciences, we call 'identity'. It is a resource which individuals could utilize in doing what I now formally conceptualize as 'identity work'.

The thinking process of human individuals is theorized in the study as a 'rhetorical' one (Billig 1987) with use being made by these managers in their inward- and outward-facing identity work of a variety of *discursive resources* (ranging from sources in childhood experience to the talk of management change agents) to help them cope with both the existential and the mundane challenges of managing their lives at the same time as they have to manage the work of others. I got personally close to a lot of these managers, by working closely with them and discussing day-in and day-out the pleasures and pains of the work we were doing (as well as many interpersonal, career and family problems that a lot of colleagues sought me out to speak about). But a significant element of my 'closeness' to the managers can be understood in terms of that fact that I, in coming out of the academic world into the rough and tumble of commercial life in a threatened factory, had as much challenging identity work to do to 'stay sane' and to meet the often over-numerous and indeed contradictory demands of a variety of work tasks as did the managers themselves.

The pressures on me as a researcher in this situation were considerable, as indeed they would be on any organizational ethnographer, especially if he or she were participating in the sort of performance-focused activities that managers carry out. And the pressures on the managers were no less considerable. A threat of losing their jobs hung over many of these men and women. I did not face the same threat of redundancy as these people, of course. But I did experience such agonies as that of being involved in decision-making processes which led to the selection for redundancy of one's own managerial colleagues. In that year, the managers of GPT were challenged in their notions of who they were and what they were doing with their lives. So was I. Identity work for everyone involved in that company during that year was hard work, it could be said. And I have only been able to tell the stories of those managers and provide glimpses into their experiences by relating them to my own story. As is often, if not always, the case when one writes about the lives of others, I can only write about stories of these managers in the context of telling my own.

A continuing story

After completing the GPT ethnography and writing the *In Search of Management* book (a research monograph which, I believe, has sold well over 10,000 copies), I have examined human identity work, in the spirit of the sociological imagination, in a number of other contexts. These vary from 'whole' managerial careers (Watson 2001b) and ethical aspects of managerial work (Watson 2003a) to strategy-making work (Watson 2003b) and entrepreneurship (Fletcher and Watson 2007). I am currently researching in a small business context where attention is being paid to the ways in which the principals in the business have simultaneously shaped their personal lives and their business over several decades. I am also following up the GPT study and looking in depth at the lifetime's identity work engaged in by one of the managers who worked there (Watson forthcoming).

In this continuing work I am very conscious of my own presence within the research and the significance of what Johnson and Duberley call *epistemic reflexivity*. The present chapter meets the call that these authors make for researchers to account for themselves in a spirit of epistemic reflexivity where 'systematic attempts are made to relate research outcomes to the knowledge-constraining and -constituting impact of the researcher's own beliefs which derive from their own socio-historical location or "habitus" ' (Johnson and Duberley 2000: 178). I have written about some of my research in this chapter and put it in the context of 'where I have come from' intellectually, historically, philosophically and so on. This has not been done as an end in itself but as a means towards contributing to more general thinking about identity work. In this spirit, perhaps, a tentative theoretical generalization can be put forward, to the following effect. Most of the time, we human beings do not reflect consciously about 'who we are' and how we 'fit into society'. If we did, we would probably go mad. Instead, our culture does this worrying for us, in a way parallel to how institutions can be said to do a lot of our *thinking* for us (Douglas 1986). Although it is normal for people to worry away 'at the edge' of such matters, most of us take our identities for granted most of the time, given the templates, roles, labels, social categories and all the rest that our culture provides for us. However, once we find ourselves operating between or across cultures we can no longer take for granted who we are and how we should behave. This means that the more culturally marginal a person is, the more significant both their both inward- and outward-facing identity work becomes in their lives.

The matter is nowhere near as simple as this tentative theorizing suggests, I am sure. Just considering my own experience, I suspect there will always be an element of personal temperament at play. That is something that will have to be considered in future theoretical work, as will the issues about the moral and emotional dimension of identity work which have surfaced in the process of writing this chapter. But what will personally have to be considered in future work will be the danger of allowing my personal predilection towards strong control over self, career and social location to push me towards over-emphasizing theoretically the role of conscious agency and choice in the identity work that people do generally. Doing research on relatively self-assertive people like managers, professionals and entrepreneurs, as opposed to studying the lives of the poor and dispossessed of the earth, might also lead one into such a danger.

We all need to be epistemologically reflexive and conscious of how our own life experiences and our own identity work can both inspire and constrain our research creativity. And we need also to keep in mind the sociological imagination and remain aware at all times that personal circumstances and experiences can only ever be understood within the public, historical and structural contexts of which they are a part. This applies equally to ourselves as researchers and to the people we involve in our research.

References

Bendix, R. (1966) *Max Weber: A Sociological Portrait*. London: Methuen.

Billig, M. (1987) *Arguing and Thinking: A Rhetorical Approach to Social Psychology*. Cambridge: Cambridge University Press.

Cohen, L. and Musson, G. (2000) 'Entrepreneurial identities: Reflections from two case studies'. *Organization* 79(1): 31–415.

Dent, M. and Whitehead, S. (eds) (2001) *Managing Professional Identities*. London: Routledge.

Douglas, M. (1986) *How Institutions Think*. Syracuse, NY: Syracuse University Press.

Fletcher, D. E. and Watson, T. J. (2007) 'Entrepreneurship, management learning and negotiated narratives: 'making it otherwise for us – otherwise for them', *Management Learning*. 18(1): pp. 9–26.

Hatch, M. J. and Schultz, M. (eds) (2004) *Organizational Identity: A Reader*. Oxford: Oxford University Press.

Johnson, P. and Duberley, J. (2000) *Understanding Management Research*. London: Sage.

Mills, C. W. (1970) *The Sociological Imagination*. Harmondsworth: Penguin.

Roethlisberger, F. J. (1945) 'The foreman: master and victim of double talk'. *Harvard Business Review* 23.

Sveningsson, S. and Alvesson, M. (2003) 'Managing managerial identities: organizational fragmentation, discourse and identity struggle'. *Human Relations* 56(10): 1163–1193.

Watson, T. J. (1977) *The Personnel Managers: A Study in the Sociology of Work and Employment*. London: Routledge and Kegan Paul.

Watson, T. J. (1982) 'Group ideologies and organisational change'. *Journal of Management Studies* 19(3): 259–275.

Watson, T. J. (2000) 'Managerial practice and interactive social science'. *Science and Public Policy* 27(3): 31–38

Watson, T. J. (2001a) *In Search of Management (revised edition)*. London: Thomson Learning (Originally Routledge 1994).

Watson, T. J. (2001b) 'The emergent manager and processes of management pre-learning'. *Management Learning* 32(2): 221–235.

Watson, T. J. (2002) 'Speaking professionally – occupational anxiety and discursive ingenuity among human resourcing specialists'. In Whitehead, S. and Dent, M. (eds) *Managing Professional Identities*. London: Routledge.

Watson, T. J. (2003a) 'Ethical choice in managerial work: the scope for managerial choices in an ethically irrational world'. *Human Relations* 56(2): 167–185.

Watson, T. J. (2003b) 'Strategists and strategy-making: strategic exchange and the shaping of individual lives and organisational futures'. *Journal of Management Studies* 40(5): 1305–1323.

Watson, T. J. (forthcoming) 'Identity work, managers and managing'. *Organization*.

Wray, D. (1949) 'Marginal men of industry: the foremen'. *American Journal of Sociology* 54.

8

Working out: lesbian and gay identity in the workplace

James H. Ward[1]

Introduction

Identities are usually seen as fundamental to our being, and the issue of identity is central to our understanding of how individuals relate to the groups and organizations in which they work (Brown 2001: 114). The study of identity is therefore one of the most popular areas of study for contemporary organizational researchers, with a lengthy pedigree (see for example, Albert, Ashforth, and Dutton 2000: 13, Brown 2001: 113, Sveningsson and Alvesson 2003: 1163). There are consequently many different approaches as well as many different theoretical positions and ways of understanding and conceptualizing identity in the workplace. And yet, although it is generally agreed that there is an almost automatic relationship between desire and self-description, self and social identity (Weeks 2003, Weeks, Holland, and Waites 2003), it is arguable that sexual identity, and minority sexual identity in particular, is one of the most taboo topics within contemporary organizational theory (Gabriel, Fineman, and Sims 2000: 183, Hancock and Tyler 2001, Klawitter 1998, McQuarrie 1998, Ward 2001), with the diversity and organizational studies literature only now beginning to make reference to minority sexual orientation (Bowen and Blackmon 2003, Bruni 2006, Bruni and Gherardi 2002, Colgan 1999, Day and Schoenrade 2000, Miller, Forest, and Jurik 2003, Ragins and Cornwell 2001, Ward and Winstanley 2003, 2004, 2005, 2006).

Coming out at work, and the act of self-disclosure, is one of the most important identity-forming events for sexual minorities in the workplace,

---

[1] This chapter has benefited from the Scholarly Contribution of Diana Winstanley before her untimely death.

151

and there is a need to understand and theorize the dynamics in operation from the individual's point of view. Understandably, therefore, the focus of many of these articles and papers is the individual, responding to the need to explain and highlight the everyday experience at work of lesbians and gay men. And yet, if we accept that identity is created not through insular self-development but through interaction with others in the work environment, then it is equally important to understand and theorize the response to coming out from others in the organization: what do co-workers and colleagues say about gay people, when confronted with gay issues in the workplace? And does this manifest itself in different ways in different organizations?

Postmodern and discursive approaches to identity have moved away from the idea that there is a 'true self' (de Levita 1965: 1) that can be revealed, or that identity is an essentialist notion (Collinson 2003: 527–528). Identities are multiple, fluid and unstable in a general sense, but in a more specific sexual sense; after all, the work carried out by Kinsey in the 1940s illustrated the spectrum of sexualities (Weeks 2003: 199). Judith Butler has described identity as a fiction, in the sense that it does not exist in any real, essentialist, pre-discursive way (Butler 1990, 1993). As Joshua Gamson says, 'Identities are multiple, contradictory, disunified, unstable, fluid – hardly the stuff that allows a researcher to confidently run out and study sexual subjects as if they are coherent and available social types' (Gamson 2000: 356). The problem of how to study fluid, unstable identities which are discursively produced led to the development of a new, narrative-based methodology which is described in this chapter. Stories were collected from gay individuals in the organizations and then, as the 'double-narrative approach' suggests, they were retold in focus groups in the organizations, which were not controlled for sexuality, and the reactions to these stories were recorded. These stories, and the reactions to them, focus on the processual aspect of identity work (Stein 2003) to provide temporary answers to the questions 'who am I?' and 'what do others think of me?'. Moreover, the stories focus on identity as 'becoming' (Sveningsson and Alvesson 2003: 1164).

The chapter is presented in five main sections: first, a brief review of coming out at work; second, a review of the literature on sexual minorities in the workplace; third, an explanation of the research methodology; fourth, the results of the empirical research from three organizations, a major banking corporation, a police department and the fire service; and lastly the chapter concludes by suggesting another angle or methodology for gay identity research in organizations, that of focusing on general discourse about sexual minorities rather than lesbians and gay men themselves. It has also drawn attention to some of the metaphors that co-workers use, and finally, demonstrated empirically the idea of dominant and dominated discourses.

Coming out at work

Coming out is an act of self-disclosure, specifically the act of disclosing previously undisclosed minority sexual identity, and one which has received much attention in the literature on sexual minorities in the workplace. It is a subject which continues to command interest and attention. Sedgwick (1991) asserts that 'gay uncovering seems if anything heightened in surprise and delectability, rather than staled, by the increasingly intense atmosphere of public articulations' (Sedgwick 1991: 67). Coming out can take many different forms; for example, the individual may make the choice to come out, perhaps having considered the issue over a long time, even years, choosing the time and the place as well as the person to tell. Sometimes the individual has no choice at all and is outed, by chance, mishap or purposeful intervention by another. Sometimes, it is not always a considered act; it can be an impulsive act in response to teasing. In our research, one gay person is put in an invidious position where they have to come out as an act of resistance; in Butler's words, 'the injurious effects of discourse become the painful resources by which a resignifying practice is wrought' (Butler 1993: 224). Whatever the form of coming out, it happens within a context of discourse created by the individual's co-workers and colleagues. And that context is important for two reasons: first because, with the constant presumption of heterosexuality, coming out, or the disclosure of self-identity, is something that the lesbian or gay man has to do in every new work situation. Second, it is important because once they are 'out', lesbians and gay men constantly have to manage their social identity, which depending on the context is potentially discrediting (Goffman 1963). So, what does the literature tell us about organizations' response to the coming out of lesbians and gay men?

The organizational context

There is an inherent contradiction in being gay and working for an organization. Whilst out, gay employees are more committed to their organization, and are likely to feel more fulfilled and do a better job (Day and Schoenrade 1997, 2000), and this is supported by much significant research that has well-documented discrimination against sexual minorities in organizations (Bowen and Blackmon 2003, Croteau 1996, Levine 1979,

Levine and Leonard 1984, Woods and Lucas 1993, Welch 1996). For sexual minorities, discrimination is a pervasive feature of the workplace (Croteau 1996, Gabriel *et al.* 2000: 174), as well as the fear of discrimination which is a regular feature of lesbians' and gay men's experience. Management of this stigma and fear means that people are either forced to remain closeted (Boatwright, Gilbert, Forrest, and Ketzenberger 1996) or people tend to separate their lives between work and leisure (Boatwright *et al.* 1996; Croteau 1996). Discrimination in the workplace can be formal and informal (Croteau 1996), such as verbal harassment, property violence and loss of credibility or acceptance (Zuckerman and Simons 1996: 40); more formal types of discrimination can include decisions not to promote, to fire or not to hire, or to pay someone less on the basis of sexual orientation (Badgett 1995). Badgett's research reported that gay men were on average paid 20% less than their heterosexual counterparts, whereas lesbians, although paid less than heterosexual men, were paid on a par with women. In the UK, 36% of employers would be less likely to offer a job to a gay man, and 31% to a lesbian (Snape, Thomson, and Chetwynd 1995). In the US, one study reported that 26% of employers would not promote homosexuals (Badgett and King 1997: 75).

Team-working and group behavior can have a tremendous impact, both positively and negatively, on the lesbian or gay individual in the workplace. For example, one heterosexual female assistant would not work with her lesbian manager because of group pressure from other colleagues (Humphrey 1999: 141). Also, managers in service roles may be out with colleagues internally, but may not be out to the public, as in the case of one lesbian social worker reported by Humphrey. One adolescent client found out and requested a change in carer (Humphrey 1999: 141), which led to a change in behavior between working with colleagues and external service provision. The issue of whether being out at work affects relationships with clients and external service provision, as well as colleagues, is an interesting one, which is addressed in our third extract of organizational discourse in the police.

And yet it is the language that people use at work about sexual minorities and the way that they talk about them which can be an important part of sexual minorities' workplace experience. Indeed, because of the invisibility of sexual orientation, compared to other diversity categories, lesbians and gay men are sometimes in the almost unique position of knowing what people think about sexual minorities before they come out, leading to a situation where sexual minorities carefully assess the prevailing organizational climate before disclosing their sexual orientation (Mintz and Rothblum 1997, Clair, Beatty, and MacLean 2002, Schope 2002). Homophobic remarks are commonplace in work organizations, and it may be no more than a joke, comment or anecdote that sets the tone. In a survey of lesbian and gay journalists reported by Woods and Lucas, 81% had heard derogatory comments about gays or lesbians in general, or about a specific employee (Woods and Lucas 1993: 16). Often, sexuality is linked to the person's ability to do the job. For example, one trader on Wall Street said of a colleague that it was bizarre 'that the guy's a fucking faggot and he's still trading' (Woods and Lucas 1993: 17). However, it is not possible to mention language without mentioning the fact that whilst vilified, sexual minorities are paradoxically also largely ignored (Woods and Lucas 1993: 5). Even in forward-thinking organizations, where progressive diversity management practices have given a voice to previously silenced sexual minorities, discourse around those very same sexual minorities may be, ironically, sometimes silenced (Ward and Winstanley 2002). The literature seems to be inconsistent in this area: there is a focus on derogatory language, with less discussion on other important areas of discourse, such as issues of stereotyping, issues of what is said and what is silent (Ward and Winstanley 2002) and also examples of language of affirmation and acceptance.

The organizational settings

In this research we have looked at three different responses to, coming out in three different organizational settings; one major UK banking corporation, which is a rare insight into a private sector organization, and the fire service and the police in the UK.

The bank

The bank is one of the largest financial services groups in the United Kingdom, made up of seven business groups, including personal and business banking, a credit card division and an investment arm, with over 78,000 employees and shareholder funds in the region of £15 billion at the time of writing.

The fire service

The Shire Fire Service is a medium-sized regional division of the UK fire service. The shire fire service employs approximately 850 people, making it the smallest organization to take part in this project. The service is in a semi-rural location, with a number of medium-sized towns, and therefore there is a mix of whole-time and retained, or part-time, fire-fighters.

The police

The Constabulary is a large rural police force in the UK. There are over 5000 employees, including 2000 support staff, making The Constabulary one of the largest employers in the area, though still one of the smaller organizations in this project.

Data collection

There are various complications in carrying out research into sexual minorities in organizations: identities are fluid and unstable; they are constantly being re-produced through discourse; and minority sexual identities present a particular challenge because they are surrounded by silence. This research project had to create an approach and research method that could break and explore this silence: a 'double or two-tier narrative approach' which went beyond individual narrative to capturing group processes, and encouraging discussion on a topic which is often left unspoken was developed; stories that were collected through individual interviews in each organization were taken to focus groups in the same organization, uncontrolled for sexuality, to get people talking about issues relating to sexual minorities, and how they, as members of the organization reacted to these stories told by their colleagues. Did they recognize the stories? How did they feel about the issues raised? Did they recognize the issues as valid?

The focus groups

Careful consideration was given to the approach of setting up the focus groups and their size and make-up. Recruitment of the right people has been described by researchers as the most underestimated aspect of organizing focus groups (Krueger 1994: 74), and this study was no exception in presenting certain challenges. Statistical representation is not the aim of most focus group research, and often qualitative sampling is used (Kitzinger and Barbour 1999: 7). In this study, no effort was made to have any statistically valid breakdown of categories in the group, since it would not have been appropriate to the study; it was not the intention to control for sexuality in the focus groups and anyway, it would be a fallacy to assume that any one individual can speak for their group, be it gender, race or sexuality (Krueger 1994: 77). We recognized that focus group work often involved increased dependency on 'gatekeepers' (Kitzinger and Barbour 1999: 10), and that there was a risk in relying more heavily on managers to organize the focus groups. However, we are confident that the selection of groups was as objective as possible. For example, the fire service was keen to select different watches who were known to have different group characteristics, some more co-operative and others more negative towards the organization, to give a selection of different views. The police did not tell divisional commanders, or any recruit to the focus groups, the topic of discussion, to avoid the problem of individual engagement with the topic. In the bank, I was able to carry out our focus groups as a 'piggy-back' exercise (Krueger 1994: 83) following regular meetings, as well as 'on location' (Krueger 1994: 83) in a call center.

The bank

In The bank, a total of four focus groups were held in three different locations around the country, with a total number of 31 participants. There were 14 women (or 45% of the total) and 17 men (55% of the total). Although there was no participation at the senior executive level, there was a good level of participation at the two next most senior grades, still senior levels within the bank.

Fire service

In the fire service, a total of seven focus groups were held in five different locations around the county, one of which was the HQ, with a total number of 43 participants. There were 5 women (or 12% of the total) and 38 men (88% of the total). All the fire-fighters who took part were male and represented 35 (or 81% of the participants). Eight other members of staff took part in the HQ (of whom 5 were the women participants), with a range of grades represented in the HQ from clerical grades to deputy chief fire officer.

Police

In the police, a total of eight focus groups were held in five different locations around the region, one location being the HQ, with a total number of 59 participants. There were 27 women (or 46% of the total) and 32 men (54% of the total). Support staff formed the largest sub-grouping and, of the 31 support staff to attend the focus groups, 10 came from the HR department. Of the sworn staff there were 20 constables, both uniformed and plain-clothed, three sergeants and two inspectors. No senior sworn staff attended.

Ethical issues in focus group research

The discussion of ethical issues is very relevant to the discussion of focus group research (Kitzinger and Barbour 1999: 17): getting the informed consent of participants is one which was always possible in this research. For example, in the police, employees did not know in advance what they were coming to, and were therefore unable to give their informed consent. Another ethical issue is confidentiality: I warned all focus group participants that these groups were not confidential in the sense that I would be feeding back their views to the organization but they would be used anonymously and I would not, at any point, link any one particular view to a participant. That said, focus groups, by their very nature, involve different members of the organization who could have talked and gossiped outside the group about views expressed inside it. For that reason, I followed the advice of focus groups researchers to set ground rules prior to running the group (Kitzinger and Barbour 1999: 17), which everyone agreed to.

These focus groups were dealing with sensitive topics, and although they did not have the aim of encouraging personal disclosure from the participants in any way, they did, nevertheless, involve the discussion of individuals' personal stories and the open discussion of taboo topics. Some researchers have even suggested that this can even introduce a certain thrill into the proceedings (Farquhar 1999: 47).

Researcher identity

The identity of the researcher is important in a number of ways: it influences the selection of the research topic; it affects data collection, especially the way that interviews are carried out (Taylor 2001: 17); it influences the way that questions are asked and the answers that are given; and it influences the way that the data is interpreted and analysed (Taylor 2001: 18). The fact that the researcher was gay was not shared with the focus groups before the discussion. The criticism might be levelled at this approach that it is not ethical and dishonest. I felt that it merely reflects and mirrors day-to-day practice in organizations where organizational members feel free to speak because of the invisibility of homosexuality. After the discussion, the groups were given the opportunity to ask any questions they wanted which included discussions of the researcher's sexual orientation.

Selecting the data

One of the ethical challenges in this sort of research is selecting the data: what is going to be included? What should be left out? In actual fact, this research generated far too much material to include in just one chapter of a book, and for that reason alone I have had to be selective about what to include and what to exclude. I feel that these excerpts of group discourse are illustrative of what we heard in those particular organizations, but recognize that in selecting these excerpts, I are also in danger of 'silencing voices from the field' (Czarniawska 1998).

Reactions to coming out in a UK banking corporation

The following extract is taken from a focus group in a call center in the bank. The discussion was created in response to a story about a gay manager in a call center. He had described how he has to take people on from induction, which involves introducing himself, describing what the job is about, what their responsibilities are, and what the new recruits can expect of him as a manager. Normally he would be introduced by name and some basic business information about him. On one occasion, however, he came into the room to the sound of little sniggers, but he carried on and introduced himself anyway. It just so happened that there was a gay man in the group of new recruits, who, in a subsequent discussion, said to him, 'You do realize that before you came into the room the lecturer said – just so that you are all aware he is *gay*.' One of new recruits was reported by the gay manager as being particularly homophobic and, he believed, as a result of this introduction, he caused all sorts of problems. The new recruit kept making comments about 'it repulses me' and 'it makes me feel sick'. The gay manager felt that he would not have had to put up with that if he had not been introduced as a gay man.

Extract 1: The bank

- *It's a bit out of order, introducing somebody as gay*
- *It's making an assumption – he didn't know, did he?*
- *Makes it sound like he's going to come onto you, sort of thing – you know – beware. Whereas if he got to know you, it would be different*
- *It's his choice if he wants to tell you*
- *There are different ways of coming out and of outing, but here he's seen as a predator, beware*
- *But even the opposite way, you know, he's gay so don't say anything bad to him, it's ignorant. It's up to the guy to tell them if he wants to*

- *It's like saying this is so and so – she were a purse-snatcher. You wouldn't say that would you*
- *I have mixed feelings about this though, sometimes I think they should know*
- *If you had someone in your team and they were struggling and they were gay, it might be appropriate to introduce them to Richard to have a chat – one-to-one might be appropriate. You know, here's someone you might consider speaking to, and by the way he's gay, but not in front of everyone. It's completely irrelevant. If you're doing sexual orientation and you say – we're going to watch this video and then have a discussion and then say this team leader that's coming in is gay and is proud of it and wants to take questions from you, that's different isn't it*
- *You need to find out how far you can go early on. You know you two if you didn't joke about it first, then no-one else would. But because you two are open about it in the first place. If someone is really serious about it and says, 'I'm gay and not a lot of people know about it,' you know that you don't go 'alright you queer', whereas with Richard you could*
- *Before Richard came I was much more of that opinion, I'd lay low, and Richard pushed the boundaries. And it's a question of numbers, once you've got more than a certain number of people, you're no longer a minority.*

The make-up of this focus group was quite unusual in that, by chance, there were three gay men in the group, Richard a very vocal individual who was a joker, and two other men, though at this point in the discussion, the third man had not yet come out to the group. There was one heterosexual man, and the rest were women. It was observed that a different sort of discussion happens when there are gay people in the room.

This group suggested that introducing someone as gay is 'out of order', but recognized the different intentions of the forced 'outing'. For example, they suggested that the message might be either 'Predator – beware!', or 'this person is gay so pity him'. They contended that either approach might be offensive for the individual concerned. Nevertheless, when trying to find a similar situation as a comparison, one of the participants suggests that it is like introducing someone as a 'purse-snatcher' or a thief, an interesting simile to use, since the opposite term would be an 'honest person'.

In this discussion about coming out, and 'outing', a female participant then 'outs' one of the gay men in the room, and later goes on to out another man in the room as well, by saying 'you two'. There is a third gay man in the group but he comes out himself, and does not do so until later in the focus group session. He may well have been out to the group, but he was not out to the researcher.

In the discussion of the story, they end up replicating the story in front of the researcher, 'Here's someone you might consider speaking to, and by the way he's gay.' Having said that, it is a particularly thoughtful suggestion if you replace the gay character with say, a female character, then introducing a new woman team member to the other woman in the team on a one-to-one basis would be a pleasant way of effecting an introduction.

One of the ways in which the group talks about the idea of a gay person is as someone who is light-hearted about their sexuality. If someone is serious, you would have to be careful around them, but if someone, like Richard in the discussion, treats it as a joke, it is a lot easier for everyone. In other words, if you are serious as a gay man or lesbian, it is problematic for everyone else; an acceptable subject position for sexual minorities is as a source of humor and banter. Goffman recounts the story of a man who would always, on entering a room, whip out a packet of cigarettes and light a cigarette ostentatiously. After a short while, when he knew people would be amazed at what he could do with no hands, he would say out loud, 'at least I never have to worry about burning my fingers!' (Goffman 1963: 142). In the same way, responsibility is placed on the shoulders of the sexual minorities for lightening the atmosphere, joking or using banter to put the heterosexual majority at their ease.

Reactions to coming out in the UK fire service

The following discussion in the fire service is about coming out, and was a discussion which was created in response to a story about a fire-fighter coming out very publicly. He had entered Mr Gay UK, although he maintained he did so by accident, having been pushed onto a stage one night in a nightclub. He got through to the final which, unbeknownst to him, was filmed for television. He then went away on holiday for a couple of weeks and when he arrived back at work, someone pulled him to one side and said, 'Oh, by the way, we saw you on telly the other night, Mr Gay UK. I think you'd better start being open to people.'

Extract 2: The fire service

- Are we only talking about your gay individuals today? Gay groups have got an advantage. They have two ways of going, haven't they? You can be gay, or you can keep it to yourself. The hoo-ha with the Deputy in Manchester; he was dead right. Absolutely dead right. It was easier for him to do what he wants as a gay white male, than as an Asian or a female. The reason they have a harder time with the bigots when they do come out is that they know that there has been a secret that has been kept. Would you trust someone who had kept a secret away from you that had worked with you for 10 years? And suddenly let you in on that secret?
- We all have secrets
- If I worked with you though and then turned round and said, oh by the way, I'm gay . . .
- It'd be a shock, but at the end of the day what one person wants to keep to himself might not be what another person wants to keep
- I know what you say, but if you've known someone for 10 years, it shouldn't affect the friendship
- You can't dislike someone 'cos they've kept something from you
- I think thats a bit naïve
- During that time you could have been asked to be my best man, godfather to my children, and then after all that time you say you're gay . . .
- It's the same principle as a little white lie; and you've got to tell a lot of little white lies
- If you are visibly a minority group relationship will be maintained – they will either love you or hate you. The problem you have is if you're gay, no-one knows until you want them to know. The problem comes when you make assumptions, and then you admit to not being heterosexual and some people are going to have the reaction – why didn't you tell me before?
- Don't you think it's because it's relatively new?
- It is, and even if you're happy with them coming out your relationship will change . . .
- . . . Gays would make great spies because they inhabit a secret world.

The group saw sexual minorities as somehow belonging to a secret society, and as 'making good spies'. They also saw sexual minorities having an advantage over other minorities because they could keep their sexuality a secret. One focus group participant was suggesting that he accepted lesbian and gay colleagues as long as they kept their minority sexuality secret. In his view, they should not talk about their partners, friends and family, nor what they do at the weekend, if it were to imply their sexuality. This respondent also equated those people who are open about their sexual orientation with those who claim to be victimized at work. Another respondent suggested that by coming out, sexual minorities were really just spoiling people's fun. Many of the fire-fighters that took part in the focus groups were at pains to point out that sexuality and gay people in particular were 'not an issue'. But as Fairclough (1995) pointed out, power can control and put limits on alternative discourses, and therefore 'not being an issue' was not without its conditions (Fairclough 1995). Having gay people around was acceptable, as long as they did not remind you that they were gay.

Reactions to coming out in the police

In the following extract, an exchange between the researcher and a participant in a focus group in the police is reproduced in full. The exchange began in response to a story about a police constable who came out to his shift because of bullying which he had been suffering at the hands of his colleagues. He had some damage to his locker, and someone wrote 'dirty faggot' on his notebook so that it would be seen by members of the public, on several different occasions. He also had messages sent to him about AIDS through the internal despatch. It got to the point where he was thinking of leaving the police altogether. However, he spoke to his chief inspector, who offered him either a full investigation or an opportunity to speak to the team and tell them the rumors were true. He did the latter in a team meeting, first on the agenda, in front of about 40 people, all with their heads hung quite low.

Extract 3: The police

- *If he works for the police, to a certain extent he's representing the police;*
- **What is acceptable and what is not?**
- *If someone comes in and does a day's work, then there's no reason to . . . ; the Job is a job of this nature – if you go around flaunting anything that's unusual . . . it isn't so much the people you're working with, but the people on the street pick up things quicker than anyone else. It can become a confrontational issue with members of the public.*

(*Continued*)

So you have to hide whatever your views are, you have to become a policeman, you can't show any undue character when you're dealing with people on the street. I can't give you an exact answer to your question . . .

– *Do you have an idea what flaunting means in that context?*

– *I can't give you an example*

– *What about talking about your partner at work?*

– *That should be OK. So long as you're doing it at work, with members of staff, so long as you don't start talking about it in front of members of the public;*

– *OK, so that's the dividing line? You can talk about your partner in the canteen, but not to members of the public?*

– *(Silence) Yeah, I suppose so. If you want a quick answer. There's not a quick answer to anything.*

– *So private life should remain in the canteen?*

– *Members of the public, especially after they've drunk several cans of beer on a Friday night are not so considerate. They're extreme bigots so if you show any sign of . . . you're asking for trouble and you'll get your colleagues in trouble. At 1 o'clock in the morning they're not so considerate . . .*

– *So that's the public divide, is there anything you can't talk about at work in the canteen?*

– *You don't want to be talking about anything at work in the canteen that may upset someone else. If you're in a group of people and someone's going to be upset by it . . . it's a balance isn't it. We're talking sexually, but it could be religion, it could be anything, and we were all religious, you wouldn't want one person there running down religion, because you're antagonizing aren't you? It doesn't matter whether it's sexuality or anything else, you should just keep your views to yourself or keep them moderate. If you're upsetting someone you shouldn't be saying it – it works two ways: obviously in the first scenario the homosexual was being victimized, but someone who had strong views against that could be upset if too many people were talking about it casually as if, you know, as if everyone accepted it. As a policeman you should be able to judge when you are upsetting people. You have to be able to see with members of the public whether you're upsetting them – use the same principle with your colleagues.*

– *So is coming out to your colleagues overstepping the mark do you think?*

– *Yeah, I don't know*

In general, the researcher took a very minimal role in the focus groups, only presenting the stories, and then allowing conversation to happen between the participants. The exchange shown in this extract comes from a focus group where contributions from participants were minimal, and the researcher took more of an active role, asking for greater clarification and examples. The researcher's questions are in bold. It is an example of a dominant discourse type (Fairclough 1989). This refers to the idea that one type of discourse is established as the dominant one in a given social domain, and, at the same time, it establishes certain ideological assumptions as commonsensical, consistent with the view of discourses as rules. Discourse as a vehicle for power can mean the domination of one discourse by another, in an oppositional relationship (Fairclough 1989: 91), and the dominated discourse is under pressure to be silenced, suppressed and eliminated. Dominant discourses can also contain oppositional discourses (Fairclough 1989), which means that the dominant discourse credits the oppositional one with a certain limited legitimacy and protection. The minority is tolerated and accepted rather than put on an equal footing. The main speaker seems quite proud to know people keep their sexuality to themselves, again justifying the limiting of minority dominated discourses. Another interesting aspect to this extract is that the speaker identifies that it is precisely those people that see themselves in the role of the victim that are the problem.

From this discussion, it seems that gay people are tolerated in the police as long as they do not 'flaunt' their sexuality; in other words they should keep it 'silent'. In order to give the dominant discourse credibility, the argument is used that it is nothing to do with the police; instead it is the people on the street. The focus group participant maintains that the public 'pick up things much quicker than anyone else'. This is a fascinating assertion to make; the job of the police is to be more observant, sharper and better able to interpret signs than the general public. He is in fact creating a limited legitimacy for gay people in the police, and protection, by warning them against being seen by the public.

The need for police officers, in particular, to hide themselves when they are dealing with the public is an example of Goffman's idea of conceptualizing certain types of work as dramaturgy, as well as Kerfoot's ideas on the use of the body in paid work (Kerfoot 2000). By identifying and occupying privileged bodily designations, the mark of a competent police officer is their ability to display the body in a manner that is culturally acceptable to their organization's body code. Most obviously this relates to dress and physical appearance (Kerfoot 2000), which relates to the use of uniform in the police, and fire service, but could just as easily refer, in the case of gay men or lesbians, to overtly effeminate or masculine behavior. They are concerned with proving that they are trustworthy and reliable (Kerfoot 2000). Although the body plays an important part amongst the contemporary theorizing about the self, and outside the workplace we are freer than ever before to construct variable self-identities from a marketplace of commodities, ideas and cultural bric-a-brac (Casey 2000), inside work we are still expected to use our bodies to conform, rather than show individuality and to show outward traits of masculinity.

Conclusion

In conclusion, this chapter has suggested another angle or methodology for gay identity research in organizations: that of focusing on general discourse about sexual minorities rather than lesbians and gay men themselves. It has also drawn attention to some of the metaphors that co-workers use, and finally demonstrated empirically the idea of dominant and dominated discourses.

The research was carried out in specific organizations, rather than research on individual experience, although it was not possible to name the organizations. Unusually, the research looked at discourse about lesbians and gay men by their co-workers, rather than relying solely on self-narratives of experience in the workplace. This forms a methodological contribution to the area of lesbian and gay studies by creating and then reporting on a method which creates discourse about lesbians and gay men in organizations, recognizing that it is exceptionally difficult to pick up this sort of data by hanging around in organizations. Second, and most interestingly, are the themes which come out of these three extracts, and the metaphors which co-workers use in talking about lesbians and gay men: thief, or purse-snatcher, when talking about someone who had not come out in the bank; in the fire service, fire-fighters likened gay men who had not come out to spies, because of their ability to keep secrets and live double lives; in the police, they talked about gay men simultaneously in the role of victim and aggressor, suggesting that if they attract negative behavior and violence, either from colleagues or members of the public, they have only themselves to blame. Finally, the data shows empirically Fairclough's ideas of a dominant discourse type, where one type of discourse is established as the dominant one in a given social domain, at the same time, establishing certain ideological assumptions as commonsensical, consistent with the view of discourses as rules. This leads to a minority being tolerated and accepted rather than put on an equal footing, with minority sexuality remaining silent if it is to be tolerated. So, we see gay people being tolerated in the police, and other occupations, as long as they do not 'flaunt' their sexuality, and remain silent.

It is recognized that the data, being qualitative in nature, is limited, there being only three examples in this chapter. It is therefore suggested that further work of this nature should be carried out to explore the ways in which lesbians and gay men are conceptualized in the workplace by their co-workers, even if we, as organizational researchers, run the risk, by breaking the organizational silence which surrounds it, of 'flaunting' sexuality.

References

Albert, S., Ashforth, B. E., and Dutton, J. E. (2000) 'Organizational identity and identification: charting new waters and building new bridges'. *Academy of Management Review* 25(1): 13–17.

Badgett, M. V. L. (1995) 'The wage effects of sexual orientation discrimination'. *Industrial and Labor Relations Review* 48(4): 726–739.

Badgett, M. V. L. and King, M. C. (1997) 'Lesbian and gay occupational strategies'. In Gluckman, A. and Reed, B. (eds) *Homo Economics: Capitalism, Community and Lesbian and Gay Life*. New York: Routledge.

Boatwright, K. J., Gilbert, S., Forrest, L., and Ketzenberger, K. (1996) 'Impact of identity development upon career trajectory: listening to the voices of lesbian women'. *Journal of Vocational Behavior* 48: 210–228.

Bowen, F. and Blackmon, K. (2003) 'Spirals of silence: the dynamic effects of diversity on organizational voice'. *Journal of Management Studies* 40(6): 1393–1417.

Brown, A. D. (2001) 'Organization studies and identity: towards a research agenda'. *Human Relations* 54(1): 113–121.

Bruni, A. (2006) 'Have you got a boyfriend or are you single?': on the importance of being 'straight' in organizational research'. *Gender, Work and Organization* 13(3): 299–316.

Bruni, A. and Gherardi, S. (2002) 'En-gendering differences, transgressing the boundaries, coping with the dual presence'. In Aaltio-Marjosola, L. and Mills, A. J. (eds) *Gender, Identity and the Culture of Organization* (pp. 174–200). London: Routledge.

Butler, J. (1990) *Gender Trouble: Feminism and the Subversion of Identity*. London: Routledge.

Butler, J. (1993) *Bodies that Matter: On the Discursive Limits of Sex*. London: Routledge.

Casey, C. (2000) 'Sociology sensing the body: revitalizing a dissociative discourse'. In Hassard, J., Holliday, R., and Willmott, H. (eds) *Body and Organization*. London: Sage.

Clair, J. A., Beatty, J., and MacLean, T. (2002) 'Out of sight but not out of mind: how people manage invisible social identities in the workplace'. *Academy of Management* August.

Colgan, F. (1999) 'Recognising the gay constituency in UK trade unions'. *Industrial Relations Journal* 30(5): 444–462.

Collinson, D. L. (2003) 'Identities and insecurities: selves at work'. *Organization* 10(3): 527–547.

Croteau, J. M. (1996) 'Research on the work experiences of lesbian, gay and bisexual people; an integrative review of methodology and findings'. *Journal of Vocational Behavior* 48: 195–209.

Czarniawska, B. (1998) *A Narrative Approach to Organization Studies*. Thousand Oaks: Sage.

Day, N. E. and Schoenrade, P. (1997) 'Staying in the closet versus coming out: relationships between communication about sexual orientation and work attitudes'. *Personnel Psychology* 50(1): 147–167.

Day, N. E. and Schoenrade, P. (2000) 'The relationship among reported disclosure of sexual orientation, anti-discrimination policies, top management support and work attitudes of gay and lesbian employees'. *Personnel Review* 29(3): 346–363.

de Levita, D. D. (1965) *The Concept of Identity*. Paris, France: Mouton and Co.

Fairclough, N. (1989) *Language and Power*. Harlow: Longman.

Fairclough, N. (1995) *Critical Discourse Analysis*. Harlow: Longman.

Farquhar, C. (1999) 'Are focus groups suitable for 'sensitive' topics?' In Barbour, R. S. and Kitzinger, J. (eds) *Developing Focus Group Research: Politics, Theory and Practice* (pp. 47–63). London: Sage.

Gabriel, Y., Fineman, S., and Sims, D. (2000) *Organizing and Organizations* (2nd ed.). London: Sage.

Gamson, J. (2000) 'Sexualities, queer theory and qualitative research'. In Denzin, N. K. and Lincoln, Y. (eds) *Handbook of Qualitative Research*, Vol. 2 (pp. 347–365). Thousand Oaks, CA: Sage.

Goffman, E. (1963) *Stigma: Notes on the Management of Spoiled Identity*. New York: Prentice Hall.

Hancock, P. and Tyler, M. (2001) *Work, Postmodernism and Organization*. London: Sage.

Humphrey, J. C. (1999) 'Organizing sexualities, organized inequalities: lesbians and gay men in public service occupations'. *Gender, Work and Organization* 6(3): 134–151.

Kerfoot, D. (2000) 'Body work: estrangement, disembodiment and the organizational "other"'. In Hassard, J., Holliday, R., and Willmott, H. (eds) *Body and Organization* (pp. 230–246). London: Sage.

Kitzinger, J. and Barbour, R. S. (1999) 'Introduction: the challenge and promise of focus groups'. In Barbour, R. S. and Kitzinger, J. (eds) *Developing Focus Group Research: Politics, Theory and Practice* (pp. 1–20). London: Sage.

Klawitter, M. M. (1998) 'Why aren't economists doing research on sexual orientation?' *Feminist Economics* 4(2): 55–59.

Krueger, R. A. (1994) *Focus Groups: A Practical Guide for Applied Research*. Thousand Oaks, CA, USA: Sage.

Levine, M. P. (1979) 'Employment discrimination against gay men'. *International Review of Modern Sociology* 9(5/7): 151–163.

Levine, M. P. and Leonard, R. (1984) 'Discrimination against lesbians in the work force'. *Signs* 9(4): 700–709.

McQuarrie, F. A. E. (1998) 'Expanding the concept of diversity: discussing sexual orientation in the management classroom'. *Journal of Management Education* 22(2): 162–172.

Miller, S. L., Forest, K. B., and Jurik, N. C. (2003) 'Diversity in blue: lesbian and gay police officers in a masculine occupation'. *Men and Masculinities* 5(4): 355–385.

Mintz, B. and Rothblum, E. D. (1997) *Lesbians in Academia: Degrees of Freedom*. New York, NY, USA: Routledge.

Ragins, B. R. and Cornwell, J. M. (2001) *Walking the Line: Fear and Disclosure of Sexual Orientation in the Workplace*. Paper presented at the National Academy of Management Meeting, Washington, DC, USA, August 5th–8th.

Schope, R. D. (2002) 'The decision to tell: factors influencing the disclosure of sexual orientation by gay men'. *Journal of Gay and Lesbian Social Services* 14(1): 1–22.

Sedgwick, E. K. (1991) *Epistemology of the Closet*. London: Penguin Books.

Snape, D., Thomson, K., and Chetwynd, M. (1995) *Discrimination Against Gay Men and Lesbians, a Study of the Nature and Extent of Discrimination Against Homosexual Men and Women in Britain Today*. London: Social and Community Planning Research.

Stein, A. (2003) 'Becoming lesbian: identity work and the performance of sexuality'. In Weeks, J., Holland, J., and Waites, M. (eds) *Sexualities and Society* (pp. 132–142). Cambridge: Polity Press.

Sveningsson, S. and Alvesson, M. (2003) 'Managing managerial identities: organizational fragmentation, discourse and identity struggle'. *Human Relations* 56(10): 1163–1193.

Taylor, S. (2001) 'Locating and conducting discourse analytic research'. In Wetherell, M., Taylor, S., and Yates, S. J. (eds) *Discourse as Data* (pp. 5–48). London: Sage.

Ward, J. H. (2001) *Setting the Diversity Issue Straight.* Paper presented at the 4th Conference on Ethical Issues in Contemporary Human Resource Management, Middlesex University, 19th April.

Ward, J. H. and Winstanley, D. C. (2002) *The Absent Presence: Negative Space within Discourse and the Construction of Homosexual Identity in the Workplace.* Paper presented at the 18th EGOS Colloquium, Barcelona, 4th July.

Ward, J. H. and Winstanley, D. C. (2003) 'The absent presence: negative space within discourse and the construction of minority sexual identity in the workplace'. *Human Relations* 56(10): 1255–1280.

Ward, J. H. and Winstanley, D. C. (2004) 'Sexuality and the city: exploring the experience of minority sexual identity through storytelling'. *Culture and Organization* 10(3): 219–236.

Ward, J. H. and Winstanley, D. C. (2005) 'Coming out at work: performativity and the recognition and renegotiation of identity'. *Sociological Review* 53(3): 447–475.

Ward, J. H. and Winstanley, D. C. (2006) 'Watching the watch: the UK fire service and its impact on sexual minorities in the workplace'. *Gender, Work and Organization* 13(2): 193–219.

Weeks, J. (2003) 'Necessary fictions: sexual identities and the politics of diversity'. In Weeks, J., Holland, J., and Waites, M. (eds) *Sexualities and Society* (pp. 122–131). Cambridge: Polity.

Weeks, J., Holland, J., and Waites, M. (eds) (2003) *Sexualities and Society.* Cambridge: Polity.

Welch, J. (1996) 'The invisible minority'. *People Management* 2(19): 24–31.

Woods, J. D. and Lucas, J. H. (1993) *The Corporate Closet: The Professional Lives of Gay Men in America.* New York: The Free Press.

Zuckerman, A. J. and Simons, G. F. (1996) *Sexual Orientation in the Workplace.* Thousand Oaks, CA, USA: Sage.

9

Choreographies of identities

Natasha Slutskaya and Stephanie Schreven

In this chapter we seek to explore the territory of loss through the enquiry into the discourse of the body in order to open categories that may allow a different understanding of embodied identity. We pass theoretical concepts of repetition and loss through the event of modern dance to show that the investigation of those concepts enables us to challenge the dichotomization of both verbal and non-verbal cultural practices by asserting the unlived possibilities of movement and the theoretical potential of bodily action (Foster 1998).

As early as 1980, anthropologist Clifford Geertz remarked on the growing tendency with the social sciences to borrow metaphors from outside their disciplines in order to derive new interpretive frameworks for study of human behavior. He senses that such borrowing might shake epistemic foundations and result in a paradigm shift. By introducing modern dance as an analogous model we attempt, not simply to bring together different disciplines and theoretical-analytical frameworks in the hope of thereby producing richer insights into identity studies, but also to show how a dialogue between two disciplines and frameworks may lead to the development of a process where the internal logic of a separate discipline can be used by the other as a resource for its own development.

The politics of identity

The contemporary organizational landscape displays a proliferation of literature discussing identity issues (Alvesson 1994, Balmer 1995, Feather and Rauter 2004, Kreiner and Ashforth 2004). The goal pursued by these researchers has been to attain a better understanding of the identity of the organization in all its complexity (Moingeon 1997). Contemporary identity theory (Sandoval 2000, Stavrakakis 1999, Varadharajan 1995, Young 1990) aims for the recognition of different, divergent emancipatory claims by addressing the tension between particularistic 'I's' and a universal 'we'. It challenges the approach in which universality has been premised on and functioned as a particularity, where 'I' is subordinated to the abstract 'we', and 'we' is set to work through exclusion of individual 'I's' (Brown 1993). Identity politics then inevitably pulsates with a pressing concern for exclusion and the pain associated with it. It cannot proceed to undo social relations of injustice and inequality without rethinking 'we'. By looking into the *productive body* where I is the 'I can', a practical sense of the body's active possibilities, we can move towards an understanding of 'we' that is potentially less exclusionary and violent and that is invested in possibilities, geared towards the future, not a painful past. We intend to emphasize the productive ways our bodies allow us to connect to the world. There is an urgent need to avoid the use of 'we' as hegemonic articulation, a strategic fiction on the basis of which acts of discrimination take place. The encounter between self and other should not be premised on closure and rejection upheld by it. Instead, the sense of self we develop is primarily based on the feel we have of our productive bodies which have specific capacities and creative powers within the multiple relations in which they grow, communicate, learn, and work (Burkitt 1999).

Bodies can easily become vehicles through which subject and object, self and other, are established. On the one hand, the sovereignty of subject manifests itself in a corporeality that is assumed to 'end' with the skin, on the other hand, the body is capable of violating the boundaries between the self and the other, self and the world, by putting emphasis on the body parts that stretch out such as the nose, pot belly, breasts, and those open to the world, such as the mouth, genitals, and anus, all of which connect us to earth and to other people (Burkitt 1999). In the modern world, bodies are often used to accentuate the individual nature of human experience, one that is closed off to the world and complete within itself. Bodily surfaces are known to demarcate social and personal boundaries; identities are formulated through the experience of self that is closed and literally self-possessed (Michelson 1999). At the same time, contemporary bodies represent hybridization: a co-mingling of incompatible elements which make possible impossible identities and unauthorized truths. It is important for the body to regain its positive connotation. Reintroducing the concepts of the body and embodied identity allows a comprehension of the world as 'a totality open to a horizon of an indefinite number of perspectival views which blend with one another and define the object in question' (Merleau-Ponty 1964: 16). It is to the works of Merleau-Ponty that address the body–subject relation that we now turn.

Merleau-Ponty's body

For Merleau-Ponty, the subject of experience is not a consciousness detached from the world, but a living body (Merleau-Ponty 1962). Thus, movements, feelings, and perceptions are primarily bodily modes. Our bodies do not present themselves to us primarily as objects of study, but as starting points for our actions and practices. The relations between the body and its environment are not external, causal relations but internal relations of *expression*. From the embodiment of the subject and its intertwining with the world, it follows that the subject is not transparent to itself, but forever *ambiguous* (Merleau-Ponty 1962). The body-subject does not belong completely to the world nor is it entirely outside the world: 'The world is wholly inside and I am wholly outside myself' (Merleau-Ponty 1968: 467). The body cannot be seen as a thing, it is a situation; it is our grasp upon the world and the outline of our identity projects. At the same time our world is not a tableau of inert objects and things that we comprehend passively, but a living and complexly interacting medium in which we as body-subjects are enmeshed (Gardiner 1998). Merleau-Ponty states, 'I am no longer concerned with my body, nor with time, nor with the world, as I experience them in the inner communion that I have with them'(2004: 84). He continues:

> My body is made of the same flesh as the world, and moreover, the flesh of my body is shared by the world, the world reflects it, encroaches upon it and it encroaches upon the world. World and body therefore exist in relation of transgression or of overlapping
>
> (Merleau-Ponty 1968: 248).

Rather than haughtily and condescendingly observing the world around us, our senses reach out to the world, actively engage with it, shape and configure it – just as the world, at the same time, reaches into the depths of every sensory being. As such, the human perceptual system is not just a mechanical apparatus that exists only to facilitate representational thinking, to produce reified 'concepts' or 'ideas'; rather, it is radically intertwined with the world itself (Gardiner 1998). Merleau-Ponty reminds us that

> We cannot remain in this dilemma of having to fail to understand either the subject or the object. We must discover the origin of the object at the very centre of our experience; we must describe the emergence of being and we must understand how, paradoxically, there is for us an in-itself
>
> (Merleau-Ponty 2004: 84).

For Merleau-Ponty the body is the vehicle of being in the world, and having a body is, for a living creature, to be inescapably connected to a definite environment, to identify oneself with certain projects and be continually committed to them. In the self-evidence of this complete world, in the force of their movement towards us, in this commitment to certain projects we do find the guarantee of our wholeness and achieve the coherence of our self-perception. The body becomes 'the potentiality of a certain world' (Merleau-Ponty 1962: 106). This potential to belong to this world is equal to your potential to make this world while it is emerging around you as the reciprocal completion of your own existence:

> I understand the world and myself because there are things near and far, foregrounds and horizons, and because in this way it forms a picture and acquires significance before me, and this finally is because I am situated in it and it understands me
>
> (Merleau-Ponty 2004: 208).

However, the world is not experienced by me alone, and therefore we must also address the problem of other people. We must supplement our openness on to the world with a 'second openness' – that of other selves (Gardiner 1998). According to Merleau-Ponty, reality can be described as a world of the unknown and the unexplored, of the visible and the invisible. The only way to master this reality is through mediating it by your unique embodied viewpoint (Kujundzic and Buschert 1994). Merleau-Ponty argues that this mechanism of mediation should not imply any form of exclusion. He insists that although our particular view is not shared identically by another person, this is no reason why we cannot establish a reciprocal, mutually enriching relationship between self, other and world.

Entering the totality of the world should not be understood as a threat to a unified, coherent and sovereign self, but should be seen as a way to embrace an external viewpoint. Having an access to an external viewpoint enables us to visualize ourselves as a meaningful whole. In this case striving for wholeness does not assume the reduction of difference and alterity to sameness. Neither does it imply incorporating and thus colonizing otherness into a unified whole. Merleau-Ponty concludes that perception must be 'understood as a reference to a whole which can be grasped, in principle, only through certain of its parts and aspects' (Merleau-Ponty 1964: 16). The decisive issue for Merleau-Ponty is that although the meaning of the world for each of us is constructed for the vantage point of our uniquely embodied viewpoint, and hence irreducibly pluralistic, we continue to inhabit the same world – that is, we are co-participants in a universe that ultimately transcends any particularistic perspective (McCreary 1995).

Other people, according to this argument, provide an important 'mirror' to enable us to evaluate our own existence and consummate a coherent self-image. They offer us an outside view on ourselves, questioning our actions and motives and forcing us to engage in debate about them. It is important to note that this encounter with the other does not imply assimilation through identification and thus fully assumes its radical alterity and unassimilable uniqueness (Evans 1996).

Repetition and embodied identity

At this stage we think it is important to discuss the role of mirroring and the mirror in the encounter with the other. The mirror is both vehicle and metaphor for our points of contact with the other and the self. Human beings are inescapably both mimetic and social; they learn by imitating others (both as a part of childhood learning and through professional training); they participate (for better or worse) in the nature of their models. Bodily behavior by which we initially develop and mature is a function of external mirroring and repetition of 'appropriate' behavior. Through repetition we learn to adopt the role of the other in relation to ourselves. In this sense the body is formed on the basis of a selection process that produces just an illusion of the body as a complete object. By mirroring appropriate behavior we express our acceptance to submit to or to be taken up by the other, thus exercising some kind of choice. On the one hand this choice entails an irremediable loss of ourselves, and on the other hand it opens up the possibilities of the future engagement with the other. It is important to gain a different understanding of the loss by accepting that the difference within radical alterity is constitutive of the self, and that the self can only be recognized to exist in a state of tension, of dis-identification that 'I am' not-I, foreign or alien to myself.

We are caught in the image, of ourselves or of another form, as an identification. The moment 'I' come into existence is a moment of misunderstanding. Unlike animals, we return to the image, again and again, repeating 'a series of gestures' that constitute for us our 'own body', 'the reflected environment', and the relation between those two entities. Repeated bodily behavior provides the body with the bodily intelligence by constricting the bodily chaos by putting itself together as an image, as a coordinated bodily movement as opposed to experienced fragmented body. It is a necessary structuring mechanism that constitutes both external and internal boundaries for the body itself. The filtering process is at the same time an in-forming of sensation. The picture that is beginning to take shape is of a bodily completeness, or integrity, which is ensured by repetitive bodily behavior that is represented, nonetheless, as only a partializing selection of elements (Stukes 2001). Loss will always persist in some form and therefore it will continue to structure identity.

The dynamic that consolidates also materializes and normalizes contours and closure and thus prevents us from recognizing and bringing the outside, the other, within it. 'I am' is established, maintained, and perpetuated by embodied repetitive acts: repetition sustains a boundary and creates closure that preserves coherence and continuity, and that, thus, allows me to recognize myself as self-contained. Repetition allows me to recognize myself as one-self, and to recognize others, as the same or as different from me. However, although set to work to create and maintain similarity and recognition, repetition embodies the potential for difference and estrangement, namely by means of that which is not repeated, which is a pool of unlived and unrealized possibilities, the site of otherness. Repetition exists and does not exist at the same time. We can say 'it happened again', holding that all elements of the 'it' and the 'happened' were the same, yet the event has taken part in the ongoingness of time and space and thus is never the same event. The only conclusion is that on the one hand repetition is itself a self-generating and self-perpetuating event, it is always involved in giving integrity to what is repeated, but on the other hand it imposes limitations and restrictions by constantly returning to a beginning. The act of repetition creates the depth of the embodied experience. It is for the same reason that I am at the heart of the other and that I am far from it: because 'it has thickness and is thereby destined to be seen by a body' (Merleau-Ponty 1968: 6).

Then bodily identity is structured around a dual and opposing dichotomy of both sustaining and configuring wholeness, and fragmenting and dismantling it by encompassing/returning to loss. In order for the subject to control its body, it first must gain an access to a conception of self as a unified whole and then it begins to fragment and dismantle it. Repeating with a difference that splits reflection from what is being repeated and thus makes it able to fold itself into itself – to reflect itself – is also what makes it, for structural reasons, incapable of closing upon itself. Through that process the subject opens itself to the thought of an alterity, a difference that remains unaccounted for the polar opposition of source and reflection, the one and the other. This opens up the possibility for an ethics of being with others differently and of organizing identity politics differently. As Ewa

Ziarek points out in a similar argument by drawing on the work of Jean-Luc Nancy:

Indeed, the paradoxical mode of solidarity with others – a solidarity which respects differences between and within subjects rather than seeking their reconciliation – does not work in the sense that it fails to produce a common essence. And yet, it is the only mode of being with others that refuses to obliterate alterity for the sake of collective identity.

(1995: 17).

Dance as an analogous model

Modern dance might seem like an unusual choice for an analogous model to explore identity issues, but thinking in dance terms allows us to re-evaluate a number of dimensions in the relationship between the body, identity and organization.

From an anthropological perspective, dance involves purposeful, intentionally rhythmical, patterned sequences of non-verbal movements and gestures regarded as having aesthetic value (Sparshott 1988). In dance the body is the locus of social relations, its sensual and perceptual experience moulded by cultural and historical circumstances. Dance can be seen as a collective practice of engagement with enduring historically and culturally specific conventions of representation. Dance brings to light the connections that such conventions have to social and political structuring of power. There is an important relationship between the training of the body, norms of civility, power relations, and identity politics.

The dancer constructs relationships of the body to momentum, stasis, impulse, and flow and articulates relationships of the body's parts one to another. In doing so, the dancer fashions a repertoire of bodily actions that may confirm and elaborate on conventional expectations, or challenge and deny them. In either case, dancing moves us from the study of self into the study of plural identities.

Dance illuminates important issues in the analysis of identity because in dance the sight of the body is both forced to bear the full weight of contradictory and unstable cultural values, and disguise and deny those tensions and instabilities at the same time. The vast majority of studies investigating identity issues have focused on written representations of identities rather than the orchestrated actions of living and moving yet non-speaking bodies. They neglect the body and at the same time use body to inflect textuality with a new vitality (Foster 1998) by constantly emphasizing the ways bodies figure in social discourse. The bodily dimensions of the identity remain buried in the text, property of the linguistic order and its engagement with the social. Dance comes through the body. In his *World History of the Dance*, Curt Sachs provided us with the following description: 'Every dancer feels himself into the living, even into the lifeless forms of nature and re-creates with his own body their appearance, actions, and their essence' (1980: 48). Thinking in dance terms allows us to address what is frequently absent from contemporary theory – an awareness of the material consequences of the lived body.

Pina Bausch's work and liquid identity

To provide texture to our theoretical exposition we will explore some examples of Pina Bausch's work. As we are not dance scholars, we have chosen Ciane Fernandes's work on Pina Bausch and the Wuppertal Dance Theatre as our guide into the world of modern dance. In 1973 Pina Bausch was worldly recognized as the leader of Tanztheatre (dancetheatre), an artistic trend of remarkable importance in contemporary performing arts, and recently she has been considered the most important choreographer of the twentieth century (Schmidt 2000).

There are a number of reasons why we have chosen to engage with her work.

Pina Bausch is well known for her interest in 'expressive dance', which looks to *everyday* movement to express *personal experience*, commenting on the emotional implications of what is happening around us. 'Expressive dance' attracts dancers who feel constrained by the formalism of ballet and post-modern dance. It also allows venturing into new ground, combining the elements of dance and theatre. Since her first days in Wuppertal, Bausch has created more than 30 full-length works. Pina Bausch's pieces balance ballet and theatre while engaging social criticism and philosophical issues, and are in the form of a revue that is not continuously choreographed, appearing fragmentary. Some distinguishing features of Bausch's style are the absence of a sustainable plot, or conventional senses of progression and continuity, or logically and aesthetically consistent character development. Her pieces are built on brief episodes of dialogue and action that are often centred on a surreal situation, prop or costume. For example, in Bandoneon, a man evolves from being in a business suit to being a dreamer in a ballerina's tutu. Actions are often multilayered and performed simultaneously. What interests us the most in her choreography is her use of repetition. Repetition is an important structuring device that is used as a means of alienation, to stop the action, so that one can consider what is presented again and again and again, from different perspectives; it is an attempt to reveal the pluralistic view of the world, and to redefine the role of the body in our mastering the totality of the world.

Dance researchers acknowledge that repetition is an integral part of dance training and the creative process. Being a habitual function, movement bears an intrinsic possibility of being repeated and copied. Daily repetition of pre-set exercises and movement sequences is a basic method for dance training. In this way, repetition constructs a movement vocabulary on the dancer's body, which will then become a vehicle for the technical dance form. More often, dance professionals (teachers, choreographers, and dancers) rearrange and confirm (repeat) already existing movement vocabularies.

Repetition is often used as a formal compositional tool to connect movements and movement phrases. There are different types of repetition that can be identified in Pina Bausch's work. Fernandes (2001) distinguishes two main categories: formal repetition and reconstructive repetition. Formal repetition includes the exact repetition of a movement phrase; the repetition of a scene with subtle changes; the repetition of the same event in different contexts; and the repetition of previously separated events simultaneously in the same scene. Reconstructive repetition includes the reconstruction of the dancers' past experiences and the reconstruction of a traditional tale. Such reconstructions do not necessarily include the formal repetition of movement and words in performance (Fernandes 2001).

What is striking and original about Pina Bausch's choreography is that repetition becomes a creative tool through which dancers fragment, reconstruct, and unsettle their aesthetic and social background. Repetition initially fragments the dancers' experiences and their movement sequences. In Bausch's creative process, repetition is not used to confirm or deny the vocabularies imposed on the dancing bodies. Instead, repetition is used to dismantle such movement vocabularies learned either by dance techniques or socialization (Fernandes 2001).

We will explore one particular piece of Pina Bausch's work called 'Arien'. The piece starts with eight dancers individually describing a unique part of their bodies:

> 'My shoulder is bony.' 'My elbow is bony.' 'My knee is bony.' 'My nose is bony.' 'My eye is bony.' 'My tooth is bony.'

The dancers are scrutinizing the parts of the body they are describing while moving closer and closer to the audience. The closer they are drawn to the audience the more surreal their descriptions become:

'My nose has two holes'. 'My belly button has two holes.' 'My stomach has two holes.' 'My shoulder has two holes.'

'I have two hands.' 'I have two feet.' 'I have two kneecaps.' 'I have two stomachs.' 'I have noses.'

Later in the performance, the conventional, normal body images are replaced by deformed, distorted, and grotesque visions, which are created in order to challenge the completeness and wholeness of our self-image as well as the possibility of identifying the 'self' through the existing order. Grotesque bodies are brought in to consecrate inventive freedom, to permit the combination of a variety of different elements and their rapprochement, to liberate – from the prevailing point of view of the world, from conventions and established truths, from clichés, from all that is humdrum and universally accepted. This grotesque body challenges the existing perception of the body, reconfirms and realizes the relative nature of the existing views (Burkitt 1998).

Stretched repetition readdresses the loss of its completeness by suggesting the possibility of rearrangement. The dancer repeats certain identity formations in order to maintain through repetition the fixity of bodily identity, precisely because bodily identity is illusory. In 'Arien', repetition dominates the body and exposes it as an unsatisfied object. The bodies are presented to us in a 'deformed manner'. It brings home the uncanny realization that things are not quite what they seem, that functions to signal that we are not quite at home in our own skin, estranging us from ourselves.

The performance continues,

'My bad tooth is loose.' 'My bad kneecap is loose.' 'My foot is loose.' 'My stomach is loose.'

The term 'loose' is part of the everyday vocabulary of some dance techniques, as dancers loosen up for performances (Fernandes 2001). Here, dancers loosen not only conventional body parts such as the neck, back, and shoulders, but also their stomach, eyes, nose, and teeth. Thus, the accent is placed on the open and unfinished body rather than on its sealed and finished nature. Approaching the audience, the performance continues with only four dancers who complain:

'I can't see my stomach.' 'I can't see my nose'. 'I can't see my foot.'

They then ask the audience:

'Have you seen my kneecap?' 'Have you seen my stomach?' 'Have you seen my nose?'

The sentences from 'Arien' described above evoke the absence of the dancer's body parts and dismantle the illusion of wholeness with an outer image. Repetition again becomes the search for wholeness and completion that can only be grasped through co-mingling of different parts and perspectives.

The audience participation provides an important mirror for dancers, reflecting back aspects of them they cannot see. This adds a whole new dimension to action. The audience offers us an outside view of ourselves. The dancers' attempts to regain the wholeness of their bodies through their engagement with the audience entail an irremediable loss of themselves. Moreover, the audience participation enables them to become the object of their own projects of coping with the encompassing loss.

What is interesting is the fact that loss itself becomes relatively unimportant. Loss becomes a process, a drive, a need to return, to recover from the sadness and pain of this experience. A sense of sudden absence is countered by a persistent sense of presence.

The experience of loss fuels the various incarnations and desires, and thus carries a dynamic potential, the possibility of undergoing transformation, or reiteration. The encounter and reminder of that loss, desired but never attainable, already lost, lies behind every discrete human act. Hence, the fact that the wholeness of the body never existed as an achieved or achievable real object in no way mitigates the force of its loss.

The show continues with the dancers pronouncing their love to their deformed bodies, accepting the liquidity of their identities:

> 'I love my nose.' 'I love my stomach.' 'My stomach is under my heart.' 'My nose is under my heart.'

The re-identification provoked by repetition reinforces and frees up their physical, social, cultural, and emotional repertoires. The sentences continue to display body parts, describing daily movements:

> 'I walk on my foot.' 'I walk on my nose.' 'I walk on my stomach.'

The dancers' statements again and again contest the notion of a coherent and unified identity. The body is an aggregate of uncoordinated parts, zones, sensations, necessities, and impulses, instead of an integrated totality (Grosz 1994). The incorporation of external images by this fragmented body is not an abstract process because it is physically intrusive.

> 'I have got another kneecap.' 'I have got another stomach.'

This sense of irrecoverable loss is a particle of what will in the future develop into something immense, but at present it is unsatisfying, it gives much less than one expects, but it possesses this potential of change that is so appealing. It signifies an infinitization of the discourse. The sense of loss drives a potential mutation, a constant transformation.

The vulnerability and the fragility of our bodies are highlighted by the dancer's next statements:

'My nose is irritated.' 'My foot is irritated.' 'My stomach is irritated'.

Dancers again explore the possibilities of engaging with the world through their bodies. Pain can never be denied or confirmed, it is sharable and not sharable at the same time. Pain does not have the origin outside us, but it always has significance and expresses our attitude towards the world.

The performance finishes with the last three dancers asserting ownership and emotional ties to body parts they acquired from others.

'I have got another nose.' 'I have got another kneecap.' 'I have got another stomach'. 'My nose is beautiful.' 'My kneecap is beautiful.' 'I like my stomach.' 'I like my nose.'

Reflections

In this dance performance repetition ensures the fluidity of identity between the singular and the universal. Repetition constantly couples continuous flow and partial objects that are by nature fragmentary and fragmented. It represents a deep inherent tendency in living things, whose overcoming is the mark of all development: the losing of oneself in the environment instead of actively asserting oneself, the inclination to let go, to sink back into nature.

Repetition is then that contradictory process whereby differentiation is produced through the inclination toward non-differentiation. Repetition is the vehicle of the desire for identity and unity that necessarily brings about their opposite. Put differently: identity is precisely that concept and inclination which brings forth the non-identical. Repetition is the method of creating likeness, structuring, consolidating, and normalizing which, by dint of the structural impossibility of being identical to what is being repeated, become after-images not of what they seek to reproduce but rather of their own movement towards being complete. Repeated movements carry the mimetic trace of their own becoming, that is, of their own failed identity. Repetition becomes an anticipation of a thing-in-itself yet to come, of something unknown and to be determined.

If the dancer is to restore the totality of the world, repetition is the means to address the unsurpassable plentitude of this totality. But, more importantly, by reconfiguring the self/other dichotomy at the embodied level, exposing the limits of one's body, we accentuate the open self and the other as the self's unlived possibilities.

The body is capable of centring a plurality of experiences around one intelligible core, systemizing them, bringing to light in them an identifiable unity when seen in different perspectives. The body is constituted by the configurations of lived significance which is felt unreflectively, by the constellation of impressions that the body resonates towards its living and non-living surroundings. Repetition is a part of artistic representation and of social discipline. It establishes a system of truths and social values (Fernandes 2001). The use of repetition by Pina Bausch unsettles stable polarities and dismantles the hierarchical by freely and irreverently blending – the private and public, the profane and the sacred, the lower and the higher, the spiritual and the material.

Through repetition, the body explores body's paradoxical existence, between personal and social, the subject and the object. Dancers' bodies are no longer seen as objects but as relations to the surrounding world, which in turn is defined by its relation to us as embodied and active beings. This means that embodied persons are not simply constructs, but they are 'productive bodies' (Burkitt 1998). They are capable of activities that change the nature of their lives rather than serving as points of overlapping between the physical, the symbolic, and the sociological.

Pina Bausch challenges the dichotomy of a ' "pre-linguistic controlled body" and "linguistic controlling society". By including its controller's method (repetition) and subverting it, the body becomes responsible for its own expression within the world. The means of domination (language) become a transforming/creative tool played through and by the body' (Fernandes 2001: 121). The body is no longer a means to an end.

Pina Bausch's dance demonstrates the creative use of unavoidable daily life repetition. In Pina Bausch's aesthetically political prospective, anything can be fluid, changeable, and unstable: body, dance, beauty, and identity. Daily repetition includes and submits to otherness. It is a constant process of re-creating your own wholeness by losing your self to the other. What is particularly important about loss is that fact 'one cannot see clearly what it is that has been lost'. Loss becomes an enabling condition, a limit used. The return to what is lost actively announces that something distant is brought close, a certain strangeness overcome, a bridge built between once and now. The compelling fact is that although return/repetition may harm us, it itself can be painful to lose. Our attachment to lost objects and our lost selves represents a significant dimension of how identities are formed in the first place (Stukes 2001). The incorporation of this loss is what in the long run determines identity. The loss is taken into the self in such a way that it becomes permanently embedded within – and continues to live on as an integral part of our identity. It is conceivable that the need to return or repeat can be explained by the fact these lost possibilities carry a vital message about the direction one needs to pursue to cultivate dimensions of its being that remain unnecessarily weak or underdeveloped. We are drawn to return because there is something in this loss that promises, in however indirect a manner, to awaken what has been locked away or ignored.

References

Alvesson, M. (1994) 'Talking in organizations: managing identity and impressions in an advertising agency.' *Organization Studies* 15(4): 535–563.

Balmer, J. M. T. (1995) 'Corporate branding and connoisseurship,' *Journal of General Management* 21(1): 383–394.

Burkitt, I. (1998) 'Bodies of knowledge: beyond cartesian views of persons, selves and mind.' *Journal for the Theory of Social Behaviour* 28: 63–82.

Burkitt, I. (1999) *Bodies of Thought: Embodiment, Identity and Modernity*. London: Sage.

Brown, W. (1993) 'Wounded attachments.' *Political Theory* 21(3): 390–410.

Evans, D. (1996) *An Introductory Dictionary of Lacanian Psychoanalysis*. London: Routledge.

Feather, N. T. and Rauter, K. A. (2004) 'Organizational citizenship behaviours in reaction to job status, job insecurity, organizational commitment and identification, job satisfaction and work values'. *Journal of Occupational Psychology* 77: 81–94.

Fernandes, C. (2001) *Pina Bausch and the Wuppertal Dance Theatre*. Peter Lang Publishing: New York.

Foster, S. (1998) 'Choreographies of gender.' *Journal of Women in Culture and Society* 24(1): 1–31.

Gardiner, M. (1998) 'The incomparable monster of solipsism: Bakhtin and Merleau-Ponty'. In Bell, M. M. and Gardiner, M. (eds) *Bakhtin and the Human Sciences*. London: Sage.

Geertz, C. (1980) 'Blurred genres: the refiguration of social thought.' *American Scholar* 49(2): 165–179.

Grosz, E. (1994) *Volatile bodies. Towards a Corporeal Feminism*. Bloomington: Indiana University Press.

Kreiner, G. E. and Ashford, B. E. (2004) 'Evidence toward an expanded model of organizational identification.' *Journal of Organizational Behaviour* 25: 1–27.

Kujundzic, N. and Buschert, W. (1994) 'Instruments and the body; Sartre and Merleau-Ponty.' *Research in Phenomenology* 24: 206–226.

McCreary, M. (1995) 'Merleau-Ponty and Nietzche: perspectivism in review.' *Metaphysical Review* 2(3): 1–11.

Merleau-Ponty, M. (1962) *Phenomenology of Perception*. London: Routledge and Kegan Paul.

Merleau-Ponty, M. (1964) *The Primacy of Perception*. IL: Northwestern University Press.

Merleau-Ponty, M. (1968) *The Visible and the Invisible*. Evaston, IL: Northwestern University Press.

Merleau-Ponty, M. (2004) *Basic Writings*. London: Routledge.

Michelson, E. (1999) 'Carnival, paranoia and experiential learning.' *Studies in the Education of Adults* 31(2): 140–153.

Moingeon, B. (1997) 'Understanding corporate identity: the French school of thought.' *European Journal of Marketing* 31(5): 383–395.

Sachs, C. (1980) *World History of the Dance*. The Norton Library, WW Norton and Co Ltd.

Sandoval, C. (2000) *Methodology of the Oppressed*. Minneapolis: University of Minnesota Press.

Schmidt, J. (2000) *Tanztheater Today: Thirty Years of German Dance History*. Seelze/Hannover: Kallmeyersche.

Sparshott, F. (1988) *Off the Ground: First Steps to a Philosophical Consideration of Dance*. Princeton: Princeton University Press.

Stavrakakis, Y. (1999) *Lacan and the Political*. London: Routledge.

Stukes, P. (2001) 'The symptomatic repetition of identity: gender and the traumatic Gestalt.' *Psychoanalytical Studies* 3: 393–409.

Varadharajan, A. (1995) *Exotic Paradies. Subjectivity in Adorno, Said, Spivak*. Minneapolis: University of Minnesota Press.

Young, I. (1990) 'The ideal of community and the politics of difference.' In Nicholson, L. J. (ed.) *Feminism/Postmodernism*. London: Routledge.

Ziarek, E. (1995) 'The uncanny style of Kristeva's critique of nationalism.' *Postmodern Culture* 5(2): 1–21.

10

Disidentity

Nceku "Q" Nyathi and Stefano Harney

> The use-value of any narrative of identity that reduces subjectivity to either a social constructivist model or what has been called an essentialist understanding of self is especially exhausted.
>
> – Jose Esteban Munoz, *Disidentifications*

The real identity politics

What anti-racist, queer activist, or feminist has not been faced with the charge of being a one-issue scholar, of bringing up the same question again and again, of being caught in 'identity politics?' Who has not been considered divisive, ill-mannered, boring, or threatening for bringing a persistent critique of this kind into the seminar room and the conference hall?

There is of course a very good reason for this hostility. This persistent critique interrupts business as usual in academia and in particular it interrupts the real identity politics which sits at the heart of the university. What would properly be called a disidentity politics, if such a naming did not already begin to undermine these critiques, sets itself against this real identity politics. These critiques seek to make us uncomfortable, to insert a silence, to undermine a position, to redouble our efforts, in any account, however critical, of the relationship, as Gayatri Spivak (1988) would put it, between subject and agency. Rather than a reduction of this question to identity, disidentity critiques seek the superadequation of the subject that might release agency. The aim is the production of a social individual who would have no need of this category of identity, for whom any question about it, any struggle over it, becomes archaic. We will try to demonstrate this in what follows. But it may be worth saying at the outset that what we are calling disidentity

185

critiques emerge in a very specific way historically. Struggles in the realm of social reproduction during the 1960s in the developed world, combined with national liberation struggles in the developing world, opened up the space in universities, journals, and the press for a previously disallowed and disavowed set of populations who had a distinct critique of capital embodied within them, a distinct experience of having their bodies used for the reproduction of capitalist relations in ways previously excluded from examination. For women, for gay and lesbian people, for colonial subjects, former slaves, and indigenous peoples, their experience of being both beyond the market and foundational to it meant that they brought forth a critique of identity as a kind of impossible (for them) disembodied exchange-value extracted from the use-value of their bodies. The entire enlightenment tradition for them required this kind of mature mastery of this distance of identity from body, exchange-value from use-value, which their experience denied and their unrecognized social solidarity resisted. Disidentity critique may be thought of then as the dangerous intrusion of this experience and solidarity in the academy in the subsequent 30 years. But it might also be worth understanding this critique as a provocation in the realm of social reproduction to which capital must respond, and the concomitant politicization of this realm in turn provokes what comes to be called post-structuralism, which produces a critique akin, if more disembodied, to disidentity critique.

Disidentity critiques whether in scholarship or in activism, of course, often get read as identity politics, and with this reading their ambition is similarly diminished. But when Eve Sedgwick (1990) proposes an epistemology of the closet, or when Patricia Hill Collins (1990) proposes a new standpoint theory, or when Sivanandan (1982) insists on the category of race, these gestures are not for identity but against it, against the assumption of a neutral, bounded, present, and ahistorical or historicist individual. Instead, for these critics identity is always not just identity but race, but sexuality, but gender, which is to say struggle, history, absence, interruption. So too with activists who promote separatism. Only the crudest of these are separatists; most from the Black Panthers to the radical communities of women in Italian social centers insist that the starting point for any project of the subject, and of humanity, cannot start at the end, with its assumption, but at the beginning with the differences struggling towards such an accomplishment. In this chapter we will try then to start with the differences against the commonality that the bearers of such critiques have both been urged to embrace and at the same time denied access to. But our intention is of course to find a path to some kind of enlarged solidarity in the readings that follow.

Left identity

At the same time, to orient ourselves in this discussion it is vitally important to say that this label identity politics, like the term political correctness, was invented and deployed on the Left before being picked up by the Right in the media. It is a classic piece of sectarianism drawing on the worst elements of the Left in history.[1] So it should not be surprising that the term has been thrown about in the field of management studies by critical realists, labor process theorists, and critical accounting scholars, the traditional 'Left' of management studies.

Nor should it be a surprise that among those who take identity seriously, among scholars associated with critical management studies, we find the most pernicious persistence of the real identity politics, and the marginalization and effacement of any disidentity critique. So in what follows we are going to take a look at the effects of this marginalization and effacement on discussions of work and identity in some examples of critical management studies, and we are going to point to the assumptions of identity that remain uninterrupted by these impolite, these rude, disidentity critiques.

This is not to say that mainstream business and management studies does not promote the most rigid and severe identity politics. Of course it does, and many critical management scholars have helped the critical social sciences in general to expose the ideology of the subject from its most egregious forms in neoclassical economics, to its subtler manifestations in the behavioral sciences, and indeed the humanities. And today when one picks up a textbook in business and management, in any of its fields, one often finds a nod to this critique. Critical management studies generally understands this nod as a cooptation but it is also, in our view, a perhaps unwanted nod of recognition, an unsolicited acknowledgement of a shared commitment that still remains to the real identity politics.

The reason to undertake this critique of some examples from the work and identity literature is not to point to either theoretical inadequacy or bad faith among the scholars concerned. It is not even to demonstrate how disidentity critiques might interrupt this discourse. In fact it is altogether

---

1 So too is it from parts of the Left that we find the argument that because the neo-fascist parties have learned the language of civil rights, so-called identity politics by black people, queer people, and others is exhausted. This is to say the least of a non-dialectic understanding of the recent history of disidentity critiques which have in fact forced whiteness, heteronormativity, and machismo into naming itself. It would be an odd sort of Left that quit at the first sign of victory.

more ambitious. As we have hinted in introducing Gayatri Spivak and her work, for us, disidentity critiques, far from being the one-issue politics with which they are slandered, are the way towards the issue of our day, the critique of capital. If disidentity critiques are forced to remind Marxists again and again of their own identity politics it is not because they do not have a critique of capital but because they do, and identity politics, whether in its Marxist form or in its bourgeois, prevents the pursuit of this critique. After all, the fact that difference needs to be brought out through critique is at the end of the day an absurdity given that the world is composed of differences, that they are manifestly everywhere. Surely an understanding of the compulsion we have all been forced into, a compulsion that makes us have to work at difference, despite its abundance, must be the starting place for any politics of solidarity.

Labor process

But when we turn to potential allies in this politics of solidarity where as Paul Thompson (1989: 213) quotes Hales 'all converge in a radical commitment to making the politics of the capitalist division of labor more transparent and subject to rational criticism and change,' we nonetheless feel compelled to issue these disidentity critiques. We will begin here with some examples from labor process theory as it begins to consider identity, in the work of Paul Thompson (1989). Here the problem is not the stereotype of the male, industrial worker, a stereotype that labor process theorists came to be aware of themselves, but a more basic problem – the assumption of the accomplishment of the individual. This basic assumption is at the heart of the real identity politics, and it persists even when 'identity' at work is called into question by these theorists.

Here is how it operates in Paul Thompson's canonical book, *The Nature of Work* (1989). In some ways it is unfair to single out Thompson given how widespread this real identity politics is in debates about the labor process and worker consciousness and identity in the 1980s. This book was more than a survey and evaluation of the labor process literature. It was also admirable for its political ambition. His conclusion argued, in the face of the pessimism of the early 1980s, that new strategies would have to be found to link the politics of the workplace with a broader politics of the state and avoid the all too common reduction of politics into either economism or idealism.

Nonetheless, his book illustrates this identity politics well. In the penultimate chapter on 'The Other Division Labour', Thompson considers the way women face both capitalism and patriarchy and surveys the debates of his time, although he excludes any consideration of Third World women and women of color, making only brief mention of racial hierarchy among women in the workplace. In this chapter workers have a gender, even if an assumed and accessible and fixed one, but only in this chapter. The consideration of this special case concluded, Thompson returns to the figure of the generic worker. It is his task on his return to this worker to understand his consciousness both in what Michael Burawoy (1982) called relations in production as well as in relations of production. And yet by fixing the position of women in a special chapter, he also fixes the identity of his worker in all the other chapters; and any consideration of class-in-itself and class-for-itself, a theme of the concluding chapter, remains hopelessly abstracted. The whiteness (or otherwise) of these workers, their masculinity (or otherwise), their heteronormativity (or otherwise), their ethnicity (or otherwise), these are absent from a discussion where a certain notion of the subject – whose accomplishment as individual depends on the absence of these questions – obtains. These are not additional sociological categories but critiques of the assumed sociological categories with which Thompson operates. The point is that an inclusion of such challenges to the assumption of accomplished identity might have prevented Thompson's identity politics from blocking the very strategies for which he calls.

Of course despite its merits, the reader might counter that labor process theory is an easy target in this regard and critiques of labor process theory in management studies, and particularly in what would come to be called critical management studies, often relied on its blindness to worker creativity, culture, and resistance, something even Thompson acknowledges. And yet these critiques of labor process theory did not in fact escape this identity politics. Indeed, identity politics became even more firmly embedded in this scholarship.

Identity construction

Take for example a major article by Mats Alvesson and Hugh Willmott on identity and work in a 2002 issue of the *Journal of Management Studies*. Almost 20 years between these pieces of scholarship have seen the surfacing of identity and its mainstreaming, as their extensive list of references makes clear. No longer hidden in the generic worker or relegated to a special chapter, identity emerges in this paper as the key term in understanding power in the workplace, as the labor process tends to be called today.

Alvesson and Willmott focus on identity work as it is 'located in the regulation of identity within the contemporary, post Fordist context.' They argue for 'a conception of micro-emancipatory possibilities,' and they urge students of organization theory to put identity regulation at the heart of their considerations. They commend those who understand organizations as 'fluid, unstable and reflexive,' where identity work, self-identity, and identity regulation come together. This kind of organization, they conclude, makes both micro-emancipation and 'new forms of subordination and oppression' possible, according to the authors (2002: 15).

From what position is it possible to achieve such a generic set of conclusions about the organization and regulation today? As Gayatri Spivak (1988) showed us 20 years earlier in her discussion of a conversation between Michel Foucault and Gilles Deleuze, there are at least three moves at work here in Alvesson and Willmott's (2002) article that see them reinstating fixed identity despite themselves. In Spivak's famous article she argues that Foucault and Deleuze reconstitute the privilege of the intellectual precisely through its disavowal. This is achieved by way of the elision of the two meanings of representation. On the one hand Foucault and Deleuze agree that what Spivak will call the subaltern should not, and need not, be represented by intellectuals in the political sense. The subaltern according to Foucault and Deleuze know their own interests and can speak for themselves. On the other hand, this very statement remains a representation in the other sense of the word, a claim to know the subaltern well enough to portray them as capable of identifying their own interests. What Spivak astutely notes, as a literary critic, is that the elision, or full separation, of these two senses of representation takes away the politics, and as she puts it, the ideology of representation as a constant question of responsibility in portraying others and an insistent awareness of the misfit between that portrait and the object. Her reading of Marx's *Eighteenth Brumaire* is a lesson in this misfit of interests rather than their easy alignment. But it is also a correction to a second assumption in the conversation between Foucault and Deleuze. Their emphasis on power and desire, so much today in organization theory what Alvin Gouldner used to call a background assumption, presupposes according to Spivak an alignment between subject and agent where the unity of desire or the liquidity of power makes it possible to imagine that the subaltern knows her interests. Spivak uses Marx's analysis of a profound disjuncture of class positions among the French small-holding peasants to call into question any such undivided concept of interest, any such transparency unmediated by ideology. Finally this allows Spivak to ask how the rise of the undoubtedly important conceptions of desire and power in Deleuze and Foucault can lead so ironically to this fixing of both the identity of the intellectual and of the subaltern, and she suggests, again very aptly for our present reading, that to complete this reconstitution of the subject, the regime of what we might today call immaterial, post-fordist labor has to be taken for a generalized global condition, effacing the international division of labor. This effacement permits the 'reestablishing' of 'the subject of socialized capital' (1988: 272), a subject that takes its own effects as universal. In the end, Deleuze and Foucault have it both ways in their identity politics. They speak of those who struggle, but disavow this as speech. They abstract from their place in capitalism, but disavow the constitutive contradiction of abstraction. They try to dissolve the subject position as if ideology were not materially resistant to reduction, as if ideology held together this position rather than constituted it. In her words, 'they reintroduce the constitutive on at least two levels: the Subject of desire and power as an irreducible methodological presupposition; and the self-proximate, if not self-identical, subject of the oppressed' (1988: 279).

Disavowals

We can see the high costs of these moves in this article by Alvesson and Willmott. These authors too consider 'cultural-ideological modes of control' as 'broad-brush categories' (2002: 8) and offer instead 'empirical analysis of identity regulation' where nine modes of 'organizing practices address the actor, the other, motives, values, expertise, group membership, hierarchical location, rules of the game, the wider context, etc.' (2002: 11). This examination of forms of identity regulation is one of two goals in the paper. The other is to show how this regulation is 'balanced with other elements of life history forged by a capacity reflexively to accomplish life projects out of various sources of influence and inspiration' (2002: 4).

Yet, in this article we find the trappings of the disavowal at the heart of the conversation between Deleuze and Foucault. Ideology is rejected in favor of a concern with how desire works in regulation and how power works in the accomplishment of 'life projects.' We find also the 'subject of socialized capitalism' renewed as an identity politics, as for instance in the un-reflexive use of employee rather than worker or in the lack of attention to language as means of production. The worker, workplace, regulatory form, and intellectual are all strangely generic here. Though the terms 'post-fordism' and 'advanced capitalist economies' are both mentioned, there is no attempt to show that the coming together or breaking apart of this worker, workplace, regulation, or intellectual as identity requiring the non-identity of some other, elsewhere. This is not the same as saying the other might be 'used' in regulation. But rather to suggest that regulation itself is brought into being by this absent other. Nor does this faith in the ability of these generic workers to construct life projects produce anything like Deleuze and Foucault's intentional disavowal as intellectuals. Alvesson and Willmott make no mention of their relations to the generic employees they represent. Finally, these authors become content with precisely that trap Spivak suggested Foucault and Deleuze set for themselves. Without a critique of ideology to both separate subject and agent and link the micrological with the macrological, politics becomes mired in a micrological affirmation of identity, what Alvesson and Willmott call 'micro-emancipation.' It is perhaps enough here to ask who has the privilege to be content with such a micro-politics where a quasi-autonomy of the subject might arise. Disidentity politics, it is worth reminding ourselves, is so often taken to be strident precisely because it cannot ever allow itself this position, cannot ever allow itself this luxury, cannot ever imagine a complacency based on this kind of accomplished identity, and at its best, would not wish to.

Advances

Like labor process theory, the work of Hugh Willmott and Mats Alvesson, so full of political compromise, might be said to be an easy target. Much of the promising scholarship of the 1990s on work and identity, such as Paul Du Gay's *Consumption and Identity at Work* (1996) or Catherine Casey's *Work, Self and Society* (1995) or Roy Jacques's *Manufacturing the Employee* (1996), seemed to offer more than this capitulation through micro-emancipation – the very suggestion that we should settle for this strategy is insulting to those who fought and died for emancipation, discounting their achievements, and denying their ability to perceive the contradictions of emancipation. But neither Du Gay nor Casey nor Jacques locate any of these possibilities in this history of emancipation either. Instead, seeing possibilities only in what is happening to the generic worker in the face of the blurring of consumption and production, or of a new corporate culture, or the forgotten history of this category. Their work is important, but it starts as if no one has even been in the position before, nor do they pay much attention to who remains outside of this position. As much as they are sensitive to identity in their context, they remain identitarians structurally.

We introduce these three authors and their books not to summarize all the scholarship on work and identity, nor even to emblemize all of this scholarship, but because we regard these as examples of good books, by good scholars, that nonetheless need to be subjected to a disidentity critique; and here it is necessary to say something else about this critique in order that it does not appear that our purpose is to dismiss all efforts in the field of business and management studies. Disidentity critique might also be understood as the anticipation and development of what Randy Martin (2001) explains as the Marxist moment of post-structuralist thought, the moment when language, argument, and concepts are themselves recognized as circulating commodities invested with meanings that themselves issue from the social relations of capital, even as they invest those relations with new dimensions, even new possibilities. Disidentity critiques aim at the subject of language, argument, and concepts that shield a recognition of the material and ideological quality of these commodities. In other words, so long as capital exists, critique must follow it into every word, sentence, and statement of intent or fact. We say anticipated because of course the post-structuralist death of the subject is only possible where the subject was said to exist, and was not possible in the colonized, enslaved, conquered world, nor the patriarchal household. We say developed because rather than lapse into 'micro-emancipation' at the death of the subject, disidentity critiques insist that, as Fred Jameson says, 'it is a mistake to assimilate this view of theory to relativism or skepticism (leading fatally to nihilism and intellectual paralysis); on the contrary, the struggle for the "rectification" of wording is a well-nigh interminable process, which perpetually generates new problems.' (2002: 1).

If one wants to imagine Spivak's superadequation, one could do worse than start with the notion of a surplus of new problems generating a surplus of new possibilities for agency after subjectivity. And to this end, we will read Du Gay, Casey, and Jacques for what more might be made of them, starting with Du Gay. Du Gay ends on a note of pessimism, seeing something similar in the fate of identity subjected to new kinds of production relations when he writes that boundary crossing is advocated by both the 'cultural Left' and the new Right with their advocacy of entrepreneurship of the self, a discourse Du Gay dissects so well in this book (1996). Du Gay is on to something important here. But he needs to redouble his efforts here, not conclude that his critique of identity has led to a distressing conclusion – because this boundary crossing implies distinct territories. One of the lessons of post-colonial critique is that identity is not just other, not another country, but rather often a shadow, a mimic, a virtuality for post-colonial populations. And this in turn is a way to scope the important critique of capital as one shadowed by communism, an immanent critique that uses capital's efforts at self-sameness against it, in favor of the difference of communism. In this kind of disidentity critique, the closeness of certain kinds of critical efforts on the cultural Left is not a sign of weakness, vulnerability, or capitulation to the entrepreneurship of the Right but a tracing of the possibilities beyond entrepreneurship called into being by entrepreneurships efforts at realizing itself, impossibly.

Corporate identities

Catherine Casey (1995) also presents us with the possibility of exceeding her critique. She details the traps of what she calls a new culture of productionism. But she concludes that this culture 'thwarts . . . the conditions for self-transformation that will herald new forms of social life that are truly beyond industrialism' (1995: 196). Yet what remains of an identity politics in her analysis is precisely the place to challenge this industrialism and begin a transformation that critiques this new corporate culture – because she describes this corporate culture as one that draws on a sense of community and assembles a new kind of family within the corporate frame. She decries this invasion by corporate forces of these realms; but were these realms historically just in opposition to industrialism or also complicit with it? Is the implicit nostalgia for family or community not the place for us to redouble our disidentity critique?

Casey (1995: 189) critiques this corporate culture as 'a simulation of a caring, purposeful, related family of nostalgic, pre-industrial myth. It provides a simulated community that is manufactured for a vital function of production. It is the reification of the displaced hope and desire of a diminishing, increasingly colonized self – a self that in its emptying is re-filled and re-stored with a replica of religious virtuosity and for the more pathologically troubled self, the comfort of a resurgent narcissism.' This is a powerful critique, well wrought. Her efforts to think about how this culture of self-denial through productivity mixes with the culture of self-permission in consumption is very useful. But perhaps her sense of Max Weber, as having been interested in a singular disenchanted wrought by capitalism now displaced, is as she says, by this latest corporate culture, allowing for a kind of identity politics to creep back in. A disidentity critique would want to recognize disenchantment itself as an ongoing collective critique rather than a single historical tragedy. The dialectical process of disenchantment of modes of community and forms of family would draw on the way communities exclude foreigners from within and without, and on the way families distribute work and sex rights. Casey's work could then lead us, like Du Gay's might, to ask what kinds of superadequation of the subject can come from critiquing not just its simulation but the origins such simulation draw upon and reveal.

Social obstruction

Jacques's book is the most problematic. It is a deeply conservative book, despite its trappings. In this book, to paraphrase E. P. Thompson (1975), the employee is *not* present at his own birth. Indeed with Jacques, despite how the field of management and organization studies has advanced, much of which is on display in Jacques's book, we are strangely enough back to the identity politics lurking in Paul Thompson's book.

The argument in this book is that the employee is a product of the American Dream, which itself comes out of Puritan and Quaker settler colonies in the American territories. Jacques suggests this ethos survives industrialization and its conflicts by way of management, a management that comes into being against the background of the rise of finance capital, the social sciences, and welfare work. Industrial knowledge succeeded the common sense of the craftsman, and the consumer replaced the yeoman. This is to simplify Jacques's sweeping summaries of American history. But what it does not simplify is the generic quality of the worker at the center of this history. Like Thompson's worker has only his origins in the class struggle, Jacques's employee has only his origins in the settler colonies. Despite some genuflections to feminism, this employee is unmarked by ethnicity, race, sexuality, or gender for most of the account. This produces an employee who is unsurprisingly malleable at the hands of Jacques's highly structuralist and elite view of their construction. (His chief historians for instance seem to be Hofstader and Boorstin – class apologists of the finest order.) Jacques manages to hide this idea politics behind a story of the construction of identity, but it is as a tautological story.

Most obviously, this American dream comes into being repeatedly, as Jacques notes, against other kinds of dreams, more collective, inclusive, and spiritual than the one Jacques privileges. A very different history of the employee would have been told by a theorist versed in whiteness studies, or one who grasped the centrality of nativism and anti-communism to the moment of industrialization, or sexuality and anti-communism after the Second World War. But it would have to be a theorist who did not mask his identity politics with social constructionism, and instead regarded the problem of the subject and its agency among slaves, immigrants, women, queer people, and others marginal to his account, as central, as, indeed, they were to forcing the proper American dream of Jacques's account into its present protective and restrictive covenant.

Reflexivity

One would think this might be the moment to speak of the reflexive, but such a turn cannot be an excuse to cease the disidentity critique. The reflexive turn in business and management found in Hardy and Clegg (1997), for instance, is not a disidentity turn, but rather its opposite, securing identity politics by another means. Here, access to the self is unproblematic, in the way Foucault and Deleueze assume of the subaltern – with the same result that subject and agent seem to match and the point of disidentity, or the critique of the present absence of identity, is thoroughly misunderstood as a psycho-sociological problem. When Patricia Hill Collins (1990) uses reflexivity, it is to call into question the possibility of achieving the position of scholar as subject, and it is designed to ask who has the power and the right not to speak of themselves, or equally and crucially in the case of Hardy, Phillips, and Clegg, to speak of themselves, much less of a community of reflexive selves (2001). This ability to look upon the possession of oneself and evaluate this self-possession requires both a separation from the body and a proprietary relationship to it. Hill Collins's work stands sharply against this kind of self-possessive turn in Hardy, Phillips, and Clegg, where research is asked to account for itself and, by extension, its owners.

Nor is this proprietary relationship to one's subjectivity undermined by the evaluation of the relationship itself. A notion of working upon the well-tempered self (Miller 1993), or perhaps we should say in this context the value-added self, perhaps presupposes even more certainly the measurement of that self, its potential sale, and ultimately an obfuscation of the fact that the body will accompany the purchase of labor-power, and will remain an immeasurable resistance no matter how much self-reflection is applied (Virno 2007). In short, there is no getting away from disidentity critiques through reflexivity, but this ought to be welcomed instead of avoided.

What disidentity critiques, coming from an anti-racist, feminist, or queer perspective, challenge is the very idea of building a habitable self under capitalism. Such a project must always be at the expense of others. Any scholar who attempts such a construction at the micro-level without an attendant critique of capital, just as any scholar attempting a critique of capital without an attendant reconstruction of the social individual, will continue to participate in that very identity politics that has cost others so much. Disidentity critiques in management and organization studies are thus all too rare, given that work of most scholars in the field fall into one of the two categories above.

References

Alvesson, M. and Willmott, H. (2002) 'Identity regulation as organizational control: producing the appropriate individual'. *Journal of Management Studies* July 2002, 39(5): 619–644.

Burawoy, M. (1982) *Manufacturing Consent: Changes in the Labour Process Under Monopoly Capitalism.* Chicago: The University of Chicago Press.

Casey, C. (1995) *Work, Self and Society: After Industrialism.* London: Routledge.

Du Gay, P. (1996) *Consumption and Identity at Work.* London: Sage Publications.

Hardy, C. and Clegg, S. (1997) 'Relativity without relativism: reflexivity in post-paradigm organization studies'. *British Journal of Management* 8(Supplement 1): 5–17.

Hardy, C., Phillips, N., and Clegg, S. (2001) 'Reflexivity in organization and management theory: a study of the production of the research subject'. *Human Relations* 54(5): 531–560.

Hill Collins, P. (1990) *Black Feminist Thought: Knowledge, Consciousness, and the Politics of Empowerment.* Boston: Unwin Hyman.

Jacques, R. (1996) *Manufacturing the Employee: Management Knowledge from the 19th to 21st Centuries.* London: Sage Publications.

Jameson, F. (2002) *A Singular Modernity: essay on the ontology of the present.* London: Verso.

Martin, R. (2001) *On Your Marx: Relinking Socialism and the Left.* Minneapolis: University of Minnesota Press.

Miller, T. (1993) *The Well-tempered Self: Citizenship, Culture and the Postmodern Subject.* Baltimore: Johns Hopkins University Press.

Munoz, E. J. (1998) *Disidentifications: Queers of Color and the Performance of Politics.* Minneapolis: University of Minnesota Press.

Sedgwick. E. (1990) *Epistemology of the Closet.* Berkeley: University of California Press.

Sivanandan, A. (1982) *A Different Hunger: Writings on Black Resistance.* London: Pluto Press.

Spivak, G. C. (1988) 'Can the subaltern speak?' In Nelson, C. and Grossberg, L. (eds) *Marxism and the Interpretation of Culture.* Urbana, IL: University of Illinois Press.

Thompson, P. (1989) *The Nature of Work: An Introduction to the Debates on the Labour Process.* London: Palgrave.

Thompson, E. P. (1975) *The Making of English Working Class.* New York: Penguin Books.

Virno, P. (2007) Recording the Present: Essay on Historical Time translated from the Italian by Nate Holdren for Generation Online, http://www.generation-online.org/p/fpvirno11.htm

part 2
Methods

11

Large scale identity research: the potential of causal cognitive mapping

Gail P. Clarkson

Introduction

Over the past 30 years there has been a huge growth in the field of managerial and organizational cognition (MOC from herein), as scholars increasingly recognized that in order to understand individual and organizational behavior a knowledge of participants' relevant cognitions is required (e.g. Bougon, Weick and Binkhorst 1977, Eden and Spender 1998, Huff 1990a, Meindl, Stubbart and Porac 1996, Porac, Thomas and Baden-Fuller 1989, Walsh 1995). At the risk of over simplification, MOC research can be broken down into two branches, each with their own distinctive features (see Lant and Shapira 2001). The first, the computational approach, examines how managers and other organizational members *process information*. The second, and the focus of this chapter, is the interpretive approach, which investigates how *meaning* is created around information in a social context.

A key concept supporting recent MOC research from the interpretive perspective has arisen from Weick's work regarding sensemaking and the interrelated notion of the enacted environment (see, for example, Weick 1979, 1995, 2001). The term 'enactment' is used to mean that in organizational life people often produce part of the environment they face. In other words, by doing something that produces some kind of outcome, constraints are then placed upon what that person does next (Weick 1979: 130). The multifaceted concept of sensemaking is grounded in identity construction and Weick (1995: 20) succinctly summarizes the complex, on-going, two-way process of identity formation:

> Depending on who I am, my definition of what is "out there" will also change. Whenever I define self, I define "it", but to define it is also to define self. Once

201

I know who I am then I know what is out there. But the direction of causality flows just as often from the situation to a definition of self as it does the other way.

Researchers in MOC have investigated various aspects of identity, such as top management team members' perceptions of identity and image under conditions of change (Gioia and Thomas 1996), and the consensual identity and causal beliefs constructed by top managers (Porac *et al.* 1989) and other organizational members (Hodgkinson 2005) to make sense of transactions within their competitive environment. In a study of the Scottish knitwear industry, Porac *et al.* (1989) discovered that beliefs about organizational identity to be central to the organizations that they studied. Furthermore, to make sense of their environment firms collectively set themselves apart as distinct from others who made sweaters and then individually differentiated among themselves, thus enabling members to define the competitive space and their place in it. This activity subsequently guided strategic choices (enactment) (see also Peteraf and Shanley 1997). In all, from an interpretive perspective, people are seen to be shaped by, and to shape, their environment.

In parallel, researchers of social identity have paid increasing attention to cognition. Turner (2001: xiii) points out that organizations are not merely 'stimulus settings' which constrain or facilitate behavior from outside, and change what we do, but that they also shape our cognitively represented self, changing our subjective experience of who we are and the psychological meaning of the environment. In particular, Ashforth and Mael's (1989) work on the Social Identity Approach focused on the cognitive dimension of identity. Moreover, a considerable body of theory and evidence (reviewed in Haslam and Ellemers 2005) proposes that identification with particular groups in the workplace is much more than a product of contextual variables, with different features of the same social identity coming to define the self-category in different situations. Rather, identities in the workplace, as in other settings, are *actively* managed through the adoption of strategies that maintain a distinctive self-concept and enhance self-esteem (see also Dukerich, Golden and Shortell 2002, Dutton, Dukerich and Harquail 1994).

A theoretically interesting and practically challenging issue in identity research concerns the ways people are encouraged to increase or reduce their identification with the organization (Haslam and Ellemers 2005). Van Dick (2004) suggests it could be argued that growing globalization and practices such as organizational alliances that cross national boundaries, international mergers and outsourcing require a *greater* degree of psychological attachment and social identification for both the individual's well-being and the success of the organization. There is some empirical support for this (Wiesenfeld,

Raghuram and Garud 2001), but building a strong evidence base requires further work whereby individually meaningful data is collected from the same participant over time and/or from multiple participants and/or at multiple levels of analysis.

Drawing upon institutional theory (DiMaggio and Powell 1991, Scott 2001), it can be seen that similar data-intensive, large-scale explorations are needed in order to address key questions concerning the nature and extent of macro-influences (e.g. trade associations, trade unions and the state) upon collective and individual identities and, in parallel, how group members *shape* macro-level identities. Clearly, disentangling the myriad influences from multiple sources of identity on, and active management of, the individual's (or group) self-concept in the global workplace (and the influences that this has on shaping organizational identities) poses a range of methodological dilemmas.

As revealed in the MOC literature, causal cognitive mapping has been used as a potentially powerful means of representing actors' belief systems (e.g. Bougon *et al.* 1977, Fahey and Narayanan 1989, Markóczy 2001). These appear to hold considerable promise for social identity research and, indeed, as will be seen later in this chapter where quite limited dimensions of just three maps are examined, it is possible to demonstrate deep insights into the socio-cognitive dynamics with very small-scale studies. However, it is apparent that many issues related to the current cognitive agenda in the field of identity can be subjected to adequate empirical scrutiny only by use of relatively large-scale data. While it is clearly inappropriate to capture data that is, in reality, not actually meaningful to participants, it is also clearly less than helpful to acquire a mass of potentially non-comparable material, and this chapter has a particular focus upon causal cognitive mapping elicitation procedures that ultimately hold maximum potential in the context of large scale studies.

The chapter is organized in five principal sections. The first section places causal cognitive mapping in the wider cognitive mapping context. In the second section, an overview of causal cognitive mapping methods is presented and a number of issues concerning knowledge elicitation that researchers need to take into account, if they are to make well-informed mapping choices, are highlighted. One empirical study, set in the context of the call-center front line, is analysed in the third section. This investigation of individual perceptions of personal and organizational identity was undertaken as one component of a larger agenda. It is utilized in this chapter not only to draw upon three illustrative examples of individual causal cognitive maps but also as a means by which to demonstrate the key decisions which need to made in developing a study utilizing causal cognitive mapping techniques. Next, in the fourth section, the issues of causal cognitive map comparisons are discussed and, in the fifth section, the chapter concludes by offering reflections of the proposed method and areas for future development of casual cognitive mapping.

Causal cognitive mapping in context

As adopted in the MOC literature, a wide range of cognitive mapping techniques has been applied in an effort to capture the essence of how people think, how they understand their world, and their belief systems (for comprehensive reviews, see, for example, Hodgkinson and Sparrow 2002, Huff 1990a, Sparrow 1998, Walsh 1995). The diversity of mapping methods employed results partly from the variety of potential relationships between constructs within the map, which could, for example, denote simple connotative relationships (A reminds me of B), relative values (A is more important than B) or causal linkages (A exerts a causal influence on B). The choice of mapping method also depends on whether the model of cognition is seen to be relatively simple, where simple counting and weighting of words in a text might be acceptable, or rather more complex, requiring methods which may involve considerable interpretation on the part of the researcher. Huff (1990b) describes and summarizes the continuum of mapping choices, from simple to complex, under five main headings (noting that there is some degree of overlap between these categories). These are maps that (1) assess attention, association and the importance of concepts (e.g. Bowman 1984), (2) show dimensions of categories and cognitive taxonomies (e.g. Hodgkinson and Johnson 1994), (3) reveal understanding of influence, causality and system dynamics (e.g. Bougon *et al.* 1977), (4) attempt to show the logic behind conclusions and decisions to act, including depictions of paths of past evaluations and/or future strategic options (e.g. Newell and Simon 1972), and those which (5) seek to explore value and meaning systems by inferring links between linguistic patterns and the underlying schemas and perceptual codes (e.g. Fiske and Linville 1980).

Causal cognitive mapping (Huff's third category) is currently the most popular form of mapping. Axelrod (1976) developed a cause mapping method used in political science. The rationale here being that when a map is pictured in graph form it is then relatively easy to see how each of the constructs and causal relationships relate to each other and the overall structure of a particular domain as perceived by an individual. Thus, cause maps cope with dynamics and encourage a holistic synthesis of an actor's view of the world (Bougon 1983, Weber and Manning 2001). Moreover, as the individual essentially explains the current situation by reference to previous events and in terms of future expectations, they focus on action (Huff 1990b), and the direct links to action implicit within this approach render it a powerful method, applicable across a wide range of contexts. By opening up a more dynamic conception of identity formation and change in the global workplace, this form of mapping appears to hold considerable potential for many aspects of identity research.

An overview of causal cognitive mapping methods

Despite their widespread popularity, there is currently no agreement concerning the most appropriate way to elicit actors' causal belief systems. Methods of data elicitation for causal mapping construction range from post hoc analysis of data, in the form of analysis of text (Barr, Stimpert and Huff 1992, Fletcher and Huff 1990) or individual interviews (Calori, Johnson and Sarnin 1992, Jenkins and Johnson 1997), to the elicitation of maps in situ (Markóczy 2001, Markóczy and Goldberg 1995), sometimes prescriptively, as a basis for intervention through 'action research' (Cropper, Eden and Ackermann 1990, Eden and Ackermann 1998). As with other research methods, fundamental epistemological beliefs, in particular the acceptable level of researcher intrusion, dominate issues of validity and reliability.

Axelrod (1976) considered individual maps separately to trace the antecedents of some event or policy, but mapping choices become more complex when the research context requires almost any form of mapping comparison. There is no easy solution to resolve the dilemma between the requirements of allowing the natural-language form of the study participants (thereby ensuring that the research tasks are meaningful) and ensuring comparability of data (within or between participants). While a detailed discussion of the pros and cons of different mapping choices are, of necessity, beyond the scope of this chapter, the comparative overview which follows provides the main features which need to be taken into consideration (for further details of key decisions influencing mapping choices see, for example, Hodgkinson and Clarkson 2005, Jenkins 1998).

Axelrod's preferred stance was that cognitive maps are derived from documentary evidence, as, while potentially problematic in terms of issues of sincerity, this form of mapping is non-intrusive and not likely to influence thought process. However, the data contained within such documentary sources is often only peripherally relevant to the investigator's purpose. For those researchers investigating a wider pool of organizational members than those who occupy top-tier positions, the potential of documentary evidence is particularly limited. For example, in many studies of work identities there are unlikely to be appropriate company documentation from which it would be possible to ascertain the views of those occupying formally non-strategic roles. Moreover, the fact that secondary source documents such as letters to shareholders are, by definition, prepared for particular audiences renders it difficult (if not impossible) for the researcher to ascertain the extent to which they genuinely reflect the originator's perceptions or are a deliberate attempt to influence the perceptions of the stakeholders to whom they were initially directed.[1] Using such documentation, the researcher must also face the difficult question as to how the maps so derived are to be coded and subsequently validated.

Axelrod suggests other forms of elicitation may also prove beneficial, for example interviews have the 'advantage of allowing the researcher to interact actively with the source of his data' (1976: 8). Similarly, Huff and Fletcher (1990) balance the advantages gained by using documentary evidence against the subtleties available to the researcher who interacts directly with the subject. Interactive methods may, under conditions ensuring confidentiality, have the capacity to reveal complex relationships (Huff 1990b), but they are also associated with people imposing more order on recollected events (Schwenk 1985) or seeing links once asked questions (Huff and Fletcher 1990), which in the context of different epistemologies is considered to be more or less acceptable. For example, in the extremely labor-intensive Self-Q [questioning] Technique (Bougon 1983, Bougon, Baird, Komocar and Ross 1990) participants both devise and answer questions, the aim being not to mention any concept, 'lest they become "planted" in the interviewee's mind' (Bougon 1983: 182). However, as with maps derived from secondary sources, interview transcripts generated in narrative form by the researcher require what can be extremely labor-intensive and problematic post hoc coding and validation (e.g. Calori *et al.* 1992, Jenkins and Johnson 1997). Nomothetic techniques, which entail the use of standardized lists of constructs supplied by the researcher, typically in the form of highly structured questionnaires, are particularly helpful in respect of comparative analysis (e.g. Roberts 1976,

---

1 Such methods could provide potential benefit for researchers of corporate identity, for whom the recipients of identity messages are external stakeholders or audiences who require persuasion (e.g. Christensen and Cheney 2000).

Swan 1995), but are criticized on the grounds that this might yield less salient data (Eden, Ackermann and Cropper 1992).

Markóczy and Goldberg (1995) developed a middle ground or 'hybrid' approach to causal cognitive mapping. Using this procedure, a wide pool of potentially salient constructs is developed prior to the causal mapping procedure. This common pool is presented to all participants, who select a fixed number of personally meaningful constructs to form the basic content of their map. Each participant then assesses the influence of each of her/his chosen constructs in a pairwise manner, which bypasses potentially problematic coding procedures, and supports subsequent map comparisons. Advocates of selection from a construct pool (e.g. Hodgkinson and Sparrow 2002, Markóczy 1997, 2001, Markóczy and Goldberg 1995) emphasize analysis and conclude these techniques are particularly helpful for comparative measures, the idea being that systematic elicitation of beliefs lays the ground for systematic comparison and analysis.

At this juncture, it is important to reiterate that the question as to what constitutes the most appropriate methodological choices can only be answered by carefully considering the precise nature of the inquiry being undertaken and the context in which the investigation is taking place. However, as revealed in the illustrative study presented in the next section, the hybrid method has particular utility in large-scale causal mapping, and recent developments in computer software have made this type of approach technically feasible.

Illustration of causal cognitive mapping process

Study context

The call-center organization reflects a mass production approach to customer service and the sector employs a large and growing number of the global workforce (Batt 2002). While call-center organizations are not uniform, their working practices are typically viewed as being particularly controlled and a source of stress. Consequently, it is perhaps unsurprising that the sector has attracted largely adverse media attention, with front-line workers acquiring a reputation as white-collar production lines, and call centers the new 'sweatshops' (Garrett, Jacques and Wynne 2002). Belt, Richardson and Webster (2000) reported the concerns of workers regarding the bad image attached to working in the sector, to the extent that one agent admitted to lying to people on occasion when asked about her job because if you work in a call center, people assume you 'aren't very bright' (p. 376).

The study was undertaken as a first step for gaining understanding of the pathways through which reality is socially constructed and legitimated for organizational front-line workers, more generally. It concerned an investigation of the dominant institutional and individual influences that feature in contact-sector front-line workers' cognitive maps of their work domain, including individual perceptions of organizational and personal identities. The study questions posed demanded large-scale data sets, and the maps of 200 individuals were constructed. These came from five contrasting sites, which were selected with a view to being representative of the contemporary call-center sector.

Mapping method

Data was collected using a variant of the Markóczy and Goldberg (1995) form of causal mapping, supported by Cognizer™ (Clarkson and Hodgkinson 2005), which is a software package designed to meet the requirements of researchers looking to elicit and compare large numbers of maps (on a longitudinal or cross-sectional basis). As noted in the above section, the first step in this procedure entailed developing a wide pool of constructs prior to the mapping procedure. Construct pools vary considerably in their formation, for example Jenkins and Johnson (1997) advocate development via a series of exploratory interviews, the transcripts of which are then coded off-site. This form of construct pool development may be entirely appropriate where the investigation concerns very localized and specific issues but rather less so in contexts where the pool is required to cover a broader domain, as in the illustrative investigation. Nevertheless, and however derived, the crucial issue to be addressed is that ultimately the pool should be representative of a particular domain for the participant sample involved in the mapping exercise.

The study pool was constructed on the basis of a detailed review of a diverse range of literatures from the fields of MOC (e.g. Eden and Spender 1998, Hodgkinson and Sparrow 2002), industrial, work and organizational psychology (e.g. Parker and Wall 1998, Warr 1994) and specialist call-center literature drawn from practitioner and academic sources (e.g. Garrett *et al.* 2002, Holman 2002). The construct language was refined during the pilot study, which involved opportunistic sampling of a variety of personnel with call-center experience and fieldwork carried out in one large call center. The pool was balanced in terms of five in each of eleven broad topic areas/categories (including 'employment conditions', 'management and employee relationships' and 'identity'). The 'identity' category included five potentially salient constructs, which ranged from media portrayal of the sector overall ('sweatshop image') through to individual identification with team colleagues ('identify with team').

The pool ultimately comprised 55 constructs, that is broad enough to provide participants with real choices but not overly lengthy and therefore unlikely to cause difficulties in the selection process (see Markóczy and Goldberg 1995). To minimize bias, the construct pool was individually randomized for each participant. Each identified those they considered pertinent in their job roles and the wider context in which they were situated. The final participant choice was restricted to a maximum of 13 constructs (with an ideal range of 10-12). This figure was based on a combination of the recommendations of Markóczy and Goldberg (1995) (who set a maximum of 10 constructs) together with personal experience. The individual then systematically considered the causal influences between constructs on a pairwise basis. Systematically considering all pairwise effects should significantly diminish the possibility that important effects are omitted (Hart 1976), and is also helpful in overcoming the potential problem of coding accidents, which tend to be common with cause maps, because of the problematic nature of determining the interviewee's view about what is cause and what is effect (Eden *et al.* 1992).

If the participant believed there was no influence between an individual pair of constructs, the default option of zero applied. When a participant indicated that there was a relationship, they were further instructed to consider the extent to which they believed the constructs in question were causally related to one another using the scale -3, -2, -1, 1, 2, 3, where -3 denotes a strong perceived negative causal relationship and $+3$ denotes a strong perceived positive causal relationship. (Simpler versions do not permit differential weighting.) From Figure 11.1 it can be seen that this front-line worker (Participant A) reports that the call-center 'sweatshop image' is personally salient (see top left-hand quadrant of the map). As one construct in a network, 'sweatshop image' is interconnected to other constructs by a series of arrow-headed pathways, terminating in each case on what the participant reports to be the dependent variable. Thus, for example, as perceived by this participant, the call-center 'sweatshop image' increases moderately (2) the call-center 'turnover [attrition] levels' (top right quadrant).

The salience of a given construct is not only determined by its presence or absence within a map, but also by the strength of its relationships with

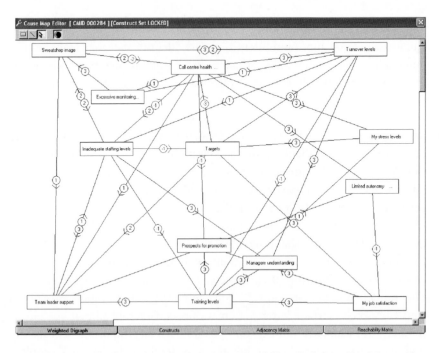

Figure 11.1 An illustrative cause map in weighted digraph format (Participant A)

the other constructs. Outdegrees indicate the extent to which a particular construct exerts a direct or indirect causal influence on another construct, while indegrees are indicators of the extent to which a construct is directly/or indirectly influenced by another construct. Generally, the greater the number of outdegrees emanating from and indegrees into a given construct, the more important (or salient) that construct is considered to be within the map (Axelrod 1976, Weick and Bougon 1986). Thus, Participant A perceives there to be several causal relationships between the sector's 'sweatshop image' and other constructs identified to be of salience. This image is influenced by four constructs (it is strongly increased by 'turnover levels' and 'excessive monitoring' and moderately increased by 'call-center health and well-being' and 'inadequate staffing levels'). In the view of this participant, the 'sweatshop image' of the call-center sector also exerts influence on four constructs (slightly increasing 'team leader support', moderately increasing 'turnover levels' and 'inadequate staffing levels' and moderately decreasing 'call-center health and well-being').

As the final step of the mapping procedure, participants immediately viewed their elicited cause map in the form of a weighted digraph (Figures 11.1, 11.2 and 11.3) for potential editing (adding or clearing links and changing the magnitude of effect) until the participant was satisfied with her/his cause map. In an attempt to ensure that participants do not try to rationalize their maps at this point, some researchers do not permit editing after the pairwise procedure (Markóczy and Goldberg 1995). Again, this kind of decision needs to be made within each specific study context and needs to contemplate whether the study employs elicit and construct causal cognitive maps solely using methods of visual representation (see, in particular, the work of Eden and his colleagues, e.g. Eden 1992, Eden *et al.* 1992). However, while a visual mode of map elicitation may be appropriate in the context of smaller-scale, idiographic applications and intensive interventions, it is considerably less useful in the context of larger-scale, hypothetico-deductive work.

Comparison of causal cognitive maps

Differences in key features of map content

Maps can be compared in terms of their content and/or structure. Content measures relate to differences in the constructs that individuals perceive as being relevant to a particular domain of interest and the ways in which they believe these constructs are related to one another. Contrary to this, structural measures pertain to differences in the overall structural features of the map, in terms of, for example, its level of complexity. This form of comparison largely relates to the computational approach to MOC, which, as outlined in our introductory section, examines how managers and organizations process (rather than make meaning of) information (for additional details regarding this aspect of map comparison see, for example, Hodgkinson and Clarkson 2005, Walsh 1995).

Four types of content difference can be identified in causal cognitive maps (Langfield-Smith and Wirth 1992). The first relates to the existence or non-existence of constructs (i.e. one person believes X is important, the next person does not). Thus, for example, in contrast with Participant A's map, the map of Participant B (Figure 11.2) does not contain the construct 'sweatshop image'. Participant B's map suggests a more localized focus regarding issues of identity and features constructs related to the employing call center ('CC good name/ reputation', see bottom left-hand map quadrant) and the work team ('identification with the team', see top left-hand map quadrant).

Some identity researchers have argued that individuals attach considerable importance to their organization's identity (Ashforth and Mael 1989) and

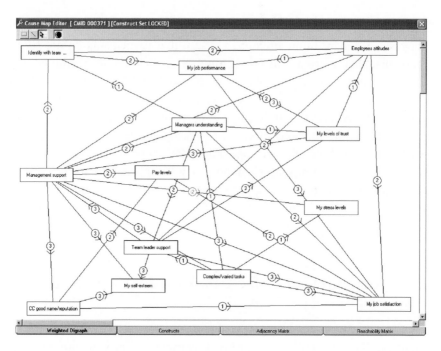

Figure 11.2 An illustrative cause map in weighted digraph format (Participant B)

that a person can acquire a more positive (or negative) social identity through associations with organizations that have positive (or negative) identities (Dutton *et al.* 1994). However, as already noted, it is clear that people are not content to have their identity determined by context (e.g. Hogg and Terry 2000) but actively manage this through the adoption of strategies that maintain a distinctive self-concept and which enhance self-esteem. Unlike Participant A, Participant B's map presents a positive employment situation. For example, the level of her 'identification with the team' is perceived to moderately increase both her personal performance ('my job performance') and the stance of her peers ('employees' attitudes'), while the level of 'management support' and 'manager's understanding' is believed to increase this identification (moderately and slightly respectively). In a similar vein, the good name of the employing call center ('CC good name/reputation') is said to strongly increase this participant's 'self-esteem' (see bottom left-hand quadrant of the map).

The second difference between maps pertains to the existence or non-existence of relationships between constructs (one person believes X influences Y, the next person does not). Participant A (Figure 11.1) perceives there to be no relationship between 'sweatshop image' and 'manager's

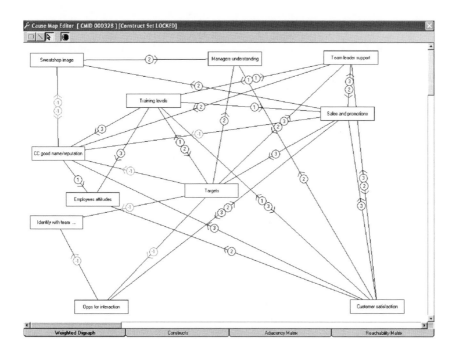

Figure 11.3 An illustrative cause map in weighted digraph format (Participant C)

understanding'. Contrary to this, as can be seen in (Figure 11.3), as viewed by Participant C, there is a relationship and this 'sweatshop image' is believed to (moderately) increase the level of her 'manager's understanding'.

The strength of relationships between constructs provides the third area of potential difference. This applies in the situation where, for example, one person thinks there is a strong positive relationship between X and Y, but the next person believes this to be moderate or only slight. For example, while Participant A perceives there to be a strong relationship between 'training levels' and 'team leader support', Participant C believes the relationship to be only slight. The polarity of those links (for one person any increase in X causes a decrease in Y, while for the next person the perception is that an increase in X results in a corresponding increase in Y) provides a fourth potential area of difference in terms of map content.

As noted, overall the maps of 200 individuals, from five contrasting sites, were constructed and these revealed a variety of differences in the subjective perceptions of the front-line worker within and between organizations. However, for illustrative purposes, quite limited dimensions of the maps of just three participants (female front-line workers, employed on a part-time basis and having similar tenure of approximately five years) are detailed. Yet, as shown, even with this small number of maps it is possible to demonstrate deep insights into the socio-cognitive dynamics of identity formation.

Such maps also provide a framework for deeper discussion, providing even richer insights and understanding. For example, when questioned further regarding the fact that 'sweatshop' image was a salient construct in her map, one participant explained: "The representation of call centres as sweatshops *is* an issue because a lot of people *think* this is how it is." Similarly, another front-line worker concluded: "This [team leader support] can personally decrease people's perception of the sweatshop image but it can't affect the public perception." Yet another stated: "My observations are that our call centre is undervalued and the job completely undervalued ... I feel it's all to do with the use of language, the term 'call centre' has a bad press and so the story begins there." Clearly, work extending beyond in-depth quotations and cross-sectional, small-scale samples is also required to fully exploit the potential promise of causal cognitive mapping in many instances, and in the next section examples are provided of the type of large-scale comparative analysis possible following systematic hybrid-mapping techniques.

Large-scale comparative analysis

Aggregated maps do not necessarily reflect the views of any individual and thus their use can be viewed as controversial (Bougon 1992). Nevertheless, collective patterns of individual cognition may be detectable within and between organizations (Sitkin 2001) and there are occasions when aggregation procedures can prove insightful, insofar as they enable the detection of *overall* group tendencies and/or theoretically meaningful, systematic variations within or between groups (Bougon *et al.* 1977). For example, aggregation allows the identification of mean subgroup response in terms of the perception of how much a construct influences, or is influenced by, other constructs, and the overall perceived detrimental or beneficial effect.

Langfield-Smith and Wirth (1992) proposed a rather more sophisticated analytical approach using a series of distance measures for the quantitative comparison of cause maps in terms of their content similarities and differences: measures, in particular known as distance formula 12, was advocated because this represents the most complete formulation of inter-subjective belief (dis)similarity; and the formula seeks to summarize on a construct-by-construct and link-by-link basis the differences between a given pair of maps; range between zero and one, with larger numbers reflecting greater dissimilarity. A parameterized version of this formula takes into account minor considerations that may need to be taken into account, depending upon the method of map elicitation, for example whether only the strength of causal relations is considered or polarity judgements are also incorporated, and the number of strength values incorporated within the mapping system (Markóczy and Goldberg 1995).

The use of distance ratios in conjunction with multidimensional scale (MDS) techniques (Wish and Carroll 1982) can be highly insightful, enabling the visual detection of meaningful patterns of variation and/or the exploration of the correlates of subgroup membership, using cluster analysis (Everitt et al. 2001). In the case of this call-center investigation, distance ratios calculated in accordance with the revised Markóczy-Goldberg formula were submitted to a cluster analysis using Ward's procedure (as implemented within SPSS™). Following on from which a combination of multinomial (polytomous) logistic regression (Cohen et al. 2003) and separate logistic regression analyses were carried out, in an attempt to predict membership of one of six empirically derived clusters. A detailed consideration of these findings lies beyond the scope of this chapter, but in brief a combination of variables reflecting organizational membership and a variety of employment attitudes and work experiences were found to be highly significant within both the multinomial analysis and the subsequent individual logistic regressions. In this connection, Markóczy (1997, 2001) has reported a series of investigations in an attempt to ascertain the extent to which exogenous variables such as functional background, education and nationality are related to the membership of empirically derived clusters based on an analysis of the map content. Thus, in summary, the use of more structured elicitation techniques gives rise to the possibility of being able to analyse the similarities and/or differences between the maps of the participants using well-known statistical techniques (Daniels, Markóczy and de Chernatony 1994).

Conclusions

As revealed in the MOC literature, causal cognitive mapping has been used as a potentially powerful means of representing actors' belief systems (e.g. Bougon et al. 1977, Fahey and Narayanan 1989, Markóczy 2001), and MOC researchers have investigated various aspects of identity (e.g. Gioia and Thomas 1996, Hodgkinson 2005, Peteraf and Shanley 1997, Porac et al. 1989). Nevertheless, and as stressed throughout this chapter, despite their widespread popularity, there is no current agreement concerning the most appropriate way to elicit participants' causal belief systems, and choices become more complex when some form of map comparison (over time or context) are required. Whilst it is clearly inappropriate to capture data that is, in reality, not actually meaningful to participants, it is also less than helpful to acquire a mass of potentially non-comparable material. If maps are to be compared systematically, then the maps to be subjected to the comparison process need to be elicited on a systematic basis. For this reason, the contribution of this chapter has been to focus upon the hybrid method of data collection, which, arguably, provides the optimum solution in such contexts.

While comprehensive, the pool of (55) constructs presented to the participants in the illustrative study was clearly unable to fully represent all possible issues of salience to each individual. Nevertheless, it did permit the systematic examination and capture of the perceived interactions between a wide range of theoretically and empirically informed issues, representing an individual's causal beliefs regarding a particular domain. In parallel, the hybrid method employed also made it possible to compare maps using a range of descriptive and inferential statistics (see Clarkson and Hodgkinson (2004) for additional details).

As illustrated, by opening up a more dynamic conception of identity formation and change in the global workplace, this form of mapping demonstrates particular promise for many areas of social identity research, as identified at the outset of this chapter. There is some evidence of the predictive value of cognitive maps (Bonham and Shapiro 1976) and, to the extent that these subjective understandings drive variations in a range of outcomes, this method may throw light on various additional dilemmas in identity research, once again particularly in relation to social identity. For example, it may provide insights regarding the extent to which group membership and/or the relative strength of different identities are predictors of facets of behavior, why social identity can contribute both to an increase in output and to a reduction, and why social support can increase stress or, alternatively, reduce it. Moreover, as recently concluded by Haslam and Ellemers (2005: 97):

> Some traditional areas of research in organizational psychology (such as motivation, leadership, power, and communication) have only just begun to be explored from a social identity perspective. The initial results of these efforts hold out great promise for the development of a broader and deeper understanding of these organizational phenomena.

In terms of theoretical considerations, Haslam and Ellemers further conclude that more will be found if 'unhelpful barriers to illumination are removed' (ibid.). As with all disciplines, the appropriate empirical investigations required to enable the validation and development of theory are dependent upon the availability and development of suitable methods. Causal cognitive mapping appears to hold considerable potential for many aspects of identity research and is, at least, worthy of additional consideration.

Acknowledgements

The financial support of the UK ESRC/EPSRC Advanced Institute of Management Research (AIM) in the preparation of this chapter is gratefully acknowledged.

References

Ashforth, B. E. and Mael, F. (1989) 'Social identity theory and the organization.' *Academy of Management Review* 14(1): 20–39.

Axelrod, R. (1976) *Structure of Decision: The Cognitive Maps of Political Elites*. Princeton, NJ: Princeton University Press.

Barr, P. S., Stimpert, J. L., and Huff, A. S. (1992) 'Cognitive change, strategic action, and organizational renewal.' *Strategic Management Journal* 13(Special Issue): 15–36.

Batt, R. (2002) 'Managing customer services: human resource practices, quit rates, and sales growth.' *Academy of Management Journal* 45(3): 587–597.

Belt, V., Richardson, R., and Webster, J. (2000) 'Women's work in the information economy: the case of telephone call centres.' *Information, Communication and Society* 3(3): 366–385.

Bonham, G. M. and Shapiro, M. J. (1976) 'Explanation of the unexpected: the Syrian intervention in Jordan in 1970.' In Axelrod, R. (ed.) *The Structure of Decision: The Cognitive Maps of Political Elites* (pp. 113–141). Princeton, NJ: Princeton University Press.

Bougon, M. G. (1983) 'Uncovering cognitive maps: the self-Q technique.' In Morgan, G. (ed.) *Beyond Method* (pp. 173–188). Beverly Hills: Sage.

Bougon, M. G. (1992) 'Congregate cognitive maps: a unified dynamic theory of organization and strategy.' *Journal of Management Studies* 29(3): 369–89.

Bougon, M. G., Baird, N., Komocar, J. M., and Ross, W. (1990) 'Identifying strategic loops: the self-Q interviews.' In Huff, A. S. (ed.) *Mapping Strategic Thought* (pp. 327–354). Chichester: Wiley.

Bougon, M., Weick, K., and Binkhorst, D. (1977) 'Cognition in organizations: an analysis of the Utrecht Jazz Orchestra.' *Administrative Science Quarterly* 22(3/4): 606–639.

Bowman, E. H. (1984) 'Content analysis of annual reports for corporate strategy and risk.' *Interfaces* 14(1): 61–71.

Calori, R., Johnson, G., and Sarnin, P. (1992) 'French and British top managers' understanding of the structure and the dynamics of their industries: a cognitive analysis and comparison.' *British Journal of Management* 3: 61–78.

Christensen, L. T. and Cheney, G. (2000) 'Self-absorption and self-seduction in the corporate identity game.' In Schultz, M., Hatch, M. J., and Larsen, M. H. (eds) *The Expressive Organization* (pp.246–270). Oxford: Oxford University Press.

Clarkson, G. P. and Hodgkinson, G. P. (2004) 'Sensemaking on the front line: the key implications for call centre performance.' In Neely, A., Kennerley, M., and Walters, A. (eds.) *Fourth International Conference on Performance Measurement and Management: Public and Private*, 28–30 July 2004, Edinburgh, UK (pp. 251–258). Stirling, UK: Centre for Business Performance (ISBN 0-9533761-3-3).

Clarkson, G. P. and Hodgkinson, G. P. (2005) 'Introducing Cognizer™: a comprehensive computer package for the elicitation and analysis of cause maps.' *Organizational Research Methods* 8(3): 317–341.

Cohen, J., Cohen, P., West, S. G., and Aiken, L. S. (2003) *Applied Multiple Regression/Correlation Analysis for the Behavioral Sciences* (3rd edn). Mahwah, New Jersey: Lawrence Erlbaum Associates, Inc.

Cropper, S., Eden, C., and Ackermann, F. (1990) 'Keeping sense of accounts using computer-based cognitive maps.' *Social Science Computer Review* 8: 345–366.

Daniels, K., Markóczy, L., and de Chernatony, L. (1994) 'Techniques to compare cognitive maps.' *Advances in Managerial Cognition and Organizational Information Processing* 5: 141–164. JAI Press Inc.

DiMaggio, P. J. and Powell, W. W. (1991) 'The iron cage revisited: institutional isomorphism and collective rationality in organizational fields'. In Powell, W. W. and DiMaggio, P. J. (eds.) *The New Institutionalism in Organizational Analysis* (pp. 63–82). Chicago: The University of Chicago Press.

Dukerich, J. M., Golden, B. R., and Shortell, S. M. (2002) 'Beauty is in the eye of the beholder: the impact of organizational identification, identity, and image on the cooperative behaviors of physicians.' *Administrative Science Quarterly* 47: 507–533.

Dutton, J. E., Dukerich, J. M., and Harquail, C. V. (1994) 'Organizational images and member identification.' *Administrative Science Quarterly* 39: 239–263.

Eden, C. (ed.) (1992) 'On the nature of cognitive maps' (Editorial). *Journal of Management Studies* 29 (Special Issue): 261–265.

Eden, C. and Ackermann, F. (1998) 'Analysing and comparing idiographic cause maps.' In Eden, C. and Spender, J.-C. (eds.) *Managerial and Organizational Cognition: Theory, Methods and Research* (pp. 192–209). London: Sage.

Eden, C., Ackermann, F., and Cropper, S. (1992) 'The analysis of cause maps.' *Journal of Management Studies* 29(3): 309–324.

Eden, C. and Spender, J.-C. (1998) *Managerial and Organizational Cognition: Theory, Methods and Research*. London: Sage.

Everitt, B. S., Landau, S., and Leese, M. (2001) *Cluster Analysis* (4th edn). London: Arnold.

Fahey, L. and Narayanan, V. K. (1989) 'Linking changes in revealed causal maps and environmental changes: an empirical study.' *Journal of Management Studies* 26 (Special Issue): 361–378.

Fiske, S. T. and Linville, P. W. (1980) 'What does the schema concept buy us?' *Personality and Social Psychology Bulletin* 6(4): 543–557.

Fletcher, K. E. and Huff, A. S. (1990) 'Strategic argument mapping: a study of strategy reformulation at AT and T.' In Huff, A. S. (ed.) *Mapping Strategic Thought* (pp. 165–193). Chichester: Wiley.

Garrett, N., Jacques, T., and Wynne, B. (2002) *Managing Human Resources in Call Centres*. Oxford: Chandos Publishing.

Gioia, D. A. and Thomas, J. B. (1996) 'Identity, image, and issue interpretation: sensemaking during strategic change in academia.' *Administrative Science Quarterly* 41(3): 370–403.

Hart, J. (1976) 'Comparative cognition: politics of international control of the oceans.' In Axelrod, R. (ed.) *Structure of Decision: The Cognitive Maps of Political Elites* (pp. 180–220). Princeton, NJ: Princeton University Press.

Haslam, S. A. and Ellemers, N. (2005) 'Social identity in industrial and organizational psychology: concepts, controversies and contributions.' In Hodgkinson, G. P. and Ford,

J. K. (eds) *International Review of Industrial and Organizational Psychology* 20:39–118. Chichester: Wiley.

Hodgkinson, G. P. (2005) *Images of Competitive Space: A Study of Managerial and Organizational Strategic Cognition.* Basingstoke, UK: Palgrave Macmillan.

Hodgkinson, G. P. and Clarkson, G. P. (2005) 'What have we learned from almost thirty years of research on causal mapping? Methodological lessons and choices for the information systems and information technology communities.' In Narayanan, V. K. and Armstrong, D. J. (eds) *Causal Mapping for Research in Information Technology* (pp. 46–79). Hershey, PA: Idea Group Inc.

Hodgkinson, G. P. and Johnson, G. (1994) 'Exploring the mental models of competitive strategists: the case for a processual approach.' *Journal of Management Studies* 31(4): 325–351.

Hodgkinson, G. P. and Sparrow, P. R. (2002) *The Competent Organization: A Psychological Analysis of the Strategic Management Process.* Buckingham: Open University Press.

Hogg, M. A. and Terry, D. J. (2000) 'Social identity and self-categorization processes in organizational contexts.' *Academy of Management Review* 25(1): 121–140.

Holman, D. (2002) 'Employee wellbeing in call centres.' *Human Resource Management Journal* 12(4): 35–50.

Huff, A. S. (ed.) (1990a) *Mapping Strategic Thought.* Chichester: Wiley.

Huff, A. S. (1990b) 'Mapping strategic thought.' In Huff, A. S. (ed.) *Mapping Strategic Thought* (pp. 11–49). Chichester: Wiley.

Huff, A. S. and Fletcher, K. E. (1990) 'Conclusion: key mapping decisions.' In Huff, A. S. (ed.) *Mapping Strategic Thought* (pp. 403–412). Chichester: Wiley.

Jenkins, M. (1998) 'The theory and practice of comparing causal maps.' In Eden, C. and Spender, J.-C. (eds) *Managerial and Organizational Cognition* (pp. 231–250). London: Sage.

Jenkins, M. and Johnson, G. (1997) 'Entrepreneurial intentions and outcomes: A comparative causal mapping study.' *Journal of Management Studies* 34(6): 895–920.

Langfield-Smith, K. and Wirth, A. (1992) 'Measuring differences between cognitive maps.' *Journal of the Operational Research Society* 43: 1135–1150.

Lant, T. K. and Shapira, Z. (eds) (2001) *Organizational Cognition: Computation and Interpretation.* Mahwah, New Jersey: Lawrence Erlbaum Associates.

Markóczy, L. (1997) 'Measuring beliefs: accept no substitutes.' *Academy of Management Journal* 40(5): 1228–1242.

Markóczy, L. (2001) 'Consensus formation during strategic change.' *Strategic Management Journal* 22: 1013–1031.

Markóczy, L. and Goldberg, J. (1995) 'A method for eliciting and comparing causal maps.' *Journal of Management* 21(2): 305–333.

Meindl, J. R., Stubbart, C., and Porac, J. F. (eds) (1996) *Cognition Within and Between Organizations.* Thousand Oaks, CA: Sage.

Newell, A. and Simon, H. A. (1972) *Human Problem Solving.* Englewood Cliffs, NJ: Prentice-Hall.

Parker, S. and Wall, T. (1998) *Job and Work Design: Organizing Work to Promote Well-being and Effectiveness.* Thousand Oaks, CA: Sage.

Peteraf, M. and Shanley, M. (1997) 'Getting to know you: a theory of strategic group identity.' *Strategic Management Journal* 18(51/Summer Special Issue): 165–186.

Porac, J. F., Thomas, H., and Baden-Fuller, C. (1989) 'Competitive groups as cognitive communities: the case of Scottish knitwear manufacturers.' *Journal of Management Studies* 26(4): 397–416.

Roberts, F. S. (1976) 'Strategy for the energy crisis: the case of commuter transportation policy.' In Axelrod, R. (ed.) *Structure of Decision: The Cognitive Maps of Political Elites* (pp. 142–179). Princeton, NJ: Princeton University Press.

Schwenk, C. R. (1985) 'Management illusions and their biases: their impact on strategic decisions.' *Long Range Planning* 18(5): 74–80.

Scott, W. R. (2001) *Institutions and Organizations.* Thousand Oaks, CA: Sage.

Sitkin, S. B. (2001) 'The theoretical foundations of organizational cognition.' In Lant, T. K. and Shapira, Z. (eds) *Organizational Cognition: Computation and Interpretation,* (pp. 73–79). Mahwah, New Jersey: Lawrence Erlbaum Associates.

Sparrow, J. (1998) *Knowledge in Organizations: Access to Thinking At Work.* London: Sage.

Swan, J. A. (1995) 'Exploring knowledge and cognitions in decisions about technological innovation: mapping managerial cognitions.' *Human Relations* 48: 1241–70.

Turner, J. C. (2001) 'Foreword'. In Haslam, S. A. (ed.) *Psychology in Organizations: The Social Identity Approach.* London: Sage.

Van Dick, R. (2004) 'My job is my castle: identification in organizational contexts.' In Cooper, C. L. and Robertson, I. T. (eds) *International Review of Industrial and Organizational Psychology* 19: 169–203. Chichester: Wiley.

Walsh, J. P. (1995) 'Managerial and organizational cognition: notes from a trip down memory lane.' *Organization Science* 6(3): 280–321.

Warr, P. (1994) 'A conceptual framework for the study of work and mental health.' *Work and Stress* 8(2): 84–97.

Weber, P. S. and Manning, M. R. (2001) 'Cause maps, sensemaking, and planned organizational change.' *The Journal of Applied Behavioral Science* 37(2): 227–251.

Weick, K. E. (1979) *The Social Psychology of Organizing* (2nd edn). McGraw-Hill Inc.

Weick, K. E. (1995) *Sensemaking in Organizations.* Thousand Oaks, CA: Sage.

Weick, K. E. (2001) *Making Sense of the Organization.* Oxford: Blackwell Business.

Weick, K. E. and Bougon, M. G. (1986) 'Organizations as cognitive maps: charting ways to success and failure.' In Sims, H. P., Jr., Gioia, D. A., and Associates (eds) *The Thinking Organization: Dynamics of Organizational Social Cognition* (pp. 102–135). San Francisco, CA: Jossey-Bass Inc.

Wiesenfeld, B., Raghuram, S., and Garud, R. (2001) 'Organizational identification among virtual workers: the role of the need for affiliation and perceived work-based social support.' *Journal of Management* 27: 213–229.

Wish, M. and Carroll, J. D. (1982) 'Multidimensional scaling and its applications.' In Krishnaiah, P. R. and Kanal, L. N. (eds) *Handbook of Statistics.* Vol. 2 (pp. 317–345). Amsterdam: North Holland Publishing Company.

12

Action research and identity

Julie Wolfram Cox and Bill Cooke

> Examining how we draw lines will ... reveal how we give meaning to our environment as well as to ourselves. By throwing light on the way we distinguish entities from one another and thereby give them an identity, we can explore the very foundations of our social world, which we normally take for granted. (Zerubavel 1991: 3–4)

In this chapter we propose an understanding of action research as an ongoing project of identity formation. In particular, we argue that it is the making of claims for disciplinary and practitioner distinctivenesses which make action research action research. Ours is not the circular argument that the identity of action research (if there is such a thing) and/or action researchers are defined by its distinguishing features. Rather, it is our suggestion that it is the ongoing claiming of such distinctivenesses and the bases of these claims which have sustained an action research identity as such over time. This is notwithstanding the contradictions and paradoxes in these identity claims.

We proceed by discussing the changing complexities of the action research role from the 1940s/50s on, when the organizational action researcher was likely to be described as an external consultant to senior management. Drawing on work from our edited collection *Fundamentals of Action Research* (Cooke and Wolfram Cox 2005), and elsewhere, we map out some of the changes in representation over this period. We present the practice of action research throughout as a relational endeavor that is (variously) dependent on/distinguishable from the practice of normal science, traditional consulting and organization development but is rarely discussed in its own terms. We then contrast current efforts/varieties of action research (e.g. participatory action research, action learning, appreciative inquiry) in terms of their relative modesty/ambition, and the implicit and explicit identity claims embedded therein. Indeed, we show how changes in both the nature of action research and the identities of the action researcher cannot be disentangled. What are, however, identifiable as problematic are the claims to social change and grand science agendas in some varieties of action research practice. We conclude by arguing for a return to greater modesty in action research.

On being an action researcher – early and more recent contributions

From its early days, action researchers have always represented theirs as a complex endeavor. Part of this complexity derives, they typically argue, from the multiple sources of influence of the field, influences that, in turn, have led to divergences in emphasis among contemporary varieties of action research (AR in parts from herein). Indeed, an important sub-genre of action research is the taxonomizing narrative, which categorizes and compares varieties of action research according to criteria prevalent at the time, the most recent example of which at the time of writing is Cassell and Johnson (2006).

The process of identity construction for action research(ers) involves differentiations within the field as much as it does between action research and the rest of the world. Thus in 1970, Rapoport distinguished four streams of 'development' (1970/2005: 26) as institutional and disciplinary identifications. Thus there were the Tavistock stream of experience in the United Kingdom during and after World War II, the Operational Research stream which also developed out of the War, the Group Dynamics stream attributed to Kurt Lewin and his followers in the United States and the Applied Anthropology stream. Rapoport (1970/2005: 26) suggested that the emphasis at Tavistock was 'to get collaboration from members of an organization while attempting to help them to solve their own problems', while the Operational Research stream led to a larger-scale focus, including attention to multi-organizational and public sector projects by the 1960s. However, while Tavistock researchers had a specific interest in cross-disciplinary research aimed to assist the solution of social problems, the emphasis of the Group Dynamics stream 'has been somewhat more on individual and small group processes than on the relations between individual and larger social systems' (Rapoport 1970/2005: 28). Different again, the Applied Anthropology stream 'emphasized the culture concept and the need to approach social problems ... in cultural and sub-cultural terms' (Rapoport 1970/2005: 28).

The point here is not that this derivation is overly simplified and readily contested (though it is, e.g. Cooke (2003/2005) on the influence of John Collier; also see Fals-Borda 1984/2005). Rather, it exemplifies the intertwining of the action researcher identity with that of action research per se, and the centrality of differentiation in the construction of these identities. One key axis of differentiation has been around the basic social scope of action research, and the consequent social role of the action researcher. For example, Whyte's (1961/2005) famous account of an AR project at the Tremont Hotel in the late 1940s and early 1950s concerned the symbolic importance of small, concrete changes such as the placing of a new water spigot closer to the dining room in alleviating what he describes as severe human relations problems within the hotel. The emphasis of such early work was on descriptions of how such changes were achieved; they were material changes assessable in the short term, and usually conducted by an outside consultant identified as a professional who is psychologically external to systems of power and dependence in which the client is located (e.g. Lippitt 1959/2005).

Lippitt's model of the external consultant was also extended, and differentiated from, by attention to internal consultants who lose both the remoteness and the impartiality of the unfamiliar, detached 'expert' (e.g. Coghlan 2001/2005, compare Dickson and Green 2001/2005, Frohman, Sashkin and Kavanagh 1976/2005), and to longer term client–consultant relationships in AR settings (Ledford 1985/2005). In such settings, Ledford suggests that the psychotherapeutic concepts of transference and countertransference may inform understanding of demands placed on the action researcher and help them 'to better understand their role and the nature of effective helping relationships' (Ledford 1985/2005, see also Wilson 1947/2005). However, Schein (1995/2005) later attempted to clarify what he saw as a confusion among notions of process consultation, action research and clinical inquiry in terms of researcher and client needs and interests, joint ownership of interventions and recognition that entry into a diagnostic relationship is itself a major intervention. While Schein viewed both process consultation and clinical inquiry as client-centred, action research may be more consultant-driven, unlikely to surface valid data, and may even cause damage to the client. In all these narratives, though, there are at least two processes in hand – of differentiation and of specification, of what is and is not required of the authentic practitioner. Schein, for example, makes clear the centrality of certain modes of professionalism and professional development in his proposition of clinical inquiry (Schein 1987).

Contrasting with the local and material locus of action research work typified by Whyte and also argued for by Lippitt (Cooke 2006), there are those who depict its purpose as broader social change. Sustenance for such a position is seen as having been provided by Lewin. As early as 1945 he supported an extension of the reach of action research on the basis that its focus on the *how* of social interventions obscured the bigger *why* questions of their purpose and legitimacy. As Lewin (1945/2005: 20) asked:

> How is economic and social discrimination to be attacked if we think not in terms of generalities but in terms of the inhabitants of that particular main street and those side and end streets which make up that small or large town in which the individual group worker is supposed to [do] his job?

This interest in larger societal issues is also evident in Lewin's (1946/2005) account *Research on Minority Problems*. In this, Lewin presents his argument for action research as social engineering, with particular concern for challenging 'the so-called minority problem' (1946/2005: 34) and stereotyping at all levels of society, be it racism in communities or of groups in society. Referring to the development of the atom bomb, Lewin argued that it was important now to 'promote social science in such a way that both natural and physical [*sic*] science become equally vigorous and successful' (1946/2005: 33), going on to argue that '[s]ocial management on all levels should benefit much from an experimental social science which could offer a clear scientific understanding of the dynamics of social living' (1946/2005: 42). In this way, Lewin establishes the legitimacy of action research both in terms of its potential contribution to solving social problems and in terms of its capacity to extend the principles of experimental science. His experimental social science is, therefore, defined in terms of the natural sciences, heralding the relative status if not the later complexity of AR's developing identity.

But it is impossible not to see Lewin's commitment to scientific social progress as embedded within his own Jewish identity, and his personal commitment to fighting anti-Semitism. Lewin was, after all, advocate of the concept of 'Jewish self-hatred' for assimilating Jews; and much of his early action research work was undertaken by his Committee for Community Interrelations (CCI) of the American Jewish Congress. Several other early papers on action research also addressed issues of racism and ethnicity (e.g. the work of Lewin collaborators Lippitt and Radke 1946/2005; Watson 1949/2005; Sellitz and Cook 1948), and its social change imperative started to gather momentum. From the United Kingdom, Curle (1949/2005) drew from then current ideas about structural anthropology and psychoanalysis to recognize the need both to change behavior and to change the social context in which it occurs. Referring to the work of Moreno and of earlier generations of sociologists in the late nineteenth and early twentieth century, Bain (1951/2005) stated that '[a]ction research deals with what sociologists have been calling social problems and social conflict for over fifty years' (Bain 1951/2005: 320). Holding a tacit definition of action research as any research aimed at social change, Bain uses irony, through his suggestion that there be a 'Groupometer' for measuring group behavior, to argue against narrow scientism in researching and applying knowledge that concerns social phenomena. Such an interest was also implicit in Shumsky's (1958/2005) *Action Research and Modern Man*, for while Shumsky retained an interest in the 'scientific endeavor' (1958/2005: 9), in experimentation and in the generalization of knowledge, he does so in the interest of the 'action research movement' (1958/2005: 5) as a grass-roots social movement aimed at the bettering of mankind through the development of a common social orientation (1958/2005: 9). Shumsky's (1958/2005: 10) interest was in encouraging a 'spirit of experimentation', exploration and hope in accordance with the spirit of America's new world pioneers.

By 1983, though, while still in the diffentiation genre, Brown and Tandon's point of comparison was not between natural and social science but, instead, between First-World and Third-World priorities. Comparing First-World action research with the tradition of participatory research that had emerged in the Third World, Brown and Tandon (1983/2005) state that the First-World tradition has focused on individual and group levels of analysis while that of the Third World is concerned with societal change. While both action research and participatory research 'explicitly reject the irrelevance of more traditional conceptions of social science research' (Brown and Tandon 1983/2005: 32), participatory research was seen to be concerned more with conflict than consensus social theory and to place more emphasis on promoting system transformation and problems of equity, self-reliance and oppression than on promoting reform and problems of efficiency and growth within a client system. They examined the prospects for beneficial, but inevitably problematic, interactions between the traditions.

While Brown and Tandon (1983/2005) distinguished action and participatory research, the latter has become known as the conflation 'participatory action research ('PAR')', itself subject to different variations of meaning (see Brown 1993/2005). For example, Orlando Fals-Borda (1984/2005), the foremost developer and advocate of PAR, aimed to use action-research-type techniques for progressive social change. PAR, according to Fals-Borda, is a combination of scientific research, adult education and political action, for 'PAR implies the production of serious and trustworthy knowledge with and for oppressed and exploited groups and social classes' (Fals-Borda 1984/2005: 3). The science that is present in this combination is both the means and the subject of transformation, for as Fals-Borda (1984/2005: 4) stated:

> Academic knowledge plus popular knowledge and wisdom give as a result a total scientific knowledge which is revolutionary as it helps to end the previous intellectual monopoly of the dominant classes. This dialectical tension in praxis leads [us] to reject the asymmetry implied in the subject–object relationship which characterizes traditional action research.

Identity is central to this differentiation for Fals-Borda. Endogenous people's science, and, tacitly and explicitly, its practitioners, are distinguished from so-called universal science, itself a cultural product that 'carries those class biases and group values which scientists as a whole hold' (1984/2005: 5). This requires the explicit use of action research for overcoming oppression, here on the basis of a class-based analysis, in which she or he who controls knowledge is the key to oppression/emancipation. Indeed, Fals-Borda later set the ability to effect radical political change as a test for the success of PAR (Fals-Borda 1987/2005).

His approach can be compared with that of W. F. Whyte (Argyris and Schön 1989/2005, Whyte, Greenwood and Lazes 1989/2005). Lacking the societal praxis of Fals-Borda, Whyte's PAR is hard to distinguish from 'normal' action research when participation is a defining feature. In this version, PAR is explained as an applied research strategy, unusual in its recognition of the value and legitimacy of labor unions and affinity with traditions of industrial democracy. Whyte and his co-authors also connected PAR to wider understandings of the nature of science in society.

In the same year, Argyris and Schön (1989/2005) sought to locate action research by comparing it with PAR (Whyte's version) and action science, the latter two being 'members of the same action research family' (Argyris and Schön 1989/2005: 139). The authors drew attention to tacit practitioner theories-in-use that serve to distort and undermine action research findings and interventions if they are not surfaced, and state that action science emphasizes such surfacing and learning from tacit theories-in-use through which affective feelings of embarrassment and threat develop. According to Raelin (1989/2005), action science goes deeper in such surfacing for more profound organizational learning than does action learning, although both show the same 'action' perspective.

This ongoing search for similarity and difference among the variants of action research is also evident in Brown's (1993/2005) discussion of the two approaches to PAR. Presenting an analysis of an organization development project aimed at non-government organizations seeking social change, he outlines differences in ideology and then the development of some shared perspectives between the First-World/Northern/Whyte form of PAR and the Third-World/Southern/Fals-Borda version. However, the idea that 'development' is itself ideological, and that there may be power imbalances beyond the participatory arena, was ignored (cf. Cooke 2003/2005, Fals-Borda 1987/2005). Such reflexive awareness is more evident in Fine and Torre's (2004/2005) exploration of how PAR projects can retrieve, reconstruct and reveal how race, ethnicity and class configure and shape – inequitably – engagements with public institutions. More aligned with that of Fals-Borda than of Whyte, Fine and Torre's emancipatory PAR can be seen as 'strong' rather than 'weak' (Peters and Robinson 1984/2005) in its emphasis on reframing questions of social justice for those who have paid the greatest price for the neoliberal state, people of color and/or poverty.

By 2000, Ellis and Kiely (2000/2005) compared action research with PAR, action learning and action science, commenting that each shares an emphasis on a cycle of action and reflection, each is interventionist and each involves (to varying degrees) collaboration and co-inquiry, and can be seen as a version of action-inquiry, '[a]t the heart of [which] is a recurring action-reflection cycle predicated on the relationship of improved knowledge through action, and new or revised action based on imaginative reflective learning' (Ellis and Kiely 2000: 86). The four variants were then compared in terms of ideology, procedure and validity criteria.

Thus, the various and changing identities of action research, and, tacitly and explicitly of action researchers, have been represented through a series of differentiation and comparison processes, the divisions within which have shown increasing specification while remaining highly normative (e.g. Cooperrider and Srivastva 1987/2005, Reason 1999/2005). Some reactions to such differentiation have been to claim that there is no simple guide nor single definition for action research (Robinson 1993/2005, see also Altrichter, Kemmis, McTaggart and Zuber-Skerritt 2002). We argue that the ongoing and shifting debate over the identity of action research(ers) is important in mapping the history of contestation among the domains of research and intervention.

Action research as a relational endeavor

Although in our account of accounts we have concentrated on intervention and action thus far, action research has also emerged as a relational endeavor in terms of its status as research. In this section we extend our discussion of action research both as and in relation to science, for it is here that the (shifting, processual) identity of action research and the researcher is framed as one of both differentiated and relational status.

Using the tactic of not naming action research as such, Sellitz and Cook (1948/2005) set out the case for it to be brought to a wider audience. They described the need to bridge a gap between 'pure' research aimed at identifying general social principles, and 'applied' research so narrowly designed as to have no relevance other than to the often artificially constructed scenarios it investigates. Required, instead, they argued, was research that addresses real and immediate social problems but uses the traditional scientific method and produces actual social change (see also Alderson 1951/2005). Adding to this, Rapoport (1970/2005: 25) wrote that 'Action research aims to contribute both to the practical concerns of people in an immediate problematic situation and to the goals of social science by joint collaboration within a mutually acceptable ethical framework' (cf. Corey 1949/2005).

Taking a more pessimistic perspective toward action research at the time, Sanford (1970/2005) adopted the tone of a premature and indeed mistaken obituary in his comparison of action research of the 1940s and 1950s with that of the late 1960s, by which time, he argues, there has been little emphasis on the study of actions, and the separation of action from research had meant that action research had had little influence in the social sciences, except in education, his chosen context. His preference was for 'research-action' with the aim of promoting liberation and growth through the processes of research.

Such reference – and deference – to science, even to social science, is common even from the early days (see Chein, Cook and Harding 1948). For example, Lippitt (1950) considers some of the decisions facing the social scientist who is considering participation in action research, questions that had to do with the nature and status of scientific knowledge, its separation from application and the responsibilities of the researcher. Cooke (2006), drawing on contemporary materials, details the extent to which scientism was embedded by Lippitt into his constructions of the action research derived 'change agent' identity.

But while the notion, tacit and explicit, of action researcher as change agent still prevails, and some forms of action research retain a positivist epistemology and commonality with the scientific method (Aguinis 1993), most do not (Ellis and Kiely 2000/2005). Action researchers have moved from the somewhat defensive claim that action research 'transcends the sterile specialization of the social sciences' (Blum 1955/2005: 316) to a careful differentiation of themselves *from* positivist scientism, albeit through such (scientific) terms of validity (Ellis and Kiely 2000/2005), generalization and rigor (Melrose 2001/2005).

Such differentiation is well illustrated in Susman and Evered's (1978/2005) *Assessment of the Scientific Merits of Action Research*. This review was published at a time when concerns with the limitations of positivist science had reached what the authors describe as a crisis of relevance and of epistemology. Susman and Evered located the action researcher within a 'different' science, one that also requires different criteria and methods; namely, understanding rather than explanation, making things happen rather than prediction, conjectures rather than deduction or induction, engagement rather than detachment, and action rather than contemplation. They argued that action research can contribute to a contingency view of science, in which different principles are appropriate for different situations (see also De Cock 1994/2005).

More specifically, McTaggart (1998/2005) put forward the view that the discourse of validity has been colonized by positivist thought. In a strongly worded paper concerned with PAR, McTaggart considered validation to be a social and political process concerned with making commitments transparent to participants through appropriate communicative structures (see also Checkland and Howell 1998). He argued that PAR is not valid unless it meets the criteria of defensibility, educative value, political efficacy and moral appropriateness, and aimed to expand the concept of validity in order to allow greater attention to the defensibility of the knowledge claims that frame changing practice.

In terms of external validity, in particular, Schön (1995/2005) places discussions of rigor and of relevance within the institutional context of the research university and in relation to the new scholarship advocated by Boyer, with its emphasis on integration and application. Schön argues for the need to legitimize a new type of generalization: that of 'reflective transfer', where actionable knowledge can be carried over to new practice situations through the use of models or prototypes. Such broadening of frame of reference is also evident in Melrose (2001/2005), who argues that rigor is a broader concept than validity and, instead, is one that can be established both as a principle internalized by researchers and as something that is dependent on the expectations of external audiences.

Thus, the changing identity of action research/the action researcher has seen a growing boldness where points of reference and of distinction have moved from development of varieties of action research within the span of activity that bridges consultation and science, to some effort to breach that span altogether and to establish broader criteria for the assessment of action. However, such efforts can also, ironically, be viewed as themselves conservative, for it is noteworthy that both McTaggart (1998/2005) and Melrose (2001/2005) acknowledged the importance of social and political expectations and that Schön's (1995/2005) argument, that the new scholarship implies action research, is framed within an institutional context.

Contemporary action research and the grand ambition

This tension between boldness and constraint is perhaps most evident in recent forms of action research, namely the popular appreciative inquiry (e.g. Cooperrider and Srivastva 1987/2005) and in ecological action research (Reason and Torbert 2001, Reason 2003). Avoiding – or is it denying – social frames of reference to distinguish their contributions, these authors drew instead on metaphysics, ancient inspirational archetypes (Cooperrider and Srivastva 1987/2005) and ecology (Reason and Torbert, 2001/2005) to argue the importance of their works. In their widely cited paper, Cooperrider and Srivastva (1987/2005) argued for the replacement of value-free science with the more active, invested, appreciative and transformative emphasis of 'socio-rational' science, stating their 'conviction that action-research has the potential to be to the postindustrial era what "scientific management" was to the industrial' (Cooperrider and Srivastva 1987/2005: 52).

Also aiming for a transformational social science, Reason and Torbert (2001/2005) argued that the action turn will place primacy on practical knowledge and on 'critical inquiry in action' (2001/2005: 234). The action turn, which is distinguished from the linguistic turn and its emphasis on the role of language constructing of reality, gives emphasis to inquiry that contributes directly to the flourishing of human persons, their communities and the ecosystems of which they are part. By 2003, Reason explored and interrogated Rorty's pragmatism in relation to action research, suggesting that just as Rorty is redescribing philosophy, so is action research redescribing inquiry.

However, despite a combination of grand ambition, aspirational comparison and great length, such efforts are also conservative in the interests that they serve. For example, the paper by Cooperrider and Srivastva (1987/2005) accepts social arrangements as arising from agreement (unlike Fals-Borda 1984, Rahman 1982) and is exclusively organizational/managerial when it comes to intervention (cf. Shumsky 1958/2005). Similarly, Reason and Torbert (2001/2005) argued that good theory is not just descriptive, inductive or deductive, universalizable and analytic, but normative, analogical, timely and implementable so as to sustain personal, social and community development (see also Reason 2003/2005).

Arguably, ongoing provocations that action research is dead, dying or not living up to expectations may have sparked the search for novelty and unfamiliar grandeur in these efforts to distinguish the future of action research from its past; what it might be from what it is not. And bound up in all this, for all the differentiations and the claims to science, is the existence of the social formation of action researchers. In terms of form, both Cooperrider and Srivastva (1987/2005) and Reason (2003/2005) make liberal use of antinomies in their carving out of potential futures for action research, supplementing these with persuasive illustrations to drive home their arguments. This approach is very different from the early grounded studies of Lewin (1944/2005) or of Collier (1946/2005), and deliberately so, for it is itself an identity claim, or at least an identity difference claim among an ever-increasing array of approaches that are not quite science (or 'good science'), not quite practical (or practical enough) and, in many cases, not critical in the sense that they work for the betterment of the status quo rather than its interrogation through the representation and liberation of marginalized interests. As argued by Regehr (2000/2005), for example, there is a growing number of critics commenting on whether action research's potential to redress oppressive social relations has been realized. Regehr argued that the larger society in which the research is conducted never disappears and may dissuade researchers from asking uncomfortable questions (cf. Greenwood 2002/2005, Minnis 2000/2005), but she was also concerned that there may be active deception when researchers fail to disclose their values. Like McTaggart (1998/2005) and Checkland and Howell (1998/2005), Regehr outlined some means by which researchers can allow greater scrutiny of their value positions, while pointing out that increased awareness of victimization may not always assist advocacy.

Both Regehr (2000/2005) and Greenwood (2002/2005) call for action researchers to show greater courage in these endeavors. We see such courage in recent writing on the limits of PAR (e.g. David 2002/2005), including reflexive and processual accounts of partial successes and failures (e.g. Williams, Srivastava, Corbridge and Véron 2003/2005) and most evident in recent feminist PAR (Gatenby and Humphries 2000/2005, Katila and Meriläinen 2002/2005, cf. Reid 2002). These works present dilemmas faced by the authors as action researchers while also addressing the precarious identity of action research; and in their small, localized contributions to assisting the understanding of both, they both engage and transform.

Future directions – a call for reflexive modesty

It is such works that, for us, epitomize progress in action research. Always a provisional endeavor, their writing about that provisionality, whether in terms of epistemology, practice or reflexivity, refers to the foundational works of action research as a humble endeavor. Such humility, we feel, is lacking in the recent cosmological and ecological variants of action research and we call for a return to greater humility and modesty in describing and accounting for action research projects and processes (cf. Wolfram Cox and Minahan 2006 on organization development).

In many ways, the calls for grand statements about action research are quite understandable, for they represent one response to its provisionality and somewhat secondary status in relation to positivist science. They are certainly not new, for Shumsky (1958) presented a manifesto in which he suggested the need for an action research 'movement', which may indeed be what we have now, with all, good and bad, that 'movement' in this sense implies. This, we would argue, is where the requirement for future research on action research and identity lies.

The very notion of 'movement' however suggests, to us, some kind of collective – yes, of course – identity. However, what Wilson's (1947/2005) call for a meaningful self-awareness on the part of the action researcher launched was what we see throughout the literature we have summarized here as another dominant trope in this movement, which too connects to notions of identity. This is the need for reflexivity. Action researchers are by and large no longer required to undergo psychoanalysis, as was the case for those who worked for the Tavistock Institute in its early days (Trist and Murray 1990). Yet the framing of reflexivity as primarily a personal and individualistic concern remains. What the body of this chapter, and the more recent feminist work mentioned above, implies is that notions of identity do need to be incorporated into practitioner reflexivity at the personal level.

But while necessary, this is not sufficient. If action research is to make claims, tacit or explicit, as a movement, and at the same time for reflexivity, then surely these two strands must be combined. Action research needs to surface the tacit and explicit social constructions of identity embedded in action research. Among all the normal meanings that might be attached to 'social' in this context, our argument here is that it should specifically apply to those constructions that occur within the action research community and through its institutions, recognizing that these in themselves are social inventions, and that there are therefore iterations and nests of meaning and identity (re)production. For action research, we would argue that this is not an abstract or merely conceptual concern. Action researchers chose not to leave things as they are but, rather, to intervene to try and change things. As we have just seen, the claims for the scale and the social significance of action research are increasing. Claims to legitimacy in this role are buttressed by claims to reflexivity. That claim to reflexivity must now, we argue, engage with notions of (self) identity formulation. That it has yet to do so is one more reason for action research to keep its ambitions limited.

References

Alderson, W. (1951/2005) 'A systematics for problems of action.' In Cooke, B. and Wolfram Cox, J. (eds) *Fundamentals of Action Research*. vol. 1, London: Sage. pp. 305–317.

Altrichter, H., Kemmis, S., McTaggart, R., and Zuber-Skerritt, O. (2002/2005) 'The concept of action research.' In Cooke, B. and Wolfram Cox, J. (eds) *Fundamentals of Action Research*. vol. 4, London: Sage. pp. 101–113.

Aguinis, H. (1993/2005) 'Action research and scientific method: presumed discrepancies and actual similarities.' In Cooke, B. and Wolfram Cox, J. (eds) *Fundamentals of Action Research*. vol. 3, London: Sage. pp. 347–367.

Argyris, C. and Schön, D. A. (1989/2005) 'Participatory action research and action science compared: a commentary.' In Cooke, B. and Wolfram Cox, J. (eds) *Fundamentals of Action Research*. vol. 2, London: Sage. pp. 137–147.

Bain, R. (1951/2005) 'Action research and group dynamics.' In Cooke, B. and Wolfram Cox, J. (eds) *Fundamentals of Action Research*. vol. 1, London: Sage. pp. 319–366.

Blum, F. (1955/2005) 'Action research – a scientific approach?' In Cooke, B. and Wolfram Cox, J. (eds) *Fundamentals of Action Research*. vol. 3, London: Sage. pp. 309–317.

Brown, L. D. (1993/2005) 'Social change through collective reflection with Asian nongovernmental development organizations.' In Cooke, B. and Wolfram Cox, J. (eds) *Fundamentals of Action Research*. vol. 3, London: Sage. pp. 57–83.

Brown, L. D. and Tandon, R. (1983/2005) 'Ideology and political economy in inquiry: action research and participatory research.' In Cooke, B. and Wolfram Cox, J. (eds) *Fundamentals of Action Research*. vol. 2, London: Sage. pp. 25–49.

Cassell, C. and Johnson, P. (2006) 'Action research: explaining the diversity.' *Human Relations* 59(6): 783–814.

Checkland, P. and Howell, S. (1998/2005) 'Action research: its nature and validity.' In Cooke, B. and Wolfram Cox, J. (eds) *Fundamentals of Action Research*. vol. 3, London: Sage. pp. 423–437.

Chein, I., Cook, S., and Harding, J. (1948/2005) 'The field of action research.' In Cooke, B. and Wolfram Cox, J. (eds) *Fundamentals of Action Research*. vol. 1, London: Sage. pp. 151–164.

Coghlan, D. (2001/2005) 'Insider action research projects: implications for practising managers.' In Cooke, B. and Wolfram Cox, J. (eds) *Fundamentals of Action Research.* vol. 3, London: Sage. pp. 229–244.

Collier, J. (1946/2005) 'United States Indian administration as a laboratory of ethnic relations.' In Cooke, B. and Wolfram Cox, J. (eds) *Fundamentals of Action Research.* vol. 1, London: Sage. pp. 69–98.

Cooke, B. (2006) 'The Cold War origin of action research as managerial cooptation.' *Human Relations* 59(5): pp. 655–693.

Cooke, B. (2003/2005) 'A new continuity with colonial administration: participation in development management.' In Cooke, B. and Wolfram Cox, J. (eds) *Fundamentals of Action Research.* vol. 4, London: Sage. pp. 207–225.

Cooke, B. and Wolfram Cox, J. (eds) (2005) *Fundamentals of Action Research.* London: Sage.

Cooperrider, D. and Srivastva, S. (1987/2005) 'Appreciative inquiry in organizational life.' In Cooke, B. and Wolfram Cox, J. (eds) *Fundamentals of Action Research.* vol. 2, London: Sage. pp. 51–97.

Corey, S. M. (1949/2005) 'Action research, fundamental research and educational practices.' In Cooke, B. and Wolfram Cox, J. (eds) *Fundamentals of Action Research.* vol. 1, London: Sage. pp. 257–262.

Curle, A. (1949/2005) 'A theoretical approach to action research.' In Cooke, B. and Wolfram Cox, J. (eds) *Fundamentals of Action Research.* vol. 1, London: Sage. pp. 263–277.

David, M. (2002/2005) 'Problems of participation: the limits of action research.' In Cooke, B. and Wolfram Cox, J. (eds) *Fundamentals of Action Research.* vol. 4, London: Sage. pp. 107–205.

De Cock, C. (1994/2005) 'Action research: in search of a new epistemology?' In Cooke, B. and Wolfram Cox, J. (eds) *Fundamentals of Action Research.* vol. 3, London: Sage. pp. 369–375.

Dickson, G. and Green, K. L. (2001/2005) 'The external researcher in participatory action research.' In Cooke, B. and Wolfram Cox, J. (eds) *Fundamentals of Action Research.* vol. 3, London: Sage. pp. 243–263.

Ellis, J. and Kiely, J. (2000/2005) 'Action inquiry strategies: taking stock and moving forward.' In Cooke, B. and Wolfram Cox, J. (eds) *Fundamentals of Action Research.* vol. 4, London: Sage. pp. 85–119.

Fals-Borda, O. (1984/2005) 'Participatory action research.' In Cooke, B. and Wolfram Cox, J. (eds) *Fundamentals of Action Research.* vol. 2, London: Sage. pp. 3–24.

Fals-Borda, O. (1987/2005) 'The application of participatory action-research in Latin America.' In Cooke, B. and Wolfram Cox, J. (eds) *Fundamentals of Action Research.* vol. 3, London: Sage. pp. 33–55.

Fine, M. and Torre, M. E. (2004/2005) 'Re-membering exclusions: participatory action research in public institutions.' In Cooke, B. and Wolfram Cox, J. (eds) *Fundamentals of Action Research.* vol. 3, London: Sage. pp. 137–166.

Frohman, M. A., Sashkin, M., and Kavanagh, M. J. (1976/2005) 'Action-research as applied to organization development.' In Cooke, B. and Wolfram Cox, J. (eds) *Fundamentals of Action Research.* vol. 2, London: Sage. pp. 367–405.

Gatenby, B. and Humphries, M. (2000/2005) 'Feminist participatory action research: methodological and ethical issues.' In Cooke, B. and Wolfram Cox, J. (eds) *Fundamentals of Action Research.* vol. 2, London: Sage. pp. 261–288.

Greenwood, D.J. (2002/2005) Action Research: unfulfilled promises and unmet challenges, In Cooke, B. and Wolfram Cox, J. (eds) *Fundamentals of Action Research.* vol. 4, London: Sage. pp. 173–196.

Katila, S. and Meriläinen, S. (2002/2005) 'Metamorphosis: from "nice girls" to "nice bitches": Resisting patriarchal articulations of professional identity.' In Cooke, B.

and Wolfram Cox, J. (eds) *Fundamentals of Action Research*. vol. 4, London: Sage. pp. 275–296.

Ledford, G. E., Jr. (1985/2005) 'Transference and countertransference in action research relationships.' In Cooke, B. and Wolfram Cox, J. (eds) *Fundamentals of Action Research*. vol. 3, London: Sage. pp. 201–217.

Lewin, K. (1944/2005) 'The solution of a chronic conflict in industry.' In Cooke, B. and Wolfram Cox, J. (eds) *Fundamentals of Action Research*. vol. 1, London: Sage. pp. 3–17.

Lewin, K. (1945/2005) 'Action research and minority problems.' In Cooke, B. and Wolfram Cox, J. (eds) *Fundamentals of Action Research*, vol. 1, London: Sage. pp. 19–31.

Lewin, K. (1946/2005) 'Research on minority problems.' In Cooke, B. and Wolfram Cox, J. (eds) *Fundamentals of Action Research*. vol. 1, London: Sage. pp. 32–42.

Lippitt, R. (1950/2005) 'Action-research and the values of the social scientist.' In Cooke, B. and Wolfram Cox, J. (eds) *Fundamentals of Action Research*. vol. 3, London: Sage. pp. 301–307.

Lippitt, R. (1959/2003) 'Dimensions of the consultant's job.' In Cooke, B. and Wolfram Cox, J. (eds) *Fundamentals of Action Research*. vol. 3, London: Sage. pp. 191–199.

Lippitt, R. and Radke, M. (1946/2005) 'New trends in the investigation of prejudice.' In Cooke, B. and Wolfram Cox, J. (eds) *Fundamentals of Action Research*. vol. 1, London: Sage. pp. 107–120.

McTaggart, R. (1998/2005) 'Is validity really an issue for participatory action research?' In Cooke, B. and Wolfram Cox, J. (eds) *Fundamentals of Action Research*. vol. 3, London: Sage. pp. 395–421.

Melrose, M. (2001/2005) 'Maximizing the rigor of action research: why would you want to? How could you?' In Cooke, B. and Wolfram Cox, J. (eds) *Fundamentals of Action Research*. vol. 3, London: Sage. pp. 439–461.

Minnis, J. (2000/2005) 'Action research, the state and legitimation in Brunei Darussalam.' In Cooke, B. and Wolfram Cox, J. (eds.) *Fundamentals of Action Research*. vol. 4, London: Sage. pp. 139–155.

Peters, M. and Robinson, V. (1984/2005) 'The origins and status of action research.' In Cooke, B. and Wolfram Cox, J. (eds) *Fundamentals of Action Research*. vol. 4, London: Sage. pp. 45–58.

Raelin, J. A. (1989/2005) 'Action learning and action science: are they different?' In Cooke, B. and Wolfram Cox, J. (eds) *Fundamentals of Action Research*. vol. 2, London: Sage. pp. 159–180.

Rahman, M. A. (1982/2005) 'The theory and practice of participatory action research.' In Cooke, B. and Wolfram Cox, J. (eds) *Fundamentals of Action Research*. vol. 2, London: Sage. pp. 11–24.

Rapoport, R. N. (1970/2005) 'Three dilemmas in action research with special reference to the Tavistock experience.' In Cooke, B. and Wolfram Cox, J. (eds) *Fundamentals of Action Research*. vol. 4, London: Sage. pp. 25–44.

Reason, P. (1999/2005) 'Integrating action and reflection through co-operative inquiry.' In Cooke, B. and Wolfram Cox, J. (eds) *Fundamentals of Action Research*. vol. 2, London: Sage. pp. 235–259.

Reason, P. (2003/2005) 'Pragmatist philosophy and action research: readings and conversation with Richard Rorty.' In Cooke, B. and Wolfram Cox, J. (eds) *Fundamentals of Action Research*. vol. 4, London: Sage, pp. 297–319.

Reason, P. and Torbert, W. (2001/2005) 'The action turn: towards a transformational social science.' In Cooke, B. and Wolfram Cox, J. (eds) *Fundamentals of Action Research*. vol. 4, London: Sage, pp. 229–266.

Regehr, A. (2000/2005) 'Action research: underlying or undermining the cause?', In Cooke, B. and Wolfram Cox, J. (eds) *Fundamentals of Action Research*. vol. 4, London: Sage, pp. 157–172.

Reid, C. (2002/2005) 'Seduction and enlightenment in feminist action research.' In Cooke, B. and Wolfram Cox, J. (eds) *Fundamentals of Action Research*. vol. 3, London: Sage, pp. 265–286.

Robinson, V. M. J. (1993/2005) 'Current controversies in action research.' In Cooke, B. and Wolfram Cox, J. (eds) *Fundamentals of Action Research*. vol. 4, London: Sage, pp. 59–84.

Sanford, N. (1970/2005) 'Whatever happened to action research?', In Cooke, B. and Wolfram Cox, J. (eds) *Fundamentals of Action Research*. vol. 4, London: Sage, pp. 3–23.

Schein, E. H. (1987) *Organizational Culture and Leadership: a dynamic view*. San Francisco: Jossey-Bass.

Schein, E. H. (1995/2005) 'Process consultation, action research and clinical inquiry: are they the same?', In Cooke, B. and Wolfram Cox, J. (eds) *Fundamentals of Action Research*. vol. 2, London: Sage, pp. 149–158.

Schön, D. (1995/2005) 'Knowing-in-action: the new scholarship requires a new epistemology.' In Cooke, B. and Wolfram Cox, J. (eds) *Fundamentals of Action Research*. vol. 3, London: Sage, pp. 377–394.

Sellitz, C. and Cook, S. W. (1948/2005) In Cooke, B. and Wolfram Cox, J. (eds) *Fundamentals of Action Research*. vol. 1, London: Sage, pp. 165–173.

Shumsky, A. (1958/2005) 'Action research and modern man.' In Cooke, B. and Wolfram Cox, J. (eds) *Fundamentals of Action Research*. vol. 3, London: Sage, pp. 3–13.

Susman, G. and Evered, R. (1978/2005) 'An assessment of the scientific merits of action research.' In Cooke, B. and Wolfram Cox, J. (eds) *Fundamentals of Action Research*. vol. 3, London: Sage, pp. 319–345.

Trist, E. and Murray, H. (1990) 'Historical overview.' In Trist, E. and Murray, H. (eds) *The Social Engagement of Social Science: A Tavistock Anthology*. vol. 1, pp. 1–37.

Watson, G. (1949/2005) 'The problem and the next moves.' In Cooke, B. and Wolfram Cox, J. (eds) *Fundamentals of Action Research*. vol. 3, London: Sage, pp. 121–130.

Williams, G., Srivastava, M., Corbridge, S., and Véron, R. (2003/2005) 'Enhancing pro-poor governance in eastern India; participation, politics and action research.' In Cooke, B. and Wolfram Cox, J. (eds) *Fundamentals of Action Research*. vol. 3, London: Sage, pp. 321–346.

Wolfram Cox, J. and Minahan, S. (2006) 'Organizational decoration: a new metaphor for organization development.' *Journal of Applied Behavioral Science*. vol. 42, pp. 227–243.

Whyte, W. F. (1961/2005) 'An action research program for the personnel man.' In Cooke, B. and Wolfram Cox, J. (eds) *Fundamentals of Action Research*. vol. 2, London: Sage, pp. 291–315.

Whyte, W. F., Greenwood, D., and Lazes, P. (1989/2005) 'Participatory action research: through practice to science in social research.' In Cooke, B. and Wolfram Cox, J. (eds) *Fundamentals of Action Research*. vol. 2, London: Sage, pp. 99–136.

Wilson, A. T. M. (1947/2005) 'Some implications of medical practice and social case-work for action research.' In Cooke, B. and Wolfram Cox, J. (eds) *Fundamentals of Action Research*. vol. 1, London: Sage, pp. 131–149.

Zerubavel, E. (1991) *The Fine Line: Making Distinctions in Everyday Life*. New York: The Free Press.

13

Identity trajectories in participative organizational research

Paul Hibbert, Robert MacIntosh and Peter McInnes

Introduction

A traditional perspective on identity is that it consists of the characteristics of individuals which remain consistent and unique over time (Albert and Whetten 1985, Ford and Ford 1994). The way that we come to know others is through recognizing facets of their character that are repeatedly expressed over time with little variation. In some settings, such recognition is allied to fitting people into social categories (Tajfel and Turner 1979) which have functions both for insiders and outsiders. Those inside social categories become aware of how they should be thinking (Granitz and Ward 2001) and acting (Brewer 1999). Those outside the category become aware of how they should approach, and relate to, those within. When the categories are working well, the result should be a fairly smooth interaction both within and between different identity groups. The setting that we are concerned with is where different identity categories – researchers and practitioners – come into contact in order to collaborate in the development of local (and potentially more generalizable) knowledge.

In our experience, the process is not generally one of 'smoothness of interaction' between distinct social categories. Rather, the whole process of interacting and working on shared issues/projects leads to a far less fixed, and a far more dynamic, experience of identification. Identities are regarded as being socially constructed (Gergen 1999) in that they are partly projected by the self towards others, and partly projected by others onto the self (Hatch and Schultz 2002). These projections may be interpreted

237

in various ways and hence the potentiality for a lack of 'smoothness' is considerable (Czarniawska 1997). Multiple mis- and re-interpretations of identity projections are possible, and the nature of such interpretations, or 'readings of the situation', can be strongly influenced by the perceiver's membership of a particular interest group (Alvesson and Willmott 2002). On other occasions, the preferred view of interest groups (or the micro-political agenda) may be further in the background, but social expectations established through sensemaking (Watson and Bargiela-Chiappini 1998) and theory-led perception (Beech and Huxham 2003) can be enormously influential in framing the identities of self and other. Hence, the issues of working between identity boundaries and of being able to integrate or collaborate across such boundaries (Gabriel 2003) are particularly problematic.

Attempts to work in an engaged way with practitioners clearly challenges some identity norms. For researchers, there is a challenge of moving beyond the concern for theoretically identified research questions into taking a genuine concern with the issues and problems of practitioners. There is also a stepping into the practitioner mindset in order to work in a way that is useful for practice. For practitioners, there is a move away from one of two potential identities. Practitioners could be research subjects, in which case their role is to submit to having data extracted from them by the researcher. Alternatively, they could be a client, commissioning the work of an academic on a particular topic, for a particular purpose. When engaging in participatory research, there is a need for the practitioner to also step outside their normal role and become more involved in the researcher mindset. Such movements are potentially problematic (Ybema 2004) and may bring significant pain to the participants (Sveningsson and Alvesson 2003), and hence there is a need to better understand and manage these processes. Our interest in this chapter is to explore the flow of these shifts in identity and to seek to better understand the potential problems and opportunities.

In the remainder of this chapter we engage with these issues in three steps. First, we briefly discuss participative modes of research and – through a focus on a particular mode, as an example – begin to outline the identity dynamics that are entailed in such approaches. Secondly, we elaborate the identity issues in more detail through the presentation and discussion of a brief narrative of a particular research situation. Finally, we integrate the inferences in a concluding section which considers the implications for future research.

Participatory modes of researching organization

There are many ways of conceptualizing, describing or labelling participative modes of organizational research. These include a range of styles of action research (Bartunek 1993, Greenwood and Levin 2000, Quoss, Cooney, and Longhurst 2000), ethnography or partial ethnography (Alvesson and Deetz 2000, Golden-Biddle and Locke 1997, Hibbert and McQuade 2005, Humphreys, Brown, and Hatch 2003, Weeks 2000) and, more generically, participant observation (Vinten 1994). These modes of research share many common issues and debates. Many of these debates are most fully developed in the context of discussions of action research, and for that reason we briefly discuss that particular example of participative research at this point.

Action research is perhaps one of the most popular yet most contentious labels in the field of organizational research. It has been described as 'an umbrella term [describing] a host of activities intended to foster change.' (MacIntosh and Wilson 2003). Kurt Lewin introduced the term in 1946 to denote a new approach to social research where theory generation and attempts to change social systems went hand in hand. Action research provided a step-by-step framework for diagnosing, implementing and evaluating a change process. It also emphasized collaboration between research practitioners and clients to distribute knowledge and understanding within the organization. One of the most frequently quoted definitions of action research is this: 'Action research aims to contribute both to the practical concerns of people in an immediate problematic situation and to the goals of social science by joint collaboration within a mutually acceptable ethical framework' (Rapoport 1970: 499).

Lewin saw action research as a means for improving group decision-making and commitment towards a change strategy. Despite the subsequent impact of action research, Lewin himself never wrote a systematic statement on the topic (Argyris *et al.* 1985); in fact, he wrote only 22 pages on the topic (Peters and Robinson 1984), and died suddenly in 1947. His original model was five steps (analysis, fact finding, conceptualization, planning, execution, more fact finding or evaluation, then a repetition of the circle of activities), but in some instances he expanded his model to fit the needs of the situation (Dickens and Watkins 1999, Lewin 1948).

Our interest here is in participatory research, of which action research is a well-debated example, because of the nature of the identity work participatory research promotes and provokes within the research setting (Heracleous 2001). Participatory research focuses on participation and empowerment, and is described as a process whereby some of those in the organization under study participate actively with the researcher throughout the research process, from the initial design to the final presentation of results and discussion of their implications (Whyte 1991). In forming relationships between the researcher(s) and the researched, identity dynamics are generated which have implications for the epistemological dimensions of the research and the ontological claims of the knowledge produced. Participatory action research claims not to privilege the researcher as 'expert' over the other participants in the research process (Harrison and Leitch 2000). In longer term research engagements, participatory approaches to research can assume quasi- or partially ethnographic qualities. Our focus in this chapter is upon the ways in which such methodological stances impact upon the identity dynamics in the research process. Hence, we now turn our attention to identity work in the context of four suggested phases of research work, illustrated with examples from our own practice.

Four phases of the participatory research experience

In this part of the chapter we suggest that the participatory research experience can be described and characterized in relation to four possible phases of the process. The first of these we have described as 'a foot in the door', in which the researcher gains access to the research situation. The second we have labelled 'getting comfortable', in which the researcher begins to gain understanding of, and acceptance within, the situation. The third phase we have described as 'playing a part and being apart' – this describes the phase in which the researcher becomes fully embedded in the research situation, but perhaps struggles to avoid assimilation. The final phase we have characterized as 'the end of the affair' – in this phase the researcher seeks to withdraw from the situation. We do not suggest that these phases are universal nor cleanly bounded, but in the discussions leading to the development of this chapter we found that they were a useful way of relating and comparing the insights that all of the authors had experienced in their research projects. We therefore offer this a discursive framework rather than a prescriptive model for participatory research practice.

Each of these phases are described in relation to the experience of one of the authors in a particular research situation. This focal case was concerned with the establishment of a number of overlapping national science groups, each with a focus on the same niche area of science but promoting collaboration within a different end-user sector. Each of the four groups established over a three-year time period involved representatives from small and large organizations from both the public and private sectors; 12–15 (largely different) members were centrally involved in the establishment of each group. There were some centrally involved actors in the programme, and these are described in more detail in the discussions of each phase which follow below.

Each of these phase descriptions comprises of two parts. In the first, the researcher's narrative describing that particular stage is introduced; each narrative excerpt was developed through independent reflection and subsequent questioning by the other authors of this chapter. In the second part of each phase description, we discuss the issues arising in each phase narrative, and in some cases illustrate some alternative possibilities, through brief references to a second, rather different case.[1]

A foot in the door

Narrative: It is difficult to locate the start of my relationship with the lead institution orchestrating the creation of national science groups as part of a government-sponsored programme. It seems likely, however, that they would have first noticed me as a competitor – I was working for a small consultancy that won another part of the government programme, which was competitively tendered, against their incumbent bid.

Once this project was underway, however, it was vital that the relationship should change to a degree as fulfilment required that I gain access to some key inputs from the lead institution. We seemed to be dancing around each other; when we had to meet at this stage I was seeking to present myself as a neutral government contractor and the lead institution managers I was consulting seemed to be trying to appear cooperative without actually delivering much in the way of helpful information – perhaps just enough to appear to be compliant. They seemed to be operating way below their reputed ability: they were difficult to get to see and were very slow in delivering documents that the government sponsor required them to provide to the project. There was little in the way of friendliness or interest in personal interaction from

---

1 This was concerned with an organization in the cultural sector. Its main 'products' are two international music festivals which run each year and the operation of three large and complex concert venues. The intervention in this second case was aimed at improving the organization of the main festival.

their side and occasional brusque rudeness about the 'little company' where I was employed.

Whilst this was, at this stage, merely a competitive, commercial consulting situation, I was interested in the lead institution's potential role in coordinating science networks – I was conducting research into inter-organizational collaboration on a part-time basis, as I thought at that time that a doctorate would boost my consultancy career, both as a marketable specialization and by informing my practice in supporting networks. For that reason I sought to try to change the working relationship with them. This I did by giving the senior manager the opportunity to comment on the final report for the project. I did not have to do this, but it gave them the opportunity to forestall any major embarrassments or inconveniences in this report, which might have impacted on their competitive position in future projects. I think that giving them access to this report perhaps achieved two things. First, it communicated the impression that I was not trying to engage in competitive 'points scoring', at their expense. Secondly, it meant that the senior manager actively engaged with my work – and could see that it was sound, since he actually suggested very few changes. This seemed to be helpful, since when the project to develop national science groups was initiated, I was engaged by the lead institution as a sub-contractor.

Discussion: We can see in this first part of the narrative that an identity shift is asserted on the part of the researcher – from 'competitor' to collaborator. However this also requires a corresponding identity shift on the part of the other (in this case, a group of others) since competition is a relational notion. In this case, these shifts seem to occur at rather different rates, with three processes being indicated. First, the narrator suggesting that there was a period of *analysis*, in which the performative manoeuvres of the lead institution managers were reflected on as indicators of their construction of the researcher's identity. Secondly, there was *disruption* through the deliberate execution of an action which was inconsistent with the (presumed) expectation of competitive behavior. Finally, there was a process of *co-option* initiated by the lead institution. It can be argued that the researcher, despite arriving at the start of the relationship through a competitive process, saw the other as a collaborator from the outset whereas this regard was mirrored by the lead institution managers only much later.

This seems to suggest that there is potential for some kind of 'phase lag' in the realignment of identity positions, but it would be too simplistic to view this as a simple switch from one state to another. In particular, the narrative also suggests that there are multiple identity conceptions in play in the situation; the researcher could have approached the situation from a perspective informed by his contractual, formal role as a commercial consultant, but instead focused on his interests and self-positioning as a part-time doctoral researcher. A consideration of reflexivity seems to be important here, perhaps both in the sense of a distinct focus on the self-in-action (Cunliffe 2003, 2004) and also as unconscious self-confrontation (Beck, Giddens, and Lash 1994); both modes suggest that reflexivity describes a process which acts upon itself in such a way as to modify that very process. In particular, at this early stage in the relationship the researcher was intending to continue with a consultancy career, which the research degree was to enhance – but by the end of the case things had changed somewhat.

Getting comfortable

Narrative: Becoming at home in the research situation was both deliberate and accidental. On the deliberate side, I made the lead institution managers that I was working with fully aware of my own background in the natural sciences – in fact, in their own niche sector. They had not been aware of this in our competitive, business process interactions in the past and it was something of a transformative revelation. One of them actually apologized for not realizing that I was 'one of us' and for 'talking down' in discussions. Being a scientist – like them – made me something more of an insider and meant that subsequent conversations flowed a little more freely. I also tried deliberately to anchor my position by presenting myself as an expert on collaborative facilitation. On reflection, I think that I did believe this to be true – at least to a degree – but others in the firm could probably have undertaken the contracted work. However, this role was providing me with a legitimate position in the scientific communities I was researching and my emphasis on my expertise in collaborative processes was intended to persuade the lead institution managers to insist on my personal involvement – rather than risking my transfer to other assignments.

Whilst I had therefore made considerable effort to consolidate my position, a greater level of openness in the research input was actually a result of chance conversation, in which we realized that there was a common acquaintance that the senior manager and I shared. Although I had not talked to the third party in question for seven years (in fact, I didn't really get on with him), this started a round of nostalgic diversions. After this event I seemed to be treated as part of the social circle – not just the professional community – of the senior manager and his colleagues.

Discussion: In this second phase of the narrative another facet of the researcher's identity is in play: that of a natural scientist *manqué*. The scientist identity is deliberately constructed through the relation of personal history, but the degree of ambivalence that the researcher has to this identity allows him to use it, to put it in play (or at risk). There may have been much less willingness to play (or 'trade') with an aspect of identity to which he was deeply attached.

This manoeuvre seemed to result in an identity/identification shift and was perhaps effective because it relied on something already developed and intrinsic to the researcher's story, rather than something that had to be built up during the relationship – earned, learned or imitated. The researcher was able to assert the claim and simply 'be' a scientist since the necessary patterns of speaking and interpretation had already been learned over many years in the community of practice (Lave and Wenger 1991). This was perhaps also possible because the language of the natural sciences at least claims to be built on consistent and universal principles; perhaps more than any other community of practice, natural scientific disciplines are relatively free of theoretical diversity and paradigmatic controversy – hence, there is a linguistic smoothness and agreement is easy and expected. Trust was therefore easy to develop on such a basis and a second implicit identity shift seems to follow, from collaborators to members of the same professional community.

Alternatively, it might be better to suggest that another identity facet was exposed and turned towards the light; since the collaborative project was still the framework for interactions, the identity notion of 'collaborator' was still live. In addition, a new facet seemed to be cut as coincidental overlap in personal histories became the basis of a rather more personal level of interaction. Taking up the theme of reflexivity once more, we can see that the researcher's identity is again put in play in both deliberate and uncontrolled ways. The outcomes may have been somewhat different if the conversation had uncovered a mutual acquaintance that the manager liked but the researcher disliked, or vice versa. In addition, at the time of accepting the personal relationship on the basis of an assumed attitude to a common acquaintance that was actually the reverse of what was felt, the researcher is seemingly moving from a professional relationship to a more open, personal relationship whilst at the same time actually becoming – to a degree – somewhat less honest. Once again the identity moves are out of phase, but it is now the other, rather than the researcher, who is running ahead.

In contrast to the developing connection between researcher and client on the basis of a shared expertise in science, in the case of the cultural organization the researcher had no expertise in the specific activities or sector of the organization. Getting comfortable resulted more from initial differences moderated through contact. The researcher was seen as having expertise (in business and organization) that lay outside the normal scope of the organization, and this was valued. However, the members of the organization also had the impression that such expertise would be applied in a formal and distant way. Once the intervention started, the interviews and focus groups were fun to do. People were dedicated to the cultural mission of the company and they were interesting people. The problem, however, was related to complex constructions that various parties were making of each other, subsequent prioritizations and a lack of communication. Hence, the problem was also very interesting. Friendships in the organization, particularly with the CEO and with a middle manager, developed and the researcher became personally engaged with the mission. Therefore, in this case, getting comfortable was based on professional difference and personal empathy.

Playing a part and being apart

Narrative: Having seemingly been established as 'one of us' within the professional community, and a trusted member because of common social connections, I seemed to be called upon to enact this identity. This was exemplified by my co-option to a long-established national committee on standards in the lead institution's niche area of science, at the request of the senior manager (who also served as the chair of this committee). Whilst this added more depth to my ethnographic study of science networks, it also meant that I had to exercise my (natural) scientific knowledge, which had rather atrophied – I felt that I might expose my limits at some inopportune moment. Whilst this exposure and shame never actually occurred, I was also conscious that I was getting 'bedded in' a little more than was comfortable; some of the committee members had served for decades (one was over 80, and still chairing his scientific materials firm) and everything seemed to run by rote.

There was plenty of opportunity to observe, but little opportunity to question or provoke – this was problematic since there seemed to be little to learn after the first couple of meetings. Was I 'really' a researcher or 'really' a committee member? Perhaps I was blurring into a kind of micro-establishment, and beginning to go native ...

Discussion: Later in the narrative the researcher's careful manoeuvring seems to be resulting in unexpected identity outcomes, as he finds himself having to enact, 'for real', the identity of a natural scientist. At such times, when research projects are most active and intense, it seems that the researcher is necessarily enacting different identities inwardly (researcher) and outwardly (participant) and there is a tension between which one is (or should be) the most important or 'real' – although perhaps both are essential. There also seems to be a risk that the researcher stumbles into a particular micro-community of practice, and in learning to make sense of it for a research purposes becomes a legitimate and fluent participant within it; through repeated enactment, the identity becomes meaningful (Boyer 1990, Shils 1981).

In the cultural organization, playing a part entailed running some workshops which meant that the researcher had to play a somewhat detached role. More significantly, the researcher was involved in assisting managerial decision-making about organizational structure, people's roles and reporting relationships. This meant that some people felt betrayed and for some there was anger towards the researcher. For others, taking the actions led to an increased level of trust and friendship as 'we had come through a difficult time together'. There was an entanglement between having to be part of difficult decisions and being 'authentic' within the relationships that were emerging. Ultimately, this meant prioritizing the actions that were needed by the organization, and risking the relationships.

The end of the affair

Narrative: Getting out of the situation was eventually executed relatively cleanly. I changed my job, joining academia full time, and explained the position to the lead institution. I had not intended to make such a radical change at the start of the research project, but I had begun to find the tension between the two halves of my life to be insupportable.

I was becoming increasingly cynical about the possibility of making a difference through consultancy, and switching between academic and consultancy styles of discourse was difficult. I was able to make the transition easier by taking a colleague from the consultancy firm along to my last round of meetings with the various groups and committees, and began to let him lead the interactions towards the end of my time of employment with the firm. He is still involved with the lead institution, and still attends the national committee on standards – a privilege for which he does not thank me ...

Discussion: In the conclusion of the narrative, the exit strategy from the research situation is relatively dramatic and presents a 'clean break' to the relationship, but perhaps it need not necessarily have been handled in this way. Possibly, this might have been an opportunity for the researcher to seek to stay engaged, but in a differently balanced relationship which more explicitly emphasized his identity as a researcher and occluded the other aspects (consultant, collaborator, friend, professional colleague ...), although some negotiation around this might be expected.

However, what is interesting is that this shift in emphasis was achieved anyway, in the breaking of the relationships not just with the managers in the scientific institution but also with the researcher's commercial employer. On reflection, it seems that this career identity outcome – although not predicted or desired by the part-time researcher at the start of the project – might have been implicit in the choices that were made at the outset of the project, when commercial considerations were given less attention than research questions. It is difficult to be certain whether the processes and tensions brought into play in the deliberate manipulation of identity for research ends always carry such personal risks for the researcher, but it seems likely and there are other outcomes that we have collectively experienced that are perhaps less dramatic but still uncomfortable or problematic.

In the cultural organization example, the break was far less 'clean'. The organizational intervention was complete, but the relationships were ongoing. As things have settled down in the organization, parts of the agreed future have slipped back into old practices. In this case, the researcher has remained engaged with the CEO and middle manager on an informal basis, offering support and advice on how to deal with the emerging situation.

Conclusions

There are three particular implications about identity issues associated with participatory research that can be gleaned from the preceding discussion. These also have potential relevance to other areas of organizational practice, or at least to the study of identity in such areas.

The first and second of these implications are concerned with the identity shifts – in relation to both researchers and practitioners – within and across phases of the research process, and the manner in which they seem to occur. It seems clear that such shifts can have a range of different time frames and involve processes of interpretation (Beech and Huxham 2003). At shorter timescales, these can be connected to instances of framing in a particular, contested, micro-political context or in response to some particularly provocative or significant moment in the processes of interaction (Alvesson and Willmott 2002, Heracleous 2001), as we observed in parts of the research narrative presented earlier. At the longer timescale, there is the possibility of identity shifts occurring in association with developmental change – on either side of the research–practice relationship – in a more gradual manner, although in the narrative presented earlier this is clearest in the case of the researcher. This might perhaps be expected in modes of research that often seek to change accepted modes of organizing, and therefore to alter patterns of sense making in a particular context (Lewin 1948, MacIntosh and Wilson 2003, Watson and Bargiela-Chiappini 1998)

The third implication follows naturally from the first two. The varying instances and processes of identity shifts can have relatively enduring consequences. As we noted in relation to the narrative presented earlier, the researcher eventually found himself in an uncomfortable position, straddling multiple-notional identity boundaries – consultant, scientist, researcher – from moment to moment (Gabriel 2003, Ybema 2004). He eventually acted to reduce the tension and pain of the situation (Sveningsson and Alvesson 2003) by abandoning a commitment to two of these roles. However, this suggests that there are some ethical implications here for research and practice. There is a question of how far we are able and willing to allow 'play' or 'trade' with aspects of our identities in order to build the relationships necessary for participatory research. There is also the question of how one should proceed (and at what speed) through the phases outlined above. Clearly, if different participants move at different paces there is the potential for tension and conflicting views/interests.

References

Albert, S. A. and Whetten, D. A. (1985) 'Organizational identity.' In Cummings, L. L. and Straw, B. M. (eds) *Research in Organizational Behavior*. London: JAI Press.

Alvesson, M. and Deetz, S. (2000) *Doing Critical Management Research*. London: Sage.

Alvesson, M. and Willmott, H. (2002) 'Identity regulation as organizational control: producing the appropriate individual.' *Journal of Management Studies* 39(5): 619–644.

Argyris, C., Putnam, R., and Smith, D. (1985) *Action Science: Concepts, Methods and Skills for Research and Intervention*. San Francisco: Jossey Bass.

Bartunek, J. M. (1993) 'Scholarly dialogues and participatory action research.' *Human Relations* 46: 1221–1233.

Beck, U., Giddens, A., and Lash, S. (1994) *Reflexive Modernization*. Oxford: Blackwell.

Beech, N. and Huxham, C. (2003) 'Cycles of identity formation in inter-organizational collaborations.' *International Studies of Management and Organization* 33(2): 7–21.

Boyer, P. (1990) *Tradition as Truth and Communication*. Cambridge: Cambridge University Press.

Brewer, M. B. (1999) 'The psychology of prejudice: ingroup love or outgroup hate?' *Journal of Social Issues* 55: 429–444.

Cunliffe, A. (2003) 'Reflexive inquiry in organizational research: questions and possibilities.' *Human Relations* 56(8): 983–1003.

Cunliffe, A. (2004) 'On becoming a critically reflexive practitioner.' *Journal of Management Education* 28(4): 407–426.

Czarniawska, B. (1997) *Narrating the Organization: Dramas of Institutional Identity.* Chicago: The University of Chicago Press.

Dickens, L. and Watkins, K. (1999) 'Action research: rethinking Lewin.' *Management Learning* 30: 127–140.

Ford, J. D. and Ford, L. W. (1994) 'Logics of identity, contradiction and attraction in change.' *Academy of Management Review* 19(4): 756–786.

Gabriel, Y. (2003) 'Your home, my exile: boundaries and "otherness" in antiquity and now.' *Organization Studies* 24(4): 619–632.

Gergen, K. (1999) *An Invitation to Social Construction.* London: Sage.

Golden-Biddle, K. and Locke, K. (1997) 'Constructing opportunities for contribution: structuring intertextual coherence and "problematizing" in organizational studies.' *Academy of Management Journal* 40: 1023–1062.

Granitz, N. A. and Ward, J. C. (2001) 'Actual and perceived sharing of ethical reasoning and moral intent among in-group and out-group members.' *Journal of Business Ethics* 33: 299–322.

Greenwood, D. J. and Levin, M. (2000) 'Reconstructing the relationships between universities and society through action research.' In Denzin, N. and Lincoln, Y. (eds) *Handbook of Qualitative Research.* London: Sage, pp. 85–106.

Harrison, R. T. and Leitch, C. M. (2000) 'Learning and organization in the knowledge based information economy: initial findings for a participatory action research case study.' *British Journal of Management* 11: 103–119.

Hatch, M. J. and Schultz, M. (2002) 'The dynamics of organizational identity.' *Human Relations* 55(8): 989–1018.

Heracleous, L. (2001) An ethnographic study of culture in the context of organizational change, *Journal of Applied Behavioural Science*, 37(4) 426–446.

Hibbert, P. and McQuade, A. (2005) 'To which we belong: understanding the role of tradition in interorganizational relations.' *M@n@gement* 8(4): 73–88.

Humphreys, M., Brown, A., and Hatch, M. (2003) 'Is ethnography jazz?' *Organization* 10: 5–31.

Lave, J. and Wenger, E. (1991) *Situated Learning: Legitimate Peripheral Participation.* Cambridge, Cambridge University Press.

Lewin, K. (1948) 'Action research and minority problems.' In Lewin, G. W. (ed.) *Resolving Social Conflicts.* New York: Harper.

MacIntosh, R. and Wilson, F. (2003) *Publishing Action Research*, 19th EGOS Colloquium, Sub-Theme 25: Challenges Faced by Action Researchers in Bridging the Gap Between Micro-Sociological Processes and Desired Macro Changes, Copenhagen, July.

Peters, M. and Robinson, V. (1984) The origins and status of action research. *Journal of Applied Behavioral Science*, 20(2), 113–124.

Quoss, B., Cooney, M., and Longhurst, T. (2000) 'Academics and advocates: using participatory action research to influence welfare policy.' *Journal of Consumer Affairs* 34: 47–61.

Rapoport, R. N. (1970) 'Three dilemmas of action research.' *Human Relations* 23: 499–513.

Shils, E. (1981) *Tradition.* Chicago: University of Chicago Press.

Sveningsson, S. and Alvesson, M. (2003) 'Managing managerial identities: organizational fragmentation, discourse and identity struggle.' *Human Relations* 56(10): 1163–1193.

Tajfel, H. and Turner, J. C. (1979) 'An integrative theory of intergroup conflict.' In Austin, W. G. and Worchel, S. (eds) *The Social Psychology of Intergroup Relations.* Monterey, CA: Brooks/Cole, pp. 33–47.

Vinten, G. (1994) 'Participant observation: a model for organizational investigation.' *Journal of Managerial Psychology* 9: 30–38.

Watson, T. J. and Bargiela-Chiappini, F. (1998) 'Managerial sensemaking and occupational identities in Britain and Italy: the role of management magazines in the process of discursive construction.' *Journal of Management Studies* 35(3): 285–301.

Weeks, J. (2000) 'What do ethnographers believe? A reply to Jones.' *Human Relations* 53: 153–171.

Whyte, W. F. (1991) 'Comparing P.A.R. and action science.' In Whyte, W. F. (ed.) *Participatory Action Research*. Beverly Hills, CA: Sage.

Ybema, S. (2004) 'Managerial postalgia: projecting a golden future.' *Journal of Managerial Psychology* 19(8): 825–841.

14

Exploring culture and collective identity with the radio ballads

Stephen Linstead

Introduction: identity, performance and aesthetics

Culture is a notoriously paradoxical organizational phenomenon to explore – to the extent that it is the product of organic cultural process, it tends to be taken for granted and left largely implicit; to the extent that it is publicly announced and presented, it often displays a superficial glitter that masks some more deeply held characteristics that subvert the culture as displayed. In the last decade, the concept of organizational identity has tended to displace that of organizational culture as it is both easier to isolate and has both inward- and outward-facing aspects, relying less on the taken-for-granted (Hatch and Schultz 2002). Yet organizational culture is not by any means a dead concept, having a good deal to do with what organizational members think and feel in common, and can critically shape the mindsets that are brought to the decision-making process and associated environmental assessments. The understanding of culture depends on the dynamic understanding of cultural processes, not on their abstraction and rationalization – on those things that, precisely because they are intuitive, unconscious and taken for granted, respondents cannot always readily make available for discussion.

Almost by definition, questionnaires will not be able to access such data. Other methods are necessary, of which participant observation offers traditionally the richest resource, but has limitations of scope, is demanding on time, is not always possible and may sometimes be a hostage to fortune depending on how organizational circumstances unfold. Depth interviewing, serial interviewing, story and narrative interviewing, life history interviewing and group interviewing have all been deployed ethnographically in pursuit of culture, and attempts to involve research participants in co-authorship by feeding back early forms of research accounts to them and incorporating their voices more explicitly have become more common in recent years. Yet co-production means that accounts cannot be written for academic audiences alone, and attempts to make ethnography more powerful and intuitively accessible through the use of aesthetic techniques for data presentation including performance ethnography have been persuasively advocated (Denzin 2003, McCall 2000). In this chapter I explore how one form of performance ethnography – and the methods it used – can be applied to hold up a mirror to organization as a means of facilitating more sensitive understandings of culture, identity and change.

Aesthetics is the study of forms and appearances, and is often associated solely with beauty, although ugliness is part of aesthetics too. What people regard as beautiful, particularly how everyday objects and events are seen differently by different groups, is increasingly an important aspect of the investigation of the aesthetic life of organizations, with the recognition that aesthetics is connected to meaning, and is therefore subject to social negotiation just as socially constructed meaning is (Strati 1999). So aesthetics can make us aware of paradox and pain as well as pleasure, and looking at the aesthetics of a particular group can reveal powerfully how identity is sustained by the symbolic revalorization, within the group, of phenomena, tasks, objects, activities, and so on, that are devalued by other groups or wider society. Additionally, the poetic dimension of art and music is that which creates and captures significant moments, moments where our awareness changes, where things are seen in a new light, or where we experience insight or revelation. When attempting to gain some insight into another group's culture, this sort of experience is exactly what data collection instruments and cultural metrics cannot provide and what the use of aesthetics – art, music, poetry, theatre and dance – does provide, literally and *sensation*ally. The point of performance ethnography, as I use it here, is not the performance itself as entertainment – although its success *as* performance is a paramount factor in the selection of material. Where ethnography might wish to achieve a comprehensive representation of the elements of a culture or subculture, and attempt balance in such representation, it tends to rely on two-dimensional and primarily textual representations. Performance ethnography seeks to restore additional dimensionality to ethnography, with an immediacy that opens windows into the data, rather than replace text-based ethnography entirely. As such, we can use performance ethnographies to enable us to reinterrogate our own data, as well as offering new approaches to data collection and representation, and we can learn from performance ethnography without necessarily needing to produce performance ethnographies of our own.

In this chapter I will introduce the Radio Ballads as a dramatic form that draws upon ethnographic research and presents ethnographic data in a powerful and compelling way, but only listening to the programmes themselves will convince the reader of their remarkable range and motility. Drawing on writings by Ewan MacColl and Charles Parker that discuss their methods, and on some transcriptions from the programmes, I will discuss five of the most salient aspects of this work for the study of collective identity – recording the background culture; listening to language (rather than discourse); intermittent interrogative methods; collective identity and narrative myth; collective self-discovery and catalytic interviewing. I will conclude by addressing some potential criticisms of the approach.

The radio ballads

[*Background noise of machinery – it is as if we are standing in a foundry. The noise punctuates and accompanies the speech, and the sound of the huge drop-forge hammer rises in intensity . . .*]

Male voice: Dark, dank, noisy, smelly, dangerous . . . and I wouldn't recommend any kid of mine to work in a steel foundry

Female voice: The air would be yellow with sulphur

Older male: Looking back on it I shudder to think that I worked in such conditions . . . it told on everybody . . . I mean no . . . no protective clothing . . . you damaged your lungs and your eyesight . . . and . . . every part of your body you abused it (*The Song of Steel* 2006).

At 21.03 GMT on 27 February 2006, a BBC Radio 2 announcer uttered a phrase that had not been heard in the context of the introduction of a new radio production for over 40 years: 'We present *The Song of Steel*, a radio ballad featuring the men and women who worked in the steel industry of Rotherham and Sheffield'. *The Radio Ballads 2006* were a series of six programmes reviving and modernizing a form first developed in the late 1950s and 1960s for a series of experimental but seminal radio documentaries. The original programmes were devised by writer, lyricist and singer Ewan MacColl, with orchestration and music direction by Peggy

Seeger, and production and editing by Charles Parker, a radio producer with the BBC Home Service [although after the first programme Seeger was involved in every part of the creative process (MacColl 1990: 314–315)]. They were not originally planned as a series, but began as an idea for one programme about a specific incident (the heroic death of Stockport train driver John [Jack] Axon) initiated by Parker. As they became successful the producers discovered their emerging mission and broadened the scope of the programmes. Nevertheless, even to the last the series was never planned as a systematic whole, although it covers a wide range of experience from the micro (the psychology of pain) to the macro (the dispossession of a migrant community) and the individual programmes complement each other very well.

The 2006 programmes were devised by producer John Leonard (himself also a former singer and musician), musical director, musician, singer, writer and actor John Tams, and a production team of tape editor Annie Grundy and interviewers Vince Hunt and Sara Parker (daughter of Charles), to deal with six topics that were different from the original themes but represented significant issues that had emerged to prominence out of and during the period since the original series was broadcast. What the two series have in common is a concern not with work or social processes themselves but

> people's attitudes and responses to those processes: in other words, not with things, but the way people related to things and the way in which those relationships were expressed in words
>
> (MacColl 1990: 318).

and a willingness to utilize the capabilities of the medium and the available technology to represent what they found.[1] One significant difference is highlighted by the first programme of the new series on steelmaking and confirmed by the final one on shipbuilding – the shift from recording experiences of a part of an industrial subculture at or close to its most extensive and vibrant, towards experiences of a culture that is largely recollected and identity faded, as the industry is either dead or in decline (although the original series *Singing the Fishing* contained elements of both). It could be argued from the point of view of a traditionalist or archivist

---

1 Not that this was the intention from the beginning – rather it was arrived at after the second programme attempted, under political pressure from within the BBC, to combine the format with the more traditional radio documentary format and try to achieve a balanced representation of views. Whilst the second programme was a critical success, MacColl considered it to be a 'débâcle with a few bright spots' (MacColl 1990: 316).

that the omission of shipbuilding (British shipbuilding was at its peak in the early 1950s) and steelmaking (similarly successful in the post-War period) from the original series of ballads was a weakness – indeed there are other industries such as cotton in Lancashire and wool in West Yorkshire that remain unexplored in either series. But this illustrates precisely the point that from its inception the series was not about the nostalgic collection of stories and reminiscences even from a living and active culture – the Radio Ballads were *experimental* and looked to explore new *methods* as much as new content.

The concept as it developed was simple – field recordings would be made of interviews and conversations with key informants and hours of tape would be edited and clustered so that only the words of the people would be used to tell their own stories, without the intervention of a narrator or interviewer.[2] Instead, incidental music would be punctuated by songs, specially written by MacColl, using the words and images of the informants. The programmes would dispense with narrators and actors, and be woven together from the three elements of original lyric; a combination of specially composed, arranged and improvised music incorporating a range of styles including folk and jazz; and 'actuality' or field recordings with sound effects [this actuality could also include traditional songs by the informants from their own repertoires]. MacColl developed a technique of improvising around traditional tunes as a base for his songs, ending with a finished product that 'felt' like a traditional song but sounded nothing like the tune that he had used as his original base. He performed the songs back to the informants and checked for errors, inaccuracies and generally whether they liked or approved of the songs. His greatest compliment, received from an 80-year-old fisherman, was 'I've known that song all my life'. Of course he hadn't as MacColl had only just written it, but the statement was testimony that it had the ring of authenticity about it that MacColl had hoped to achieve. The songs were not necessarily used as complete songs in the

---

2 In an unpublished paper, MacColl (n.d. ms circa 1981: 1–2) notes that the Radio Ballads did not pioneer either the use of the tape recorder to present 'actuality' or dispensing with the narrator in programmes. He gives examples of the producer and poet John Pudney replacing narration with song as early as 1937, and D. G. Bridson in 1944 and Denis Mitchell in 1949 using field recordings in the production process. The difference was that with the increased availability of broadcast-quality standards from new technology, Parker saw 'actuality' as being 'central to the whole business of broadcasting', not marginal. He also saw the need for an organic rather than artificial link between the songs and the spoken word. It was this combination that made the Radio Ballads so innovative.

programmes, but verses were often scattered here and there to emphasize, link or illustrate at different points in the programme – verses also might be performed more slowly, or in a different key for effect.

The broadcasting and recording detail for both series is as follows:

Title	Subject	First broadcast	Topic label CD #
Original Series			
The Ballad of John Axon	Railways	02.07.58	TSCD801
Song of a Road	Construction	05.11.59	TSCD802
Singing the Fishing	Sea-Fishing	16.08.60	TSCD803
The Big Hewer	Mining	18.08.61	TSCD804
The Body Blow	Polio	27.03.62	TSCD805
On the Edge	Teenagers	13.02.63	TSCD806
The Fight Game	Boxing	03.07.63	TSCD807
The Travelling People	Gypsies	17.04.64	TSCD808
Radio Ballads 2006		*Website Download**	
The Song of Steel	Steelmaking	27.02.06	Yes
The Enemy Within	HIV/AIDS	06.03.06	Yes
The Horn of the Hunter	Hunting	13.03.06	Yes
Swings and Roundabouts	Fairgrounds	20.03.06	Yes
Thirty Years of Conflict	Sectarianism	27.03.06	Yes
The Ballad of the Big Ships	Shipbuilding	03.04.06	Yes

Recording the background culture

Perhaps the first area that invites our attention in recording for broadcast (however limited the audience) rather than simple transcription is that of the aural environment, which Parker (1965a: 17) argues is an important dimension of 'man's (sic) relationships to his natural and social environment'. Although the foundational works of ethnography in social and cultural anthropology and ethnology did not neglect the significance of music and sound in the cultures under study, this has not been the case for subsequent ethnographies and in particular studies of organizational communities (see Nissley [2002] for a relatively rare contrasting view).

What I want to draw attention to here, however, is twofold. First, it is probably true that as research interviewers we pay insufficient attention to the quality of our recordings. We could pay attention to the quality of direct sound (i.e. mouth to microphone); reflected sound (from the body to the walls, floor, ceiling, furniture reflected back to the microphone) and background noise (phones ringing, traffic noise, etc.) with the objective of maximizing the quality of the first and eliminating the latter two.

Generally speaking, any microphone in use should be close but not too close to the speaker's mouth. Lapel mikes are now of a good enough quality to use for broadcast recordings but researchers may well not have the resources to afford them, although high-enough quality lapel mikes for research recordings can be within reach. If a radio-controlled mike can be afforded, it can enable a more relaxed and less self-conscious atmosphere for what Parker (1965a: 6) calls the 'deliberately created conversational situation (never *ever* an "interview" situation)'. For Parker here, the objective of what is sometimes called the 'documentary' is to create the antithesis of the 'document' – that is, something capable of evoking intense and individual experience and capturing 'the speaking likenesses of human life itself'. This means paying attention to the social quality of the interaction and not allowing the interview to become an adversarial battle of wits; a sort of fact-finding mission rather like a political poll with specific answers required to carefully prepared questions; or the interview as self-adulatory (whether of the interviewee or, sadly, on occasion the interviewer). But interestingly, it also means recognizing that the acoustic qualities of familiar surroundings may be what the interviewee's voice is attuned to, and this will immediately give them a sense of congenial familiarity. As Parker (1964: 6–7) notes, 'the reflected sound is itself important to the character of the speaker – often the timbre of his (sic) voice is in tune to this particular condition'. Nevertheless, unwanted and unnecessary background noise should be minimized.

Yet the second point is that whilst this noise is minimized for the purpose of hearing the spoken words clearly, the ambient sound is crucial to the texture of what is being conveyed. Although the actual recorded sounds were not necessarily usable on broadcast recordings, other sound sources could be used to accurately produce their effects; so Parker and MacColl spent a lot of time recording ambient noise of machines working. They recorded in the locomotive sheds in Edgeley, and even on the footplate of an engine of the same type as Jack Axon's, travelling at the same speed (Parker 1965b: 2–3). For *Song of a Road* they recorded 'in hostels, dormitories, pubs, canteens and shelters . . . . in the cabs of bulldozers and earth-moving machines and helicopters, in offices and plant headquarters' (MacColl n.d.2: 2). In *Singing the Fishing* they went perhaps even further.

We kept [the tape recorders] running while we sat at meals in the galley and in the wheelhouse, where a radio-receiving set kept up a continuous chatter of information from every drifter within a fifty-mile radius . . . . We recorded the rhythmical clacking of the winch as the two-mile long nets were played

out . . . [I stood] there on the deck, terrified, clinging desperately with one hand to a steel cable while in the other I [held] up a microphone to record the storm
(MacColl 1990: 322–323).

In *The Body Blow*, looking at the experience of pain in polio victims who spent months in hospital, often on the artificial respirator called the 'iron lung', they realized that the constant sound of this machine – it literally pumped every breath, 24 hours a day, became a huge part of the experience of their interviewees. In the programme, one of the most powerfully realistic sections appears to be a montage of comments given against the background of the monstrous but life-saving beats of the iron lung. The sound itself was added in the studio by the use of the breather button on the English concertina of Alf Roberts, a device that allows the bellows to work without sounding the reeds.

The point in all cases was the same: to recognize the importance of the auditory environment to shaping the shared experience and common aspects of identity of those embedded in it, and who offered their personal testimonies from out of that cultural milieu. The beginning of the 2006 series emphasizes this dramatically, as the opening sequence proceeds to the sound of the drop-forge hammer and local people telling how it dominated their lives.

Listening to language

Culture is importantly sustained by communication as well as interaction, as it sets the template for how interaction is to be interpreted. If communicative styles are creating language communities, then the existence of cultural differences is to be expected. *The Song of a Motorway*, featuring some of the 19,000 people who worked on the construction of the first sections of the M1 in the United Kingdom, provides wonderful material on what binds migrant workers together, but particularly, by simple juxtaposition of language styles, contrasts managerial and worker cultures dramatically. In the multi-ethnic environment of the construction workers, there is a huge difference between the colorful mixture of images used by the workforce to convey meaning and the cool, dry abstractions of management:

The labourers . . . used both similes and metaphors liberally. They changed tense constantly, often to emphasize a point or to sharpen an argument. They made use of extended analogies and emphasized verbs in such a way as to give every sentence an effort-peak. Almost all of them used the first person singular and the present historical with equal effect.... A project manager drew attention to the two language groups in the course of defining the functions of a ganger: 'He's the link between us and them. *I sometimes think we'd be no worse off if they were speaking Swahili.'*

(MacColl 1990: 326).

One mechanic, interviewed vividly and with startling economy, conveys the sense of excitement he gets from travelling with his work by saying that working in a garage is 'a rusty old life'. Yet managerial informants

tended to use an extremely small area of the vocal effort spectrum.... Irrespective of the subject under discussion they scarcely ever varied the tempo of delivery. Almost all of them made constant use of the impersonal pronoun.... Verbs were given no more vocal weight than nouns, and similes and metaphors were almost totally eschewed

(MacColl 1990: 326).

In the programme, this is illustrated in a song (*Song of a Road* in Seeger 2001: 120) which sets parts of an interview with Sir John Laing, who manages to drain all the life out of an epic enterprise, against a jolly, well-orchestrated music-hall tune with a knockabout comedy feel, which develops into a mournful blues and ends up as chaotic New Orleans–style traditional jazz:

Sir John Laing (somewhat languidly, slightly bored): *We are the consulting engineers . . . aah . . . we are responsible to the Ministry of Transport for the whole design of the road . . . and . . . We are employed to design and supervise the construction . . .*

Sung [Voice 2 – tenor, vigorously]: Every time you want to build a road from there to here

The first thing that you need is a consulting engineer

He will do your thinking for you; he'll put your plan in gear

He's the brainy bloke that's got the know-how

Chorus [heartily]: With his surveyors and designers and his peggers and his liners

With his plans and elevations and his endless calculations

He was there [trombone slide] when it began [trombone slide]

He's the man who put the detail in the plan [trombone slide]

Sir John Laing: (sighs) *Now we actually surveyed four different routeser . . . for this road, there were certain standard radii, curves, gradients and so on . . . and of course . . . minimum amount of property to be demolished . . .* [Solo concertina begins in background] *. . . Well we planned four different routes in four different places . . . we'd been on . . . on this particular road for eight years*

[Brushed snare, followed by solo clarinet, mournful, lonesome blues]

Sung [Voice 2 – baritone]: Been on the road so long, been on the job so long

Engineer 2: *It was one of the longest surveys carried out by a private firm*

Sung [Voice 2]: Travelled the line, been time after time along the fifty miles

Engineer 2: *I knew every field, and met every farmer personally on all of the length of the 53 miles*

Sung [Voice 2, with gusto]: Cut a million hedges culverts, streams,

Built embankments in my dreams

Been on the road so long, been on the job so long

Engineer 2 [ponderously]: *It was necessary to ensure that the line that we had provided was the best line and the ratio of the amount of land that was surveyed to the amount of land that is now occupied by the road was something in the region of about four to one . . . I would say . . . we . . . my surveyors and I . . . covered some 200 hundred miles for the . . . London . . . Yorkshire . . . motorway*

Sung [Voice 2, deeper, more staccato] [typewriter starts very fast in background]: Wrote a thousand letters to the Ministry, "Dear Sir, your memo of August 3, re: reference BL/CT. . . .

This section brings out the contrast between the world out on site and the world of the bureaucracy, which is the one that clearly dominates the engineers' thinking and their experience of the world. There is also an element to which the management of the company involved was concerned not to expose itself. With what were quite active trade unions at the time, the managers seem at times to be reading from a rehearsed script, or internally scrutinizing their own thoughts before committing them to words. Depending on the research context, whether there are possible interventions or feedback sessions, or simply as a resource for teaching managers about culture, this passage is an excellent medium to use to get managers reflecting both on their own language, the ways in which they relate to their colleagues and employees through that language, the significance of that language to their sense of who they are, and issues of power, control and information. If using an analytic device such as Johnson's 'cultural web' (1987), for example, acts as a stimulus for data recollection by managers themselves, it is a very helpful way of accessing language and symbols in use and bridging into power relations.

When we listen to recordings obtained as part of ethnographic interviewing, we usually listen in the act of transcribing, or we listen for the transcript contained in the words. As quickly as possible, we tend to move on to analysis of the written transcript and rarely if ever return to our tapes. But MacColl worked differently. As he realized:

> The typed transcript is a useful guide to subject matter, but it is limited. Your choice [of which passages to concentrate on or use] must be based on additional factors, such as speed of utterance, rhythm, pitch and timbre of voice and the speaker's effort pattern. By the tenth time you have listened to a forty-five-second passage of actuality, you begin to feel that the words originated in your own mind and took form in your mouth with breath taken from your lungs. You have become familiar with every vowel and consonant, with every hesitant pause, every inflection, and – most important of all – *you have discovered whether there is anything to be found beyond the words*
>
> (MacColl 1990: 318 *emphasis added*).

Although we are not making choices of extracts for broadcast, it is nevertheless important to consider whether we are missing what might be 'found beyond the words' – and it is these things that are often clues to where informants implicitly ground their identities – to which paying attention to the sound and enunciative properties of the recording can alert us (and which might be restored in a performance-oriented presentation of the data). This requires listening to our data with different ears.

Life history and the formation of labor: intermittent interrogative methods

When MacColl (1990: 312–313) first heard the tapes from the *John Axon* fieldwork which he played and replayed over and over again, he was struck with the power of the language. He felt that they had captured

> a remarkable picture of a way of life, a picture in words charged with the special kind of excitement which derives from involvement in a work-process . . . . the excitement of an experience relived and communicated directly without the dilution of additives, living speech unglossed by author's pen or actor's voice.

It was with the idea of such a way of life in mind that, after the compromises of *Song of a Road*, they moved on to the two big industrial canvasses addressed by *Singing the Fishing* and *The Big Hewer*. The latter deals with mining communities in Wales, the Midlands and the North-East of England. The former focuses on two herring-fishing communities, one in Scotland and one in Yarmouth, England, where the programme makers were lucky to find three informants who had skippered and crewed boats across the three great ages of sail, steam and diesel, and obviously loved both the work and the storytelling – of the everyday, of characters, of struggles, triumphs, tragedies and comedies. In this programme the technique of great song writing interspersed with hypnotic actuality is nowhere better illustrated than in the song *The Shoals of Herring*. The song itself allegorizes the journey through life, whilst the actuality between each verse tells vivid stories of the early progress of the young fisherman. Elements of the song are added or reprised during the later stages of the programme as the story unfolds. Only part of the actuality with the song is presented below as the complete transcription would occupy several pages. Tune A, though part of the song, does not appear close to the main body of the song in the programme itself.

[Tune A] **wistful prologue**

Ronnie Balls: When you fish for the herring, they rule your life. They swim at night – you've got to be out there at night waiting for them to swim . . .

Singer 1: With our nets and gear we're faring

Ronnie Balls: Course it's a wonder too you see; you pick one of these little fish up and it's vibrant with life . . . Brrrr . . . like that!

Singer 1: On the wild and wasteful ocean

Ronnie Balls: When you think of the numbers . . . you realize that's only one of millions and millions and millions. When the little people swim up properly they really do it!

Singer 1: It's there on the deep
That we harvest and reap our bread

Ronnie Balls: There's no lazy man when herring are about

Singer 1: As we hunt the bonny shoals of herring . . . . . .

. . . . . . [Tune B] **to jaunty ensemble accompaniment**
Singer 1:

Oh, it was a fine and a pleasant day
Out of Yarmouth harbour I was faring
As a cabin boy on a sailing lugger
For to go and hunt the shoals of herring

Now the work was hard and the hours were long
And the treatment sure it took some bearing
There was little kindness and the kicks were many
As we hunted for the shoals of herrin

Sam Larner (82-year-old ex-herring fisherman):

Real old bulldog breed they were: they didn't care for nothing, neither God nor man, they didn't; they didn't! That's the truth; they were wicked old men. Now and again you'd find a kind man but some of them oh they

were . . . cruel! You weren't allowed to speak and they'd take you and give you a rope's end afore they'd look at you . . . put the rope onto your backside if you give 'em yer trouble! . . .

Oh, we fished the Swarth and the Broken Bank

I was cook and I'd a quarter sharing

And I used to sleep standing on my feet

And I'd dream about the shoals of herring

Sam Larner:

And d'you know what? Sometimes I been sleepy and they'd throw a bucket of water on you to wake you up . . . "Wake up you young beggar!" . . . and they'd chuck a bucket of water on you to make you shake your feathers. That'd wake you up!

Well, we left the home grounds in the month of June

And to canny Shields we soon was bearing

With a hundred cran of the silver darlings

That we'd taken from the shoals of herring

Sam Larner: (to mournful single concertina accompaniment)

Away we went to Shields . . . I was looking on deck and I could see the Shields pier . . . I could see 'em a-coming! O that felt funny going into Shields pier . . . strange and – excited to see different affairs of life you see, I'd never been away from home before . . . away from home!...............

.... Singer 2: (to shanty style accompaniment, following the rhythms of pulling a rope)

Now you're up on deck, you're a fisherman

You can swear and show a manly bearing

Take your turn on watch with the other fellows

While you're following the shoals of herring

In the stormy seas and the living gales

Just to earn your daily bread you're daring

From the Dover Straits to the Faroe Islands

While you're following the shoals of herring

Singer 1: (to mournful accompaniment)

Well, I earned my keep and I paid my way

[More actuality]

And I earned the gear that I was wearing

[More actuality]

Sailed a million miles, caught ten million fishes

We was following the shoals of herring......

...... [Tune A] slow, reflective

Night and day we're faring

Come winter wind or winter gale
Sweating or cold,
Growing up, growing old and dying
As you hunt the bonnie shoals of herring

The words themselves were based round the words of the fishermen – for example, the metaphor 'living gale' was taken directly from field-recorded actuality. As with all the Radio Ballads, each song was conceived 'either as an extension of a specific piece of actuality recording, as a comment on that recording, or as a single frame for a collection of actuality pieces', and echoed the speech patterns and accents of the informants, whether conveying the feeling of trying to coax the herring to 'swim-up', the atmosphere of anticipation of coming into port, the crises of battling through force 11 gales and tempestuous seas, and the occasional fatal tragedy. So successful was the veracity of this song, even as a faux-traditional creation, that not only was it taken up by a wide variety of folk singers, but it has reappeared in the repertoires of Irish traditional singers as 'The Shores of Erin'. Indeed, it works not just as a telling of the fisherman's journey through a career, but as a metaphor for the journey through life, which means that parallels are easy to draw with other spheres of activity. But in particular it illustrates, as Charles Parker observed, the way that

> the men have been formed by the strange seasonal movements of the shoals of herring around the coast of Britain and by the ships and gear they have devised to catch them. They have also been formed by the methods of treating and marketing the fish

> (Parker 1960).

To get the fullest sense of the vitality of this formation, MacColl approached the task of interviewing differently. In contrast to *John Axon*, he was not seeking background to an incident, but stories and life histories, so the stimulus for the interviewee was different. Interviews were still one-to-one, but the scope of the life history was beyond a single interview – what was necessary was a series of encounters that enabled informants to reach a point where they were able to reach a break-through level of communication. This meant adopting a deliberate strategy geared to the particular informant. After establishing over the first few days the broad outlines of his or her life and work, they would listen to the recordings made and note carefully what sort of questioning elicited what appeared to be the best response. Breaking down the chronology of the narrative into manageable sections, they would then record intensively over a two-week period, taking each area in detail. *Sometimes* they would ask the same question in different ways over a two- or three-day period, with the resulting tension and frustration in the informant at not having communicated effectively often leading to a more charged and vivid response. As Parker (1964: 9) noted elsewhere it was often an advantage for the informant to think you were a little hard of hearing, or stupid, or both. As MacColl puts it in relation to Sam Larner:

> We probed and constantly changed the perspective of our questions, until his emotion-memory was in full flight and he began to relive and refeel the experiences and emotions of three quarters of a century earlier . . .
>
> (MacColl 1990: 319).

The concept of the emotion-memory seems to be central to what the ballads were trying to achieve. Identity is forged through processes and events that leave their mark, after which it is impossible for the informant to be quite the same. Conveyed with speech 'as active as his life had been', which grew richer the deeper he entered into his past, Larner was able to create the same effect in the listener – so memorable that it did not allow you to see his work and his life in quite the same way as before. Combining attention to releasing the emotion-memory alongside the fact-memory, which is rarely done in most ethnographic work, and not in the depth that MacColl, Seeger and Parker achieved, not only requires us to pay attention to the aesthetics of the interview situation, but it also produces a natural aesthetic output.

The highly material and corporeal culture accessed, expressed and incorporated in the aesthetic presentations of the Radio Ballads differs markedly from the way culture is discussed in more standard presentations of organizational and corporate culture and yet has greater intuitive veracity. It offers evidence of the sorts of things we are usually encouraged to look for in organizational culture – common values and experiences, symbols, language, objects, and so on – but we also find evidence of other things that are clearly cultural but missing from consideration in organizations, such as a broad sense of history, a sense of lived social identity, the engagement of the body in the work that shapes it, religious belief, or a loyalty to the work rather than the employer as such. Culture is experienced much more as a way of life than simply a way of working.

Collective identity and narrative myths

We're concerned with the effect on human beings of a type of work or a technological advance, and as soon as we become primarily concerned with people rather than with processes, we are up against the problem of finding out what is the essentially most important characteristic of a particular group of people or a particular individual: in searching for the typical, we are led to the myth

(MacColl 1961 cited in Parker 1965a: 13).

MacColl's view of the 'essentially most important characteristic' might well be challenged in terms of its specific formulation, but it is clear that what he was looking for was similar to what investigators of social and organizational culture have also been interested in locating (and sadly in the case of organizational culture, in manufacturing if they did not find it or remaking when they did). Although studies of identity have emphasized symbolic dimensions of the identity process, and some have located this in narrative, the early emphasis in cultural studies of organization on myth has largely slipped from view. Yet myth – understood as a discursive means for raising contradictions and paradoxes within a culture to attention, and holding them in an ambiguous space without resolving them whilst making them easier to live with – is an important part of cultural sense- and non-sensemaking. Peggy Seeger (2001: 154) notes:

> British coal miners have many stories of a superhuman worker who is known by a variety of names: Temple, Tempest, Torrs, Towers and (in Wales) Isaac Lewis. He is also known as The Big Hewer and The Big Miner. The British colliers created this man . . . so persistent was the legend throughout the coalfields that we named the whole Radio-Ballad after the big man.

Myth of this nature usually asserts some values in the face of a common problem, and the Big Hewer myth is no exception in its celebration of strength and resilience in the face of both danger and exploitation, as is brought out in the song of the same name. What is remarkable though is the dimension of culture here that is clearly an industrial identity and not a local one, although the regions sampled in the programme had themselves strong cultural identities, born, as culture tends to be, out of common experience, common problems and challenges and sometimes common solutions. Miners across the country, despite strong regional variations in dialect and even a completely different language as in Wales, spoke their own variety of talk which they termed 'pitmatic', which MacColl (1990: 329) described as the 'bold, biter, ribald, beautiful talk of miners' and 'the conversation of men who can make words ring like hammer blows on the face of anthracite'. This commonality is brought out in a short, simple song that looks at the production of everyday mythology that seeps into the society around it – crossing regional and national boundaries, the myth of the miner is enacted and enforming identity even before the young men get anywhere near the pit.

Voice 1 Sung (Louis Killen, Northumberland):
> Schooldays over, come on then John,
> Time you were getting your pitboots on
> On with your shirt and moleskin trousers
> Time you were on your way
> Time you were learning the pitman's job
> And earning a pitman's pay

Voice 2 spoken [English, West Midlands]: I was 14 when I first went down the mine . . . November 5th, Guy Fawkes night, on am Monday.

Voice 3 sung (Ewan MacColl, Scots):
> Come on then Jim, it's time to go
> Time ye were working down below
> Time to be handling a pick and shovel
> You start at the pit today
> Time you were learning the collier's job
> And earning a collier's pay

Voice 4 spoken [English, West Midlands]: I was 12 when I left school, and as soon as I reached the age of 14 I went to the pit . . . the pit was the place.

Voice 5 sung (A.L.Lloyd, Ango-Welsh):
> Come on then, Dai, it's almost light
> Time you were off to the anthracite
> The morning mist is in the valley
> Time you were on your way
> Time you were learning the miner's job
> And earning a miner's pay

Voice 6 spoken (Welsh): When I was a boy we always thought of the mines . . . when I was at school I used to parade with my . . . er . . . long trousers and my naked lamp parading on the road in the night . . . as colliers. . . . Months before I had the job, you see Oh yes . . .

[EDIT].

Voice 2 [English]: No I'll never forget that day, not as long as I live

Here, what appears to be a folk song could never be so because of the trans-regional perspective it adopts, with each verse being from a different region, with a different voice, yet describing a common experience: the excitement of becoming a miner, the first day at work. Whilst a good deal more could be said about the critical workings of this song, what is of relevance here is that the song was created from a methodology that consisted of a way of relating to the data. Parker (1965b) observes that a large amount of actuality must be recorded in the field, 'so as to cover every conceivable facet of the subject which might bear upon the final work'. Accordingly, the investigators must 'be able not only to forecast immediately the likely form of the final work, but must be prepared radically to revise that forecast in the light of the actuality that is being recorded', indeed to recognize the creativity of the informants they encounter, the output as a co-creation with the investigator as facilitator and stimulus. It may be surprising that this awareness was in practice in the field of work and organization some 40 years before its existence was hinted at in the form of reflexive interviewing (Alvesson 2003, Alvesson and Skjoldberg 2000). The flexibility here is in responding to and recognizing the organic creation of everyday myth that binds an industrial community together intuitively across geographical distances, with an identity that is perhaps one explanation for the long-standing industrial strength of the miners both as communities and nationally as networks.

Collective discovery of subjective identity: catalytic group interviewing

Some groups of course do not necessarily have a strong formal grounding for their identity, although the basis for such an identity may be present. For MacColl and Seeger, teenagers presented such a group – clearly the conditions surrounding youth culture had changed in the post-War period and the experience of being young, with all its tensions, possibilities, choices, mysteries and problems had changed with it. The term 'teenager' had been used in the media but little serious sociological work had been done at that time, although it was to come. The question at the very heart of much of what concerned these young people was identity, but precisely because of instability: physically, psychologically, socially, they did not know who they were becoming, who they were or who they could be, as individuals or as a 'generation'.

MacColl and Seeger had been warned that teenagers were uncommunicative and it would be impossible to get them to talk, so they decided to begin with some exploratory sessions to see what might work and what would not. Via a friend of a friend they were able to arrange a discussion with five teenage boys and two teenage girls one Saturday morning. They had no experience in group interviewing but found that for three hours the teenagers spoke non-stop about everything that concerned them from the bomb to the generation gap, and 'all of it was interesting, much of it profoundly moving' (MacColl 1990: 333).[3] They arranged a follow-up one-to-one interview with a girl, Dot Dobby, who seemed to be a key informant, in line with anthropological tradition, and found that

> We had stumbled on one of those rare human beings, who can give utterance to their most secret thoughts, while at the same time recreating emotions that they have experienced.... [Dot] would just close her eyes and after a few minutes of preliminary questioning, retreat into some private world and then, in stream-of-consciousness fashion, recall scenes, moods, conversations and events. We were completely bowled over by her ability to articulate her perceptions of reality and those shadowy areas of feeling which overlap with the unconscious
>
> (MacColl 1990: 333).

What they found was that they had to adapt their methods – they interviewed some 52 individuals from a wide range of backgrounds both singly and in groups, in twenty locations from Stirling to Reading and Brixton to Bristol. They used groups that were known to each other, and in locations where they had no contacts, they obtained permission to approach prospects at the school gates, and random groups were generated. Where they were used to having to pay attention to making the subject feel at ease, looking and sounding casual whilst concentrating fully and feeding interesting questions, they found these respondents were different.

> Our intervention was reduced to naming a topic... and off they would go... until we mentioned another word, then off they would go again. Often when one person was holding forth on some intensely personal subject, another would burst out "I didn't know anyone else felt like that", indicating that they rarely got down to those depths of communication amongst one another. It had taken a catalyst – us – to start them off
>
> (MacColl 1990: 333).

The metaphor that they adopted in the presentation of the work was that of the journey, which in this case was barely a metaphor as the pain of doubt and the vitality of the simultaneous discovery of subjectivity and shared subjective elements were constantly emergent. Perhaps the major point to be made here is that contrary to the implicit approach taken in much of the interviewing, that what there is to discover is already there, already known by the informants, some types of knowledge are not pre-known and may

---

3 MacColl was influenced by the concept of emotional memory found in Stanilavski's acting 'method'.

in fact be discovered or generated by the interaction of the interview, and this is even more so if the form of interaction is a group session. What happens is a matter of discovery for all concerned. This requires flexibility in response and responsiveness in the interviewer and the willingness to be a catalytic rather than a controlling or even interrogative presence, ready to be surprised, even bowled over, by what emerges. The constant principle, however, seems to be to try to anticipate every eventuality, to collect as much data as necessary to cover all those eventualities (a sort of expansive sampling strategy) and be prepared to change and adapt as new dimensions emerge.

Critical questions on the aesthetic approach

The first question that needs to be addressed is whether the method is intrinsically *nostalgic* – does the nature of the material in the programmes offer a romanticized picture of the culture of the past that can get imposed on the present? Is the identity so presented a fanciful and sentimentalized version of history? The answer here is affirmatively no – although Parker and MacColl argued that they were not 'realists' in claiming to portray 'reality' without any artifice, they nevertheless had a commitment to their respondents' experiences as well as their own perspectives. They always talked to far more people than they could use – indeed, for one hour of documentary they would typically record around 90 hours of tape, and often much more (300 hours for *The Travelling People*). So they did not offer hugely idiosyncratic perspectives. But there were others and they acknowledged that, after all, MacColl was a dialectician rather than simply an ideologue. They also stood back from any final judgement on matters, which was helped by the absence of any narrating voice and is a feature particularly taken up by the 2006 series. What they produced was a text sufficiently rich in resource and sufficiently open-ended to allow the listener to take an active role in interpreting – or rewriting – the data. The programmes make rich information available to us for our interpretation, and occasionally some of this is characterized by sentiment as well as emotion, but it is not finally in any sense nostalgic. Indeed, the fishermen who remember steam and sail are mindful of both the beauty and the problems of working under these regimes, and appreciative of the different benefits of diesel. Similarly, miners have no intrinsic objection to technological progress. What the programmes do is take the emotional impact of technological and social change seriously and make it available for debate – which makes it easier to encourage contemporary managers to recognize that new knowledge and information technologies have emotional impact too.

Was the method too *political* – after all, MacColl was a lifelong unreconstructed Marxist of a fairly traditional sort committed to dialectical materialism (MacColl 1990: 337)? But he was also an artist, a professional writer, singer, composer, playwright and performer who had an interest in his art as well as an interest in politics. In short, the quality of the art was never delivered by the politics. And the politics was never compromised by the art. The art succeeded on the basis of astute observation, sensitivity to others' perspectives, and the quality of words and music applied to the insights so delivered. This often raised our attention to issues of power, disadvantage, inequality and suffering, but as part of human experience, not as political issues. Indeed when MacColl let the politics swamp the art, as he frequently did in his other work, what resulted was peculiarly inhuman at times or very quickly dated. What the programmes do is help issues of organizational power and politics to be raised and recognized as part of the meshwork of culture, part of the very fabric of identity, where this is often difficult to achieve.

The realist nature of the programmes is paralleled in contemporary research initiatives on oral history, where the recognition that social security records and instruction manuals are not enough to convey the experienced realities of living a life in contemporary society, whether one is a lorry driver or a stock exchange trader. Culture is founded, at least in part, on narratives, on the accounts of themselves, their work, their relationships and their lives that people develop and share to render collective experience commonly meaningful. So the programmes underline the fact that organizational culture is an intertext of interlocking narratives, without necessarily having a master narrative – that patterns unfold, that there is ritual and drama present, but that plots are often plural and paradoxical, no matter how much corporate efforts might seek to engage in strong forms of emplotment.

An *artistic* criticism – that the programmes were based around folk music and this is not an appropriate medium for discussing contemporary life – needs to be addressed, as its social implication is greater than its artistic significance. It implies that the experiences that were so effectively addressed through the folk medium have themselves faded into irrelevance at the same time as the musical genre may have fallen from fashion. This in itself is contestable, but looking at the way that MacColl and his colleagues approached their task, it is clearly mistaken to suggest that these were essentially 'folk' programmes. They sought to use what musical form seemed most appropriate to the task in hand and the culture expressed, including blues, jazz, music-hall and modern jazz, all adapted freely. Listening to the programme about pain, with interviews from recovering polio victims, the music is very different to that in the industrial programmes, as it is for the programme about teenagers. Whilst the series does show the power and adaptability of folk methods, it also shows the adaptability of the Radio Ballad methods in being able to handle a breadth of expressive challenges stretching from the micro detail of individual experiences of pain to the epic scope of a whole industry. What the method does challenge us to do is to take it on and find the appropriate forms of expression, old or new, that fit the experiences of new forms of living in twenty-first–century society. But most particularly, what music does is to capture commonalities of experience that usually elude other forms of expression, especially those predominant in the managerial and organizational sciences.

So with particular issues in organizations, the programmes raise the level of reflection on communication and language; the extent to which experiences are shared across levels of the organization; the depth of history attaching to these issues; the extent to which cultural attachments outside the organization continue to be important within it; questions of identity and self-hood; the specific features of work activity of all types and how they are valued by people who do them; power and vulnerability; the importance of hearing the stories of individuals within the organization; and the importance of meaning in the processes of change. Whilst processes of rationality will always be important in management, the poetic and aesthetic approaches that the radio ballads exemplify illustrate the often unacknowledged but equally powerful importance of processes of emotionality.

References

Aston, L. (2000) *The Radio Ballads 1957–64*. London: Topic Records (booklet to accompany the reissue of the programmes on CD).

Alvesson, M. (2003) 'Beyond neopositivists, romantics, and localists: a reflexive approach to interviews in organizational research.' *Academy of Management Review* 28(1): 13–33.

Alvesson, M. and Skjoldberg, K. (2000) *Reflexive Methodology: New Vistas for Qualitative Research*. London: Sage.

Denzin, N. (2003) *Performance Ethnography: Critical Pedagogy and the Politics of Culture*. Thousand Oaks, CA: Sage.

Hatch, M. J. and Schultz, M. (2002) 'The dynamics of organizational identity.' *Human Relations* 55(8): 989–1018.

Johnson, G. (1987) *Strategic Change and the Management Process*. Oxford: Blackwell.

MacColl, E. (n.d.) 'The Radio Ballads', undated manuscript circa 1981, *The Ewan MacColl and Peggy Seeger Archive*, Oxford: Ruskin College.

MacColl, E. (n.d.2) 'Song of a Road', undated manuscript circa 1981, *The Ewan MacColl and Peggy Seeger Archive*, Oxford: Ruskin College.

MacColl, E. (1990) *Journeyman*. London: Sidgwick and Jackson.

McCall, M. (2000) 'Performance ethnography: a brief history and some advice.' In Denzin, N. and Lincoln, Y. (eds) *The Handbook of Qualitative Inquiry*. Thousand Oaks, CA: Sage, pp. 421–434.

Nissley, N. (2002). 'Tuning-in to organizational song as aesthetic discourse.' *Culture and Organization* 8(1): 51–68.

Parker, C. (1960) Letter to Art Editor *Radio Times*, 1 July, BBC Archive WR33.

Parker, C. (1964) 'Folk music series – field recording techniques', unpublished manuscript, *Critics Group of Folk Song Studies*, December.

Parker, C. (1965a) 'Some aspects of traditional song: tradition and the tape recorder', unpublished manuscript 23/6/65, *The Ewan MacColl and Peggy Seeger Archive*, Oxford: Ruskin College.

Parker, C. (1965b) Sleeve Notes to *The Big Hewer* [1967] Argo Records DA140 (notes are separately dated).

Seeger, P. (ed.) (2001) *The Essential Ewan MacColl Songbook: Sixty Years of Songmaking*. New York: Oak Books.

Stanislavski, K. (1980) *An Actor Prepares*. London: Eyre Methuen.

Strati, A. (1999) *Organization and Aesthetics*. London: Sage.

15

Identities and interviews

Christine Coupland

Introduction

In this chapter I will briefly examine the concept of identity and how this approach has implications for what we as researchers think we are able to do through interviews. Interviews as appropriate media for the exploration of identities and how the interview context operates as a particular venue for the construction of identities will be considered. I illustrate and problematize how the notion of analysing identities using data generated in this way requires the researcher to be reflexive (Alvesson and Skoldberg 2000) about identities as co-constructions (Leudar and Antaki 1996). I then discuss the implications of seeing identities as practices, co-constructions which are *worked up* in and through interaction, for doing interviews.

What I mean by 'identity practices' are those activities we all engage in as we go about our everyday business; for example, you by reading this book, me by writing this chapter. In an interview situation, as in all socially located exchanges, there are rules surrounding appropriate responses in interactions relevant to the context of those interactions. Identity practices, of both the researcher and the researched, are available for scrutiny as we analyse, interpret and translate our interactions and the meaning they have for our selves.

Key concerns regarding understanding identity include how it may be examined. One argument is that identity practices occur, and hence become visible, in narration in particular contexts. The question of whether the self is preconceived prior to speaking about one's self (e.g. in interview interactions) is not one that is possible to answer from within any research perspective. However, from a narrative theory perspective, Ricoeur (1992) proposes that speakers occupy a position from which we are able to mediate between looking backwards to practical concerns while looking forwards to ethical concerns – that is, character, or sedimented acts of the past, are recounted with a concern for what they say about the speaker today and for the future. This has relevance for the narrative nature of material constructed from research interviews. Furthermore, the research interview highlights questions surrounding the extent that we are able to construct selves in interaction.

In this chapter the focus is on identity as constructed (or available) through language, although it is acknowledged that there are other processes through which identity practices (e.g. the body, consumption) are constructed and analysed which are important but that are bracketed for the time being. The structure of this chapter is as follows, first I will outline the nature of identity that I adopt in my research and how from this perspective it may be researched. Second, three perspectives on interviews will be discussed to highlight the different assumptions which underlie the theoretical research perspectives and which have implications for interviews in terms of material collection, analysis and subsequent re-presentation. These assumptions have consequences for research interviews, a primary aim of which is to understand identity. Finally, I will discuss how future research may build on our current understanding of identity and interviews.

Understanding identity

There has been increased research attention to the concept of identity recently. How identity is to be conceived, defined, examined and understood is subject to a wide-ranging and continually changing set of practices based upon theoretical assumptions made by researchers in the social sciences and in wider society.

It is not possible to cover all possible approaches in so short a space so, for the purposes of this chapter, I will conceive of identity as a researcher's or interviewer's and an interviewee's resource or set of resources (these resources may be termed 'identity markers' but their designation as such are rhetorical not factual). The idea that what we say *says* something about us is relevant to both lay and academic accounts of identities. This highlights a view of identity as something we do, as available for use and embedded in social activities, rather than something that we are. Thus, in the context of a research interview for example, an important question that may be asked is how identity-features are ascribed to self or others. Hence, identity may be regarded as an 'analyst's *and* a participant's resource' (Widdicombe 1998: 191). It is not so much that someone cannot be classified from the outside as belonging to particular categories of people; it is that assumptions surrounding the relevance of identity markers should be questioned. For example, gender, or color, may not be relevant to particular studies of 'identity'; classifying participants as gendered runs the risk of creating a logic that suggests participants are speaking as members of that group. Instead perhaps we should consider how participants invoke a gendered subject, that is, by saying, 'speaking as a woman', or, 'if I were a man'. This kind of talk constructs alternative subject positions, enabling speakers to carry out subsequent discursive work, which is open to interpretation by the interview participant (in the ongoing interaction), the analyst (in deciding how to make their meaning of the identities being invoked) and the eventual reader of the analysis (in deeming the interpretation plausible), in all stages of the research process, that is the material construction, analysis and re-presentation.

Research participants work up experiential identities, that is sedimented accounts of self made plausible through accounts of experiences, as the interview progresses. These identities then go on to be re-interpreted, or re-constructed, on many levels during the life of the research process and beyond, as they are theorized, written and read. One way to theorize this approach is to consider self-identity as developed through narrative. Ricoeur (1992) argues that the self is discovered in its own narrational acts. Self-hood is the kind of entity that is characterized by its ability to reflect upon itself, thus identity is a narrative construction, that is, the product of the reflective process of self-hood (Ezzy 1998). Hence, speaking of one's self (describing the acts of everyday living), whether in interview or other types of conversation, is an opportunity for practices of identity to be made visible through a narrated self. A narrative identity provides a subjective sense of self-continuity as it symbolically (and linguistically) integrates the events of lived experience in the plot of a story an individual tells of his or her experiences. It is proposed that the narrative imagination works with lived experience by providing a symbolic structure and temporal schema of action (Ezzy 1998). This account, or story, with its themes, or plots, mediates between the individual and events – encounters lived experience in the world of the listener, or reader, who refigures the story. It functions as a resource as it influences his or her choices about how to act in the world. That said, researchers from different epistemological positions question the degree to which the subject actively constitutes the self as 'resources' for identity practices may be proposed, suggested or imposed by culture or social group (Foucault 1988), and hence highlight how identity is constructed in and through power relations.

With this view of identity it is useful to look at the interpretive practices of everyday life. These include but are not limited to 'naturally occurring' (non-research initiated) interactions – interviews are taken to be particular forms of interaction in which we construct and reflexively manage who we are. That said, all interactions are subject to contextually relevant rules where language games discursively construct the self as having the semblance of a more or less unified subjectivity centred in experience (Wittgenstein 1967). From this perspective, self and truth, or authenticity, are not universal truth values but are seen in relation to interpretive communities (Fish 1980) and within a particular language game. In the context of interviews therefore, the self is not simply a sea of images (Denzin 1991), hyper-real (Baudrillard 1983) or 'anything goes' (Gergen 1991) but a practical project of everyday life, locally articulated, locally recognized and locally accountable with authenticities situated and plural (Holstein and Gubrium 2000: 70). Identities are put to work as practical, discursive accomplishments. This shifts the focus to the practice of subjectivity and language games (rules) used in practice. I shall now consider the interview situation as a particular context for identity practices.

Perspectives on interviews

Interviewing is far broader than merely having methodological significance; the interview is not just a research procedure, but is a constitutive feature of everyday lives (Holstein and Gubrium 2003: 11). Contemporary views suggest we are in an 'interview society' (Silverman 1997), where it may be assumed that everyone in society will be familiar with what an interview looks and feels like. Before raising epistemological awareness in the following discussion, in everyday terms the interview is regarded as an interactional accomplishment. It is generally understood that interviewees and interviewers ask and answer questions in interviews resulting in an inter-change of views about a theme of mutual interest (Kvale 1996).

The types and methods of interviewing, whether they should be structured versus unstructured interviews or group interviews for example, have been discussed elsewhere (see Fontana and Frey 2005). However, since my area of interest is identity as a co-construction, a social phenomenon that may only be glanced at sideways, I will explore researcher assumptions about what it is legitimate to say in and about interviews. Other writers have signalled different epistemological approaches in interview-based research (e.g. Alvesson 2003), which have implications for what may be said from the research. Furthermore, it may be that acknowledging this provides an unusual and potentially creative ground for interview work. It is well understood that there are three, broadly defined, approaches to research in terms of epistemological positions (although at times this labelling is debated and demarcation lines appear more fluid than 'real'). I acknowledge that this is a gross oversimplification but for the purposes of remaining attentive to interviews, a necessary one. Although 'Neopositivists', 'Constructionists' and 'Poststructuralists' have varied and nuanced interpretations within their general fields of inquiry, they share certain perspectives which are related to material generated using interviews and which will be discussed next.

Neopositivists regard interviewees as vessels of answers to both internal and external worlds. The role of interviewer is also regarded as a passive, aiming to be a neutral, subject in this encounter, whose role includes not contaminating the accurate, authentic reports from the interviewee (cf. Fontana and Frey 2005). The interviewer stands apart from the material – collecting what is already there or speculating on the hidden forces that make the interviewees say things. In this model, the vessel-of-answers image of the subject is not an agent engaged in production of knowledge. Interviewing has typically been seen as an asymmetrical encounter in which an interviewer solicits information from an interviewee, who responds relatively passively to enquiries. Interviews from within this research perspective are often regarded as stimulus–response activities and have been criticized (e.g. Mishler 1986), where the interviewee is treated simply as an object of research. If we want to find out about items relevant to the research we just have to ask the right questions and the other's 'reality' will be revealed. Researchers who adopt a neopositivist approach emphasize exclusively the referential function of language which raises questions particularly for the role of interviews in research around identity practices.

Constructionist positions vary quite dramatically across a range from a conversation-analytic focus on 'naturally occurring' material which eschews the use of interviews in research, to a social constructionist approach which acknowledges that the interview is a complex social event in which knowledge is produced. This latter approach assumes active interview subjects (e.g. see Holstein and Gubrium 2003) where researchers work with an awareness of the interview as a site of production of meaning as animated participants co-construct versions of reality in interaction. All interview participants, both interviewer and interviewee(s), are regarded as practitioners of everyday life, which includes the interview context. This transforms the participant subject behind the interviewee from being a repository of information and opinions into a productive co-constructer of knowledge. This perspective is particularly relevant for studies of identity. The interviewee, construed as an active subject, describes details of life experience and in interaction with the interviewer actively shapes the information. One charge levelled at some versions of constructionist research is that it focuses on interviews primarily as a topic in its own right (Silverman 2001). However, this is a narrow view with particular reference to understanding identity, as the interview 'account' is only one part of the world being described.

A conversation-analysis perspective also presumes active subjects and illustrates how interactants mutually monitor each other's speech exchanges (e.g. Antaki and Widdicombe 1998, Peräkylä 2005, Sacks 1992, Widdicombe 1998). They jointly construct their sense of the developing agenda in interactions, resulting in exchanges which are linguistically animated. Despite radical conversation-analytic proponents not engaging with interview material, except as a focus of analysis, the techniques of this approach have provided a source of analytical tools which may be utilized from other perspectives sharing an interest in the fine detail of talk. With specific regard to identity, how the self is constructed in interaction, through pronoun use (e.g. Malone 1997 drawing on Goffman 1959) and positioning (see Harre and van Langenhove 1999 for a broader description of this concept), is relevant to investigations. Another example of the analytic utility of this approach using material generated through interviews is where the context of the interaction is made relevant in the talk (see Duranti and Goodwin 1992). The conversation analytic's focus on detail enables us to investigate what is made salient and how this is oriented to and made plausible and legitimate in talk.

A *poststructuralist* perspective sees the individual as constituted within discourse, researchers are regarded as passive onlookers or willing participants in creating new practices for legitimating social inequality (Briggs 2003: 504). Hence the interview is regarded as of interest due to the discourses at work, providing an opportunity to examine identity as a permanent state of becoming as powerful discourses vie with one another (Thomas and Linstead 2002). In addition, Foucault (1973, 1978, 1980) proposes that the discursive organization of subjectivity is constituted by 'the technologies of the self' transforming the way we view the sources of our subjectivity. With reference to the interview, this is the agent who stands behind the 'facades' (Holstein and Gubrium 2003: 7) of the interview participants. With regard to interviews and research into identity practices, these socially and historically located institutional practices advance the idea that each of us has a self and can reflect on our own experience. It may be argued from this perspective, therefore, that the individual interview is a function of technologies of surveillance, governmentality impressed on us by inquiries into our lives. The interview may be one of the twenty-first century's most distinctive technologies of the self (Holstein and Gubrium 2003). Nevertheless, power relations that emerge in interviews may be regarded not as a source of contamination or silencing, but as a source of insight into interviewing processes and the social worlds they seek to document (Briggs 2003: 496). Discourses of difference lie at the center of producing and resisting structures of social inequality. Discourses of difference are drawn on to construct and resist versions of the self in interaction too.

Leading from this diverse range of approaches, we need to consider what the practical consequences are for understanding identity. Narrating the self has been described as an everyday technology of self-construction which stands at the intersection of discursive practice and discourses in practice (Holstein and Gubrium 2000). This intersecting position offers multiple dimensions for our attention. Thus, I suggest that one way to examine this is to consider how material which is constructed in interviews occupies three dimensions for analytical purposes: description, action and representation. These are helpful to illustrate what happens in the interview research process for several reasons. The dimensions:

1. may be applied to a greater or lesser extent across all research perspectives and therefore collapses the purism often attached to working within different positions;
2. work simultaneously within each part of the research process, that is in material construction, analysis and re-presentation;
3. may appear to take a sequential or linear process which privileges this way of thinking and working. I propose that there are flows of activities that surge and ebb, in terms of relevance, in and out of our awareness (as speakers and researchers) specifically with regard to identities which require a more nuanced manner of thinking about processes.
4. appear to mirror how we speak of our and other selves, or identities. In theoretical terms they also seem to work loosely within Ricoeur's (1992) triad of describe, narrate, prescribe.

Description

Participants in interviews describe events and inner feelings, whether real or imagined, for the consumption, or understanding, of the other. In these descriptions, selves are constructed and ascribed to others. Various roles are played and identities/selves drawn upon, made relevant, plausible and legitimate according to the rules of the particular language game (see Wittgenstein 1967) of the interview. The content of these descriptions are treated as real for the participants and have relevance for the researcher in different ways according to their theoretical perspective. The relationship that this has with a study of identity is how it offers opportunities to engage with what the content *says* about the interactants. One way this may be examined is through how participants link substantive matters to biographical descriptions. Put simply, examples may be:

"speaking as an engineer" or
"I'm not really a manager" or
"If I were a senior manager".

It is clear that people may occupy distinct, sometimes plural, sometimes contradictory, positions from which to talk.

From a neopositivist perspective this categorization is what the interview is designed to elicit or capture as it is assumed that the interview gives access to 'facts' about the speaker and the world. The self-labelling (even through the denial of a label) would be taken as self-categorization and followed by an assumption that the categorization is salient and has relevance for the speaker. So, from this research perspective the description is taken as fact; even if it is an aspirational self-categorization, the 'fact' would be analysed to represent a desire or other internal state which may be available to the researcher in order to understand the participant's identity.

Constructionists are frequently accused of not paying any attention to the content of 'talk', being generally too preoccupied with its structure. However, this is an oversimplified version of constructionism, which does not deny that language both describes and does things (see Edley 2001). 'Most constructionists also want to preserve a concern with what interviewees are saying as well as how they are saying it' (Silverman 2001: 97). From this research perspective there would be a concern with how identity relevant categories are constructed *and* what discursive business is being carried out by claiming (or denying) membership.

Poststructuralists would challenge the notion of an autonomous individual as a bearer of meaning. The language which constructs the description element of interview material would be regarded not as an expression of subjectivity; rather it is seen as what constitutes subjectivity (Foucault 1980). The examples given above may be taken as instances of participants performing their own marginalization. Discourses of 'engineer identity', for example, may be performing social ordering by mapping subjects onto a hierarchized space with central and marginal positions (Fournier 1998). In contrast to neopositivists' interest in description, poststructuralists would argue that research participants do not necessarily internalize these categories as norms or expectations, instead they subsume them in their own accounts of organizational 'reality' and thus the framework operates as a regulatory system (e.g. Grey 1994, Fournier 1998).

Action

This aspect of the research process focuses upon how the identities achieve discursive ends specifically in an interview context. It presupposes that identities are available for use, something that we do which is embedded in social activities. This conceptual thinking is based originally on Austen's (1962) speech act theory, which proposes that words are descriptive and active; they describe and do things simultaneously. An interest in identity leads us to consider what the various selves, identities, subject positions adopted enable the speaker to say (or do) or to not say (or not do). Examples may be:

> "engineers are dinosaurs, slow and becoming extinct" (non-engineer, bemoaning lack of status of MBA-educated managers), or
> "I'm new here".

The analytic question being asked here of interview material is – what claims are being made and about the world, self, or other from this position? What may be done and/or legitimized from the subject position being adopted? How does the way people define and interpret one another's actions become the basis for adjustment of one's own action? Joint action is therefore one of the basic features of social behavior (Blumer 1969), of which the interview context is an exemplar.

Neopositivists would deny this element of analysis, initially from an expectation that there is an internal reality which would be encouraged to be expressed in the form of an authentic self as an outcome of research into identity. However there is an acknowledgement of the influence of impression management on the research process whereby roles are acted out through scripts in social situations, of which the interview is one (e.g. Goffman 1959). Inability to 'capture' the authentic self would be regarded as a design fault of the research process.

Constructionists, on the other hand, would focus largely on this element as the local accomplishment of identity work through attempts to accuse, persuade and make claims (see Potter and Wetherell 1987). There is a general interest in the descriptive tools and techniques that enable a speaker to talk about self and other. Hence, there is an evident focus on the speaker as creative, as able to construct multiple and at times contradictory selves, in order to do discursive business. Categories are drawn upon, which have entitlements and costs attached (Sacks 1992). Nevertheless, communicative practices are contextually situated, and participants make available particular positions for each other; moral grounding for claims being made about identities may be established or shaken through validation or rejection in subsequent talk (Carbaugh 1996).

Poststructuralists would be more inclined to see this as a struggle for meaning and hence would consider what participants may be unable to do or say. Powerful discourses which predominate in a particular historical and social context are assumed to speak through participants. Texts and practices are regarded as inseparable; they establish and maintain boundaries between ideal objects and spaces for individual identity (Armstrong 2002, Peräkylä 2005). Interview material, its analysis and subsequent re-presentations are thus regarded as sets of statements through which objects and subjects are constituted.

Re-presentation

This may be called construction, or re-construction (as re-presentation implies positivist rhetoric), but it describes interpretations of meaning from the interview interactions at several levels. At its most simple level, in interaction the speaker and others' lives are re-presented – this refers to all research participants including the interviewer. Beyond the initial interaction, the transcription of material involves decisions regarding how much material and in what form to transcribe. How much of the context is relevant. How will background events prior to the research interaction be included. In analysis, another layer, and often several layers, is added in choosing what to highlight and what to ignore in terms of material and analytical options. This activity is mirrored in the production of articles, books, conference presentations all of which present a particular account of the research process and the identities of the participants. These layers of meaning re-present identities.

Neopositivists would not consider this aspect of analysis as it is inconsistent with their views on language as a mirror or conduit onto reality. Methodological protocols would ensure the researcher aims for a neutral representation of the 'facts'. Hence, the most authentic representation is the object of the research.

Constructionists would focus on this element as it is indicative of their approach to research; each analysis is but one version of many possible versions, each vying for (at least) temporary supremacy due to the plausibility of the account, while acknowledging it is one from many possible. The most plausible version is the object of research.

From a poststructuralist perspective, language (and all representations of it) is not regarded as an expression of subjectivity but subjectivity is constituted through language and discourse. In particular, in interview research terms, discourses are drawn on as the individual constructs and maintains their identity through the process. The object of research then is to examine how discourses are presented in the interview situation.

Discussion

It is apparent that the inter-relationship between identity and interviews may be understood from a range of theoretical assumptions. In this chapter I have discussed interviews and identity practices from three perspectives – neopositivism, constructionism and poststructuralism. I have focused on the implications of the assumptions of these perspectives in order to better understand identity. The three perspectives are not teased apart to pit them against one another; rather, they have been described in terms of what characteristics they may share. Neopositivist concerns may be summed as an interest in descriptions and labels of identity, poststructuralist research perspectives explain that there are conditions of possibility that enable or constrain what may be described and constructionist perspectives are concerned with how identity practices are displayed within these conditions and how they are put to use. Interview generated material provides access to how people account for their selves in usual and unusual activities. It may be that a new dialogue between what have been deemed as opposing theoretical positions emerges from the interest in the area of self and identity. In research terms, researchers solicit responses to questions such as, 'tell me about yourself?' and then depart in different directions to work out what this means to us as researchers – to what forces do we attribute agency for the responses we evoke, or co-construct? From my empirical research on narrative and identity, the very thing on which we wish to cast our gaze often slips away under our focus. I propose that the interview itself is part of the process of creation, continuing through the research process and on each subsequent reading. My examination of differing epistemological positions suggests that there are opportunities for understanding identity practices from interview based research within each approach. Awareness of what may be said from within the perspectives enables a reflexive stance on the researchers' identity practices, which are also intimately linked with issues of authenticity, plausibility and the prevailing conditions which make the argument possible. Doing identity appears to be very much like doing engaged research.

The framework of description, action and re-presentation presented in this chapter could be applied to any research process in order to make comparison, but it appears to be particularly relevant to research which is intent on understanding identity, as it explains differences in the processes of identity practices and how we come to *know* them. Our identity practices are evident in our *descriptions* (of self and other) and what these descriptions allow (and do not allow) us to do or legitimate, in other words, to *act*. These descriptions/actions are then recounted, drawn on in interactions, and function to *represent* our and other selves in an ongoing dialogue. With particular reference to interview research processes, these activities are continuous through all the stages of research, that is, for example, re-presentation is not simply confined to a final draft of a research report, it begins with the articulation of the problem which initiates the research.

It is apparent that a poststructuralist concern with broad contextual political forces within interviews should be addressed (e.g. Foucault 1988). The conditions of possibility have a historical and temporal location relevant to any knowledge produced. It is proposed that a narrative theory of identity (not limited to but including the stories we tell about ourselves and others) addresses the temporal and ethical self in identity (Ricoeur 1992). If the interview may be regarded as an interaction, a conversation of sorts, then enquiries may lead to a regard for what the participants say as their/our construction of self in the moment, not necessarily being reflective but undoubtedly relating to the other. Furthermore, if poststructuralist concerns may be described as prescriptive and neopositivist concerns as descriptive, narrative theory occupies a middle ground which may be shared with constructionists' major concerns with analysis (those of how identity is practised). This mirrors Ricoeur's (1992: 115) triad of 'describe, narrate and prescribe' as an explanation of the constitution of action and the constitution of the self, which has been drawn upon in this chapter.

It has been argued that it is in the very narration that identity practices occur in a particular temporal context. In an interview situation the participants are invited to speak. The act of speaking positions the speaker reflexively, placing attention upon the 'I' and the 'you' of the speech situation, thus highlighting the co-constructed nature of identity practices of an interview encounter. In order to examine identity practices it is not always (or often) relevant to make direct enquiries; from accounts of experiences, researchers endeavor to recognize signs or re-presentations that enable a consideration of the sort of subject that is constructed in this way (Ricoeur 1992). Ricoeur (1992) appears to offer one way to theorize self and identity which may be usefully applied to future empirical research. Utilizing a framework of description, action and re-presentation, which may be seen in people's identity practices in and out of research encounters, it has been possible to examine how each approach investigates identity across common interests – the question of identity.

References

Alvesson, M. (2003) 'Beyond neopositivists, romantics and localists: a reflexive approach to interviews in organizational research.' *Academy of Management Review* 28(1): 13–33.

Alvesson, M. and Skoldberg, K. (2000) *Reflexive Methodology: New Vistas for Qualitative Research*. London: Sage.

Antaki, C. and Widdicombe, S. (1998) 'Identity as an achievement and a tool.' In *Identities in Talk*. London: Sage, pp. 1–14.

Armstrong, D. (2002) *A New History of Identity: A Sociology of Medical Knowledge*. Basingstoke: Palgrave.

Austen, J. L. (1962) *How to do things with words*. Oxford: Oxford University Press.

Baudrillard, J. (1983) *Simulations*. New York: Semiotext.

Blumer, H. (1969) *Symbolic Interactionism*. New York: Prentice Hall.

Briggs, C. (2003) 'Interviewing, power/knowledge and social inequality.' In Holstein, J. and Gubrium, J. (eds) *Inside Interviewing*. Thousand Oaks, CA: Sage, pp. 495–506.

Carbaugh, D. (1996) *Situating Selves: The Communication of Social Identities in American Scenes*. Albany: State University of New York.

Denzin, N. (1991) *Images of Postmodern Society: Social Theory and Contemporary Cinema*. Newbury Park, CA: Sage.

Duranti, A. and Goodwin, C. (1992) *Rethinking Context*. Cambridge: Cambridge University Press.

Edley, N. (2001) 'Unravelling social constructionism.' *Theory and Psychology* 11(3): 433–441.

Ezzy, D. (1998) 'Theorizing narrative identity: symbolic interactionism and hermeneutics.' *The Sociological Quarterly* 39(2): 239–252.

Fish, S. (1980) *Is There a Text in this Class? The Authority of Interpretive Communities*. Cambridge, NA: Harvard University Press.

Fontana, A. and Frey, J. H. (2005) 'The interview: from neutral stance to political involvement.' In Denzin, N. K. and Lincoln, Y. S. (eds) *Sage Handbook of Qualitative Research*. Thousand Oaks, CA: Sage, pp. 695–727.

Foucault, M. (1973) *Madness and Civilization: A History of Insanity in the Age of Reason*. New York: Vintage.

Foucault, M. (1978) *The History of Sexuality, Vol. 1 An Introduction*, Trans. by R. Hurley, New York: Vintage.

Foucault, M. (1980) *Power/Knowledge: Selected Interviews and Other Writings, 1972–1977*. In Gordon, C. (ed.), Trans. by L. Marshall, J. Mepham and K. Soper, New York: Pantheon.

Foucault, M. (1988) *Technologies of the Self*. Amherst: University of Massachusetts Press.

Fournier, V. (1998) 'Stories of development and exploitation: militant voices in an enterprise culture.' *Organization* 5(1): 55–80.

Gergen, K. (1991) *The Saturated Self: Dilemmas of Identity in Contemporary Life*. New York: Basic Books.

Goffman, E. (1959) *The Presentation of Self in Everyday Life*. New York: Doubleday.

Grey, C. (1994) 'Career as a project of the self and the labour process discipline.' *Sociology* 28(2): 479–498.

Harre, R. and van Langenhove, L. (1999) *Positioning Theory*. Oxford: Blackwell.

Holstein, J. and Gubrium, J. (2000) *The Self We Live By. Narrative Identity in a Postmodern World*. New York: Oxford University Press.

Holstein, J. and Gubrium, J. (2003) 'Inside Interviewing, New Lenses, New Concerns.' In J. Holstein and J. Gubrium (Eds.) *Inside Interviewing*. Thousand Oaks, California: Sage (3-30).

Kvale, S. (1996) *InterViews: An Introduction to Qualitative Research Interviewing*. Thousand Oaks, California: Sage.

Leudar, I and Antaki, C. (1996) 'Participant status in social psychological research.' In T. Ibanez and L. Iniguez (eds.) *Critical Social Psychology*. London: Sage (273-290).

Malone, M. J. (1997) *Worlds of Talk: The Presentation of Self in Everyday Conversation*. Cambridge: Polity Press.

Mishler, E. G. (1986) *Research Interviewing: Context and Narrative*. Cambridge MA: Harvard University Press.

Peräkylä, A. (2005) 'Analyzing Talk and Text.' In Denzin, N.K. and Lincoln, Y.S. (eds.) *Sage Handbook of Qualitative Research*. Thousand Oaks, California: Sage.

Potter, J. and Wetherell, M. (1987) *Discourse and Social Psychology: Beyond Attitudes and Behaviour*. London: Sage.

Ricoeur, P. (1992) *Oneself as Another*. Translated by K. Blamey. Chicago: University of Chicago Press.

Sacks, H. (1992) *Lectures on Conversation* (Ed. G. Jefferson). Oxford and Cambridge MA: Blackwell.

Silverman, D. (2001) *Interpreting Qualitative Data: Methods for Analysing Talk, Text and Interaction*. London: Sage.

Silverman, D. (1997) *Qualitative Research: Theory, Method and Practice*. London: Sage.

Thomas, R. and Linstead, A. (2002) 'Losing the Plot? Middle Managers and Identity.' *Organization*, 9, 71-93.

Widdicombe, S. (1998) *Identity as an Analysts' and a Participants' Resource. In Identities in Talk*. London: Sage (191-206.).

Wittgenstein, L. (1967) *Philosophical Investigations* (3rd ed.) trans G.E.M. Anscombe. Oxford: Blackwell.

16

Narrative methods for identity research

Nic Beech and David Sims

In this chapter we explore an approach to understanding the nature of *homo narrans narratur* (Christie and Orton 1988), the person who understands herself and others by telling stories about them, both to themselves and to others. Identity is understood by differentiation; we know and tell who we and others are by contrast. In particular, we tell stories which illustrate the differences between those we are wishing to identify with and those from whom we want to 'disidentify'. The following example is taken from the kinds of things that people say just after telling a story about someone else in the office:

> Of course I'm not the sort to moan. I mean, if she goes round saying those sorts of things about people, well that's up to her. But I think you have got to have some standards; I don't know how she faces herself when she sees herself in the mirror (fragment of office conversation).

This extract (a composite, but so reminiscent of many office conversations) illustrates the kind of identification that takes place everywhere. 'Of course I'm not the sort to moan' differentiates the self from others, who are the sort to do just this. It is apparently said to warrant the statement that is about to be made – I'm not the sort to moan, so when I do, I should be taken seriously. But like most statements it shines both ways, illuminating the speaker as much as the supposed topic. In addition, in researching the narration of identities, the researcher is also building other people's stories (or fragments of stories) into their own stories, some of which are about the self, and some of which are constrained by what one can (and cannot) write in research. In what follows we will seek to set out an approach which enables the researcher to analyse stories in order to reveal their connotations of identity.

Why research identity through narratives?

Narratives are frequently used to explain complex ideas and propositions where a more direct, or simpler, mode of speaking is likely to under-represent the complexity (Pye 1995). Parables, stories and metaphors in the mode of narrative are all used in this way. It may be a conscious strategy of the storyteller as they grapple with a difficult topic, or may occur 'naturally' as people exchange their stories of experience and of the actions of others (Rhodes and Brown 2005). Identity is clearly one of the 'difficult topics' in organizational life. Who are the in-people and who are 'out'? Who should be trusted? Who should be followed? And who should be opposed? are just some of the multifarious questions that inform everyday behavior in the workplace. Judgements and perceptions about identity are fundamental to how people answer these questions for themselves. The way in which I see myself, and how I regard others, will have a significant impact on whether or not my relationship with that group of others will be typified by trust and cooperation, suspicion and opposition, a position in between, or possibly combining these extremes.

As people interact, perceptions of identity and relationships are built and stories are simultaneously constructed (Rhodes 2000). Stories are both descriptive of what happens and prescriptive of what should happen. Prescriptively, stories lay out scripts in advance of interaction (Goffman 1961). When people interact, they often already have predispositions about the role and character that they and others will take. For example, in seeking to lead a change, a manager may be predisposed to see a trade union representative as a (somewhat faulty) means by which to communicate with the workforce. Hence, the natural thing to do would be to feed particular messages to the union representative, which are designed to be passed on to union members. The expectations that the trade union representative has of the manager, however, will mediate his/her actions. For example, if the union representative's expectation is that managers in general, and this one in particular, deal in 'spin' and partial truths, he/she is likely to treat any messages from the manager with caution and will reinterpret the message for the union members. The stories that each actor tells of the event (of the message being passed from management to union members via their representative) to their own in-group will typically reinforce the group's predispositions about the self and the other. The managers tell each other the story that follows the 'well-trodden pathway' (Beech and Huxham 2003) of faulty communication told by the trade union representative, and the union members tell each other the story that follows similarly the well trodden pathway of the unforthcoming manager. As such stories are rehearsed and repeated, they lead in-group members to have ever strong predispositions about what to expect from out-group members. And hence, future interactions are flavoured by such expectations before they even begin (Humphries and Brown 2002).

Therefore, storytelling is both descriptive and formative of processes of identity construction. The analysis of stories in identity research seeks to reveal the implications of stories for ways of thinking and behaving, and the implications of thought and behavior for identity.

We have argued that stories can be used as ways of engaging with 'difficult topics' and, for example, the research of Martin *et al.* (1983) has shown that stories can provide the answer to difficult questions such as, 'is the boss human?' and 'what will happen if I make a mistake?' Such questions can be answered directly – the boss either is or is not 'human' – but the direct form of answer still leaves the audience without a full or contextualized understanding. Brown (1995) provides an example.

> In the Revlon Corporation, there was a story about Charles Revlon. He required staff to be on time and sign the sign-in sheet, which should not be removed. Revlon himself, however, was not normally on time. One day he arrived late and took the sign-in sheet to examine. The new receptionist, not knowing who he was, told him to replace the sheet. He refused and there was a short 'debate' which was concluded when Revlon said " 'do you know who I am?' and [the receptionist] said 'No sir, I don't'. 'Well, when you pick up your final paycheck this afternoon, ask 'em to tell ya'."
>
> (Brown 1995: 15).

This short story leaves the listener quite clear that the boss is not human, but it also provides a perspective on how the boss should (and should not) be approached, what the relationship between the boss and workers is like and how workers are likely to be treated. In short, in a few sentences, significant clues are given to the relative identities not only of Revlon and the new/ex-receptionist, but also to the identity constructions of owner and workers in this situation. The story may or may not be true, but, as it was taken to be true by the actors in the situation, it provides the researcher with potentially valuable insights into how the organizational actors make sense of themselves and others.

Stories carry a number of messages (Currie and Brown 2003). Some messages are basically concerned with the content or moral of the story. The story of Revlon is mainly targeted at telling us what a bad person he is, and there is a moral that he should be avoided and not crossed. However, the story also carries messages about the storyteller. It has been argued that some stories say more about the storyteller than they do about the story per se (Gergen 2001). In this case, the storyteller is positioning him/herself as anti-Revlon and as de-powered. The implication of the story is that there is nothing *we* can do about it – so beware!

In this chapter we will explore some of the techniques for analysing stories and narratives. Our aim is to show how stories can be used as a basis for researching identity. We will discuss the gathering of narrative data, the process of analysis and the sorts of conclusion that can be drawn from this type of research.

Narrative data

The data (stories) used in analysing narratives come in different forms. The key dimensions are whether the stories are elicited or unelicited and whether they are complete or composite. The first dimension relates to the mode in which the researcher gets access to the story. Elicited stories are ones that the researcher has asked a respondent for. For example, a respondent might be asked for the story of their experience in a particular setting, or with a particular person. Sometimes a respondent will tell a story in response to an open question – particularly when they are trying to explain something that is complicated and which needs a degree of contextual understanding. When stories are elicited, the audience (researcher) is playing a significant role. In effect the researcher has commissioned a performance and from the perspective of the respondent, the performance will have a specific purpose, such as answering (or warding off) a question. Hence, the telling of the story is conditional on the researcher as well as the respondent and this can have implications for the analysis and conclusions.

Unelicited stories are those which are told naturally in the course of a conversation. The most 'natural' are those told by one organization actor to another, outside a research setting. However, the researcher can get close to such situations, particularly when undertaking ethnographic or observational research. When a story has not actually been asked for, the frame of the performance is different. This is not to say that the researcher (and others) do not constitute an audience – they do – but it is an audience of a different type. In this case, the audience has not commissioned the storytelling and hence the process is different. For example, at the beginning of the story the storyteller might seek to 'sell' the story to the audience by stressing its relevance to them, or to some concern that they have. As with elicited stories, the framing of the performance can have consequences for analysis and conclusions and it is important to acknowledge the elicited/unelicited nature of the story during analysis.

The second dimension is whether stories are complete or composite. Complete stories are those which are told in their entirety in 'one sitting'. The Revlon story above is one such. The whole story is conveyed (in this case in one paragraph) as one piece of speech. A variant of this type of story is one that is told in one sitting by a storyteller but rather than it being a monologue, there are prompts and questions from the audience that assist the story on its way.

Composite stories are those which are drawn from disparate sections of data. For example, the research may have been conducted by interviewing the same respondents once a month for six months. In such circumstances it is often possible to string together a story across time, drawing elements of talk and interaction from the various interviews. These stories might take the following form: our initial intentions were W, we undertook action X, subsequently Y happened and so we are now at point Z. The advantage of this is that the story is not simply a 'snap-shot' view of what is going on. The potential disadvantage is that the researcher is fairly active in selecting which pieces of data fit together and in framing them as a story. However, it should be acknowledged that the researcher is active in selecting which data to show and which to hide and in forming the overall narrative of the research story in any case.

Analysis of narratives

There is a long tradition of narrative analysis that operated under structuralist assumptions (De Saussure 1983, Silverman 1993). These assumptions were, first, that the 'surface manifestation' of a story was underpinned by a 'depth structure', like a grammar of stories; secondly, that the deep structures were relatively few but that they led to many variants on the surface; and lastly, that the depth structure was more fundamental and in some sense 'more true' than the surface manifestations. The latter were regarded as fleeting and changeable, whereas the depth structure was relatively constant and predictable. Much of the current narrative research in Organisation Studies has rejected the epistemological assumptions of structural narrative analysis. Current research tends not to assume that there is a deep structure that is more true than surface stories. Rather, stories are regarded as projected images which, if taken to be true by the storytellers and audience, are true in their effects (Sims 2003). The social constructionist position (Gergen 2001) is that in telling stories, people are in the process of trying to construct a state of affairs. For example, if a new entrant to Revlon were told the old story about Charles Revlon firing the receptionist, this may have some impact on how they understand their own position vis a vis the organization. And hence, the story has had some role in the construction of the individual's identity within the organization. It is not the only influence – the individual's life story before joining Revlon, their self-assurance and so on will also impact on how they react to the story. However, from a constructionist narrative perspective these other factors are part of how the individual absorbs (or rejects) the story of the fired receptionist into their own story. Hence, the object of research is to unpick the constructions that occur in the various stories as they come together in a particular setting.

Some researchers who work with narrative have reacted to these changes in epistemological assumptions by dropping many of the techniques that were used by structural narrative researchers. We want to argue, however, that it is possible to use some structural techniques without adopting structuralist beliefs. We will argue that it is possible to analyse stories to show underlying plots and character structures without then regarding the plot structures as somehow more real than the stories themselves. The point of such analysis is not to unveil the underlying true deep structure. Rather, it is a way of unpicking some of the implications of the stories that might not at first sight be apparent.

Propp (1975) was interested in revealing the underlying *plot summaries* of stories. For Propp, the point was to cut through the superficial 'decoration' of the story in order to produce a series of statements that told the essence of the story. This technique could be applied to the Revlon story above as follows:

1. Charles Revlon required staff to sign-in on time and not remove the sign-in sheet.
2. A new receptionist was appointed, and was told that the sheet should not be removed.
3. Charles Revlon arrived late one day and removed the sign-in sheet.
4. The receptionist challenged him.
5. Charles Revlon fired the receptionist.

The advantage of this technique of laying out the plot summary is that it highlights in simple terms 'who did what to whom, in which order'. There is an order of activities and choices. For example, Revlon could have chosen to remove the sign-in sheet or not; the receptionist could have chosen to challenge him or not. In doing this, a second step of analysis is revealed. This is the *establishment of character*. At one level, characters are the actors named in the story. However, the analysis needs to go further than simply naming. The important feature is what Silverman (1993) termed the '*spheres of action*'. The spheres of action are what the character is allowed (and not allowed) to do. For example, a hero is expected to have good intentions and do good things, whereas the villain is expected to have bad intentions and do bad things. Confusion occurs if characters act outside their sphere of action (Czarniawska 1997). So, for example, in the Revlon story, Charles Revlon is clearly cast as villain. He could have reacted in a number of ways to the receptionist. He could have explained the situation to her, he could have admonished her but taken it no further and so on. However, in the way the story is constructed, he had bad intentions (or at least predispositions) and carried them out.

In addition to acting in a sphere of action, actors will adopt a *style* when they act (Sims 2005). In this case, the villain acts with relish. He could have been matter-of-fact in the way that he dismissed the receptionist, but his villainy is confirmed not only by his wielding of power, but also by the dismissive, malicious trickery in his style. This is in contrast to the character of the receptionist. The receptionist is cast as victim. The character of the victim must be undeserving of punishment and lack power. The victim's sphere of action is to be victimized. In this case, the receptionist acted reasonably in denying Revlon access to the list, given the information she had, and hence was undeserving of the punishment. However, even though the punishment was unfair, she had no power to resist and had to go along with the action. The style of action is submissive.

Hence, at this stage of analysis, the story as told has produced a plot summary and list of characters with their spheres of action and styles of enactment. Each of these steps of analysis can tell us something about identity. In the plot summary the order of activities tells us who acts first and who is in the reactive mode. The choices made give us an indication of the person's approach to the situation and their preferences. The characters are established through defining what they are permitted to do (being the villain or the victim, for example) and the style (aggressive or submissive, for example) with which they carry out their role.

The significance of narratives

The next phase of analysis is to unpick the significance of the plot and characterization. There are alternative schema for achieving this. Six 'narrative style factors' can be used as analytical questions as follows (Beech 2000):

1. the lesson learned/moral
2. integration/differentiation
3. causal attribution
4. efficacy of action
5. temporal perspective
6. behavioral style of dominant characters.

The first factor concerns the central lessons that the storyteller is trying to convey to the audience. The second factor concerns the social positioning of the actors. A high degree of integration would be a narrative that shows the actors to be part of the same in-group. A high degree of differentiation could show certain actors to be isolated or even alienated from others. Often, though not always, there is opposition or conflict between differentiated groups/individuals. The third factor focuses on how actors attribute cause, praise, blame and agency. Some actors may be seen as being able to make things happen, whilst others may be subject to the will of others or the whims of fate. Some will believe that individual or group action can overcome 'the system', whereas others will believe that their best efforts will be quashed by the system. The fourth factor, the efficacy of action, is the belief that if a particular actor tries to achieve an outcome, it will be achieved. Conversely, there can be a belief that actions will not result in their intended outcomes, and where this is the case there is a propensity for inertia. The fifth factor explores the orientation to time and the degree of optimism/pessimism. In essence, stories can be centred on the past, present or future, or can trace a track from past to future. In doing so, the view might be that the future will be better than the past. Alternatively, the future might be worse than the past. The last factor is the behavioral style of the central characters. This can range from highly assertive to highly passive (or submissive). The factors are typically interlinked. For example, passivity can follow from a belief that personal action will be defeated by the system and that others hold power. Conversely, assertiveness can follow a belief that individual action will be effective and that the future can be better than the past.

When applied to the Revlon story the factors show the following:

Moral of the story	Do not cross the boss
Differentiation	The boss is different to everyone else
Causal attribution	The boss has power to make things happen. The receptionist has no power
Efficacy of action	Whatever the receptionist does will not have any effect
Temporal perspective	The future is not likely to be any better than the way things are now – hence the need for this warning
Behavioral styles	Revlon – aggression Receptionist – passivity

An alternative schema is provided by Gabriel (2000, 2004). Gabriel identifies 'poetic tropes' which are the interpretive devices storytellers use to make sense of events. He identifies eight tropes as follows:

1. Attribution of motive – the conscious or unconscious aims of the actors
2. Attribution of causal connections – the notion of earlier events in the sequence (plot summary) causing subsequent ones
3. Attribution of responsibility – the evaluation of events and characters as being praised or blameworthy
4. Attribution of unity – where a class (or category) of people is treated the same and in which any individual within the class is substitutable for any other individual
5. Attribution of fixed qualities, especially in opposition – people or classes of people, or objects, are regarded as having particular immutable qualities (such as strength, intelligence or cunning) which will persist unless the plot incorporates a transformation
6. Attribution of emotion – individuals acting in emotional ways or deriving emotional outcomes from events
7. Attribution of agency – where inanimate objects (e.g. machines, the weather, natural forces) are seen as acting in a motivated way
8. Attribution of providential significance – where an event is seen as inevitable within the plot (e.g. a negative outcome is inevitable in a tragedy).

This schema can be applied to the Revlon story as follows:

Attribution of motive	Charles Revlon may have a subconscious motive to belittle the receptionist
Attribution of causal connections	The setting of the rule about the sign-in sheet is a necessary precursor to the receptionist's adherence to the rule, without which the rest of the plot would not occur
Attribution of responsibility	Revlon is to blame
Attribution of unity	In the on-telling of the story, workers are a unified class. Anyone who displeased Revlon would have suffered a similar fate
Attribution of fixed qualities	Revlon is regarded as unreasonable and merciless
Attribution of emotion	Revlon may relish the event. The receptionist is likely to be upset
Attribution of agency	In this story, Revlon is the key agent
Attribution of providential significance	There is a sense of inevitability from when the receptionist applies the rule to Revlon, to her dismissal. In effect, she has accidentally sealed her fate

For the identity researcher, the point of the application of these schema is what they can tell us about identities and identity dynamics. In the first schematic, the nature of actors and what they can do are elucidated. Further, how those actors stand with regard to each other, the effectiveness of action in the face of social structures and systems, and the passage of time are highlighted. This will not necessarily say all there is to say about identities, but it will give insight into how a story can form and reinforce predispositions and perceptions of the self and others. In the second schematic, certain tropes have particular significance for identity research. The attribution of unity – groups/classes to which actors are ascribed – is particularly important. The collection of group memberships that one has says a lot about one's identity. Group memberships are often used as a shorthand for ascribing identity (for example, groups such as 'managers', 'workers', 'strategists' and 'trade unionists' are commonly used in Organisation Studies).

Similarly, the attribution of fixed qualities can be very important for identity. For example, 'managers' and 'workers' might regard the other group as having particular qualities which lead to them acting towards the other in particular ways and selectively perceiving the actions of the other so as to reinforce the perceived association of the group with the quality. For example, managers might be associated with a concern with 'spin' and impression and hence, their words are likely to be regarded with suspicion. Some factors/tropes are shared between the two schema presented above, whilst others provide different emphases. It is appropriate for identity researchers to make selection/combinations from the two lists as befits the data being analysed; however, in making such selections it is important to ensure that certain basics are covered:

1. the nature of actors (individuals, classes, roles, integrated or differentiated)
2. attribution of qualities and styles to the actors
3. attribution of agency (to actors, structures and objects)
4. attribution of causal connections and outcomes over time.

Having taken the analysis to this stage, quite a lot can be said about the identities of those involved in the story. The nature of events, how they flow into each other and where the characters stand with regard to each other are all now laid out. However, there is another layer of complexity that we need to deal with and this will be addressed in the next section.

Multiple narratives and silence

The Revlon story seems like a simple narrative, but most stories in organizations are complicated and often involve more than one set of interpretations woven around others. Boje (1991, 1995) introduces the metaphor of a play called *Tamara* as a way of conceptualizing this. *Tamara* is a play where the audience is more active and mobile than normal. As an audience member you would choose which character to follow and watch them in a particular scene with other characters. At the end of that scene you would then choose who to follow to the next scene. As a result you might be following the character of the spy who is posing as the chauffeur. You are aware that he is really a spy from the interactions you have observed. However, other audience members who have been following other characters will be unaware of this. So, for example, when they follow the maid to a meeting with the chauffeur, they see a chauffeur, not a spy. Consequently, they will make sense of his actions framed through their understanding of his role. Depending on which characters you follow to which sequence of scenes, you might see radically different versions of the play on different nights. And audience members attending on the same night, but following different characters, can see quite different versions to each other.

Boje argues that organizations are like *Tamara*. There are many scenes going on at any one time. Characters move in and out of them, revealing some facets of their character in some settings and other facets in other settings. Interpretations and reinterpretations will be made continuously. It is not that there is a true version of the play. Rather, there are multiple possible interpretations of different plot strands, many of which will impact on each other, sometimes in unplanned ways. Boje's style of analysis draws our attention to the significance of *who is telling the story* and how they choose to project images.

In the Revlon story, although Charles Revlon is the central character, to whom causal agency is attributed, he is not the storyteller. The story is told as a tragedy from the perspective of someone sympathetic to the receptionist. The same set of events might be narrated differently from Revlon's perspective. For example, the story might be as follows:

> The latest in a line of insubordinate receptionists had been appointed. She was highly impolite and clearly this was a problem, not only for me (Revlon) but also for customers and visitors who will come to the building. I had to take decisive action, which is what is required of a leader.

This rendering of the story would be analysed differently. For example, rather than Revlon acting in an inappropriately aggressive way towards his victim, here he is seen as being forced to dismiss someone because of *their* ineptitude. Thus, cause is differently attributed, there is a different attribution of unity – it is not that all employees would be treated this way, only those who were rude and inept – and the providential significance of the plot is pushing Revlon to act in this way. As a result, quite different identities are constructed for the characters. When applying this approach in organizations, it is therefore important to gather different perspectives on a story from the actors involved and from others who have a perspective. The purpose of this is not to 'triangulate' to see which is true. The point is to present the versions of the story that are taken to be simultaneously true.

The last point of analysis we want to make is to focus on what is *not* there. Watson (1995) refers to a work of Arthur Conan Doyle to draw our attention to elements that appear to be missing from a story, whose absence we can question. In a Conan Doyle story, Sherlock Holmes is able to unlock the mystery because of the clue that a dog did not bark in the night-time. If the prevailing view of the event had been correct, one could reasonably expect the dog to have barked. Everyone else overlooks this 'absence' as they are focused on the clues that can be seen and observed, but Holmes outwits not only the villains, but also his colleagues. The point in narrative analysis is that we can learn about people's identities through what they refrain from doing. In the Revlon story the receptionist does not appear to fight back at all. As far as we know she does not try to explain her side of the story; she does not go to the trade union; she does not go to a lawyer. The question is – why not? This sort of pattern has been detected amongst workers by critically oriented researchers, who focus on hegemony (for example, Alvesson and Willmott 2002). Workers who might be expected to resist managerial efforts to intensify their work do not. The reasons for this include the workers' perceptions of themselves as powerless, and it is possible to show how workers come to this view of themselves through narrative analysis.

Conclusions

In summary, stories are told in organizations to perform a number of functions: to entertain; to inform; to answer 'difficult questions'. The position of narrative analysis is that such stories can tell us much about the identity of the storyteller and their perspective on the identities of others. Through applying the analytical techniques outlined above, it is possible to reveal assumptions and beliefs that people hold about their (and others') characters, associated qualities, abilities, relationships and place within the social structure. Further, it is possible to see stories told from different perspectives as ways of understanding the complex web of relationships and reciprocal interaction that exists in most organizations.

However, narrative analysis has its limitations. It does entail interpretation and reinterpretation of talk in organizations. Hence, it fits most easily with an intepretivist or social constructionist paradigm of research. It fits less well with positivist forms of research and hence is less likely to be used for large-scale generalizations or for uncovering the 'real essence' of an individual's identity. Stories have a temporal aspect to them. They track a series of actions and commonly project both forwards and backwards in constructing the moral or point they are making. However, it must be acknowledged that stories are fundamentally about the time they are gathered. They express current views of the future/past rather than being actually representative of the future or past. Lastly, given that the nature of stories is that they do not absolutely close-down interpretation, it is in the nature of things that interpretations made by researchers are contestable. Others may pick up different nuances to stories, or read different significances in them. Hence, in writing up narrative research of identity, it is important for the researcher to be open about what interpretations are being made and why, and it is important to express multiple (*Tamara*-like) interpretations as a matter of course.

References

Alvesson, M. and Willmott, M. (2002) 'Identity regulation as organizational control: producing the appropriate individual.' *Journal of Management Studies* 39(5): 619–644.

Beech, N. (2000) 'Narratives styles of managers and workers: a tale of star-crossed lovers?' *Journal of Applied Behavioural Science* 36(2): 210–228.

Beech, N. and Huxham, C. (2003) 'Cycles of identity formation in interorganizational collaborations.' *International Studies of Management and Organization* 33(3): 28–52.

Boje, D. (1991) 'The storytelling organization: a study of story performance in an office-supply firm.' *Administrative Science Quarterly* 36: 106–126.

Boje, D. (1995) 'Stories of the storytelling organization: a postmodern analysis of Disney as "Tamara-land".' *Academy of Management Journal* 38(4): 997–1035.

Brown, A. (1995) *Organizational Culture*. London: Pitman.

Christie, J. R. R. and Orton, F. (1988). 'Writing a text on the life.' *Art History* 11(4): 543–563.

Currie, G. and Brown, A. D. (2003) 'A narratological approach to understanding processes of organizing in a UK hospital.' *Human Relations*. 56(5): 563–586.

Czarniawska, B. (1997) *Narrating the Organization: Dramas of Institutional Identity*. Chicago: University of Chicago Press.

De Saussure, F. (1983) *Course in General Linguistics*, Trans. R. Harris, London: Gerald Duckworth & Co.

Gabriel, Y. (2000) *Storytelling in Organizations: Facts, Fictions, Fantasies*. Oxford: Oxford University Press.

Gabriel, Y. (2004) 'Narratives, stories and texts.' In Grant, D., Hardy, C., Oswick, C. and Putnam, L. (eds) *The Sage Handbook of Organizational Discourse*. London: Sage.

Gergen, K. J. (2001) *Social Construction in Context*. London: Sage.

Goffman, E. (1961) *Encounters*. Indianapolis, IN: Bobbs-Merrill.

Humphries, M. and Brown, A. D. (2002) 'Narratives of organizational identity and identification: a case study of hegemony and resistance.' *Organization Studies* 23: 421–447.

Martin, J., Feldman, M. S., Hatch, M. J., and Sitkin, S. B. (1983) 'The uniqueness paradox in organizational stories.' *Administrative Science Quarterly* 28: 438–453.

Propp, V. (1975) *Morphology of the Folktale*. Austin, TX: University of Texas Press.

Pye, A. (1995) 'Strategy through dialogue and doing: a game of "Mornington Crescent"?' *Management Learning* 26(4): 445–462.

Rhodes, C. (2000) 'Reading and writing organizational lives.' *Organization* 7: 7–29.

Rhodes, C. and Brown, A. D. (2005) 'Narrative, organizations and research.' *International Journal of Management Reviews* 7(3): 167–188.

Silverman, D. (1993) *Interpreting Qualitative Data*. London: Sage.

Sims, D. (2003) 'Between the millstones: a narrative account of the vulnerability of middle managers' storying.' *Human Relations* 56: 1195–1121.

Sims, D. (2005) 'You bastard: a narrative exploration of the experience of indignation within organizations.' *Organization Studies* 26(11): 1625–1640.

Watson, T. J. (1995) 'In search of HRM: beyond the rhetoric and reality distinction or the case of the dog that didn't bark.' *Personnel Review* 24(4): 6–16.

17

Negotiating identities of consumption: insights from conversation analysis

Nick Llewellyn and Robin Burrow

Introduction

Conversation analytic studies of work identities are distinctive because they reveal how matters of identity are demonstrably relevant for the actual material accomplishment of work activities, processes and practices. Such studies reveal what the work of different people consists of and how matters of identity are relevant and consequential for the accomplishment of that work. All such enquires are based on audio and/or video recordings of people working and all are exclusively concerned, in one way or another, with identity as a *members' phenomenon* (Eglin 2002); occasions where members' themselves orient to, or variously draw upon, aspects of personhood in the 'concerted activities of their daily [working] lives' (Garfinkel 1967: vii).

This chapter illustrates methodological principles and practices character- istic of conversation analytic studies of work identities. It does so by drawing on an extended corpus of audio/video recordings that capture the work of buying and selling in a public setting; a busy urban street in a British city. Whilst the analysis is bound up with and seeks to explicate the work of selling the *Big Issue* magazine, matters discussed – such as the production of 'sales pitches', the management of customers and the cultivation of a body of 'regulars' – have a broader relevance for more conventional work settings. First and foremost, however, the chapter is concerned with work identities on the street. It is curious that Organisation and Management Studies should have so privileged the 'enclosed sphere of work' (Foucault 1977, in Gordon 1980), at the expense of settings which – whilst less conventional – have nevertheless always been places of work. Variously, urban streets are conventional and familiar settings for selling (products such as food, newspapers, double glazing, motor breakdown cover, etc.); canvassing; consumer research; leafleting and promotion; trade in 'deviant' goods and services such as drugs and prostitution; soliciting charitable donations. What this work consists of and the various accountabilities and identities that are established by the location of such work on busy urban high streets have been overlooked. For exceptions it is necessary to look to Sociology (Pinch and Clark 1986), and Urban Sociology in particular (Duneier 1999, Duneier and Molotch 1999).

Through three empirical sections, this chapter considers different ways in which magazine sellers and those who engage with them orient to identities, including 'Catholic', 'guy', 'customer', 'regular', 'donor' and 'homeless'. Such identities are approached as positions within a fluid web of accountabilities that are locally invoked and negotiated; not as deeply embedded features of personal biographies or psyches. The matter of whether people really are 'X', 'Y' or 'Z' is bracketed from consideration and supplanted by a study ethic that privileges how people accomplish, *do*, or otherwise draw upon, various ways in which they are availably identifiable in the 'concerted activities of their daily lives' (Garfinkel 1967). In practice, this means looking in detail at 'live' social conduct. Matters considered below include, but are not exhausted by: greetings, bodily movements and inclinations, smiles, hands gestures, the speed, direction and way that people walk, and so on.

The first empirical section considers the problem of *identifying* intended recipients of sales pitches. Of all the people walking past, who is targeted as a potential customer? In part, this problem was solved by the seller describing passers-by as members of gendered identity categories, such as 'bloke', 'sir' and 'ladies'. In Eglin's (2002) terms, the seller *found* passers-by to be members of such categories and *used* their gender-status to identify them as the recipients of sales pitches. He never once used their height, weight or dress sense to do this work. Reference terms such as 'bloke' and 'couple' are well suited to the work of identifying 'strangers', but not all passers-by were unknown to the seller. A core task for *Big Issue* sellers – and for those selling goods and services more generally – is to cultivate a body of 'regulars'. A second empirical section considers how 'sellers' recognize 'regulars' and how 'regulars' recognize themselves in concerted activities on the street. Finally, the momentary reconfiguration of scenes brought about by acts of charity is considered, to illustrate the fluid, negotiated and continually accomplished character of identities on the street.

In addition to giving an overview of the chapter, this introduction has alluded to the ethic or 'study policy' underpinning conversation analytic treatments of identity. The matter of 'who people really are' is bracketed from consideration (Garfinkel 1967) by a policy that privileges how people *find* and practically *use* available identities in the context of their work. This policy can be translated into research practice in a number of different ways (see Baker 1997, Fitzgerald and Housley 2002, Hester 1991, McHoul 1990, Potter and Hepburn 2007). What links these studies is an interest in identity 'as a members' phenomenon' (Eglin 2002), as a complex of problems that people confront and practically manage in the context of doing work. In the first instance, identity is a puzzle people resolve in the course of their ordinary affairs; conversation analytic approaches explore how they do this.

Principles and practices of conversation analysis (CA)

The following sections work-through some video-audio data,[1] applying principles and practices associated with CA. The clips are taken from an extended collection of recordings of a *Big Issue* seller working on a busy street in the center of Coventry, a medium-sized city in the United Kingdom. The *Big Issue* magazine is produced for and sold by the homeless.

Pitches and the identification of sales targets

Part of the work of street selling involves positioning passers-by as 'potential customers' through the production of 'sales pitches'. This positioning may only last a few moments but routinely has material consequences for the conduct of passers-by. Once recognized as the recipient of a sales pitch, people face new accountabilities: whether and how to accept or decline the invitation to buy some product. In one way or another, people respond to the new circumstances. This section considers how these circumstances are generated, through an analysis of a five second video clip.

To position others as potential customers, street sellers have to get the attention of passers-by, who face the problem of whether and how to recognize themselves as recipients of sales pitches. Such problems are resolved through an intricate choreography of movement, gaze and speech which are by no means distinctive to the work of street sellers. A great many more conventional sales or service encounters begin with resolutions to such problems. This is known by anyone who has ever tried to get served at a busy

---

1 The three clips reproduced in this chapter are all publicly available; they can be observed through the author's website (http://llewellyn.nick3.googlepages.com/home).

bar, or attempted to get a busy waiter's attention. How people get another's attention is amenable to research using resources from CA.

In this instance, the work of gaining another's attention starts before the 'pitch'. The seller takes two clear steps towards the path of the sales 'target' and then stops. The seller's trajectory is matched to the target's; had the seller not stopped, evasive action would have been required to avert a collision. The second of these steps, the matched trajectories and the stationary position finally occupied by the seller, are captured by the first two images in Figure 17.1 As pedestrians co-ordinate their physical movements on busy city streets to avoid collisions, the act of walking directly towards another person may be rare, 'noticeable', and thus a device for gaining that person's attention.

As the seller is walking towards the 'target', he produces the 'pitch' ('hello, big issue guy'). As the 'pitch' begins, the passer-by has not demonstrably recognized the seller. He may have *actually* noticed the seller's presence, but he has not *done* noticing him. He has not looked at, spoken to or adjusted his trajectory towards the seller. The pitch begins with a loud and stretched 'hello' (stretched from the 'o' and produced with upward intonation). In this context 'hello' is not produced as a greeting. The seller leaves no space for a return greeting and does not receive one after the pitch's completion. In this context, 'hello' is a preliminary to a pitch; one more little thing that might get the target's attention.

The pitch ends with a 'person reference' (Sacks and Schegloff 1979) fitted to the 'target'. He is referred to as 'guy'. This is another way the seller shows 'I am speaking to you'. Across the corpus as a whole, the seller exclusively uses these 'single reference forms', never combined forms such as 'young guy', that allowed passers-by to recognize themselves. Almost all were gendered categories. For this seller, and perhaps more broadly for all sellers, it would seem gendered categories are very usable for the work of publicly identifying strangers.

As the pitch is being produced, for the first time the target publicly orients to the seller, by casting his gaze to the product, which the seller is displaying in a prominent position, using his right arm (see image two especially). At the point the target is adjacent to the seller, his gaze moves upwards and they exchange a glance just as he is about to walk past (see image three).

Precisely at this point, as they exchange glances, something happens which is both remarkable and easily missed. The 'target' has declined the invitation to buy. How can we see this? From a conversation analytic perspective, social actions are nothing more or less than 'members' methods for making those . . . activities visibly rational and reportable' (Garfinkel 1967: vii). So

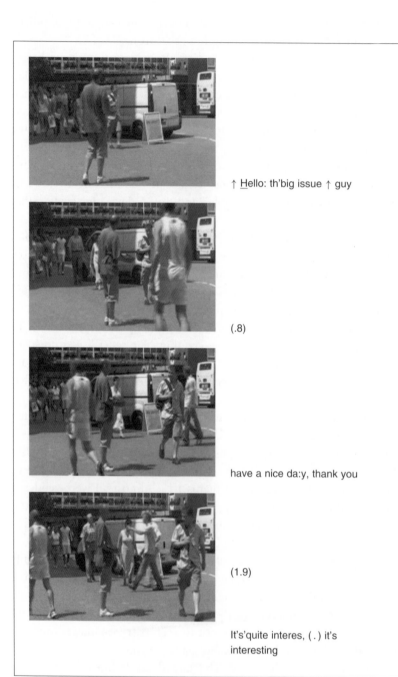

Figure 17.1　Images and verbatim of extract 1

how is the declination made 'visibly rational and reportable'? The answer is – by the seller's response 'have a nice day thank you'. Such an utterance, which orients to ending of the encounter, is a practical method for 'noticing' a declination. By saying 'have a nice day thank you', the 'target's lack of interest in buying a magazine is publicly noticed. What evidence might he have drawn upon? Perhaps he found, in (a) the absence of any response to his pitch, (b) the 'target's unaltered trajectory along the pavement and (c) the continuing pace and rhythm of his movement and gait, no evidence of a forthcoming sale.

The analysis has started to recover ways in which people are momentarily positioned as they move through busy urban settings. In building such an appreciation, we are starting to explicate a local system of signification that renders conduct amenable to assessment and evaluation in this context. In this brief extract, the passer-by does not say anything, but is 'heard' loud and clear.

The encounter does not finish there. There is a nicely choreographed sequence of activities at the close. Arguably, in and through the organization of these activities, the participants enact a more general concern for the 'other'. Following the negotiated declination, the 'target' keeps looking at the product (image four); even though he has walked past the seller. In response, the seller further adjusts his bodily position through 45° and maintains the magazine in a position of prominence. As the passer-by continues to look, the seller says 'it quite interes, it's interesting'. Through this utterance the 'target's gaze is made accountable as 'curiosity about the product'; there is a momentary possibility that a sale could be back on the agenda. But there is something more; in this utterance both participants find something to smile about. Whilst the 'target' keeps walking, he has not declined the pitch with hostility, annoyance or ambivalence. He has manufactured and taken part in a moment that acknowledges the seller's presence on the street.

Selling to regulars

In the first extract, the seller deals with a 'stranger' who had no prior plans to purchase a magazine. Whilst *Big Issue* sellers participate in such encounters a great deal, many of their sales come from 'regulars' and from people who have plans to buy the magazine. Like many in local service or sales occupations, *Big Issue* sellers both recognize and consciously cultivate 'regulars'. But what is a 'regular' and how, as an analyst, do you identify them?

For conversation analysts such questions can only be addressed by analysing specific instances. Rather than asking *who* are 'regulars', the challenge is to recover *how* and *when* the identity 'regular' is an oriented to feature of some work task.

In the extract of figure 17.2, which lasts approximately 16 seconds, the seller seems to be dealing with people he knows. As an analyst, how is it possible to see this? For the business of practically doing CA, this is perhaps the key question. In this data, how is it possible to see people doing 'recognition' and displaying 'familiarity'?

First, consider how the seller acknowledges the buyer and his associate as they walk directly towards him. As they approach, the seller's gaze is cast upon them and he stops his continual movement back and forth across the pavement; he waits for them to come to him. As they are motioning towards him, he looks at them directly, leans back slightly and then smiles. This seems to display an appreciation both of their desire to purchase a magazine *and* a level of familiarity with them as individuals (image one is an attempt to capture something of this).

Second, consider the production and management of *greetings*. In extract 1, 'hello' was not produced or oriented to as a greeting, but in the second extract, 'hello' *is* produced and responded to as a greeting. Alone, of course, this does not evidence familiarity; it is perfectly possible for strangers to exchange greetings, and street sellers will often manufacture such exchanges to draw passers-by into encounters. But this is not happening here and there is something about the way the seller says 'hello' which embodies familiarity. But what is this?

This brings us to a key tension in doing CA: what level of evidence is required to support the analysts reading of the data? CA *is* an evidential approach, analysts' accounts have to tally with the displayed orientations of members; but are these 'displayed orientations' always obvious and easy to capture? Sometimes they are, sometimes they are not.

The only place conversation analysts' look to recover evidence – that an utterance is doing this or that – is the data. Going back to extract 2, the buyer certainly finds nothing unusual or remarkable in the sellers 'hello'; a return greeting is produced which also arguably embodies familiarity. But this alone does not really explicate *how* the seller's greeting embodies familiarity. A second place to look would be the design and production of specific grammatical units, such as 'hello'. Comparing the 'hello's' in extracts 1 and 2 reveals them to be quite different. The first is louder, begins from a higher pitch, the 'h' is more prominent and the word is stretched from the 'o'. The second is quieter, more compact, the 'h' is barely audible (the first sound is 'el') and there is upward intonation on the final syllable. The analyst might even deploy an element of intuition here and argue, where someone to

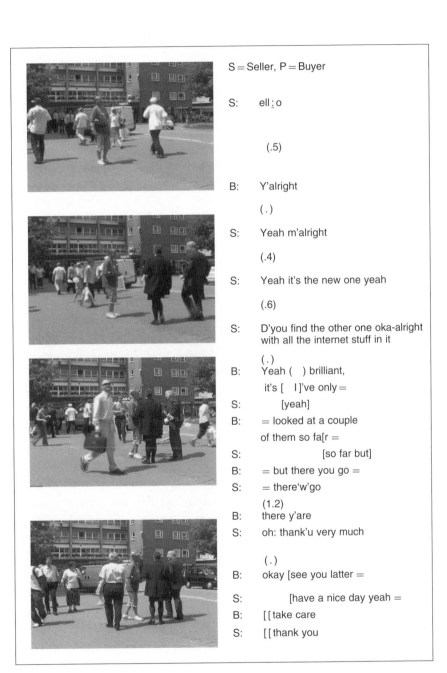

S = Seller, P = Buyer

S: ell:o

(.5)

B: Y'alright

(.)

S: Yeah m'alright

(.4)

S: Yeah it's the new one yeah

(.6)

S: D'you find the other one oka-alright with all the internet stuff in it

(.)

B: Yeah ( ) brilliant,
     it's [I]'ve only =

S: [yeah]

B: = looked at a couple
     of them so fa[r =

S: [so far but]

B: = but there you go =

S: = there'w'go

(1.2)

B: there y'are

S: oh: thank'u very much

(.)

B: okay [see you latter =

S: [have a nice day yeah =

B: [[take care

S: [[thank you

Figure 17.2 Selling to a regular: images and transcript

produce the second 'hello' to a stranger, it would be 'disruptive', precisely because it embodies familiarity (Garfinkel 1967).

Even though CA is an 'evidential approach', something often escapes rational discourse and codification through transcription. This is recognized within the community of CA scholars. In extract 2, for example, you have to see how the seller's smile, his 'hello' and his bodily positioning all combine in the moment. For this reason, it is essential that – where it is possible to do so – data is made public.[2] To ensure reflexively, the operation of the researcher's descriptive competencies has to be open to public scrutiny. In this tradition, the reader of this chapter can consider my rendering of extract 2 against the data itself.

* * *

In this data, the most obvious way both parties display their 'relationship' is through talk about a prior edition of the *Big Issue* magazine ('the other one'), which we might assume the buyer purchased from the seller some previous week. The seller both solicits an assessment from the buyer ('was it oka, alright') *and* displays his knowledge of this buyer's interest in the Internet which, again, must have been accrued from previous interactions. Here we see the seller crafting a narrative that links previous encounters to the present one. In contrast to much 'narrative research', which analyses manufactured stories and narratives, *this narrative is part of the world it reflects upon*. It is part of a process through which the seller gets to know his customers.

The analysis has taken some initial steps towards addressing how it is possible to see 'regulars', considering (a) the production of initial glances and acknowledgements, (b) initial greetings and (c) narratives that trade upon prior encounters. Perhaps it is precisely through such glances, greetings and narratives that sellers 'recognize' regulars and buyers recognize themselves as 'regulars'.

But there is something quite uncomfortable about the analysis produced thus far. The identities 'regular' and 'stranger' have been invoked purely by the analyst and not by members. This has not been done flippantly. There are major differences between extracts 1 and 2. Where people orient to a prior relationship, there are significant consequences for the way people come together and organize exchange. But the labels have come from the researcher, not the field. One reason for selecting this clip, however, is for what happens right at the end.

---

2 Please refer to footnote 1

Following the sale, the seller walks past the camera which is set up at the side of the pavement. He says to the operator, *'that's one regular'*. What is the relevance of this? It does not somehow prove the passer-by really was a regular, but it does illustrate that 'regular' is a familiar and recognized identity on the street. It is not simply an analyst's invention. More broadly, such comments are themselves amenable to analysis, as a way of appreciating consequences of filming people as they work. In this case, the camera's presence on the pavement gave the seller an opportunity to discourse upon his approach to selling. He alludes to a lively sense in which his work is subject to various techniques and strategies.

Giving not buying

Thus far no mention has been made of charity, even though the 'regular' in extract 2 lets the seller 'keep the change'. This final section briefly considers an episode where identities of consumption are displaced through an act of charity. The moment by moment negotiation of accountabilities and identities on the street is massively apparent in the brief exchange.

In Figure ?? below, an individual walks towards the seller and is initially seen as a customer. How is it possible to see this? Following the 'pitch' she walks directly towards the seller. Following a brief pause, she looks in her bag. It is this searching, rather than anything that is said, which occasions the sellers *'oh bless you'*. Through this utterance, the 'donor's activities have been seen to embody an intention to purchase a magazine. As she is searching, the seller thumbs a copy of the *Big Issue* from the pile he is holding (image 2). We can see he is expecting a sale. These are the accountabilities in play, within which the 'donor' is momentarily caught.

We can also see the 'donor' recognizes this definition of the situation. Easily enough, she says, 'I don't want the magazine'. Even though the seller responds by saying 'that's fine', the 'donor' produces an elaborate narrative account that locates her reasons for giving in the conditions of her own life. She has lots to read, by dint of being a Catholic. Again, the interest is not *who* people are, but *when* they are (Eglin 2002). In this instance, the 'donor' is a 'Catholic' in the context of an account for giving. Rather circuitously perhaps, her donation is not framed as a good deed via Catholicism, but as a rational response to being overwhelmed with reading materials. In and through this framing of her actions, the individual expresses and enacts a more general concern for the 'other'; the donation is handled gently, with due concern for the social implications of acts of charity.

S = seller, D = donor

S: Hello the big issue mam

(1.1)

S: arh bless you, thank you very much

(1.1)
S: havin a good day

(.7)

D: not to bad [( )
S: [arh that's good

(3.4)

D: I don't want the magazin, I hope you don't mind

(.)

S: no::[I don't mind ( )
D: [it's just that ( ) I'm a catholic and ([ ) =

S: [okay alright (.) hoo]
D: = (a lot of) catholic

stuff   and huh

S: [alright whatever]

((continues))

Figure 17.3 Giving not buying: images and transcript

Discussion

Conversation analytic studies of identity try to find how matters of identity are relevant and consequential for the daily activities of people. In the above sections, the work of street selling has been shown to consist of such things such as (1) describing passers-by ('guy'), (2) recognizing intentions to buy ('arh bless you'), (3) gaining the attention of passers-by and (4) recognizing repeat buyers or 'regulars'. An attempt has been made to reveal how matters of identity are relevant for these activities. In one way or another, the analysis has been concerned with identity as a *members' phenomenon* (Eglin 2002), with occasions where sellers and those who deal with them orient to, or variously draw on, aspects of personhood in their concerted activities. Despite considerable interest in identity over recent years, research within Organisation and Management Studies arguably remains far removed from 'the work itself' (Strauss 1985), not least because of the empirical materials that are conventionally analysed: interview data and *post hoc* recollections from ethnographic journals.

How best to characterize conversation analytic approaches? In relation to familiar conceptual distinctions, CA is firmly anti-realist. Identity is viewed as an 'ongoing accomplishment' (Garfinkel 1967). What is interesting is how people *do*, or otherwise draw upon, aspects of personhood in everyday life. But the approach is also materialist, in the sense analysts are concerned only with interpretations that are part of the social world they reflect upon. More broadly, CA might be seen as part of a broader theoretical movement that decouples identity from individuals. In CA, identity is akin to a position within – or a property of – accountabilities that open, close and change with every ongoing utterance and action. As in post-structuralism and structural linguistics, in CA, identity is not owned by individuals.

But such conventional distinctions fail to capture the most interesting and radical feature of conversation analytic approaches. In the history of Organisation Studies, and Social Science more generally, analysts have allocated identities to persons such as 'manager', 'entrepreneur', 'employee' or 'professional' without explicating how those identities are 'relevant' and 'consequential' (Schegloff 1991) for the concerted activities of the workplace. This is a considerable omission which reflects the longstanding tendency within Organisation Studies to approach identity – and other core categories – from within an analyst's frame of reference. But in the first instance, such matters are resolved by members and it is their solutions, not those of analysts, which are implicated in the constitution of social scenes. Whether a *Big Issue* vendor is a 'salesperson' or a 'homeless person' is not resolvable from within an analytic attitude. It is only resolvable by members *in situ.* Practical scenes of work are filled with sentient actors who, in building their work activities,

> Orient to their context under some formulation or formulations; who grasp their own conduct and that of others under the jurisdictions of some relevancies and not others; who orient to some of the identities they separately and collectively embody and, at any given moment, not others. And, because it is the orientations, meanings, interpretations, understandings, etc., of the participants in some socio-cultural event on which the course of that event is predicated, it is those characterisations which are privileged in the constitution of socio-interactional reality, and therefore have a prima-facie claim to be privileged in efforts to understand it
>
> (Schegloff 1997: 166–167).

Historically, researchers in Organisation and Management Studies have accommodated the actor's perspective by talking with them, getting to know them and by observing them, often over extended periods. Such approaches allow researchers to describe how particular identities are relevant for people *personally*, but unless the researcher can analyse 'live' recordings, they will not be able to reveal how identities such as 'manager', 'entrepreneur', 'employee' or 'professional' are relevant for the activities and practices of the workplace. The absence of this account is a problem for Organisation Studies, whose practitioners are yet to thoroughly demonstrate how work identities are demonstrably relevant for the actual 'real time' activities of people at work.

References

Baker, C. (1997) 'Ticketing rules: categorisation and moral ordering in a school staff meeting'. In Hester, S. and Eglin, P. (eds) *Culture in Action: Studies in Membership Categorisation Analysis*. Washington, DC: IIEMCA.

Duneier, M. (1999) *Sidewalk*. New York: FSG.

Duneier, M. and Molotch, H. (1999) 'Talking city trouble: interactional vandalism, social inequality and the "Urban Interaction Problem" ' *American Journal of Sociology* 104(5).

Eglin, P. (2002) 'Members gendering work: "Women", "Feminists" and membership categorisation analysis.' *Discourse and Society* 13(6): 819–825.

Fitzgerald, R. and Housley, W. (2002) 'Identity, categorization and sequential organization: the sequential and categorical flow of identity in a radio phone-in.' *Discourse and Society* 13(5): 579–602.

Garfinkel, H. (1967) *Studies in Ethnomethodology*. Cambridge: Polity.

Gordon, C. (ed.) (1980) *Michel Foucault: Power/Knowledge*. Harlow: Harvester Wheatsheaf.

Hester, S. (1991) 'The social facts of deviance in school: a study of mundane reason.' *British Journal of Sociology* 42(3): 443–463.

McHoul, A. W. (1990) 'The organization of repair in classroom talk.' *Language in Society* 19: 349–377.

Pinch, T. and Clark, C. (1986) 'The hard seller: patter merchanting and the strategic (re)production and local management of economic reasoning in the sales routines of market pitches.' *Sociology* 20(2): 169–191.

Potter, J. and Hepburn, A. (2007) 'Chairing democracy: psychology, time and negotiating the institution.' In *Rhetoric, Discourse and Ordinary Democracy.* Tuscaloosa, AL: University of Alabama Press.

Schegloff, E. A. (1991) 'Reflections on talk and social structure.' In Boden, D. and Zimmerman, D. H. (eds) *Talk and Social Structure.* Berkeley: University of California Press, pp. 44–70.

Schegloff, E. A. (1997) 'Whose text? Whose context'? *Discourse and Society* 8/2: 165–187.

Strauss, A. (1985) 'Work and the division of labour.' *Sociological Quarterly* 26(1): 1–19.

CA transcription symbols

(.7)	Length of a pause.
(.)	Micro-pause.
=	A latching between utterances.
[ ]	Between adjacent lines of concurrent speech indicates overlap.
.hh	Inbreath.
hh	Outbreath.
(( ))	Non-verbal activity.
-	Sharp cut-off.
:	Stretching of a word.
!	Denotes an animated tone.
( )	Unclear fragment.
° °	Quiet utterance.
CAPITALS	Noticeably louder.
> <	The talk in-between is quicker.
< >	The talk in-between is slower.
↑↓	Rising or falling intonation.
Word	Underline indicates speaker emphasis.
zz	Audience buzzing
zzZZ	Buzzing becoming louder.

18

Becoming a researcher: gendering the research self

Alison Pullen

Introduction

This chapter begins from the position that research is a social practice. In this practice, researchers not only perform the customary research functions by constructing the field and representing the other, gathering, questioning, and interrogating data, but also produce and reproduce the researcher. This is the researcher as self, as identity, as authorial voice, and even as research subject. In recognizing this and seeking an alternative to objective scientific rigor for subjective qualitative research accounts, there have been increasing demands for reflexivity and self-reflexivity in recent years (e.g. Clegg *et al.* 1996/2006, Martin 2002). These calls however often underestimate the difficulties of knowing and expressing the 'self', especially insofar as the self is socially constructed and even co-constructed and may be legitimately acknowledged as being multiple (Stone 1995). Additionally, the gendered nature of research and researcher identity is almost always under-acknowledged. Research frequently renders the feminine abject and always marginal in an academy that reproduces masculinity in the form of gender-neutral procedures, processes, criteria and forms of output and evaluation. Surviving in such an academy that marginalizes difference will always pose dilemmas for the identity of researchers who are methodologically qualitative, ideologically feminist or post-feminist and sexed as women.

The central problem of positioning self in research requires us as researchers to go beyond reflexive tales of doing research (see Fletcher 2002) in which reflexivity is, more often than not, processed instrumentally. It entails questioning how rewriting the self – rewriting the feminine – involves challenging authoritative frameworks which suppress difference and multiplicity and encourage *writing multiplicity*. This is a *corporeal* writing that rests on multiplicity. Bringing back a little of both, the other and the self, into the process and discovering ways to rewrite the self in relation to dominant theoretical paradigms relies on three basic assumptions – moving beyond the fixity of dualistic thinking by exploring ontologies of becoming; finding more fluid forms of resistance to incorporation for achieving praxis; and enabling multiple selves to be revealed as immanent within the account rather than 'brought back in' (Martin 2002).

In this chapter I develop a model which identifies two approaches which may be taken to the conceptualization of 'self' and 'gender' – the discursive/textual approach, which is characterized by the work of Foucault and early Judith Butler; and the social practice/performance approach, characterized by Sylvia Gherardi and late Judith Butler. I also argue that these can be both bridged and augmented by a third approach that I term 'corporeal multiplicity'. This third approach uses the work of Gilles Deleuze and Deleuzian feminists such as Grosz and Olkowski to reintroduce the body into the matrix. Finally I suggest three strategies to help operationalize this third approach in reflexive research texts. The first is *re-citing* which entails a deliberate playful strategy of redeploying discursive resources to expose the intertextuality of self-making. The second is *re-siting*, which is a transgressive attempt to change the positioning of the self in power/knowledge relations by reinscribing, or writing power into self-narratives and the self into power narratives. The third is *re-sighting*, which is a creative opening up of new, virtual visions of possibility within the 'findings' or 'conclusions' of accounts. These strategies both foreground and problematize the very character of what it might mean to enter the identity of the researcher.

Gendering the research self: the textual, social and corporeal

My starting assumption is that there is a common paradox in researching others: when offering to represent multiple voices in research, the researcher simultaneously suppresses his or her own voice. In addressing this paradox, this chapter explores the reflexive and gendered production of researcher self-identity within research texts and the ways that this production might be accounted for methodologically. To do so, the strategy I develop is one that opens out the compass of the idea of reflexivity towards that of multiplicity. Multiplicity, I argue, is customarily and unremarkably attenuated by the relationship between self and research text being corporeally grounded and gendered. This suggests that multiplicities of the self do not just occur at the textual level nor just at the level of practice, but corporeally as well.

It is noteworthy that the manner in which the self is reflexively written into 'normal' qualitative research is largely divorced of corporeal experience. Building on the heuristic distinctions sketched in the introduction to this chapter, two bifurcations are apparent. The first is a distinction between the self as constructed in discourse and the self as emergent from practice. The second is the distinction between the self as constructed and the self as corporeal. These distinctions are represented schematically in Figure 18.1 and discussed below. It is by exploring the seams between these distinctions that I develop the notion of corporeal multiplicity in research that explicitly accounts for gender.

As researchers, we are constantly creating, recreating and representing the lives of others through narrative or stories (discursive practices and discursive artefacts retrospectively, after Gherardi 1996, in Gherardi and Poggio 2002), and in doing so produce and reproduce our gendered lives as researcher, colleague, child, lover and so forth within our phenomenological experiences. Schutz's social phenomenology highlights how 'intersubjectivity' 'is an ongoing social accomplishment, a set of understandings sustained from moment to moment by participants in interaction' (Holstein and Gubrium 1998: 140). Considerations of the socially constructed nature of gender, however, go beyond the exploration of gender in specific social situations given that the very concept of *sociability* (that we think of ourselves as social beings) has phenomenological relevance even when we are not engaged in interaction. Outside of specific interactions, our consciousness of ourselves

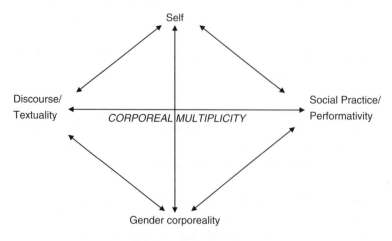

Figure 18.1 Corporeal multiplicity

as social beings informs our thought processes and experiences. In terms of research practice, this means that writing – even in solitude – is an inevitably social practice. For researchers, therefore, constructing the self, and constructing a gender, involves both textual and social practices. In the horizontal axis of Figure 18.1, I have tried to represent this tension as running in two directions such that both the individual self and the socially constructed category of gender have discursive textual and social practice/performance dimensions to their construction. Each of these are explained below.

The discursive/textual approach

The discursive/textual approach to both gender and power is strongly informed by the legacy of Michel Foucault (see 1976, 1977, 1979a, 1979b, 1980). In gender studies, a greater awareness of the political and epistemological dimensions of language, and the inseparable relation (though not deterministic connection) between language, symbolic forms, social institutions and individual and collective behavior, has to a large extent arisen from the use of Foucault's work which explores how 'the self is constructed in discourses and then re-experienced within all the texts of everyday life' (Parker 1989: 56). That said, long before Foucault's rise to popularity, feminism recognized the importance of the language of labelling, paying particular attention to how language creates the object, for example sexist language reproducing sexist oppression. Here I explore Foucault's work to illustrate the most significant aspects and development of this approach.

Foucault, throughout his work, was interested in the way in which the relation between power and knowledge is changed or sustained through language (and to a lesser extent by other symbolic forms). For example, powerful groups such as managers can use their power to ration and limit the distribution of knowledge about their field and also use language to define what counts as knowledge. They can also police knowledge creation through accounting and disciplinary practices. Through practices of surveillance they can identify, capture, legitimate and incorporate new knowledge, and disadvantage, render illegitimate and suppress knowledge which they deem to be threatening or challenging to the existing order. Social institutions such as professional bodies may be set up to facilitate this. Individuals may be examined and tested, formally and informally, as a matter of everyday social practice. Their positioning as social and even individual subjects, who are competent, significant, consuming, compliant citizens or otherwise, is affected by how well they pass these occasions of scrutiny under a gaze – whether it be that of the state, religion, education, professional superiors, co-workers, parents, partners, friends, subordinates, their own children and even themselves. Foucault was particularly concerned with how people police their own self-identity against competing models of the ideal self, and how such internalized imperatives literally inscribe themselves on and affect the physical characteristics of the body (see Brewis and Linstead 2000).

Key to Foucault's understanding of subjectivity is the notion of *discourse*. Following Foucault, a discourse can be any regular and regulated system of statements such that discourse analysis crucially examines the *relations* within the system. As Parker notes, 'not only are social relations stressed as social relations as they are embodied in discourse, but we may view these relations as power relations' (1989: 67). Foucault's earlier *archaeological* work looked in particular at the workings of language, how words had historically acquired specific acceptations and how the system of rules governing the discourse internally came to operate. His subsequent work, however (and in contrast to most of what we would understand as discourse analysis), examines the conditions of power and knowledge, which not only have influenced the form of a discourse, but have favored its appearance at a particular point in time, and its specific *relations* with other forms of discourse. In summary what a discourse does is:

> Determine criteria for the establishment of acceptable 'truth' and the creation of 'truth-effects', and further delimit what can and cannot be said, the normal, the abnormal, the standard and the deviation and hierarchies the field of these relations . . .

> (Linstead 2001: 226).

A discourse, however, is also concerned with establishing the position of its authorship, usually so as to appear as naturally authoritative as possible – this is particularly salient in the consideration of research identity. Discourse creates and characterizes discursive spaces or *subject positions* to which it both tries to lay claim (in the case of authorial positions) and offers to recipients through *interpellation* – that is, an implicit invitation for the discourse to be taken up. In other words, a discourse is already at the heart of processes of social structuring in seeking to position its readers in relation to an idealized reader, and establish its own authority accordingly. Discourse therefore is not dominated by language alone, and is far more than simply a linguistic phenomenon. Foucauldian discourse analysis is accordingly not trying to claim that words determine reality. What it does however recognize is that 'practices which constitute our everyday lives are produced and reproduced as an integral part of the production of signs and signifying systems' (Henriques *et al.* 1984: 99). Practices and what is said about them cannot be separated in such easy distinctions between words and deeds. Accordingly, discourse inevitably also relates to non-discursive practices which must be an important focus for discourse analysis. A *discursive formation*, which incorporates both linguistic and non-linguistic phenomena, can be identified by defining 'the system of formation of the different strategies that are deployed in it', by showing 'how they all derive . . . from the same set of relations' (Foucault 1972: 68).

Before moving on we need also to distinguish the difference between a discourse and a text. Fairclough (1992) argues that discourse analysis links the systematic analysis of spoken or written texts to systematic analyses of social contexts, taking into account formative contexts and extra-discursive effects. It looks at 'the particular configurations of conventionalized practices (genres, discourses, narratives, etc.) which are available to text producers in particular social circumstances' (Fairclough 1992: 194). In meeting their rhetorical or persuasive objectives, texts will not only draw on a variety of linguistic features, but will also draw on one or more discourses which warrant the truth of their arguments (Linstead 2001).

A consideration of Foucault's work as introduced above adds to the discussion of the identity of the researcher in seven ways. First, it introduces *increased discursive heterogeneity which surfaces* contradiction, ambiguity and suppression and alerts us to the possible operation of a wider variety of discourses in tension within the discursive processes through which we establish our gendered narratives of self. Second, *it expands the consideration of context* by linking discourse to texts and to organizational and social contexts, which constrain and enable processes of subjective identity in becoming a researcher and doing research. Third, *it provides a broader understanding of the nature of surveillance and the variety of the 'gaze'* so as to consider a greater range of social technologies which may be internally operationalized by the individual (as self-surveillance) as well as externally occasioned (as inspection) throughout the research process. Fourth, *it introduces the possibility of relational resistance* by emphasizing the importance of power relations and the political dimensions of knowledge formation and by introducing a relational element to the consideration of power. Power, for Foucault, circulates, rather than being passed down (or even up) a system, and is always two-way though not necessarily symmetrical. Actions of individuals may be prescribed by a discursive system, but there is always room for reinterpretation and manoeuvre. Resistance may arise and circulate from individual levels and itself become incorporated, or alternately institutionalized. Foucault does not theorize resistance overtly, partly because his project is primarily one of subversion, and also because of his awareness that power is intimately connected with the unsaid, the secret, and that resistance, to be effective, must also organize, if it is to be organized, around its secrets. This is particularly salient to the discussion of gendered research identity in that attention needs to be given to the relational forms of power in exploring the multiplicity of gendered identities, thereby surfacing the *ways in which men and women relationally resist* the discursive subject-positions institutionally prescribed for them through discourse. We can then surface how both the research subjects subvert the research that we hold in high regard, and how we as researchers partake in subversion and emancipation. Fifth, *it links the formation of selves and subjects.* It makes central to any consideration of rhetoric the processes of subjectivity and subject-formation. It underscores the part which individuals play in rendering themselves subject to a discourse, their potential complicity in their own domination. The question becomes, how does the researcher produce the fabric of domination that we seek to challenge? Sixth, *it draws attention to the significance and importance of boundaries.* Persuasive language is occasioned where existing social processes are themselves alone insufficient to render the need for persuasion unnecessary. This may be in policing the boundary between researcher and research subject, the research supervisor and research student, the journal and your paper submission. Seventh, *it emphasizes the embodied and gendered nature of subject-formation.* Foucault's later work treats gender as a discursive category as much as a social or embodied one (see Moss 1998). Discursive effects inscribe bodies in terms of requirements for appearance, structure or conditioning but also leave the marks of the consequences of performing as a 'good researcher' on the self – the inscription of the intellectual, emotional and physical stresses and strain of doing particular types of research on the body. I will develop this dimension in my consideration of corporeality.

In gender studies, Foucault's negation of women and his neglect of the feminine, although conspicuous in his discussions of sexuality (see Sawicki 1991), have been questioned extensively (McNay 1992, Weedon 1999). Nevertheless Foucault's work has been used to great effect by feminists. Feminists who have adopted Foucauldian notions of a decentred subject in organization studies, for example, have challenged the gender-neutrality with much organizational theorizing. Nevertheless, this has fallen short of challenging the gender blindness of our research methods and lacks the reflexivity to explore the multiplicity and fluidity of self as researcher. Most importantly, for this chapter, Foucault shows how self and gender are embedded in and emerge from discursive structures and this initiates the appreciation of the multiplicity of lived experience.

The social practice/ performance approach

As I noted earlier, Foucault's concept of a 'discourse' extends beyond language and into practice. On this basis, in this section I turn to consider those approaches which have prioritized social practice and performance in their analyses – each of these are dealt with in turn.

Gender as a social practice

I now want to build on my earlier discussion of how selves become subjects within discourse. Gherardi, in both her sole authored work and her work with others, has argued that the processes of research production – the production of research subjects and the production of the researcher as subject – are not just social but gendered (Bruni *et al.* 2004, Gherardi 1994, 1995, Gherardi and Turner 1988, see also Poggio 2006). Such a perspective, after Gherardi and Poggio, sees gender more generally is a social practice:

> . . . gender may be viewed as a social practice, or better as a set of practices, which jointly help define the relations between men and women, and between male and female. By means of these practices, people *position* [emphasis mine] themselves by aligning themselves according to the positionings of others within situated discourses; that is, discourses which have a precise location in space and time
> (2002: 247).

Drawing on Davies and Harré's concept of *positioning*, Gherardi and Poggio make a link to the discursive/textual approach I have discussed by emphasizing that 'the production of self can be analysed as a linguistic practice within the dynamic occasion one encounters. A position is what is created in and through conversations as speakers and hearers construct themselves as persons' (2002: 247). They go on to comment on how 'gender identity is constructed by a comparison activity in which male and female are perceived and positioned as alternative categories, so that belonging to one necessarily entails a discourse which highlights nonbelonging to the other' (ibid.).

Gherardi's work thus raises our awareness of the more ambiguous and fragmented nature of gender, indeed its discursive fragility, and the fact that language and discourse need to be understood in terms of their use as practices. Gherardi and Poggio further state:

> Bringing out the ambivalence present in the rituals, riles and narrative devices of gender production serves to highlight not only the intrinsic ambiguity of the concept of gender but also the ambivalent and manifold nature of social reality, which cannot be understood by being reduced to dichotomous categories but instead requires interpretative keys and metaphors able to convey a plurality of differences
> (2002: 257).

The idea that we need to move beyond dichotomies and recognize plurality is by now a familiar one, but the move which Gherardi and Poggio make is, as I have argued elsewhere (Linstead and Pullen 2006) limited to recognizing multiplicities of the same, where pluralities are varieties of masculinity or femininity, which multiply around the poles of the gender binary but still preserve its essential dualism. A move beyond this would embrace multiplicities of difference and dispersion, which derive from an ontology of desire as a creative exuberance which is motivated not by the lack or the need to resolve difference by various material and psychological ways of removing it, but by the drive for its own proliferation. Multiplicity therefore creates both overlapping and redundancy, excess of identity and difference at one and the same time, and recognizes in these overcrossings that the self always contains internal alterity – an inner otherness in which it differs from itself. Multiplicity seen as the dispersion of difference (rather than as the collection of different elements and their positioning into self-consistent 'identities') performs its identity rather than simply expressing it or constructing it in language.

From within this perspective, Judith Butler's (1990, 1993) work has moved from an early emphasis on the importance of discourse to a recognition of its limits. Butler notes that language makes things happen, often in complex, indirect and oblique ways, and that the performativity of language in the ways in which it combines to make certain types of gender positioning possible is critical to understanding gender and sexuality. But Butler also considers that we weave streams of this general performativity into specific gender performances, and it is to this consideration that I will now turn.

Gender as performance

As I have suggested, practice (including research practice) and text mediate the gendered performance of self. The implications of this, however, have not been fully accounted for in research methodology. Some organizational researchers on narratives of self and storying the self have gone beyond creating monologues as dictated by a singular researcher identity and have explored identity multiplicity. Few however have explored the fragmented and fluid nature of the subject. Where the fluidity of identity has been addressed (e.g. Grafton Small 2005a, b) these accounts have not explored the gendered experience of self. Conversely, in other disciplines, such as women's studies and sociology, women's narratives are presented widely but the fluid nature of these narratives has been under explored. More importantly, however, this research raises the gendered problems of methodology directly. Feminist ethnomethodologist Dorothy E. Smith, for example, in her work on women's work as mothers argues that social science rules out women because 'typical' research designs are insensitive to women's lived experiences (Holstein and Gubrium 1998: 151). Women researchers have to do and act in particular ways that run against their experience as women. Moreover, Spivak (1988: 104) iterates that the problem that many researchers face is 'the desire to explain (through research is) . . . a symptom of the desire to have a self (the researcher) that can control knowledge and a world that can be known (i.e. converted to the same)'. As such, rather than challenging masculine discourses inherent in organizational research, under such an epistemology of collection and coherence, research unknowingly reinforces the feminine as abject; gendered research subjects become *docile bodies* through the agency of the researcher. This is reinforced by specific modalities of validity. Spivak (1988: 105) argues that by 'explaining (through valid research), we exclude the possibility of the radically heterogeneous (the Other).' I would argue that a great deal of research on 'women in management' could be critiqued on the basis of Spivak's claims. The multiplicity of the research subjects and the researcher's subject positions get lost playing the validity game. As Benjamin comments, 'If I completely control the (O)ther, then the (O)ther ceases to exist' (1988: 53 cited in Scheurich 1997: 86).

When the claim of much research on and by women is to challenge hegemonic masculinity, the paradoxical outcome is reinforcement of the dominant norm. As such we as researchers 'eat the other' – incorporate the other into our own agenda and make them merely a projection of ourselves. This reminds us that to break out of this ecology we need to appreciate not only the multiplicity of the other but that of the self as researcher too. Moi reinforces this point, stating that

> the subject is split, decentred, fragile, always threatened by disintegration. At the same time, this split and decentred subject has the capacity to act and make choices. Such choices and acts, however, are always over-determined, that is to say deeply influenced by unconscious ideological allegiances and unconscious emotional investments and fantasies as well as by conscious motivations
>
> (2002: 177).

In this vein, some poststructuralist informed female writers in their studies of work and organization have adopted a 'confessional' approach to rewriting the self into their research and this is becoming successful in redressing the imbalance of women's voices in research, bringing the body back in and reinstating an emotional response. We may however wish to question whether this confessional approach names, inscribes and further marginalizes women as other – as abject. Foucault sounds a cautionary note in reminding us of the power of silence as: 'The limit of language, since it traces that line of foam showing just how far speech may advance on the sands of silence' (cited in Botting and Wilson 1998: 24). In other words, you are forced to *confess* because you *transgress* and thus take ownership of the requirement to *con*/form to the rules as you *per*/form – although fitting into these rules continues to reproduce the feminist stereotype of the feminine as marginal. So, do we as female writers play the marginal game by adopting autobiographical practices? Do we perform the institutionalization of our own exclusion? Botting and Wilson urge us to recognize that certain 'experiences do not give themselves up to discursive meaning . . . exceeding articulate speech, understanding, comprehension, certain experiences disclose an 'unknowing' at the heart of experience that denotes the limit of language, discourse, culture' (1998: 3). Thus the dimension of performance that remains in excess of language and the performativity of language may yet act as the resource for transgressive reinscriptions which promote positive change, which is where the idea of gender as practice and performance breaks away from the idea of gender as discourse and text. What facilitates this break is the fact that it is *bodies* which render the performances.

Much feminist research has on the whole neglected the micro- or infra-politics of the everyday through which such identities are constructed. I would also add that researcher identities, whilst being increasingly recognized as multiple in the less essentialist versions of such research (Linstead and Thomas 2002), are rarely considered as being *fluid*, with the exception of the theoretical reflections of writers such as Olkowski (1999), following Deleuze. Baudrillard (1990) identifies the feminine with that which cannot be fixed or fixed upon – that is, the feminine is always that which is and remains elusive, outside any system that tries to contain it, the essence of change. As such, the feminine is a response which may be adopted by males to create a fluid space in which they can avoid being inscribed in someone else's rules, which is quite different from the strategies of feminists who seek to enter into such systems with a redefined sense of power in order to reinscribe themselves within the system's new rules. From a multiplicity perspective, then, self-identity is only stabilized by the deferral or displacement of multiplicity. This accordingly renders such an identity project nostalgic rather than either authentic or transgressive by suppressing its essential openness.

The corporeal approach

Having examined multiplicity in relation to discourse and practice, I now wish to address the intersections of these multiplicities with a specific focus on corporeality, and consider the implications of this for identity. We can begin by noting that writing the self through autobiography raises the issue of how the construction of self is neither purely cognitive nor physically over-determined. To problematize gender as either a purely phenomenological or materialist experience, corporeal feminists (Braidotti 1994, Grosz 1994, Olkowski 1999) recognize that self is constructed in relation to bodily experience – bodies *matter* but bodies are different – they are characterized by not only multiplicity but also fluidity (Butler 1993; Grosz 1994). Post-feminists therefore are not rejecting materiality, as some feminists, particularly radical and Marxist contributions, would argue (see Sim 2000). However, despite the enormous contribution that feminism has made, some feminists have often regarded the 'female feminist subject' unproblematically, particularly in studies of work and organization (Braidotti 1994: 159). In this regard, Braidotti's work is useful in exploring and expanding an understanding of subjectivity so as to include an exploration of gender fluidity at the level of ontology (see Linstead and Pullen 2005, 2006). Indeed, Braidotti questions feminist materiality, offering corporeal materiality as a means to explore woman as a site of multiple and contested experiences which is not 'gender-centred' (Braidotti 1994: 161). That said, we also need to be mindful that she remains unresolved between her thinking of subjectivity as difference, as a desire to become, and her materialism, and in doing so falls short of challenging perceptions of gendered identities as same-different. If we see identity as a 'site of difference' (Linstead and Pullen 2005) in a way that addresses this challenge, then a 'nomadic' vision that takes into account experiences of oppression, exclusion and marginality may rest on a corporeal feminism. After Grosz and Olkowski (drawing on Deleuze and Guattari), this means striving to achieve a nomadic, disjunctive self which evades oppression by avoiding being in any static sense. The implication of this is that rethinking the subject entails rethinking the body in a way that rejects a realist ontology and an essentialist account of the body (Linstead and Pullen 2005). The body, sexuality and sexed identities might then be de-essentialized so as to move beyond the dualistic oppositions that conjugate into monological discourses. To develop this argument, gender needs to be seen as a corporeal multiplicity.

Gender as corporeal multiplicity

Above, I sketched out two approaches to gender in terms of discourse and practice, and subsequently incorporated a discussion of identity and corporeality to propose a third approach. I now bring this discussion together by offering a theorization of gender as corporeal multiplicity as it builds on the uptake of the philosophical writings of Deleuze and Guattari (1987) by feminists (such as Braidotti and Grosz) and then relating this specifically to gendered research practice. Of note here, despite the importance of Deleuze and Guattari's work for feminists in thinking nomadically and non-logically, they have themselves been criticized by writers such as Irigarary for being male-centred and patriarchical. Grosz (1994) acknowledges that these charges are not frivolous, but overcomes them in exploring 'a becoming beyond the logic, constraints and confines of being, and a multiplicity beyond the merely doubling or multicentering of proliferating subjects' (Grosz 1994: 192). Grosz argues that Deleuze and Guattari are useful in rethinking gender as 'rhizomatic' – that is as a networked, boundary crossing and expanding series of connections not controlled by any center or concept. Considering gender this way goes beyond a pluralized notion of identity by thinking of it as 'an ever-changing, nontotalizable collectivity, an assemblage defined, not by its abiding identity or principle of sameness over time, but through its capacity to undergo permutations and transformations' (ibid.).

Taking this notion of multiplicity further, then, we can see gender as a process, incorporating desire and bodies, which is 'driven by a formless desire beyond binaries and even beyond the multiple identities of individual subjects – multiplicities of the same, still in much feminism' (ibid). Grosz comments that the body itself for Deleuze and Guattari is similarly a 'discontinuous, non-totalised series of processes, organs, flows, energies, corporeal substances and incorporeal events, intensities, and durations' (1994: 193–194). This transcends the traditional conception of the mind and body as separate so as to reconfigure the subject beyond being as an entity or a relation between interior (mind) and exterior (body). The subject can be seen as a series of 'flows, energies, movements, and capacities, a series of fragments or segments capable of being linked together in ways other than those that congeal it into an identity' (1994: 198). The connective capabilities of the body become of central importance, rather than being defined and confined by its sexual and physical properties. This is liberating for rewriting the feminine without necessarily writing as woman. As discussed earlier this enables us to think of gender beyond seeing it as a linguistics or dramaturgical performance (Butler 1990, 1993) and a social construction (Acker 1990) or social practice (Gherardi 1995), to seeing gender as a connective capability, a 'productive process whose productivity is pure, that is it rests in the creativity of effulgent desire rather than being defined and delimited by the product it creates' (Linstead and Pullen 2006: 1305). As Linstead and Pullen state, 'Gender is not the construction or outcome of a performance but is immanent within those performances making them productive of new molecular connections in the meshwork of identity' (2006: 1306).

This then completes the model, with corporeal multiplicity at the heart of a process which holds self and gender in fluid and creative tension, shaped directly by textual and discursive constructions and practices and performances of self and gender, and enforming the continually emergent relationships and overlaps between them.

Self-multiplicity in research: re-citing, re-siting and re-sighting[1]

If the self is not just multiple but a corporeal practice of fluid multiplicity, and we therefore need to explore fully what it means to write gendered research in the feminine, not just as woman, some specific strategies might be useful. To rewrite the gendered self into organizational research, one approach we can take is to consider the self in terms of three textual practices – re-citing, re-siting and re-sighting.

From reciting to re-citing

In any recreation of a narrative of self, we call upon previous narrative selves that we may have created, or have received from others in the form of attributions, archetypes or stereotypes. An autobiography is always a retrospective-prospective account, recreating who we were in terms of who we would like to be. As such, when we write we *cite* the various selves which may be wholly or partially available to us as we rewrite them into

---

1 Clegg and Hardy (1995) originally used these terms in relation to subjectivity but as the ideas develop (see the chapter on representations in the Handbook [Clegg *et al.* 1996]) they did not use these terms. I use these terms with a slightly different application to explore self as multiplicity in relation to gendered ways of knowing. Nigel Thrift (2000) considers a set of 'procedures that both show up and value the new things necessary to produce 'fast' subjects, the subjects of the new managerial governmentality' (p. 677). These processes he calls sight – new spaces of visualisation; cite – new spaces of embodiment; and site – new spaces of circulation.

our self-story (Höpfl, forthcoming; Pitsis, this volume). At the level of representing voice through language, rewriting then is reciting – if the reciting is unreflexive it is a recitation – preformed, often rehearsed, a learned rather than lived performance, essentially reproducing others' recorded voices. In attempting to write as woman we are implicitly following an injunction to recite our womanly identity. If we try to escape both the womanly and masculinist recitations which inscribe the research process, we need to find a way to *re-cite* ourselves – through a process of multiple connections. *Re-citing* therefore entails a deliberate playful strategy of redeploying discursive resources to expose the intertextuality of self-making. One way to define feminine textual practice then could be as *contesting recitation through the process of re-citation.*

From siting to re-siting

Selves are not just grounded in bodies but are also importantly located in places, part of geosubjectivity, as the new social geography recognizes. But placing subjects is also about epistemological space (Knights 1992) – how you are positioned with regimes of knowing, where who you are is related to what you know or are recognized as knowing. Gherardi talks about being positioned in social practice, and how women are positioned in relation to the practices of hegemonic masculinity. Women are positioned as abject, with its attendant loss of power, because they are positioned outside the respected and legitimate sources of knowledge which are dominated by the explicit rather than the implicit and unexpressible. This reinforces the binary which literally dispossesses women through displacing feminine ways of knowing, feminine epistemology. Therefore to challenge this siting on the margin we need to re-site. Re-siting, which is a transgressive attempt to change the positioning of the self in power relations by reinscribing, or writing power into self-narratives and the self into power narratives, as power and knowledge are inseparable. Gherardi argues with a related point that 'a gender perspective within organization studies that is ironic, nomadic, and eccentric cannot be integrated into the main/male stream, but it can forge tactical alliances with other perspectives critical of the mainstream politics of knowledge and of the social practices sustaining it' (2003: 232). Gender research, then, is always a critical practice of repositioning and reconnection. Feminine research practice here then involves resiting non-hegemonic ways of knowing by combination outside and realignment within the existing epistemological spaces of research to destabilize, open out and reformulate those spaces.

From Sighting to Re-sighting

The previous two sections have highlighted that feminine research needs to proceed by exploring new ways of speaking (re-citing) and new ways of knowing (re-siting). Finally, of course, it also demands new ways of seeing, ways of re-visioning existing practice rather than simply *revising* it. Feminism has been so heavily involved in revision that it has missed several opportunities for re-visioning, such as those which Deleuze and Guattari present (Linstead and Pullen 2006).

Such post Deleuzian approaches deliver not just the functionality of a new vision but the virtuality and possibility a new way of seeing, and it is critical that we do not neglect the importance of this. Feminine research practice then needs to create new vistas through *re-sighting* its object, constantly seeking new and multiple lenses to ensure that it escapes the incrementalist traps of revisioning by working to enable re-visioning.

Concluding summary

This chapter has stressed the paradox of researching others, and offering to represent multiple voices, whilst suppressing the voice of the researcher. In doing so the reflexive and gendered production of researcher self-identity within research accounts has been explored. Its essential strategy has been to open out the compass of the idea of reflexivity towards that of multiplicity. Multiplicity, it was argued, is customarily and unremarkably attenuated by the relationship between self and research text being corporeally grounded and gendered. Three possible approaches which incorporate multiplicity and fluidity to self and gender were considered: the discursive/textual approach; the performance/social practice approach and the corporeal multiplicity approach. Building on the latter, and addressing the central problem of what it could mean to *write the feminine* in research accounts, I suggested a tripartite approach to writing gendered self-multiplicity in research which extends the possibilities opened up by the social practice approach: *re-citing*, *re-siting* and *re-sighting*.

Re-sighting refers to the opening up of new, virtual visions of possibility within the 'findings' or 'conclusions' of accounts. So in conclusion to this chapter, in what directions for future research, of writing the self as corporeal and multiple, can this quest take us? I cannot offer any objectives for further research because gendering the research self is not really an objective at all, simply a trajectory, a direction which has no point of arrival, which will move off at tangents to itself and may never return from its diversions. It does not set itself the target of creating a new language, or a new genre, but of pursuing a new relation to language, one which might be called feminine but even that category is surely destined to disappear in the process of the journey's unfolding.

References

Acker, J. (1990) 'Hierarchies, jobs, bodies: a theory of gendered organizations.' *Gender and Society* 4(2): 139–158.

Baudrillard, J. (1990) *Seduction*. New York: Semiotext(e).

Botting, F. and Wilson, S. (1998) *Bataille: A Critical Reader*. Oxford: Blackwell.

Braidotti, R. (1994) 'Toward a new nomadism: feminist Deleuzian tracks; or metaphysics and metabolism.' In Boundas, C. and Olkowski, D. (eds) *Gilles Deleuze and the Theater of Philosophy*. New York: Routledge, pp. 157–186.

Brewis, J. and Linstead, S. (2000) *Sex, Work and Sex Work*. London: Routledge.

Bruni, A., Gherardi, S., and Poggio, B. (2004) 'Doing gender, doing entrepreneurship: an ethnographic account of intertwined practices.' *Gender, Work and Organization* 11(4): 406-429.

Butler, J. (1990) *Gender Trouble: Feminism and the Subversion of Identity*. New York: Routledge.

Butler, J. (1993) *Bodies that Matter: On the Discursive Limits of Sex*. New York: Routledge.

Clegg, S. R. and Hardy. C. (1995) 'The person in the sight/cite/site of organization theory', chapter presented to the *VIth International APROS Colloquium*, Cuernavaca, Mexico, December.

Clegg, S. R., Hardy, C., and Nord, W. R. (1996/2006) *Handbook of Organization Studies*. London: Sage.

Deleuze, G. and Guattari, F. (1987) *A Thousand Plateaus: Capitalism and Schizophrenia*. Vol. II, Minneapolis: Minnesota University Press.

Fairclough, N. (1992) *Discourse and Social Change*. Cambridge: Polity.

Fletcher, D. (2002) 'In the company of men: a reflexive tale of cultural organizing in a small organization.' *Gender, Work and Organization* 9(4): 398–419.

Foucault, M. (1972) *The Archaeology of Knowledge*. London: Tavistock.

Foucault, M. (1976) *The Birth of the Clinic*. London: Tavistock.

Foucault, M. (1977) *Madness and Civilisation*. London: Tavistock.

Foucault, M. (1979a) *The History of Sexuality*. Vol. II, Vintage: New York.

Foucault, M. (1979b) *Discipline and Punish: The Birth of the Prison*. Harmondsworth: Penguin.

Foucault, M. (1980) *Power/Knowledge*. Brighton: Harvester Wheatsheaf.

Gherardi, S. (1994) 'The gender we think, the gender we do in everyday organizational life.' *Human Relations* 47(6): 591–609.

Gherardi, S. (1995) *Gender, Symbolism and Organizational Culture*. London: Sage.

Gherardi, S. (2003) 'Feminist theory and organization theory: a dialogue on new bases.' In Knudsen, H. and Tsoukas, H. (eds) *The Handbook of Organizational Theory: Meta-Theoretical Perspectives*. Oxford: Oxford University Press.

Gherardi, S. and Turner, B. (1988) 'Real men don't collect soft data.' Trento: *Quaderni del Dipartimento di Politica Sociale* 13.

Gherardi, S. and Poggio, B. (2002) 'Creating and recreating gender order in organizations.' *Journal of World Business* 36(3): 245–259.

Grafton Small, R. (2005a) 'Asymmetry and the assault on order.' In Pullen, A. and Linstead, S. (eds) *Organization and Identity*. London: Routledge.

Grafton Small, R. (2005b) 'Suits you, sir: that obscure desire of objects.' In Linstead, S. and Linstead, A. (eds) *Thinking Organization*. London: Routledge.

Grosz, E. (1994) 'A thousand tiny sexes: feminism and rhizomatics.' In Boundas, C. and Olkowski, D. (eds) *Gilles Deleuze and the Theater of Philosophy*. New York: Routledge, pp. 187–210.

Henriques, J., Hollway, W., Urwin, C., Venn, C., and Walkerdine, V. (1984) *Changing the Subject: Psychology, Social Regulation and Subjectivity*. London: Methuen.

Holstein, J. A. and Gubrium, J. F. (1998) 'Phenomenology, ethnomethodology and interpretive practice.' In Denzin, N. K. and Lincoln, Y. S. (eds) *Strategies of Qualitative Inquiry*. London: Sage.

Höpfl, H. (2007) 'The codex, the codicil and the codpiece: some thoughts on diminution and elaboration in identity formation.' In Pullen, A. and Knights, D. (eds) Undoing Gender, special issue of *Gender, Work and Organization*.

Knights, D. (1992) 'Changing spaces: the disruptive power of epistemological location for the management and organizational sciences.' *Academy of Management Review* 17(3): 514–536.

Linstead, A. and Thomas, R. (2002) 'What do you want from me? A poststructuralist feminist reading of middle managers identities.' *Culture and Organization* 8(1): 1–20.

Linstead, S. A. (2001) 'Rhetoric and organizational control: a framework for analysis.' In Westwood, B. and Linstead, S. A. (eds) *The Language of Organization*. London: Sage, pp. 217–240.

Linstead, S. and Pullen, A. (2005) 'Fluid identities and un-gendering the future.' In Pullen, A. and Linstead, S. (eds) *Organization and Identity*. London: Routledge.

Linstead, S. and Pullen, A. (2006) 'Gender as multiplicity: desire, difference and dispersion.' *Human Relations* 59(9): 1287–1310.

Martin, J. (2002) *Organizational Culture: Mapping the Terrain*. London: Sage.

McNay, L. (1992) *Foucault and Feminism*. Cambridge: Polity.

Moi, T. (2002) *Sexual/Textual Politics*. London: Routledge.

Moss, J. (ed.) (1998) *The Later Foucault*. London: Sage.

Olkowski, D. (1999) *Gilles Deleuze and the Ruin of Representation*. Berkeley, CA: University of California Press.

Parker, I. (1989) 'Discourse and power.' In Shotter, J. and Gergen, K. J. (eds) (1989) *Texts of Identity*. London: Sage.

Poggio, B. (2006) 'Editorial: outline of a theory of gender practices.' *Gender, Work and Organization* 13(3): 277–298.

Sawicki, J. (1991) *Disciplining Foucault: Feminism, Power and the Body*. London: Routledge.

Scheurich, J. J. (1997) *Research Method in the Postmodern*. London: Falmer Press.

Sim, S. (2000) *Contemporary Continental Philosophy: The New Scepticism*. Aldershot: Ashgate.

Spivak, G. C. (1988) *In Other Worlds: Essays in Cultural Politics*. New York: Routledge.

Stone, A. R. (1995) *The War of Desire and Technology at the Close of the Mechanical Age*. London: MIT Press.

Thrift, N. (2000) *Performing Cultures in the New Economy*, Annals of the Association of American Geographers 90(4): 674–692.

Weedon, C. (1999) *Feminism, Theory and the Politics of Difference*. Oxford: Blackwell.

19

Cartographies of a life

Alexandra Pitsis

A life contains only virtuals. It is made up of virtualities, events, singularities. What we call virtual is not something that lacks reality but something that is engaged in the process of actualization following the plane that gives it its particular reality. The immanent event is actualized in a state of things and of the lived that make it happen. The plane of immanence is itself actualized in an object and a subject to which it attributes itself. But however inseparable an object and a subject may be from their actualization, the plane of immanence itself is virtual, so long as the events that populate it are virtualities. Events or singularities give to the plane all their virtuality, just as the plane of immanence gives virtual events their full reality

(Deleuze 2005: 31).

The person appears before you as an elaborate smudged line. You greet them, treating them as if they were a complete entity, an essence that inhabits a reality, but at the same time your perceptions, your senses, tell you that this person is like a patch of bleeding ink. And here, even your senses absolve you of any understanding of perception of the consciousness before you. You try and look further into this person and all you see is blurred lines and a lack of any delineation. When you look closer at the blurred lines, you see there is no sense to it – there is no direction or indication of what that line defines on the map. It splinters here and there and it becomes almost impossible to follow. Look at the way the ink seeps and splinters off into an infinite number of threads that merge. You are this disintegration – and while I try to hold onto you and control the way I look at you, I am powerless and deluded. And when I stand close to your aching and joyful being, I realize I must have somehow slipped outside myself and stand there next to myself, external to my own being and locale. I close my eyes and what becomes evident is that I am an impersonal entity, my life, my history, my pain is not my own. And being is like that illusory sense of place, I quiver when I can really feel it – because all it says is that I am only the outside. I can't inhabit your sense of place without violently annihilating you, yet I think I do this out of love. And if I tore myself away from myself so many times to experience, perceive reality, and if I believed it did not exist – I was initiated into this like a baptism by fire. That I became a witness – and that is all you wished for on dying, that there was a witness in the community of death.

What has happened has changed me – I could say the events were 'out of my hands', I could say the events were like God's hands, pounding me from one palm into the other, like a vast concrete machine, unable to be gentle or touch me lovingly; yet the attempt to show love – felt like pain, dislocation and cruelty. If I could fathom the deepest esoteric mysteries about the world and my place in it, I would see that this is a paltry way of seeing a life. It was not cruelty at work, it was the sheer force of an unknown power and it was treating me as an equal. Enveloping me and sweeping me up, showing me the folding of myself. After all, this was my very wish.

Why do I persist, why does my soul persist in clinging so vehemently to this notion of self? I could relay to you events both material and ephemeral to show you who I appear to be. But more likely, I can only allow a fleeting rite of passage. And that only at times when I feel strong enough to hold onto the illusion and aporia that holds the semblance together. It is only then that I can relay who I am to you. But in essence I am as far away from myself as a distant, unknown galaxy. The best I can be is a remote landscape only discernable from a distance. When I think of knowing you I think of hurling myself into this landscape, to get closer. And yet, this landscape disappears when I am embedded into its heart. And when I come to understand anything else, whether organic or inorganic, I am tethered to bring what has been destined to caricature my soul. I try to stand near it but the closer I get, my self slides away, as if it were visceral and beside myself and inside myself at the same time. A self culminates as a coordinate in a life – a life that has some kind of alliance – and strangely emerges fleetingly in that feeling created as you sway in the presence of death.

This is like the mystical field or plane and yet it is the maternal body – when I was born, my Mother thrust me violently into the world, and her body was cut open for my existence. She told me many times that I was a piece of her own flesh; I was made of her body. So, when I came into my existence, I came into her own and yet I couldn't get a glimpse into who she was. I clung to my ability to read her like a map – but this proved difficult and complex, and when I held one of her maps in my hands, it would dissolve before I could see the lines or places, the topographies. The legends were obscured and random and the lines had no start or end – and most times these maps would not seem light and paper thin. These maps would not dissolve and disappear before me or have that air of the un-locatable to them; they were weighty and abject and they were made of flesh – flesh that had carried so many ordeals, each scar a painful groan and each a journey deeper into the flesh, and each assault and blow marking out who she was to me. It was like I would dress in this flesh, embroidered with fleshy jewels and gaping wounds seeping the very fluid running in my veins. Branching like a line pointing to life.

What does this plane point to in my understanding of a life and of a self? This field that deals with transcendence differs from all that I have come to experience, a series of events, historical locations and points in time, my genealogies and all the things that could measure me, whether accurately or not. What it is appears as the reality of my being and this is linked to everything that makes it real. Ironically, it is the virtual that makes it real because it emits the stance of negotiator.

All that she was became known to me as I floated around the rim of the abyss. I came to know my Mother on another plane through this process as 'You'. And I could look into this process and see you there, fatefully disappearing; your corporeality for all it was – became an appearance that I couldn't fathom. In my total loss I thought I was dealing with identity as a series of cartographic explorations, a systematization of all that eludes us as we gently glance at what we fail to understand and aim to capture at the same time. The lines on the maps first appeared volatile and colorless and yet they marked out ancient realms where I was made to laughingly conceptualize a soul possessed of another dimension. And lurking beneath what can be seen, the customary surfaces dialled measures and marked – and something more. I trembled each time your body underwent that horrifying journey and I ached to see you emerge again.

You were like Atlas, like those first maps made of clay, like that earthy path that I submerged with. The story of Atlas is important here because it is our story, the story of the ordeal of the human body. That we must bear life and we must dare to bear life. Atlas was one of the Titans who watched over the moon. His name comes from the root 'tla', to suffer or endure. He holds up the heavens the way we must endure holding up our being. Atlas shows us the weight of the world and the heavens within us all, displaying the impersonality of it all. That time is all but forgotten and time is not experienced through suffering. That the world is not accessed through the personal notions of who we are as individuals but as residues, our immanence that shows a map for what lies outside of ourselves. And this path, this murky, terrifying path is one filled with unknown beauty of being ripped away from the very things that give you the comfort of the known, and the comfort of the pretence of saying, this is me, I have a history, I have a true identity. I can explain myself to you and you will understand me. I am a complete individual and I am here for you to come to know me.

And while I pondered the dream life of thinking myself a complete being, thinking myself a gestalt, the very night I thought myself whole, I dreamt of myself as a pathway, and I was a pathway into myself and so this triggered the idea of etheric maps. And what is the ether to explain to me about who I am, who you are and where our transpositions occur? Do I fill the atmosphere and send a thousand unknowable waves into the air? Am I of the air, but of the air of a place that is nowhere? Gliding through a mixed terrain of nightmares and oblivion I'd like to introduce myself to you in a manner of multiple cartographies. I am, like you, the mythic Atlas – who carries a volume of psychic maps. Some of the maps intersect, overlap and disintegrate. Some are made of fine paper, some are made of flesh but all fold magically and it is only when they fold that you get a glimmer of what the map is alluding to. It shows you no sense of direction; it takes you nowhere and shows you nothing. Yet you are trapped in this series of maps, the maps of the infinite and infinitesimal. The maps of fathoming reality while unknowingly entering into a terrain that has no sign posts.

I am made of these maps that I have spoken to you about, I am also made of the maps I have been told about, the maps that I have invented and the maps that have been inflicted on me. I am a series of events that do not smoothly flow into one another. My body has experienced the visceral tunnels of existence, I have been from the onset a sensate and etheric entity, all that has happened to my body and my soul is layered and remembered, not in temporality and not spatially, but in another realm and a vastly different dimension. I am referring to this, the process of what emerges as a series of thoughts and precursors of experiences that make you believe that I am whole and yet more whole. I am nothing but trembling dust without form. I make up a multitude of other habitual planes of 'You'. If I could let go of this illusions of me, if I could honor the community of souls, then I could merge with the power that rips me away from myself. The vehicle could be the embodiment of courage and strength, and sensate notions that break into consciousness.

If I want to understand who you are and how you function in this abyss, I would like to think of all the maps that make you. Not that the maps can order you, but the ones that can only work to organize and present a schema that allows me to think that I can order you. The map is not a metaphor, it is something that cannot be substituted or replaced. I am describing my very soul in a way that fails I know. But I can only do this by attempting to understand your history. This can only be done by a starting point that teases all teleologies. I want you to start to think about who you are but I want an annihilation at the same time, I want you to want to present it, both personal and transpersonal. I know this is pure conceit but I will try. And if I were to introduce myself – who I am – I would also do the same and attempt to do this as a series of immaterial maps and corporeal maps. These maps were not like time and space neatly marked out, but like time and space folded, complex overlapping points and mutually exclusive and inclusive maps and lines. The folds that were all but hidden from view; they become those subterranean virtual maps of all that you are not and all that allows me to witness You. The lines of the poetics of self – explained against parallel histories of identity through an impersonal archive and relational aspects of the other than historic, social identity and personal histories, and these maps manifest the features of some aspects of the soul itself. If you could play with me in this ensnarement of death, then I may come to see your face. That you are no longer an individual but you pass into the realm of the nameless – yet no one could mistake your beautiful essence for any others. There is that moment of inbetweenness, like a slipping into an endless fall, where 'there is a moment that is only that of a life playing with death. The life of the individual gives way to an impersonal and yet singular life that releases a pure event freed from the accidents of internal and external life, that is, from the subjectivity and objectivity of what happens.' (Deleuze 2005: 28)

And all these notions and ideas of maps and mapping are only another launch into the unknown. That the details point to relational aspects always pointing away from the blind spot. The culmination of the series of maps, of which there is no number, is an allusion of being and the sense of being as folded in on itself, where the fold, the absence is the point that gives direction, when the point cannot be seen. So each map embodies the corporeal and the essence of the blind spot. And in the process of attempting to locate these masked areas of the map, is the destruction of what I could call identity. Identity is the illusion of center and cohesion when looking at the palimpsest, the paper and flesh folded before you allow yourself only to see a portion, and that portion is random. So, what is this blind spot that upsets being, distresses it without seeing or holding it – without even knowing of its existence.

If you stop to think about what you are constituted of and by. What your consciousness is made of, how it moves and does it move along straight lines in space or is it the interiorized sense of who you are, the compulsive guidance of everything you are and do? This is where identity is only the consciousness that you have come to know. If you come to not feel attached to this consciousness and to be aware of your lack of ownership of this consciousness, things may start to emerge. The prime emergence involves the recognition of yourself as nothing more than an impersonal and strange linking of maps, maps of multiplicities and maps that point to nothing external and yet point to something singular. The estrangement of the subjective when it collides with a reference point.

I don't remember all those stories you told me but I feel the stories, they are embedded in my body and in the sensate part of my nature. And these stories guide me where ever I go, but I cannot recall any of them easily. These stories are my little templates, my little gifts that point to the feeling of being anchored and safe. Protected and loved. But more so, these stories are the poetic implements that show me a pathway to you. The story of the man and his wife – the truest sense of what marriage is. Where the spirit is light and meets its equal. Where you become a pathway, and lovingly let someone else travel into your psyche, with an ever so gentle touch that foot prints leave no trace. There is a map of the trail these prints leave, and it looks like a road, but it is only seen in the interior.

This writing is a cartographic process. In any event all writing is a form of cartography, it is the ephemeral bridge between my interior world and the world that my interior inhabits. There is a strange phenomenon that I would like to describe – it involves the conceptualization of the unknowable. This conditional space has limitations of the human mind but if you were to break through into another realm, another aspect, another dimension of understanding of this space, you would be overwhelmed with the beauty of it all. In this space there is no power over yourself and your entry and being only traces through unknown terrain. I existed so lovingly in that space you made for me – and now I have no recourse to describe it.

All lines are merely fractured, all lines begin where they have no end – all these lines are the relational aspects of a multidimensional field. All lines are the relationships with respective lines mapped out between one aspect and another. This is the entry point to my soul. I am a series of complex immaterial terrains and I will try and allow you an avenue into conceptualizing me and my identity through discussing points on a series of stencilled maps, lines on a map that disappear as you lay your eyes on them. Am I or am I not a list of references, and ever decreasing points, a catalogue or a series of concepts that make sense or cohesively meld? Am I an index of multiplicities that contain the univocal? Does my essence come into being when I realize my habitual self?

There are an infinite number of these maps that point to who I am but I will only tell you of some of the inherited maps that have been passed down to me. First there is the map of songs, thousands of songs with words that create sadness and laughter, history and struggle and a sense of place. Songs that bring you home, to a place within yourself. There is a song of a little girl bravely facing the dark. Creating sanctuary through melody. The map of courage – in this map I see a small child walking hand in hand – traversing a dangerous land. This involved the creation of song to ward off danger and the power of melody as protective agent. This is where the lion roars within the child.

Then there is the song of the solitary white mountain flower, isolated in the icy coolness of the highlands. Portending purity and lost romance. Then there is the map of historical events, joining all the people of that time together. The famine, war and the thousand little unknown events that make up notion of the universal. The slippage between that and the personal, like a dive into the darkness of the unknown. The map of family, the loss and dislocation. The tearing yourself away from all that you know, to leave behind what is known and face the chance of knowing something better. The maps of poverty, humor, telling a good joke. Then there is the map of passion, betrayal and the map of fighting and the map of dancing. That all these maps are fleeting and centrifugal.

The map of wisdom and the map of marriage – the map of children. Protecting and nourishing what you bring into life. The many maps of the sense of love and cooking, the stories of each recipe and the knowledge behind the food cooked. The maps of hunger and the maps of war. The map of gambling. This is where the soul faces the unknown and triggers it to thrust into fate, the unknown that will become fixed. That something is fixed and unknown, that when it becomes known it somehow loosens the threshold into something else, something that smacks of the unknown and the unknowable. How could I have known the series of events that I would have to endure?

Then there is the map of cruelty. When you open yourself up to life completely. And here I got a sense of some universal force that was not benign, nor was it cruel – but the feeling and effect of its touch manifested as cruelty. And once you opened yourself to this, the trigger was there, for things to occur, for things to seem random, meaningless and cruel. The map of spiritual beliefs and the map of all that seems like death are all about this nameless terrain.

The map of the human body. The way that activity is played out on the soul is through the body. This is that universal force, one slight touch of it – on the human body and it calls us to struggle with it, to suffer with it. You are called to fight this unknown entity, to know it is physically impossible to defeat it and to proceed to fight with it anyway. What effect does this have on your body? What lines start to manifest on those etheric maps? It may look like a scratch or bruise – or even a deep gash in your flesh, a scar, something raw and painful. This is the ordeal of the human body – and only the bravest enter that arena. The realm where you fling yourself to the abyss and say – I am ready for whatever is to be inflicted on me. This is the immanence of my love.

In her melodic voice, she spoke about her maps all the time – but she never referred to them by name. The maps were transcendental and multi-relational and too complex to be explained like reference points on a scroll. We are a succession of complex fleshy maps that are connected to each other and to one another. This succession does not occur in temporality and the demarcations are like cuttings made into flesh, we sometimes believe the 'body is ordeal' and yet the body allows us the rites of passage and the ability to be a witness to our own existence. But what do these cartographies I have been discussing point to? What referencing takes place to make our travels clearer and to alleviate our destiny with our antithetical teleology? I am not discussing what could make clarity of this confusion we call the world. I am conjuring up a dimension, ever so fragile, where we can say I have attempted to see reality. And if you were to get a glimpse of what these networks look like, even a glimpse, the mind most fathomless will make a minuscule but definite turn into honoring all that comes into its path. I attempted to bring you into this fold; I did this with a pure aim in mind. I wanted to be opened up, like the ephemeral gates of the immanence of your soul.

And when the maps reconfigure, it is as though your flesh were my flesh. I can feel your body's sensations as if they were my own. The flesh, our flesh is like a measurement of life. And my heart starts slowing down and I can feel it thumping rhythmically and then missing a beat, and then it goes more slowly and softer. I can see its movements like waves across your face. Your mouth that sang a thousand songs now gapes like a last groan of defiance. And when the map finds its impermanent place – my heart feels like it has stopped along with yours.

Reference

Deleuze, G. (2005) *Pure Immanence: Essays on A Life*, Introduction by John Rajchman, Trans. A. Boyman, New York: Zone Books.

Index

management and managing, 3, 4, 5,
135–50
managerial and organizational cognition,
201–16
managerial identities, 3, 5, 135–6, 148
marketing ideology, 22–3
marketing, 11–25, 23
metaphor, 4, 44–57, 289
micro-emancipation, 190, 192–3
multiple identities, 23, 39, 62, 65, 152,
248, 301, 317, 327–32
multiple narratives, 298–300
music, 252–7
  and ethnography, 256–65
  and the radio ballads, 253–6

narrative, 12–13, 274–6, 288–301
narrative methodology, 152, 156, 291–3
  and double-narrative approach, 152,
    156
  and identity, 16, 289–91, 317
  and method, 5, 7, 240, 251–3, 288–301
  and narrative style, 295–6
  and poetic tropes, 296–8
  and stories, 151, 156, 288–91

observance, 94–5
occupational/professional divides, 73–7
organizational identity, 4, 44–57
  and cognitive framing, 47, 51–2
  and discursive psychology, 48, 52–3
  and institutional theory, 48, 53
  and organizational behaviour, 47, 51
  and organizational communication, 47,
    50–1
  and research traditions, 45–53
  and social identity, 48, 53–4
  see also metaphor
organizational restructuring, 27–8, 30–3

panopticon, 85–7
paranoid-schizoid position, 112–14
participative organizational research,
237–4
  see also action research, and
    participative action research;
    action researcher
performance ethnography, 7, 252–3
personal branding, 4, 26–41
  and anxiety, 30–4
  and authenticity, 33–9
  and conformity, 38–40
  and dissimulation, 33–40

  and homophily, 38–40
poetics, 338–9
police service, 156
  and sexual minorities at work, 162–6
popular management, 4, 27–8
possessions, 12, 13, 15, 17–18
postcolonial, 6, 193
poststructuralism, 62, 65, 78–9, 325–6
power, 4–5, 85–99, 276, 319–21
  and domination, 87
  and resistance, 4–5, 14–15, 83–97,
    321–2
  and subversion, 90
presencing, 94
professional identities, 135–6
psychodynamic approach, 5, 100–31
  and group dynamics, 102

queer, 185, 187, 195, 196

reflexivity, 8, 148, 196, 232–3, 316
research self, 158, 316–33
  and action, 282–6
  and description, 280–6
  and re-presentation, 283–6

self, 1–10
  embodied, 17
  extended, 18–19
  fragmented, 16
  ideal, 22–3
  multiple, 316–32
  social, 22–3
  see also research self
self-discipline, 84
self-esteem, 17, 21, 100, 202
self-identity, 3, 44, 136–7
self-improvement, 40
self-management, 87–8
self-surveillance, 87
  and discrimination, 153–4
  see also surveillance
sexual identity, 5, 151–67, 322
social identities, 136–7, 202, 216
social practice, research as, 316–32
spatial and functional divides, 68–70
stories, 7, 264, 272, 288–300
  complete, 292
  composite, 292
  and interviewing, 251–72
  and plot, 293–4
  see also narrative
structuralism, 4, 61–80